The Troubled Farmer

T0339026

The Troubled Farmer

1850-1900

RURAL ADJUSTMENT TO INDUSTRIALISM

Earl W. Hayter

NORTHERN ILLINOIS UNIVERSITY PRESS: DEKALB

First Printing 1968
Second Printing 1973
Third Printing 1987

All rights reserved. No part of this book may be reproduced in any form without written permission from the publisher, except for brief passages included in a review appearing in a newspaper or magazine.

Copyright © 1968 by Northern Illinois University Press
Library of Congress Catalog Card Number: 67–26267

Preface

DURING THE early part of the nineteenth century, the American farmer lived in a society imbued with an agrarianism that taught the superior virtue of the rural way of life and inspired a calm confidence in its future. In the course of the next one hundred years, this way of life was shaken by a series of vast technological and economic changes that catapulted the farmer into an industrialized society with a very different scale of values. The results of this change were disorientation, bewilderment, and loss of the traditional feelings of confidence and security. This book attempts to tell of the stress and strain introduced into the farmer's life by the new order and of how he dealt with these problems.

As a child, I grew up in a sparsely settled Dakota wheat-farm area. In my youth I had the opportunity to observe the reactions of a group of farm folk to the unsettling influence of revolutionary technological and economic changes. These people had been caught up in the northwestern land boom around the turn of the century. For a few years they produced wheat on a grand scale; then the boom collapsed, leaving a disillusioned group of people whose only recourse was to leave the land and emigrate to the towns and cities in search of a new way of life. Influenced by these early experiences, some thirty-five years ago I developed a scholarly interest in rural life, and more specifically, in the daily routine and personal behavior of farmers in their conflicts, crazes, and foibles, in their delusions, gullibilities, obstinacies, and credulities. Several chapters of this book are concerned with these aspects of rural life in a period of difficult transition for the farmer, 1850 to 1900.

I am indebted to several individuals for their assistance and encouragement. To the late Isaac J. Cox, who directed my dissertation and gave me my first assignment in this field, I am deeply grateful. The fifth chapter is a revised essay of one which I originally submitted to him as an unpublished *Festschrift*. Among others who have been generous with their advice and assistance are those early agricultural historians Edward E. Dale, Paul W. Gates, and Russell H. Anderson, as well as the late Everett E. Edwards, Fred Shannon, and Herbert A. Kellar. I would like also to thank the Perry Ellwood family for the freedom to use their valuable steel and wire collection, now in the archives at the University of Wyoming, and the American Steel & Wire Company for its collection, formerly at Worcester, Massachusetts, and now in the Baker Library at Harvard University. Special appreciation is due the many librarians and archivists in the state historical societies and universities, as well as the John Crerar, Newberry, McCormick Historical Association, and the United States Department of Agriculture Libraries. I am greatly indebted to my own Swen Franklin Parson Library and its librarians for their cheerful and unselfish assistance these many years. It is not possible for me to name those there who have aided me in one way or another, but the number is sizeable. I wish to acknowledge the contributions of my graduate students, especially Donald Seymour, Stanley Deming, Ralph Martin, Clair Heyer, and Robert Lang, whose studies were particularly helpful. My colleague, Benjamin Keen, has been generous in offering discriminating criticism of the entire text. Robert W. Schneider and J. Norman Parmer both gave helpful suggestions for individual chapters. Finally, to my wife Beulah, I owe more than to any other person for her unselfish time and assistance over the years; her unlimited devotion to this project, while still rearing a family, made this manuscript possible.

Financial assistance was secured on various occasions from the

Social Science Research Council and the American Philosophical Society for my work in Washington, D. C., and the British Museum.

I am indebted to the following copyright holders for permission to reprint revised portions of several of my articles: *Agricultural History, Iowa Journal of History and Politics, Wisconsin Magazine of History, Indiana Magazine of History, and the Mississippi Valley Historical Review.*

EARL W. HAYTER
DeKalb, Illinois

Contents

Part Three: Credulous Farmers

Part Four: Patent Conflicts

The Troubled Farmer

RURAL ADJUSTMENT TO INDUSTRIALISM

1850-1900

CHAPTER I

Introduction: The Rural Mind

in Transition

THE MIND of the nineteenth-century American farmer constitutes a rich and relatively unexploited vein for the social historian. This is especially true of the period following the Civil War. Historians have subjected to rigorous analysis many facets of agrarian discontent resulting from industrialization and the triumph of capitalism. But the more personal and technical aspects of the farmer's daily life—the reasons why he decided to do one thing and not another—have eluded a comparable investigation. Neglect of this rich mine of information is due in part to the difficulty one faces in attempting to establish a suitable model in this area for modern quantification techniques that have contributed immeasurably to the formulation of historical generalizations in such areas as economic history and voting patterns. Historians, consequently, have glossed over considerations of how and why farmers in the nineteenth century felt, thought, and acted as they did, on grounds that the reasons lie too deeply "hidden in the complex mystery of human motivations."

The difficulties that face the social historian are formidable and real, but possibilities for a broader understanding of nineteenth-century America are too inviting to ignore. And when one investigates the daily behavior of rural folk in this period, definite patterns of behavior emerge. To begin with, it becomes clear that large numbers of them were experiencing an extremely difficult and painful process of adjustment. To be or not to be became the question for millions of rural people during this period: should they wholeheartedly accept the emerging commercial system with all of its disturbing elements and conflicting values—a "culture that threatened the familiar order with strange, even dangerous ideas," or should they deny and resist the new age and remain rooted in a more comfortable rural ideology?

On the other hand, these people displayed no such lack of resolution or confidence when dealing with problems with which they were intimately familiar; when dealing with their animals, implements, tools, or in such activities as planting, cultivating and harvesting, they displayed a firm assurance and certainty. In fact, many observers of the rural scene concluded that farmers were obstinate, habit-bound, conservative, and prejudiced. One writer on rural life, Levi Lincoln, contended in 1822 that most farmers were so prone to follow traditional routines that they seldom made any improvements in any of the branches of agriculture.

Habit and *Prejudice* are powerful opponents of improvement, and they are in a great measure incident to the business of Agriculture. The cultivation of the earth, is a practical lesson, taught to the Husbandman in earliest life. He is instructed in the ways of his fathers, and the *mode* which experience has approved as safe, will be reluctantly yielded to the mere promise of experiment. Hence, from generation to generation, men pass on in the track of their predecessors: believing that the path which is explored, is in the only direction to their object, and those who deviate, wander to their destruction. To conquer this stubborn habit of reflection is the greatest effort and best results of Agricultural Associations. He is either deaf, and blind, and dumb to your appeals, or answers you in the language of distrust. . . .[1]

This "hereditary feeling of obedience to ancient usage" seriously hindered and retarded technical improvements in farming. In 1822 a certain manufacturer shipped the first two Cary or Dagon plows to Fredericksburg, Virginia, where they were placed on sale. Curiously enough local farmers displayed not the slightest interest in these devices, and they

remained in the stable yard of the Indian Queen Tavern nearly a year, before any one would even *try* them. During all this time, they lay objects of doubt and cunning suspicion; to all the knowing ones, each fearing to meddle with them, lest he should render himself a mark of ridicule to the rest, for putting any faith in so ill-looking a tool. And . . . [this] they would have continued for years, if an enterprising Yankee, . . . had not boldly resolved, at every risk, to achieve the perilous adventure of making the first trial. . . . Even after he had demonstrated the merit of this plough, . . . it was nearly ten years, before it was generally used. . . .²

Such aversion to new tools expressed itself in an inordinate mistrust of improvements produced by "outsiders," especially of implements manufactured in distant towns and cities. The same distrust attached to ideas or services offered by professional and learned men. A British visitor in the 1850's was amazed at the small regard the farmers had for the educated class. He wrote: "Every man you meet thinks himself capable of giving an opinion upon the questions of the most difficult kind; and for the most part, the masses seem, by their choice at public elections, to prefer to be guided by the less rather than by the more educated of their fellow citizens." ³

This lack of respect for educated people affected farmers' decisions about schooling for their children. There was little rural controversy on this question. A deep conviction prevailed that "schoolhouse" learning should not go beyond the common school level and should consist of a curriculum that would help the boy achieve a useful and happy life upon the farm. Moreover, the most important part of a boy's education was to be obtained through hard work at many tasks around the farm and home; then by the time he reached manhood he would have developed a constitution of "nerve and muscle," a set of broad shoulders, a stout back, but most important of all, the character and perseverance required for a successful career as a farmer. ⁴

Formal study, therefore, received little emphasis, and its purpose, according to one writer, was "to get just as little . . . as is compatible with keeping book accounts and reading the political paper." [5] In the final analysis, rural thought favored muscle over mind. If a youth by some chance developed a taste for education beyond the common school level his elders usually foretold his failure as a farmer. Love of knowledge was not only too expensive an indulgence; studious habits were also regarded dangerous to health. The young man who obstinately pursued a scholarly life might expect in a few years to have a thin, pallid, and emaciated body "completely unstrung by his close application to study, and want of exercise in the open air." [6]

This anti-intellectualism found expression in hostility to so-called book-farming. Attempts by journalists, lawyers, schoolmasters, physicians, and clergymen to break through the cake of custom were long and to no avail; farmers absolutely refused to accept advice on the simplest problem if that advice first appeared in a book or magazine. A common excuse for this resistance was that farmers had "no time to read." [7] This abhorrence of "book-farming" clearly illustrates the narrowness of the rural mind. If a man openly attempted to change his pattern of farming with ideas taken from a book or printed material of any kind, he might receive extremely unfavorable comment from his neighbors. Let a farmer discover something for himself and inform his neighbors of his innovation, and they would quickly and gratefully adopt his procedure. But

if this man, desirous of benefiting a whole community by his experience, and having too much business at home to go about repeating his success from man to man, by word of mouth, shall write out his experiment, and cause it to be printed in a book or periodical, that moment it becomes a part of book-farming, and ceases to have virtue in the eyes of many. There is a magic in types, it would seem, that converts what is wisdom when spoken into folly when printed. [8]

Another aspect of the rural mind was a traditional belief-system often referred to by sociologists as a complex of "agricultural myth and magic." This system sprang from the ancient storehouse of mythology and folklore and lacked all elements of scientific explanation.[9] Farmers believed in many forms of powers, spirits, and influences existing beyond themselves in the natural world. Some of these possessed the capacity to inflict injury, pain, or illness, while others were capable of inducing contentment, health, strength, and prosperity.[10] Farmers also believed that certain individuals were endowed with the spirit of truth, prophecy, or the power of speaking in tongues; they were the diviners who located the water veins, foretold future events, identified robbers and thieves, located runaway animals and lost property, and possessed the "never-failing Nostrum" which could cure the worst diseases of man or beast. Many farmers looked to the stars with a faith that those celestial bodies could exercise a favorable influence upon them; they also viewed comets as signs of impending calamity.[11]

By the time of the Civil War many of these age-old superstitions were beginning to loosen their grip upon the rural inhabitants, especially in the older sections of the country. Nevertheless, there was one rural superstition which maintained its influence over the rural mind for many more years. This concerned the influence of the moon upon agricultural activities.[12] Individuals who believed in this phenomenon became known as "moon farmers"; and as one of them remarked about themselves, "We plant, we sow, we reap and mow; we fell trees, we make shingles, we roof our houses, secure bacon, make fences, spread manure, when the moon is auspicious. If we are ready before her ladyship, we wait the happy moment when her aspect shall say, proceed." [13] To guide the believers through the intricacies of this type of farming there developed the well-known almanacs which carried the proper phases of the moon as well as the signs of the Zodiac.

"Moon farmers" were convinced that if such crops as potatoes, beets, turnips, and other tuber plants were not sown in the phases established by tradition they would produce mostly tops and vines, with few or no roots. Those who ignored the proper phases in growing plants that bore cereals above the earth could expect an excess of root growth and very little seed. Timber cut for fences must be "fallen" during the wane of the moon if they were to be of lasting quality; otherwise the rails and blocks would "decay and sink into the earth" much quicker. Furthermore, it was believed that fruit trees set out during the last days of the last quarter were more likely to live and flourish. Pruning, grafting, winemaking and the drawing of sap were also regulated by the phases of the moon.[14]

The same ritual was followed in the care and production of farm animals. Shearing of the sheep during the wrong phase produced a shorter wool; slaughtering of animals must not be performed during the declining phase or the flesh would "when cooked, shrink from the bone, leaving much of it exposed, when brought to the table." Rural housewives were adamant that the proper time be observed, claiming that any animal flesh butchered during the wrong time lost from a fourth to a half of its bulk in cooking; when this happened they would be held responsible, since they cooked the meat. Cattle were frequently bled for the preservation of health, which must be performed during any one of the lower phases of the moon.

In order to produce animal progeny of the proper size, color, shape, vigor, productivity, and disposition, it was believed necessary to synchronize the time of setting or breeding with the moon. Castration of the different farm animals was done according to a definite cycle: some gelders observed the proper month of the year and day of the month, while others went even further and insisted that the process be carried out only during the late afternoon.[15] All phases of gestation—birth, incubation, hatching, and even weaning—were thought to be regulated by the phases of the moon.

By 1850 this pattern of superstitious beliefs and practices in rural America was being challenged by new influences. Farmers living in close proximity to the social forces produced by urbanism, mobility, science, and technology—forces that were remaking America— naturally were the first to feel these challenges and be forced to modify their way of life. Once doubt entered a community concerning the traditional beliefs a struggle of ideas began; a cleavage developed between those who sympathized with the new views and those who opposed them. Observers of rural behavior patterns have noted that once an innovation penetrated a rural community and became well known, many farmers adopted it without hesitation; this gave rise to sporadic fevers or crazes that endured for a short time, then gave way to some new enthusiasm.

The nineteenth century saw many such hysterias wax and wane.

Now it was a craze for certain plants, seeds, and vegetables; now for fruit trees or for one crop in preference to another; at another time it would be sheep-raising, egg production, or beekeeping. Their uncontrollable enthusiasm for the current mania led farmers to use poor judgment. Sometimes they purchased too much of the new product for a successful experiment. Instead of putting in the proper amount of new seed, they would plant more than they could possibly care for. In the purchase of farm machinery and tools farmers were easily duped in respect to price, quantity and quality.[16] Moreover, these enthusiasts demonstrated little patience in prosecuting their projects, often quickly abandoning one new scheme to leap blindly into another.

On the other hand, one group of farmers in every community rejected all innovation. They were the satisfied, the conservative ones "who are never caught attempting to improve upon the old practices," who were perfectly willing to sit contentedly under their own vine and fig tree.[17] One rural editor drew attention to these two opposing types:

We take the liberty here to warn our farmer friends against two very serious and prevalent errors, which have already done much to retard the progress of desirable improvements in agricultural science—one of these is *incredulity*, which so obscures the perceptive faculties of the individual, as to prevent him from realizing the benefits to be derived from scientific investigation—the only solid basis of a really progressive agriculture; while the other is the opposite extreme—*over-credulity*, which induces improvident expenditures for new machinery, plants, seeds, manures, etc., that have not been thoroughly tested by a series of careful experiments, and their adaptation to the particular locality clearly ascertained.[18]

It is this latter group, this overly credulous element of rural America, very numerous in the decades following the Civil War, that is mainly the subject of this book. Challenged in their old beliefs, customs, habits, and traditions, they found themselves caught up in the unfamiliar world of industrial capitalism, with its emphasis upon atomistic individualism, the profit motive, and its motto of *caveat emptor*. The conflict between their traditional values and those of the strange new world in which they found themselves created a disquieting uncertainty. Looking outward, the farmer saw complexity when he yearned for simplicity; looking inward, he saw fragmentation when he longed for wholeness.

The shock of contact with this new, impersonal world of industry, commerce, and trade produced serious maladjustments in the farmer. This bewilderment and frustration found expression in a variety of attitudes and behavior traits: vacillation, anxiety, nostalgia for the past, and an excessive credulity or gullibility. It is this last trait that especially interests us here.

The bewildered farmer, thrust unprepared into the age of industrialism, was made for generations the easy prey of peddlers, impostors and fraudulent sharpers; he was a victim of what has been called the golden age of deception.[19] His susceptibility to quackery was described by an Iowa editor who depicted the farmer as an individual who

believes in quack doctors, quack lawyers, quack preachers, quack patients, quack medicine, and quack politicians; and . . . he invests in all sorts of humbugs with a faith and simplicity that it is refreshing but humiliating to see. He bows to pretenders; counterfeits of all kinds are passed on him; he pays the fiddler while others dance. The proper name however for this sort of belief is not faith, but credulity.[20]

The sway of quackery over the rural scene continued until the farmer acquired some degree of immunity and protection against fraud and deception. By the 1880's the federal government had established certain agencies—experimental stations, agricultural colleges, and farmers' institutes—that gradually raised the farmer's level of information.[21] State governments gradually enacted a series of laws giving some security to innocent consumers against the host of swindlers who swarmed in farm communities. Before the farmer could develop immunity to the "spoils" of these sharpers he had to achieve a certain sophistication which in turn required that he possess a fund of solid information. A long and difficult process of re-learning was needed to overcome the farmer's deep-seated feeling against "book-farming."

The many agencies that contributed to this educational task included various agricultural journals which, by the end of the nineteenth century, had penetrated an increasing number of farm homes.

Another source of rural enlightenment was the proceedings and transactions of the various state agricultural societies. These publications contained a wide assortment of educational materials which farmer-readers could digest during the long winter months.[22] Although these compilations had limited circulation, farm journals and journalists drew heavily upon them for editorials, columns, and feature articles; in these forms material of a technical nature reached many farmers who subscribed to rural magazines.

To these sources of information we may add the ever increasing flow of advertising pamphlets, catalogs, tracts, circulars, and placards as well as the handbills that were left in wagons, blacksmith shops, depots, and stores. This material had a definite educational value. By way of illustration, we may cite illustrated pamphlets and catalogs advertising different kinds of new machinery which enabled farmers to judge their own technical progress. Large numbers of people also attended the annual county and state fairs at which these mechanical creations were displayed and demonstrated.[23]

Confronted with the dynamism of the urban-industrial revolution of the late nineteenth century, the traditional rural way of life, with its restrictive customs and superstitions, had to change. The transition, made with such rapidity, produced bewilderment, anxiety, and an excessive gullibility.[24] In time, however, the farmer acquired the knowledge and sophistication needed to cope in a more satisfactory way with rural problems in the urban-industrial age.

PART ONE

Livestock Controversies

CHAPTER II

"The Horns Must Go"

IN THE course of man's long and intimate relationship with his domestic animals he inevitably developed a large body of notions, in part folklore, in part based on observation and experience, concerning these silent creatures. This complex of ideas included certain attitudes and criteria, some aesthetic, others utilitarian, with regard to the bodies of these animals and even to their appendages—the horns, tails, and hoofs. When, as a result of certain changes in the cattle industry in the nineteenth century, a movement arose that demanded the complete removal of horns from the heads of all American cattle, a clash developed between the traditional, tenaciously held notions concerning the aesthetic or economic value of horns and the practical needs of the industry. This clash grew into a national controversy that required nearly a decade to resolve. Farmers, cattle-raisers, breeders, veterinarians, and city-dwellers participated in this debate.

Traditionally for the farmer a bovine animal's horns represented certain symbols of value. They were frequently prized as ornaments, and cattle lacking these appendages were often considered poor, imperfect creatures. Some farmers not only insisted that their cattle have a set of horns on their heads but required that these horns

15

actually should be of a certain shape and curve. Others favored horns of a particular color, length, and thickness. Indeed, cattle were sometimes classified or evaluated according to certain features of the horns. In the British Isles, for example, there was the notable beef and tallow type assigned to the "short-horn" group; cattle popular for milk, butter, and cheese or a thicker hide were generally thought of as having the "spreading," "crumpled," or the "long" and slender horn. Finally, in some areas of these Isles there were the celebrated polled breeds, identified by their complete lack of horns.[1] Similar traditions existed in the United States; for example, most Americans were acquainted with the historic "Long Horn," which contributed so greatly to our western livestock industry during the past century.

Horns also had been desirable in cattle-raisers' eyes because they served functional purposes; for example, cattle-owners and buyers for centuries had used horns as the chief indicators in determining an animal's age. Many believed that the "ridges and rings" that appeared on horns at various intervals in the lifetime of a horned cow or bull could be used, with the aid of the proper arithmetical technique, to arrive at the approximate age of the animal.[2] Many dairymen were equally convinced that a crooked, folded, or wrinkled horn was an essential requirement for a good dairy cow, and that a stocky, thickset horn was absolutely necessary for an ox when backing a cart or plowing with the yoke.[3] In evaluating bull cattle, a common folk belief held that their horns were important symbols in judging natural male characteristics. A fine set of horns, it was claimed, imparted to an animal an appearance of greater size, strength, and beauty. Moreover, such horns were often considered primary evidence of a spirited and masterful animal, endowed with great potency and vitality and with the capacity to transmit them to his offspring.[4]

The religious proposition that horns were given by God to these dumb creatures as their only weapons of defense reinforced the traditional folk respect for these appendages. Bulls, men argued, needed horns in the fierce bovine struggle for survival; cows required them for the protection of their young.[5] Rural folklore also held that the state of the horns was a most reliable index of the amount of fever of a sick animal. Cow doctors and leeches also used the horns to diagnose a great number of folk illnesses which they usually grouped in the broad categories of ailments called "hollow horn" or "horn-ail." [6]

As happened with so many other groups in American society during the latter half of the nineteenth century, the cattlemen ultimately had to abandon traditional attitudes and practices as a result of the demands and pressures of an emerging industrial and urban society. The enormous expansion of the cattle industry following the Civil War led to an extraordinary increase in the number of western horned cattle; technological advances brought great changes in the handling and transporting of these animals. By the middle of the 1880's railroad networks had penetrated into all sections of the cattle country, making it possible to eliminate the long drives to ranges and to markets. In the same period the invention and mass production of barbed wire fencing materials inaugurated a whole new era in which the cattle were gradually removed from the free and open ranges and confined to enclosed pastures.

These and other changes led to a genuine revolution in the whole process of handling livestock. Here a special interest attaches to such elements of the process as human and animal safety, and the sheltering, feeding, watering, breeding, and transporting of cattle.

Under the new dispensation, with an ever increasing demand for better beef and more dairy products for the American and European tables, western cattlemen soon became fully aware of the delicate problem of horns. The problems of placing more and more horned cattle into feeding lots, shelters, pastures, railroad cars and on cattle boats provided experiences of a kind designed to convince the most ardent believer in the "natural virtues" of horns that something must be done to eliminate this problem.

Probably the greatest impulse for change came when farmers, dairymen, and cattlemen found it necessary to enclose their animals in smaller pastures and care for them in enclosed quarters. The situation affected not only the lives of the farmers but their entire families.[7] When horned cattle and human beings came into close proximity with each other, the incidence of horn injuries and even deaths from such injuries inevitably increased. The problem was far

more serious than in the old days, when horned beasts could roam
and feed miles from any human beings except a few horsemen who
were sufficiently well armed to protect themselves in any emergency.

Rural Americans, young and old, had from colonial times been
exposed to the perils of wild beasts, and had become more or less
reconciled to these perils, but with the vast increase in domestic
animals the problem grew to alarming proportions. Nothing inspired greater distress than to witness a friend, neighbor or member
of one's own family attacked by a bull, tossed from its horns into the
air and then trampled to death before his own eyes. Evidence
abounds of the deadly nature of those murderous spears. An Ohio
physician, William W. Crane, gave a vivid account of the problem
in a paper before the State Agriculture Society on the "Advantages
of Hornless Cattle." In his catalog of indictments of all horns he
listed, giving names and places covering a three-year period, fifty or
more people who had been "fearfully mangled, [and] nearly all . . .
mortally wounded." In a few lines he told a terrifying story of men
whose

legs have been wrenched from bodies, eyes gouged from sockets, arms
torn from shoulders, heads from trunks, hearts, lungs and all viscera
scattered over the ground, while triumphant assailants have ripped the
intestines from their dying victims, wound them about their horns and
gone bellowing down the lanes with the shreds of humanity streaming
over them in bloody ribbons. This is no picture trumped into print by
active imagery—it is an undertold but "o'er true tale." [8]

Horned bulls and goring cows injured and killed not only human
beings but frequently worked havoc on their own kind; this was
especially the case when these animals had to be confined together in
the same shelter, lot, or field. Moreover, when animals were closely
restrained in small pastures, yards or lanes, a bossy cow frequently
forced the weaker members away from the feeding troughs or hay
ricks and, if necessary, viciously fought to master and cower the
others into mute obedience. This pattern of behavior was particularly evident when cattle had been roughly treated or were strange
to each other. If the frightened and quivering animals were unable
to escape these sharp-horned tormentors, cattle-owners could expect

to find in their herds some which had been cornered and gored to death, and others with gaping paunches and torn hides.[9] The attackers in these episodes of farmyard assaults were no respecters of property rights; as a result, sooner or later the owner of a prized mare, heifer, colt, or ram might find his animal disemboweled in an angle of a rail fence, at a crowded feeding rick, watering tank, or in a narrow lane.[10] Professor W. A. Henry, a prominent experimentalist in the field of agriculture and livestock at the University of Wisconsin Experiment Station, described this aspect of the horns problem in one of his numerous publications: [11]

This is a subject upon which our farmers have shown a great deal of interest, and not without good reason; let one stand in a barn yard well filled with cattle and observe the pushing, hooking and driving about that takes place, and he soon comes to ask the question, "Of what use are horns?" A very considerable loss is entailed yearly by colts, horses and other live stock being gored and killed through the instrumentality of horns; then the loss of human life is very considerable each year by means of vicious bulls. Indeed, horns are a source of loss from every point the subject may be approached. The beauty some see in them is a barbarous beauty parallel with the fierce ivories of a lion or tiger, or the bow and poisoned arrows of a savage.

The problem had other, less obvious aspects. Farmers and ranchers, who constantly complained of the difficulties encountered with horned cattle during the winter season when they were confined in close quarters, experienced even more adverse effects when they shipped them to market.[12] Stockmen, in the absence of restraining regulations for railroad companies during this period, frequently overloaded the cars with their horned beasts for the sake of greater profits, heedless of the fact that it might cause a loss of weight for some animals and inflict on others a cruel and fatal ride.[13] If a significant number of deaths, injuries, and damages to hides occurred when shipping by rail, the losses sustained by sea during various voyages were considerably more serious. The Privy Council inspectors at the ports of entry where American cattle were unloaded often witnessed and recorded moving pictures of suffering by these unfortunate animals in rough crossings. These tragedies arose from the fact that the cattle had been loaded in such a manner as to make it impossible for many to survive under conditions of excessive rolling and pitching of the ships. Tied in long rows with no divisions between them and no slats on the floor to cling to, or "tied up in twos, in boxes just large enough for them to stand," when they made "efforts to rest, the horns . . . become entangled, resulting in injury and . . . when one does lie down his frantic struggles to rise are sure to cause hooking and ripping," resulting in wounds and bruises to some, and death to others. Moreover, many of these maimed and emaciated brutes who survived the crossing either died immediately upon landing or had to be shot due to injuries and exhaustion.[14]

These reports, widely disseminated in rural areas, soon provoked widespread revulsion against such unnecessary cruelty. In time, public opinion became sufficiently sensitive to the humanitarian and economic aspects of the problem to insist that some solution be devised. Beef-cattle-raisers in the western prairie regions were the first to look with favor upon an artificial technique of removing the horns; the dairy industry was won over to the idea four to five years later.[15] By the middle of the 1880's the idea of removing the horns was so popular in the beef cattle areas of the West that a considerable amount of literature began to appear in the livestock and farm journals. This literature covered the whole spectrum of the subject, from such minor details as the name to be given to the practice of dehorning to the major question of the effect that removal of the horns might have on the generative powers of the bull.[16] Agrarian concern over this problem found expression in a variety of possible solutions. Some were so moderate as to cause no serious conflict with traditional rural patterns of thought; others, more radical, aroused alarm and charges that they threatened the very existence of the bovine species. As a result, the introduction of some dehorning techniques into various communities of the country produced an extraordinarily large volume of protest.

Many who opposed dehorning, whatever the reason, were aware of the fact that it was an absolute necessity to protect human beings as well as their livestock from dangerous animals. But many were not yet convinced that the only solution was the removal of horns; they maintained that more humane ways and means could be used to quiet or tame the aggressive animals. One such merciful plan, practiced in England for many years, consisted in fastening a chain two or three feet in length—depending on the height of the animal—to a ring in his nose. This chain, hanging freely, or fastened to a rod, never failed to serve as a "stern authority" that prevented the beast from becoming aggressive.[17]

Another such compassionate contrivance was reported in the *Complete Grazier*, one of the prominent journals of the period. It was constructed with a small and narrow bar of iron clamped on the horns midway between the head and the tip; a chain was then fastened to the iron bar and extended down the middle of the face to a ring in the nose, so that when anything came in contact with this chain the bull was quickly and sometimes painfully reminded by the pressure that was immediately conveyed to the ring.[18]

Still another method of "dociling" bulls was to use a form of blinder which interfered neither with their eating nor drinking habits but greatly restricted their vision of objects in front of themselves; as a result of this restricted vision they seemed to become more timid and inoffensive toward human beings. This device was easily produced and usually made with a stiff piece of leather or some hardwood board large enough to cover the face; it was then securely tied or bolted to the horns with a set of hinges, permitting it only to swing in and out as the head was raised or lowered—much like a "trader's sign"—hanging over the eyes of the bull.[19]

A more sophisticated notion, but equally benevolent to animals, was for cattle breeders to adopt the new policy of securing polled animals to begin with for beef cattle. Others attempted to "breed off" horns by a simple genetic process of using mulley cows with polled Angus or Galloway bulls.[20] Many regarded this as the only practicable solution.

Acceptance of hornless breeds in America had been a slow, reluctant process and it was not until the late seventies and early eighties that interest really developed. This delay may have been primarily due to the fact that even European cattle-raisers had not taken these "kindly heads" seriously until the Paris Exposition in 1878, when the "Black Doddies" from the braes of Angus won the highest prize for beef-producing animals. Another reason for the delay in adopting hornless breeds was the fact that most rural people, inherently traditionalists, could not conceive of livestock without horns: their absence gave the animal the appearance of an oddity, unable either to defend itself or to offend another.[21] As one honest cattleman confessed, "I always looked at a hornless bull as the very homeliest animal living and not only homely but ugly looking and would never think of buying one. . . . Now this feeling all comes from habit or custom and not because there is any greater value in horned against hornless cattle." [22] A similar prejudice existed in the case of mulley cows; they were considered suitable for beef cattle only and rejected completely for dairy purposes. In the light of these attitudes, the resistance to hornless cattle that prevailed in most sections of the nation is understandable.

In time, however, this polled image began to fade, and despite weaknesses imputed to them in the production of milk and butter, increasing numbers of them were imported for beef cattle. An Iowa stockman, noting the changing attitudes of the western farmer and stock-breeder, submitted his views on the relative merits of hornless, as compared with horned cattle:

The hornless cattle mania seems liable to break out at any moment. We read of their virtues in every agricultural journal, and the pioneers in this branch of cattle breeding will reap a rich harvest. There is little claim made for the milking qualities, but their other desirable qualities are oft repeated. . . . First, they are about as harmless as a flock of sheep; second, sheep, colts and horses can run in the same pasture or yard and drink out of the same tank with perfect safety; third, it is sometimes necessary to milk in a storm, and I have only to open the cow-stable door and twelve cows will not take more room than three pairs of horns; fourth, a straw rick two rods long and twenty feet wide will make a first-rate shelter for thirty head of young mulley stock, for they will soon have the rick shelved all around and lie down like so many hogs and be comfortable under the edges of the stack, while six pairs of horns could hardly be accommodated on the same territory. Many a time have I had my patience tried to see one pair of horns hook and tear the rick in pieces and the rest of the stock stand back out of danger till the one pair of horns was done pitching straw. But I have not had any such occurence take place on my farm for the last twenty years. . . . My mulley bulls become a little cross sometimes. . . . I never have had any horses wounded, or colts, sheep, calves, children, women or men tossed upon mulley bull's horns.[23]

Theories of how to breed off the horns ran the whole gamut from the absurd to what seemed scientifically plausible in that day and age. Some sensitive individuals, recoiling from the thought of mutilating an animal's horns with a saw or clipper, advanced a variety of proposals. These individuals readily admitted the dangers and economic losses created by animals' horns, but pleaded that some method other than mutilation be found.

So popular did this subject of "breeding off the horns" become that for at least a decade it was a favorite topic of agricultural writers. Farm journals received inquiries as to whether or not it was possible to secure mulley animals by constant inbreeding of those which had had their horns removed in infancy. Was it not possible, asked one writer, to make horns totally disappear after a period of years by exclusive inbreeding of polled and short-horn breeds?[24] Amateurs, carried away by the current enthusiasm for dehorning, vied with each other in advancing pet theories as solutions for the problem.[25]

Perhaps the earliest dehorning procedure in the nineteenth century was based on the reasoning that one should not wait until the horns were fully developed, when their removal would be more painful; they must be destroyed when the calf was a few days old with a sharp gouge or a common caustic compound.[26] The first apparent reference to dehorning calves with a gouge was by a Paul Cooper from Woodbury, New Jersey, who removed only the horns of his bull calves. His method was simple: when a male calf was about a month old and the horns had penetrated the skin, he would cut off the buttons "close with a chisel, and with a sharp gouge, pare them clean from the bone: then sear the wound, and fill it with sturgeon's oil, or hog's lard."[27] A second method, used more widely following the 1840's on both male and female calves, was described as follows:[28]

When the calf is from two to four weeks old, tie the legs, the same as if you intended to kill him. Cut off the hair on and around the horn—have an iron, an inch or more in diameter, square at the end, heat it to a red heat, and sear the lump down even with the surface of the head, and put on a plaster of shoemaker's wax, . . . to keep the air from it, and no more is necessary to be done. The calves do not suffer the least inconvenience from it. If the lump is not seared down close, there will sometimes grow a loose nub of a horn.

Many dairymen considered cutting, gouging out, and searing the small buttons from the head of a four-week-old calf too cruel and continued to seek more humane methods. By the 1880's a number of effective chemical removers were on the market and advertised in numerous rural journals. Most of these killers contained patented mixtures of different sorts; products having some kind of caustic chemical in combination with kerosene and water were the most effective. They were sold throughout the farming communities in drug stores, by itinerant peddlers and circulars, and upon receipt of seventy-five cents to a dollar per bottle, were sent by mail. If properly applied, one bottle contained enough of the "Horn-Killer" to destroy the embryo horns of twenty-five calves.[29]

Some cattle-raisers employed a practice long used in England and considered more humane. It was believed that the removal of one to two inches from the tip of the horns of pugnacious animals would cure them of their aggressiveness without inflicting the slightest pain.[30] Adherents of this practice argued that once these unruly individuals discovered the loss of their pointed weapons, they would modify their behavior, becoming more tractable and less bossy. Other cattle-raisers, however, maintained that tipping their horns alone would never cure animals of their aggressive proclivities and resorted to another technique which also was borrowed from English cattle-raisers. This technique employed hardwood balls or brass knobs of a certain size which were driven onto the horns and riveted with small pins; the aim was not only to safeguard the lives of other animals and of human beings but to improve the appearance of the horns.[31]

Still another means of disarming animals by tampering painlessly with their horns was advanced by certain stockmen. These reformers proposed a delicate operation designed to redirect the horns by sawing off the end of the horn at an oblique angle from the front backwards; the result being that in a few months its direction of

growth had left only a rounded curve to be used for offensive purposes. The same results, it was suggested, could be achieved by
tying the head firmly and, with the aid of a rasp or piece of sharp
glass, shaving the inside of the horn if the purpose was to turn it
inward, and on the underside if one wished to turn it downward.
"In other words, rasp the horn on the side in the direction you wish
to turn it. By doing this you deaden the growth on the side rasped,
while the opposite side keeps on growing and naturally pushes the
horn to the desired shape." [32]

Despite all these humanitarian proposals, the controversial process of dehorning by the use of a handsaw or some other sharp
instrument grew more and more popular throughout this period.
This practice apparently originated in Ireland in the 1860's as a
result of certain difficulties that Irish cattle-raisers had experienced
in selling beef animals for the British market. It appears that English consumers had a strong preference for roast beef obtained from
hornless cattle and were willing to pay a higher price for such meat.
Since a high proportion of their cattle were horned, Irish cattlemen
were placed at a serious competitive disadvantage. This situation led
to the first attempts to produce polled cattle by removing their horns
with a sharp instrument. These initial experiments took place in
Ireland in 1868. As a result of this innovation, Irish cattle brought
premium prices in England. The dehorning process also made it
possible for them to ship larger numbers of cattle by sea and rail
with greater comfort, less cost per head, and with a marked reduction in deaths and injuries.[33] Scottish stockmen followed the Irish
example a few years later.

From Ireland and Scotland the idea of completely removing the
horns from adult cattle with sharp instruments was diffused, first to
England and then to the United States and a few years later to
Canada. In all these countries it was received initially with forceful
protests and legal actions by humane and antivivisection societies.
In England, for example, following a series of lower court cases, the
High Court of Justice in a celebrated "Norfolk dehorning trial"
interpreted the law to mean that "close" dehorning was too painful
and therefore violated a statute forbidding cruelty to animals. However, the court did not outlaw all forms of dehorning, for it per-

mitted cattlemen to remove several inches from the tip of the horn
on the ground that this operation caused no severe suffering or pain.[34]

In the United States the controversy ran a longer and more complex course. The removal of horns from the heads of calves with a
hot iron, a gouge, or a handsaw had been advocated at different
times during the first half of the nineteenth century, but few
farmers or stockmen had had the courage to perform the act on
adult cattle. Doubtless an occasional steer in the cattle country was
relieved of his long horns with a regular ax during shipment to
market, but such occurrences were rare. For the rest, there is no
evidence that dehorning was widely used before the middle 1880's.

In the United States, as in Canada, the movement for dehorning
generated intense feeling on the part of friends and foes and widespread controversy concerning its merits and demerits. From a local
dispute it soon developed into a national debate that raged over
several years before a consensus in both countries was achieved.

The Middle West appears to have produced the first successful
and continuing technique for removing the horns from adult bovine
animals with the aid of sharp instruments such as clippers or handsaws. The creator of this technique, and the leader of a long, vigorous, and ultimately successful crusade in favor of dehorning was a
certain Heman H. Haaff. Haaff came from New York to Illinois in
1854. Possessed of a fine educational background which included a
law degree, he taught school for two years in Oswego, Illinois, after
which he entered the law profession in Chicago. By 1874 he had
achieved considerable wealth which he invested in some 4,000 acres
of land and a large herd of cattle at Atkinson in Henry County.[35]

According to the scanty evidence at hand, Haaff performed his
first dehorning operation about 1878 after he had been attacked by
one of his own bulls. Angered by the animal's action, he had it
forced into a stanchion and immediately removed the horns with a
handsaw. Noting the calming effect produced by the operation, he
concluded that general adoption of the practice might benefit the
whole industry and began a controversial campaign in favor of
dehorning. His campaign had repercussions that reached well beyond the borders of Henry County, and aroused such strong feelings
that he soon faced a series of prosecutions on the grounds of "cruelty

to animals." The central issue in the trials that followed was whether or not the removal of horns with a handsaw was a cruel and barbarous act, and whether or not it was essential for the continued progress of a rapidly changing livestock industry.[36]

The most celebrated of these dehorning trials was held in Henry County in the late fall and winter of 1885–86. Haaff, the defendant, was brought into court on the charge of cruelty for removing the horns from his neighbors' animals as well as his own.[37] This extraordinary legal contest soon became a *cause célèbre* and received wide coverage in the metropolitan newspapers, the national farm journals and publications of the agricultural societies. Journalists immediately perceived the news possibilities of the testimony, filled with blood, torture, and gory accounts of hooking cows and vicious bulls. Haaff himself was a colorful character, highly vocal, intensely earnest, a fluent writer, an effective debater and orator, and eminently successful as a stockman and landowner.[38] He was an abrasive and uncompromising speaker, welcoming all opponents to debate him on this "remedial enterprise." In platform debate or in responding to hecklers in an audience at a farm meeting or a local fair he had a decided capacity for caustic language and a well-turned phrase.

He supported his almost evangelistic beliefs on this subject in two challenging books, the most popular and successful being *The Practical Dehorner, Or Every Man His Own Dehorner.* In this work he presented a complete set of instructions for the beginner. He was also an ardent campaigner with his pen. An adverse remark or criticism of his methods or his ideas in any livestock or farm journal was sufficient incentive for him to launch a series of polemic letters that attempted to set the editor or publisher straight on the matter. These attributes attracted much attention to Haaff and before the dispute had been resolved he and his favorite slogan, "The Horns Must Go," were known from coast to coast by farmers, dairymen and cattle-raisers alike.[39]

Haaff was more than a propagandist for his cause; he also provided it with its technology. Soon after his trial he began to manufacture and sell patented tools of his own invention: gouges, handsaws, clippers and a chute large enough to enclose the most vicious bulls. He traveled throughout the West and Southwest where his ideas were more quickly accepted than in parts of the Middle West. He later extended his campaign with the same impetus and vigor to the dairy interests. Wherever he went he contracted to dehorn large numbers of cattle and calves for a small fee per head, and since his instruments were all patented he often engaged stockmen and farmers as his sole agents to sell and to act as distributors for these tools and devices.[40]

Haaff's trial in Oswego, Illinois, was perhaps the most significant event in the history of dehorning for two principal reasons. In the first place, the testimony at his trial first acquainted the American public with the basic arguments for and against dehorning and the essential techniques used in the operation. Secondly, the notoriety created by the trial gave the dehorning movement such momentum and popularity that in a short time it flowered into one of the nationwide crazes that periodically swept over rural America.[41]

The plaintiff in this trial was the Illinois Humane Society. It appears that an agent of the organization happened to be in Haaff's neighborhood in November, 1885, investigating a complaint that livestock had been cruelly handled by a railroad company in this area while in transit from the West to the Chicago Yards. In the course of this inquiry the Society learned of Haaff's exploits as a dehorner and determined to move against him.[42]

Attorneys for this Society charged Haaff with violation of the Illinois anti-cruelty laws. At the trial the prosecution ably presented a number of expert witnesses, veterinarian and public health officials, brought from Chicago and Springfield, together with several depositions from other individuals, all of whom supported the contention that dehorning was inhumane and barbarous. In the judgment of these individuals it was an "atrocious cruelty," comparable to that of pulling off the nail from the finger or toe of a human being, a practice that had not been employed since the days of the Inquisition. These witnesses also argued that the operation produced no beneficial results for either the animal or the owner; on the other hand, the protracted suffering inflicted on the animals had been known to cause illness and death.[43]

When the last prosecution witness had been called, the Humane

Society and its supporters were convinced that they had won their case. But the plaintiffs had failed to take the measure of their opponent. Haaff and his attorney had made elaborate preparations for the trial. As defense witnesses they selected some twenty farmers who were eager to testify in their behalf. Haaff had also secured a few midwestern veterinarians who testified that dehorning was no more painful than some of the traditional medical practices, such as the spaying, branding, and castrating currently inflicted upon domestic animals.[44] The defense argued further that this operation was not overly painful if performed properly. To prove their point, Haaff's attorney brought into the courtroom "a whole bag of horns" which had been removed from the heads of local cattle. Using these specimens, he demonstrated the Haaff technique to the judge and the rural audience purporting to prove that proper removal of the horn was not attended by any excessive suffering to the animal. One of the clinching points of the defense was the observation that newly dehorned cattle in most cases returned to their food and drink almost immediately after the operation.[45]

Even before the defense had concluded its argument, it became obvious that the hostility toward dehorning which members of the audience displayed before the trial began had been almost completely dissolved, and most of the two hundred or more cattlemen in the courtroom had become partisans of Haaff's innovation. So evident was this reversal of opinion that the Humane Society moved for an immediate dismissal of the trial. Evidently the Society's attorney suspected that it would be impossible to obtain a judgment in its favor in such a predominantly rural community and believed that their only hope was to test the issue in court in an urban area, such as Cook County.[46] The trial had clearly shown that farmers and rural veterinarians were likely to have ideas of what constituted cruelty to animals that differed from those of urban dwellers. This divergence of views doubtless reflected the fact that the farmers were in closer contact with domestic animals than the latter and had experienced or observed the serious effects of their horns.

Haaff and his followers had not expected this sudden turn of events. At the conclusion of the trial they remained in the courtroom in order to take the fullest possible advantage of their victory by giving the maximum publicity to the evidence favorable to their cause that had been presented in the course of the trial. Accordingly, they drew up an elaborate report incorporating this evidence and distributed it to the Chicago newspapers and agricultural journals, urgently requesting that they publish this material.[47]

After the smoke of battle had cleared, heartened by the favorable verdict of the court, Haaff began another vigorous campaign to sell his ideas to the farmer and livestock-breeder. Traveling throughout the West and especially the Southwest, even invading the Indian Territory, he lectured and demonstrated at agricultural fairs and conventions, dehorning large numbers of beef cattle, until he acquired such prominence that he was frequently designated the dehorning "Apostle." [48] As a result of all this activity, a great mania to get rid of horns arose in the prairie and plains states during the latter 1880's. By the close of that decade, Haaff, having seen his ideas take firm root among the western farmers and cattle-breeders, turned his energies eastward and invaded those states where dairymen were outspokenly in opposition to dehorning their valuable purebred cattle.[49]

Haaff immediately engaged these dairymen in battle. Characteristically, he asked no quarter and gave none. The hardest core of resistance to his crusade was composed of two or three prominent rural journals, with *Hoard's Dairyman* of Wisconsin the most vociferous, and some prominent veterinarians both here and abroad. Nearly all competent English veterinary authorities and their professional organizations were agreed as to the extreme cruelty of the operation. In Scotland, on the other hand, this opinion found few supporters; one of these was the eminent Professor Thomas Walley from the Edinburgh Veterinary College faculty, who strongly disapproved of the practice of sawing off horns; his views were widely reprinted in America and frequently cited by the dairy opposition.[50] Such expert opinion naturally carried exceptional influence, for Scottish doctors and scientists educated in Edinburgh were ranked higher in America at this time than specialists trained in this country.[51]

American veterinarians also opposed this practice, as the Haaff trial demonstrated. These were especially vocal during the beginnings of the movement. But as support for dehorning grew, and the rural public became more outspoken in its favor, these professionals, who were quite often editors of columns in veterinary or livestock journals, began to mute their dissent.[52] Two prominent veterinary surgeons, however, were very decided in their opposition to the very end. Around their leadership clustered a vigorous opposition of dairymen.

One of these veterinarians was Dr. A. J. Murray, who came to this country from England with a degree in veterinary science and later assumed the editorship of a column in the influential *Breeder's Gazette*. When the dehorning controversy arose he employed his pen vigorously against Haaff, charging him with prejudice and even dishonesty, on the ground that "a person who is making money by the performance and recommendation of dishorning can hardly be considered as an impartial judge of its merits." But Murray had an even stronger arrow in his quiver. He affirmed that the "Great Dehorner" withheld important information from his followers. He failed to reveal the whole truth concerning the cruelty of his operation. Moreover, Murray declared, Haaff did not disclose to the purebred cattle interests the extent of deformity caused to the heads of their animals by dehorning and the financial losses that must ensue as a consequence of this brutality.[53]

In his reply to these criticisms, Haaff refused to concede a single point. He had little faith in or respect for the veterinary profession, especially its members from abroad. The following line from one of his sharp retorts is typical of the man's style: "I have concluded that the veterinary fraternity of the country—at least the imported part thereof—is famous for three things: pills, plasters, and purgatory—giving us always a plentiful supply of the last-named from their mouths." [54]

Another dissenter was Dr. William Horne of Janesville, Wisconsin. He was a bitter-end opponent, using two of the better dairy journals, the *Jersey Bulletin* and the *Hoard's Dairyman*, as vehicles for his views. For some four or five years, editor Hoard and Dr. Horne, in combination with their purebred Jersey and Guernsey followers, constituted, Haaff insisted, "a dirty little ring in Wisconsin and Illinois." Ultimately their pseudo-scientific objections were

swept aside by the overwhelming advance of the dehorning movement.[55] Hoard and Dr. Horne rested their objection on the hypoth-
esis that

the butter function . . . is founded on the nervous temperament of the
animal, and as that temperament finds its origin in the brain, any
process that impairs the nervous and develops a tendency towards a
lymphatic temperament so strongly as the act of dehorning, must re-act
upon the butter producing functions in both male and female.[56]

They believed, to put it more simply, that by reason of the proximity of the horns to the brain, their removal would injure the
breeding potency of the bulls by diminishing their masculinity; they
also held that the nervous shock of the operation would hinder the
transmission of butter potency to the offspring.[57] They laid special
stress on the injury done to the males who, upon removal of their
horns, tended to suffer the loss of a "strong spirit, confidence, and a
disposition toward self-assertion," lapsing ultimately into a "listless,
mild-eyed" state "with heart, liver, kidneys, spine, etc., all 'out of
whack.'" The argument ran that the horns contained a life-giving
gluey substance which supplied a nourishment to the spine, which in
turn helped to feed these basic organs. Consequently, removal of the
horns shut off the supply of this nutriment, imparting a certain
debility to the whole animal and producing serious dorsal weaknesses and deformities in his offspring as well.[58] *Hoard's Dairyman*
supplied a pathetic, alleged instance of the debilitating effects of
dehorning: [59]

The main reason . . . for objecting to dehorning Jersey bulls . . . is
that it is likely to destroy their usefullness as sires. . . . [A certain bull]
on being dehorned lost his courage so far as to refuse to face a two year
old of his own sex, after one or two weak efforts at asserting his
superiority which before had never been questioned, he turned tail and
actually cried instead of marching around monarch of all he surveyed
undaunted. He slinks off into a corner of the pasture and too crestfallen
and dejected to assert his rights against one of his own species, very
much his inferior in every respect.

Aside from these influential dairy opponents to the dehorning
practice, the only other remaining opposition came from isolated

individuals whose conscience and religious feelings revolted against the idea of sawing off the horns of their "loving friends." These persons of tender conscience insisted that if they performed such a brutal deed or ever engaged a professional dehorner they would bear a burden of guilt and remorse for being so cruel to those who had been entrusted to them by the Creator of all life and whose horns were part of the grand design of creation and whose moral right and duty it was for them to accept and respect. They believed that if the Great Architect had wanted bovine creatures to be without horns it was certain He would have created them that way.[60]

Others, who subscribed to a belief in the immortality of domestic animals, proclaimed that one who wantonly and cruelly tortured these animals on earth could not hope to receive a "joyous greeting" from them when he passed the golden gate.[61]

A Wisconsin dairy farmer who had had removed the horns of his beloved Jersey cow reveals a depth of feeling in a letter describing his reaction to the operation: [62]

It may be humane but it hurts fearfully and I know it. If the horns are ever sawed off my cows it will be when I am away from home and know nothing about it. If the horns were already off, I am inclined to think I should not wish them on again, for they certainly do a great deal of mischief. But I can never be a party to inflicting such exquisite torture on the animals I have tended and cared for all their lives, have supplied every want and comfort and shielded from every storm or cause of worry and discomfort, till apparently they come to look upon me as their best friend and protector. The night after the operation, the agonizing look in the upturned eyes of that cow haunted my dreams continually, and the next morning I felt like a criminal when I looked her in the face.

Farm women sometimes responded with a flow of tears; often they objected to the attendance of youngsters at the bloody operation. On occasions these "women folks" protested in letters "to the papers telling how cruel it is, and how ashamed John Henry appeared when he came from the barn after the operation and hung up his saw." [63]

All these arguments, pseudo-scientific or emotional, failed to stem the rapid growth of dehorning in this period. One by one, farm and livestock journals came out in its favor. After 1887 a number of state experimental stations undertook some basic research into the practice that finally provided a solid experimental basis for dehorning. Professor W. A. Henry, director of the Wisconsin Agricultural Experiment Station, initiated one of the earliest and most objective studies in the fall of 1886. His experiment coincided with the initial dehorning crusade by Haaff who at this time lived not many miles to the south in northern Illinois. This fortunate proximity gave the two men the opportunity of sharing their experiences with each other.[64] Henry was not a colorful figure like Haaff, but the objective, scientific character of his experiment commanded much respect. He also corresponded extensively with farmers and dairymen on dehorning and other subjects, and wrote numerous articles for livestock and dairy magazines.[65]

He performed his first dehorning experiments at the College Farm on a Jersey bull and twelve adult steers; dairy cows were purposely omitted. His capable foreman at the station sawed off the horns quickly once the cattles' heads were in the stanchions and securely tied. The following extract from Henry's report describes the reactions of the steers: [66]

Of course blood flowed freely, a stream from each cut surface being thrown several feet at first and the fellows made a stubborn fight from the time the saw touched the quick of the horns. "Do I believe it hurts?" Of course I do. So it does for a man to have half a dozen teeth pulled out, ... In half an hour after dehorning, the whole bunch was running playfully about the pasture. . . . Each steer bled from a pint to a quart, though I think the smaller amount nearer the average. . . . For two or three days the animals acted as though they felt the wound, but they soon grew natural and now, two weeks after, we have the most quiet lot of creatures. . . . They do not seem like the same lot of cattle, but eat like a flock of Merino sheep. The most timid ones formerly, are now the equals of any, and all crowd up to the trough when grain is put in it, fearing nothing. The change is greater than I would have believed possible and most favorable to good results for the feed given.

I wish we did not have a horn on the farm. Our dairy cows fight and push each other most unmercifully and from the boss of the herd down to the baby calf, each animal must know its place. Every one of these battles mean[s] the loss of milk if nothing worse.

In this report Professor Henry made no effort to conceal the fact that the cattle had suffered pain. However, in reporting the experiment in another publication he tended to make light of this objection: "I believe it to be greatly overestimated. Ten minutes after the horns are off the cattle are eating hay as if nothing had happened. Some of our steers tried to hook others within twenty minutes after the operation. Instead of being a cruel operation, it is, in my estimation, a merciful one." [67] Finding nothing in this initial experiment to dissuade him from continuing the practice, he became one of the early influential leaders in the movement and was instrumental in removing all the horns from the remaining cattle on the College Farm.

Professor Henry's second experiment, some two years later, focused on questions of special interest to dairymen, who wished to know what were the effects of the operation on a dairy cow's temperature and even more important, what were the effects on milk and butter production following removal of the horns. With the issues of the effect of the operation on the temperament and potency of bulls Professor Henry refused to concern himself on the grounds that these questions "can only be settled by experiment on a large number of animals extending over several years."

Addressing himself to the problem of temperature, he recorded the milk and butterfat production, as well as the temperature, of twelve dairy cows for a period of six days before dehorning. Then he collected the same information for six days following the removal of their horns and compared the two sets of data. He noted a slight, but insignificant falling off in the milk yield and an equally insignificant increase in the butter fat content; as concerned the temperature, he recorded only a fraction of a degree of fever, and this passed in a few days. [68] In less than a week the cows had returned to normalcy in regard to these three measurable factors.

Other experiment stations made studies of various aspects of dehorning; these studies extended into the early years of the new century. They investigated the savings that might result from dehorning in regard to food, shelter, transportation, injuries, abortions and deaths; the most favorable techniques to use for binding animals; the best chemical compounds for removing calves' horns; the ideal sizes and shapes of cutting instruments, and, as always, the perennial subject of cruelty and what new means could be devised to reduce it. Various state publications gave wide publicity to these findings and the Department of Agriculture and its Bureau of Animal Industry included the results in their annual reports with a view to their further dissemination among the nation's farmers, dairymen, and cattle-raisers.[69]

The history of dehorning in the northern hemisphere would not be complete without a brief discussion of its spread from the United States into Canada. There it caused a storm of controversy.

A farmer in Oxford County, Ontario, recently returned from a visit to northern Illinois, where he had observed the novel operation performed with a handsaw, was so impressed that he undertook to perform the same operation upon his father's cattle. His action inspired his neighbors to do the same, and within a few months dehorning had become a "regular mania" in the province.[70] Immediately protests arose from veterinarians and members of anti-cruelty organizations who condemned the practice for the suffering it inflicted on animals. The dehorners countered with the claims that this operation was of great utility to stockmen and that the suffering inflicted on the cattle was slight; in short, they argued that the end justified the means.

In due time opponents of dehorning initiated a test case against a number of dehorners on the grounds of cruelty. Many stock-raisers testified that dehorning had great value for them in handling livestock. These witnesses also testified that the suffering endured by the animals was neither excessive nor of long duration. The magistrate, having considered all the evidence, rendered a decision favorable to the defendants.

Having gained this initial victory the Ontario stockmen mobilized to give effect to the current slogan: "The Horns Must Go." Since most of the veterinarians refused to lend themselves to this purpose cattle-raisers found it necessary to perform the act themselves or engage those few individuals who had previously operated on their own cattle. This created a small group of "professional" dehorners who worked with such zeal that a new storm blew up; indeed several of these men were arrested, charged with cruelty and brought into court. This second trial was more prolonged and received extensive coverage in the provincial press. The magistrate finally reversed the decision in the first trial, found every defendant guilty, and fined each $50. The magistrate offered the following reasons for this reversal: (1) the justification offered for the removal of the horns did not appear a substantial one, (2) the removal of horns had little apparent effect on the disposition of cattle, (3) the removal was an excessively cruel operation, and (4) removal of horns could promote fraud since the horns were the surest means of telling an animal's age, and without them a dishonest dealer "may more easily deceive and palm off upon the purchaser an old animal." [71]

This adverse decision did not terminate the controversy in Ontario; in fact, it gave additional impetus to the dehorning movement. In the sequel the provincial government decided to enter the dispute by appointing a special commission to investigate the entire problem and submit a fair and unbiased judgment to the people.[72] This body, consisting of representatives from various groups of Canadian society, made a "full enquiry" into all aspects of dehorning, emphasizing especially its effect upon the cattle themselves. After securing testimony for a period of some three months, from ninety-eight witnesses representing all occupations with any interest in the livestock industry, the Commission submitted a report containing several pertinent recommendations on the subject. This report throws a valuable light on the views of all the interested parties.

Early in the testimony it became apparent that practically all interviewed farmers were in favor of dehorning. Those who had actually witnessed the operation were particularly ardent in their support of it. On the other hand, veterinarians differed sharply among themselves on the utility of the operation and on the amount of suffering endured by the animals. This cleavage in professional opinion placed the anti-cruelty spokesmen in a difficult position. This same division naturally influenced the final recommendations of the Commission, since it left the principal issue of cruelty, upon which most of the previous litigation had been based, more or less in doubt. Exponents of dehorning also sought to weaken the opposition case by arguing that other painful experiences were inflicted on domestic animals, such as branding, docking, and castration. Yet these practices were considered wholly legitimate and necessary on the grounds that the end justified the means.[73]

Having heard a preponderance of evidence favoring the innovation, the Commission submitted two general recommendations to the Ontario government. Briefly summarized, they were as follows: (1) they conceded that dehorning was of such importance that it should be legally sanctioned, but emphasized that the operation should be performed with reasonable skill and with the proper instruments, and (2) the Experimental Farm of the province should carry out a series of experiments using various chemicals on the horns of young calves, in order to evaluate this method.[74]

By the early 1890's the great debate over dehorning, which had engaged the rural mind for nearly a decade in both Canada and the United States, had ended. Great numbers of rural Americans gave a reluctant assent to the practice, for many retained a sentimental attachment to horned cattle and maintained to the last that the operation was cruel and painful. But in this case, as in so many others involving a clash between ideology and sentiment, on the one hand, and the demands of the new industrial order, on the other, the forces of technological change and the pressure of material interests gained the upper hand and finally created a consensus.

CHAPTER III

From Folkways to Science
in Livestock Medicine

BEFORE THE emergence of scientifically trained veterinarians in the latter part of the nineteenth century, illness and disease in livestock were the most acute and economically crippling problems facing the American farmer. Eternally confronted with normal accidents and ailments common to all farm beasts, he was further beset by epidemics and maladies which often devastated whole areas of the nation. Many of these scourges, when they struck, took a fearful toll of the farmer's horses, cattle, hogs, sheep, and poultry. It was not uncommon for entire communities to have their domestic animals wiped out by disease.

In such a crisis the farmer was forced to rely on his own empirical knowledge or that of his neighbor's—usually an amalgam of traditional superstitions and common sense. If that failed, he might turn either to the agricultural journals that printed an endless number of letters from subscribers with recommended cures, or resort to one of the variety of practitioners commonly referred to as "hoss doctors" or "cow-leeches." These men either lived in the community or were quack veterinarians passing through in search of customers. From the 1850's until the 1890's, when primitive practices began to give way to scientific procedures, it was to these early predecessors of the trained veterinarian that the farmer often turned for such livestock medical service as he could not perform himself.

In most sections of the country the problems posed by illness and disease were further aggravated by the conditions under which animals were raised and tended. Since many states had fencing laws requiring each farmer to fence out all livestock in order to protect crops, stock roamed widely in the woods and on the open prairie pastures. Under such enclosure conditions, maladies easily spread far and wide. Since many farmers and a greater number of breeders provided no shelter other than an occasional strawstack, the animals were compelled to forage outside all winter without regular food and water, making them susceptible to disease. One western observer remarked that a large percentage of livestock in his area actually lived "in a condition approaching a state of nature." Another asked, "How long will farmers neglect to take the necessary precaution to prevent starvation and disease from ravaging their stock-yards in the spring season of the year? There were thousands of cattle in our State last spring but just able to creep around, and thousands more had fallen a prey to starvation and disease."[1]

In addition to the problems growing out of epidemics and neglect there was also the problem of accident and injury, which in many cases required some form of medical service. It was fairly common for horses to become entangled in barbed wire fences, incurring serious and permanent injury; hogs—the most difficult of all farm animals as far as enclosure was concerned—were habitually dogged by the canines of the neighbors, causing not so many deaths as large gaping wounds and the loss of ears. The farmer's sheep also were attacked unless attended by a shepherd night and day, and even with expert attention an entire flock might be killed or severely wounded in a single night by marauding dogs.[2] One writer remarked that apparently the dog was the only creature on the farm able to withstand all onslaughts of "diseases, distempers, doctors, drug stores and death."

The cruelty or negligence by which livestock were often handled by their owners often required the services of the local animal doctors. Numerous contemporary accounts record the inhuman treatment practiced upon dumb animals; the editors of farm publications frequently protested against this brutality.[3] Cows were often unmilked for days at a time. During the winter season they were kept in dungy barns and sheds, the filth and stench of which had accumulated over a four- or five-month period. Animals were beaten "unmercifully and . . . crippled and ruined for life" in order to satisfy the passions of their handlers, one western journalist noted. Often overfed or not fed at all, and frequently driven hard and long until they were near exhaustion, they were then exposed to the elements, being made to stand for hours hitched to a post in the street without food or water. So common were these habits of overdriving, overloading, and overworking that they began to attract attention beyond the local communities; in time anti-cruelty societies arose in various states to cope with the problem.[4]

To deal with these difficulties—epidemics, accidents, cruelty, and neglect—the farmer and stock-breeder had to resort to such service as was available. At best such service was limited, for as late as 1890 most localities lacked a trained veterinarian. But, strange as it may seem, even if one was within driving distance, most farmers preferred the "hoss doctor cow-leech," or the community quack.

The right of these local practitioners to practice stemmed from no formal training, since most were wholly uneducated, but rested on intangibles of natural talent or revealed religion or some special powers of healing attributed to them by the rural community. It was widely believed in rural circles that some men were born to be doctors, having been endowed by heaven with a power of perception and with a virtue in their touch which obviated patient observation and study. One was fortunately born the seventh son of the seventh son and thereby was believed to possess the natural gift of healing; another was born with a caul or what some thought of as a lucky birthright.[5]

These rural medicine men came from various backgrounds. Some were former stable-keepers who, after consulting a farrier's guidebook and learning a few techniques of treating animals, began calling themselves "hoss doctors." Others were former coachmen, fallen for one reason or another from their high estate, but enjoying the prestige attached to this class of men who "know all about a hoss." Still others may have worked for a period with a practitioner who was also a part-time blacksmith, teamster, groom, ploughman, or "physic-monger"—the name often given to a rural druggist or chemist. Finally, some were former horse-dealers or jockeys. Dressed in the conventional tight breeches and cutaway coats of their professions, they carried their rods on one side, drank their "glass like a man," and swore like troopers. Such backgrounds qualified these men to practice the honorable art of "bleeding, blistering, burning and physicing." [6]

Cruelty characterized the procedures of these bogus doctors to an extent that staggers the imagination. The vogue of such barbarous techniques of treatment as bleeding, blistering, burning, and the like becomes easier to understand when we note that according to one estimate, the country had no less than 500 quacks and "cow-leeches" to every qualified veterinarian.[7] Dr. Daniel E. Salmon, a leading contemporary veterinary surgeon, declared it was impossible to mobilize rural public opinion against this cruelty to livestock.

For centuries physicians had used bleeding to cure certain human ailments. By 1865 this ancient practice was virtually extinct as concerned human surgery, but it continued to be used on farm animals in rural areas, where traditions still held sway. A livestock reporter stated that there were few horses that did not bear several scars, each testifying to an operation at the hands of an ordinary horseman or a farrier. Regardless of the animal's age, condition, or disease, the practitioner always discovered that it required bleeding, an easy operation that brought him a fee.[8] When bleeding was used for such ailments as blind staggers, colic, dysentery, inflammation, or a host of others, one to two quarts of blood was supposed to be the maximum taken; some "bleeders," however, went far beyond this amount and bled the animal until it could hardly stand up. As described by one writer, the technique consisted in the surgeon holding "up the stable pail to catch the vital current which they allowed to flow until the poor animal actually staggers. . . . The strangest fact is that most owners love to see the purple life drained as long as the horse can stand. . . . There are, . . . too many

persons . . . morally certain that every quadruped in their possession will be benefited by losing a gallon or so of blood three or four
times a year." [9]

Another practice in the "hoss doctor's" repertory, and one which
was used extensively as a catch-all for many livestock ailments, was
known as firing, burning, or blistering. In any of its various forms
the process was an operation requiring no particular skill, such as
the use of a surgeon's knife, being performed with crude irons
designed in some crossroads blacksmith shop. Instead of irons, the
more humane practitioner might substitute a blistering corrosive of
his own concoction. However, to satisfy the caprices of employers
and bystanders many preferred the more showy operation of firing
or burning with irons.

Firing was used to correct a difficulty called lampas that often
appeared in horses' mouths. A congestion of the mucous membrane
of the hard palate back of the incisors, this condition was due no
doubt to the aftermath of teething in young horses and to digestive
disorders in older ones. Usually it caused some temporary interference with the animal's eating habits. The owner, noting the swollen
condition of the animal's mouth, turned to a "hoss doctor" if one was
available; otherwise he would solicit the services of the community
blacksmith. In this latter case the technique of firing was to hold a
red-hot iron against the roof of the animal's mouth until it was
burned in a most barbarous manner; if the beast did not regain its
appetite within a reasonable time, the process might be repeated. [10]
Despite the fact that leading veterinarians throughout the nation
inveighed against the operation as useless, farmers, apparently deaf
to scientific explanations and admonishments, continued to patronize these neighborhood doctors.

Other practices of these "roasting veterinarians," as they were
often styled by more intelligent members of the farm community,
treated the spavin and ringbone disorders so often found among
work horses. The common treatment of this bone ailment was either
to burn with the irons the diseased part of the bone thought to have
caused the lameness, or to administer some potent caustic medicine.
A few practitioners acquired some prominence in this field; one in
Iowa had a reputation as being the great "bone melter," while

another gained renown for a medicine he devised to cure these disorders and sold under the name of "Magic Bone Disolvent." The claims of effectiveness for these various concoctions were such that one doctor went so far as to promise that his remedy would absolutely correct the bone ailments within a few hours without blistering or even irritating the skin! [11]

Another ailment which the doctors treated was a condition, or an imaginary disturbance, labeled "wolf-teeth" by country folk. This concerned a supplementary set of teeth which appeared in young horses but which in most cases dropped out rather early. However, while the teeth were present, the eyes occasionally had a harmless tendency to swell and show signs of irritation. Farmers frequently became alarmed—there was a traditional belief that if the teeth were not removed they would cause blindness—and called upon the horse doctor to administer his cure. With his large punch and hammer the doctor would set to work knocking out the offending teeth and leaving an almost incredible state of suffering, pain, and mutilation. [12]

Finally there was an ailment, less prominent than those previously described, called the "hooks" or "haws." When a horse had some trouble walking, which might be due to any number of causes, such as a sprained back or weakness from being overworked, a "hoss doctor" often convinced the owner that the fault lay in a diseased eye, whereupon the doctor proceeded to remove the nictating membrane, or inner eyelid. When performed by the local practitioner the result was inhuman torture, for he would have to hobble the animal, tie its head solidly and then remove the "hook" with a sharp knife. Loss of sight often followed. [13] One of the better known veterinarians in Illinois, Dr. N. H. Paaren, outraged by these practices, was provoked to remark in 1880 that such a cruel operation demonstrated that in the curing of animal diseases men still had not progressed very far along the road toward civilization.

Additional weapons in the arsenal of these so-called doctors were the strong purgatives and drenches used to combat some of the more common indispositions of horses. Unfortunately these men had no conception of the unscientific nature or the debilitating character of these so-called cures, nor did they recognize the evil results which followed their indiscriminate use. A noted veterinary surgeon, writing in one of the journals, informed his readers that incredible were the doses sometimes administered to horses. Another authority, writing in a popular magazine, stated that these nostrums were "poured down the animals" in season and out, and had been for centuries, whether the horses were well or sick; in most cases the noxious mixtures had no effect on the health of the animal. Among the favorite articles found in the purges of these local teamsters, grooms, coachmen, and ploughmen were dragon's blood, black antimony, sulphur, spices, and condiments of all kinds mixed together in various unsavory concoctions, often including the animal's excretions. In some parts of the country strong mineral poisons, acids, and preparations of arsenic, antimony, and mercury were forced down the unhappy beasts.[14]

For the complaints commonly diagnosed as colic, bots, and the like, two or three standard traditional techniques were used in administering a physic. When chemicals were administered in solid form the most prevalent method in use was called the "ball." The dose, in the form of an oblong mass of rather soft consistency but tough enough to retain its shape and wrapped up in thin paper, ordinarily ran from one-half to one ounce and was placed far down the throat by means of a balling-iron which held the mouth open. The ball's contents were ostensibly secret, but actually the elements were known by most horsemen; in fact, the physic-mongers were willing to sell the components to all. When the drench was administered instead of the ball, the concoction was usually poured down the animal's throat from an ox's horn or large bottle. Such a method was wasteful of the medicine and on occasions proved fatal, since the victim might be suffocated, especially if as was sometimes done the draught was administered through the nose.[15]

A typical drench, used when horses had the colic or bots, consisted of various combinations of strong chemical ingredients, or just plain local products found on the farm. Some doctors administered through the mouth a mixture of lard, soot, and pepper, while others might give as much as a pint of castor or coal oil through the nose. A reporter who had witnessed an instance of the latter procedure, observed, "If you were bound to destroy the poor animal, you could scarcely have adopted a more certain, though slow and cruel method." Rural newspapers and farm journals carried advertisements or descriptions of many varieties of these cures, not only for colic but for a considerable number of illnesses.[16] Though some of the treatments were quite mild, others were more severe. A good example of the latter type was reported by an observer who had actually seen a rural doctor pour boiling water down an unfortunate animal's throat in the hope of killing bots. A second observer, Dr. C. A. Woodward of Madison, Wisconsin, described a colic cure just as painful as the one noted above, except that it was an external treatment. The horse was laid on its side, a peck or so of salt was spread over the rump and dissolved by the use of cold water; then the belly was kneaded by a heavy man who wore thick boots and walked back and forth across the abdominal area where the obstruction or spasm was supposed to be located. At times, as a rubbing instrument, a chestnut rail was substituted for the man and his boots.[17]

Rural America had another type of practitioner, known as the village or neighborhood "cow-leech," who mainly tended the farmers' cattle. This type had much in common with the "hoss doctor"—a total ignorance of the nature of animal diseases and of the fundamentals of veterinary science.

In addition to administering strong drenches, the "cow-leech" often resorted, as did his "hoss doctor" counterpart, to the practice of bleeding cows for certain ailments that beset them in the spring of the year after a long and hard winter. In some sections of the country, these practitioners advocated that calves be bled in order to increase their appetites and to produce a veal with a more salable white meat.[18] One agricultural journal has offered this evaluation of the "cow-leech's" work:

The local "cow doctors" which abound in many sections, are wholly inefficient for the proper protection of our live stock, in case of . . . an epidemic like the pleuropneumonia or the rinderpest. . . . They work on the "guess" system, and treat all cases nearly alike; so that, if perchance an animal recovers under their treatment, it is in spite of it, and a case of pure luckiness, rather than a consequence of their skill.[19]

Among cattle diseases treated by the "cow-leeches" there were scarcely more than two ever described in the current veterinary books. Rural dwellers called them "hollow-horn" and "wolf-tail," the latter being sometimes vulgarized to "tail-ail." The term "ail" might be affixed to indicate any affliction of an extremity of the body, such as hoof-ail and horn-ail. They were little more than generic terms covering almost any specific sickness, and veterinarians did not regard them as prime sources of most animal diseases.

In one, the horn was thought to be the source of the disturbance. When the cow displayed signs of illness, the "cow-leech" first examined the horns, and the usual procedure was to drill through the base of one with a gimlet. Since he believed the horn was by nature a solid appendage and whereas upon examination it was revealed to be largely hollow, that fact in itself was ample proof to the "cow-leech" that the locus of the affliction was centered in this external growth. The boring through the horn alone was an intensely painful operation, but the treatment that followed the diagnosis was doubly so. In his attempt to cure the animal the "cow-leech" generally employed spirits of turpentine which he applied freely and rubbed into the hole that he had made in the horn. If this local application did not soon restore the animal's health, he would extend his rubbing with the same medication the full length from horn to tail, producing a solid blister down the entire back.[20]

A second location for a whole series of bovine illnesses was thought to be the tail. Concentration upon this appendage by the leeches probably stemmed from the fact that the bones of a cow's tail gradually diminish in size until near the extremity they finally disappear in flexible gristle. During the time of illness it was observed that both bones and gristle tended to become somewhat more relaxed and less rigid than when the animals were well, creating the illusion that some of the bones were missing. On this basis the "cow-leech" concluded that the absent bones had been devoured by a hypothetical worm, or what was then called the "wolf."

The "cow-leech" tended to diagnose a fairly large percentage of all ailments as "tail-ail." Taking from his kit a sharp knife, he split the animal's tail open near the extremity, and removed what he contended was a small worm which had eaten the gristle and flesh, leaving nothing but the skin for a space of six inches. Then he would rub red pepper and salt into the wound of the mangled and bleeding tail, thus increasing the pain and suffering. The theory was that removal of this imaginary parasite would prevent further eating away of the tail by the "wolf" and thus keep it from affecting the spine and perhaps ultimately killing the beast. If the wretched cow recovered, it was thanks to the removal of the "worm"; if she died, the operation had been performed too late and the parasite had taken its toll—so reasoned the farmer as well as the leech.[21] To trained veterinarians, this splitting open of the tail was a survival of archaic practices, surviving into the nineteenth century only because too many farmers and breeders were still opposed to scientific cures.

Although such practitioners as the horse doctor and the "cow-leech" were as ignorant of animal physiology and veterinary science as they were lacking in professional training, most farmers believed in them with a touching faith. One point can be made in their defense: cruel and barbarous as they were, the "hoss doctor" and "cow-leech" were needed. No other way existed of meeting the wants of the agri-culturist in this period. As one prominent veterinarian has observed, despite their serious errors the doctors and the leeches were able to offer certain services that helped to bridge the gap between the old and the new in veterinary medicine.[22]

Another important group of livestock practitioners was composed of community quacks who assumed the title, bought and paid for, of Veterinary Surgeon. No better than the horse doctor or the leech, in most respects they were more mercenary than either. A legitimate veterinary surgeon, writing in one of the professional journals in 1885, said of this group of frauds:

The "hoss-doctors" at the country cross-roads whom everybody knew to have no professional training, and who made no pretense of being graduates of any school higher than a blacksmith shop or a livery stable, were bad enough, but a horde of quacks, having no more theoretical knowledge and a great deal less of the practical, backed up by college diplomas would be a great deal worse; and it seems to me the authorities should protect the people from this form of quackery, and see that those who hold themselves out as veterinary surgeons are so in point of fact, and not merely by virtue of a piece of purchased paper.[23]

Few of these imposters had even a high-school education; many could scarcely speak or read their own language; and only a small percentage could lay claim to any scientific training. Most of them came from rural backgrounds and had a strong liking for animal life. Having memorized the names of a few common drugs and some of the ordinary operations described in current livestock medical books, they were ready to hang out their shingles. Bogus diplomas, enabling their owners to masquerade as doctors of veterinary science, could be secured from so-called veterinary colleges and could be framed and hung on the wall for rural patrons to see.[24] But such quacks, despite their dishonest accoutrements of learning and experience, had, as one rural editor remarked, difficulty in distinguishing "a case of glanders from one of nasal gleet and hardly a ring bone from a wart. . . . It would be impossible for a child to make greater blunders than some of these most pretentious veterinarians do." [25]

Responsibility for the traffic in bogus diplomas to all parts of the country rested on a few veterinary colleges located mainly in the large eastern cities. Founded some years before the entrance of this branch of science into the curriculums of state universities, most of these private institutions were financed entirely from fees. As a result large numbers of mediocre students were crowded into classes and graduated at the earliest possible moment—sometimes at the rate of two classes per year. To supplement their income, a few of the more disreputable colleges sold diplomas outright at a handsome sum, without any requirements in respect to scholarship or residence.[26] Philadelphia was the seat of most of these quack colleges, which in 1877 were selling diplomas for $100. Should the purchaser desire his diploma to contain a particular signature, for example, the name of a scholar in a foreign university, the price was increased to $135. The purchase of a sheepskin was generally accompanied by the supply—at an additional fee—of veterinary books which had ostensibly been written by the members of the college staff. Possession of these articles normally furnished a young man with the façade needed to begin his medical career.

This group of bogus veterinarians might be classified into two main types: those who developed a regular community practice; and those who traveled about the countryside selling their services as well as quack livestock remedies. Little need be said in regard to the work of the resident practitioners, since it was similar to that performed by the local "hoss doctor," with this difference: the quack was careful to classify himself as a bona fide doctor and employ all the learned trappings of an authentic medical man in dress, office, and manner, including the ever-present diploma on the wall.

Two anecdotes will typify the gross ignorance and ineptness of these community quacks. A veterinarian in Springfield, Illinois, was called upon to prescribe for a certain highbred horse. After very learnedly inspecting the sick animal for a few minutes, the doctor turned to the owner and remarked that the horse was suffering from "a relapse of the epizoot." The startled owner replied that the horse had never had the epizoot. "Oh, that's nothing," continued the quack, "it is nothing unusual for them to have the *relapse* first." [27]

A second story concerns a Kansas quack who signed his name with the purchased degree of "V.S." No doubt attempting to take a leaf from the book of one of the diverse medical "pathies" so prevalent in America at that time, he boldly claimed to have discovered an infallible vaccine which would cure all sorts of animal diseases. According to him, he had been able to isolate certain poisons accumulated in animals' bodies as a result of eating plants and other substances, which in time caused illnesses. He proceeded to inject quantities of this vaccine, in itself a certain poison, into the sick animals under the well-advertised assumption that like cures like or that two things cannot occupy the same space at the same time. Therefore, when these conditions prevailed, one of the poisons had to "get up and get." So humorous did this theory strike the scientific fraternity that one of its members was provoked to remark facetiously that "his pizen outpizens the other pizen."

The most highly publicized type of quack veterinarian was the itinerant who roved from one rural section to the next, hawking his wares and his numerous fraudulent cures, as was the custom of so many agents of humbuggery during the 1880's. This class of doctor-agents varied little from their disreputable contemporaries, the quack physicians, who in great numbers likewise preyed upon the simple country folk, in what, as one recent study has shown, was the golden age of medical quackery.[28] When an epidemic affecting either man or beast struck a rural community, farmers could be assured of the quack's visitation. The livestock quacks operated chiefly by advertising their remedies in the farm journals or by mailing out circulars, highly embellished with attractive pictures of healthy farm animals, designed to promote sales of their secret nostrums.[29] The rural press, with some honorable exceptions, defrayed much of its publication expenses with revenue derived from these "dead-shot" advertisements, covering the whole gamut of diseases from glanders to worms.[30] Solemnly guaranteeing a cure, the itinerant quacks were adamant that the fee be paid in advance. In time many of the farmers saw through this ruse and agreed to pay only after the animal had been treated; others offered to deposit the money in the local bank, to be surrendered when a cure was effected. The traveling doctors, well aware of their own limitations, usually rejected these stipulations.[31]

During the seventies and eighties, numerous epidemics (such as pleuropneumonia, glanders, Texas fever, and cholera) ravaged the nation periodically, sweeping away entire stocks of cattle, horses, swine, and poultry, and frightening farmers and breeders into trying many kinds of patent remedies.[32] In the case of cholera cures, the mobile quacks were able to strike it rich. Since no scientist at the time actually knew the real causes of this scourge, a general state of confusion existed in the rural mind—a condition favorable to the rise of a plethora of quack remedies which were developed and distributed not only by itinerant doctors but in many communities by the local druggists as well. A good illustration of the quack doctor's activity occurred in an Iowa community from which a Chicago quack carried off as much as $1600 gathered from sales of his patent humbug Hog Remedy.[33] This skillful operator was so bold that he remained in the neighborhood selling his cure until some of his customers had lost nearly all of their hogs; at this point he felt a sudden need to depart for greener fields. Another quack of the same type boasted of a cure so successful that it would not only prevent and cure all ills besetting poultry and swine but would actually leave them better off than if they had never had any disease.

Hundreds of these traveling charlatans circulated among the rural districts, peddling their celebrated remedies. One of the most noted of these was the cholera nostrum created by a Dr. Joseph

Haas of Indianapolis. Haas' medicine was sold far and wide by agents, doctors, and druggists; editors of various farm journals were even known to market it for certain fees.[34] Certificates confirming its curative powers were secured by the dozens from gullible farmers on the same plan as testimonials for patent medicine remedies for humans.

Two situations made it particularly easy for the quack doctor to obtain an ample stock of bogus certificates. First, when a disease like cholera struck a community, the infection eventually subsided— having run its course. Any particular cure in use at that time naturally received the credit in the form of a certificate, although nature and not the nostrum had in fact brought relief. Again, one farmer's hogs might escape the scourge, while those of his immediate neighbors were severely hit. The fortunate farmer, who may have been using a particular remedy at the time, would be more than willing to sign a certificate giving the nostrum credit for his hogs' immunity.[35]

Analyses made of these cures by reputable scientists of the day verified that they had little true merit. In 1889, a leading chemist of the New York Agricultural Experiment Station, commenting on the cures in general, said: "If these substances . . . could do what is claimed for them, the dread disease would have been wiped out of existence years ago."[36] Several others, including a trained pharmacist and a representative of the Illinois Industrial University, made similar analyses and all agreed that the ingredients used were valueless as cures, consisting only of inexpensive substances such as common salt, water, and castor oil, with small percentages of such strong ingredients as cayenne pepper and spirits of turpentine.[37]

During the 1870's and 1880's, an enormous number of livestock medical books purporting to help the farmer arrest the illnesses and epidemics among his increasing numbers of farm animals appeared on the market. Some were written by reputable American and European veterinary surgeons and were read by many country physicians; they, in turn, passed on the information to their farm patients, who sometimes consulted their family doctor concerning diseases of their livestock. Some of these books, however, were written by pseudo-veterinarians professing no scientific knowledge and who could only claim to have been born on a farm. These books of dubious value were hawked about the country by quacks and agents, of whom one farm journalist said: "Every rural neighborhood is infested with the inevitable book agent, who, with oily tongue, gulls the unsophisticated into purchasing some great 'Illustrated Stock-Book,' or 'Illustrated Horse Doctor,' or 'Complete Farrier,' or some other catchpenny, swindling affair, not worth the white paper it is printed upon." [38]

The larger farm journals proved of greater assistance to the farmers in their veterinary problems. Although most of these journals did little to expose quacks and humbugs, they did report the latest medical and scientific discoveries in the care of livestock. In a certain section of each journal was usually found a "Veterinary Department" or "Column" whose director was listed as a regular veterinarian (or medical doctor) and whose responsibility it was to extend expert advice to all inquirers and to offer an occasional commentary on the leading livestock problems. Inquiries describing as fully as possible a sick animal's symptoms would come in from readers, and shortly thereafter the journal might carry a discussion of the case. [39]

Undoubtedly, many of these columns contained a great deal of medical nonsense and many faulty prescriptions. Since persons trained in both veterinary science and journalism were rare, most editors engaged persons having only the slightest medical knowledge to write these columns. Although a few of the better farm magazines attracted well-trained surgeons as writers—especially in the late eighties—answers to inquiries in a majority of the magazines were written by pseudo-veterinarians or by downright quacks. Dr. A. A. Holcombe, professor of pathology and surgery in the American Veterinary College in New York City, while traveling in Nebraska in 1880, read some columns by a certain William Horne, M.D., V.S., who gave expert advice to farmers in that state. On returning to New York Holcombe bitterly attacked this imposter, "in order," he said, "to protect the farmers and stock owners of Nebraska from imposition." [40]

One national farm journal deplored the national dearth of properly trained veterinarians. The journal praised those practitioners who consistently disseminate correct information on veterinary matters, thus preparing the way for a more general appreciation of their profession and for the eradication of the bogus cures and the unreliable livestock books.[41] Some trained veterinarians, seeking to counteract the harm done by quacks, not only wrote for farm journals but traveled considerable distances to give professional advice. A good example was Dr. N. H. Paaren, one-time State Veterinarian of Illinois and at various times a veterinary columnist for the *National Live-Stock Journal* and the *Prairie Farmer*. Dr. Paaren notified farmers that he would serve anyone living within a hundred-mile distance of Chicago, provided round-trip fare to the nearest station were paid for in advance. He would perform surgical operations and examine and treat all forms of disease for moderate charges, especially if engaged to attend more than one customer. He also offered, for a small fee by mail, expert advice "concerning management and treatment of any species of domestic animals, in health or disease," and if desired the "properly compounded and reliable Medicine . . . together with full directions for their use." [42] Apparently Paaren's gesture bore fruit, for an increasing number of farmers began to use such services. In fact, some of the editors on various occasions reported that the veterinary departments of their journals had accumulated such a sizeable backlog of unanswered inquiries and suggested cures that they would have to refuse any more.[43]

In concluding this study of livestock practitioners, it is now appropriate to deal with the emergence of a modern scientific veterinary profession. Its growth was slow, a fact particularly striking because this period saw great strides made in other professions. By contrast with this era of mounting numbers of lawyers, physicians, and clergymen, the supply of trained doctors for domestic animals was conspicuously meager.

Why did farmers so long persist in allowing their sick animals to be practiced upon by "hoss doctors," "cow-leeches," and quacks? Why did farmers not patronize men who had been educated in the medical techniques of veterinary science when such men became available? Why was the profession so long in developing? Why, as an eastern journal asked in 1875, was it that

we Americans, a nation as enlightened as we suppose ourselves to be, so persistently ignore the claims of the Veterinary Art, and either allow our animals to suffer, and ourselves to sustain unnecessary loss at the hands of a set of ignorant men, self-styled Veterinary surgeons, who do not know the first rudiments of anatomy, pathology, physiology, or the action of drugs? [44]

There were diverse explanations for this cultural lag, but the one most frequently advanced was America's unfortunate dependence on English veterinary leadership. For many years after the veterinary art had become a reputable science in France and other European countries it remained in the British Isles in its unscientific stage, with folk doctors, farriers and grooms administering their age-old nostrums and cures. This appears inexplicable in a country that had produced a medical profession that had made notable progress in its treatment of human beings and had an outstanding record in the development of celebrated race horses and other fine specimens of livestock. But the fact is that England lagged in recognizing the need for scientific treatment of domestic animals and especially those of the cloven hoof. Veterinary colleges opened in London and Edinburgh many years after the first ones were begun on the Continent, and in view of the backwardness of these institutions it is not difficult to understand the English failure to create a scientific veterinary profession.[45] As a result of following the English lead, without trained veterinarians to draw upon for our scientific development, our country's livestock remained for most of the nineteenth century in the hands of a variety of inept practitioners.

Another plausible explanation of the American lag in the adoption of scientific veterinary medicine is suggested by a thesis developed in Richard Hofstadter's *The Age of Reform* (1955). Hofstadter suggests that for generations rural people were caught between the expanding world of commercial realities and the unreal, self-sufficient life of noncommercial agrarianism. The more agriculture developed scientifically and technologically, the more the farmer clung to the traditional ways with sentimental attachment. Those traditional rural values exalted the goodness of farming, the sanctity of living in isolation, and, above all, the benefits that ensued from being close to nature. Simultaneously, there existed in the farmer's mind his age-old suspicion, mistrust, and fear of urban society, industry, and science. To a certain extent this conflict between the farmer's cherished agrarian values and contemporary scientific realities made him incapable of choosing the new and rejecting the old; he continued to give his loyalties to the "mythical" ideals and values of an agrarian society. As a result, for many years after the establishment of an acceptable veterinary science, he continued to engage the services of folk doctors and to regard educated surgeons "as an inferior order of beings." His faith in the old remedies transcended his faith in the scientific ones, and as a consequence the demand for trained veterinarians was negligible, with the result that few young men could be induced to enter the profession.

Closely related to the hold of the agrarian myth was the farmer's traditional belief in what often modern sociologists refer to as a complex of "agricultural magic." This system sprang from centuries of rural living and had no basis in fact or scientific explanation. It was rural magic, practiced in the planting of crops, in breeding, weaning, slaughtering, castrating or dehorning of livestock, or in the cutting of rails, weeds, and bushes by the signs of the moon. One of its manipulations was the practice of divining for wells, involving the employment of a "water witch" with his carefully selected dowsing rod in the form of a Y-shaped branch.[46] These were some of the main forms of agricultural magic, but hundreds of minor signs and superstitions induced farmers to resist rational developments in farming practices and to continue to treat the illnesses of their livestock with traditional cures.[47]

These complexes of myth and magic help to explain why the farmer permitted his domestic animals to be subjected to cruel and barbarous cures at the hands of local practitioners, frequently to his own great financial loss through the death of valuable stock.[48] Reflecting on this paradox, one observer remarked that the farmer responded in very different ways to different classes of problems on the farm. When he had to select a blacksmith, a builder, a steamboat pilot, or a merchant, his judgment was on a par with that of urban people. But when he had to choose a doctor for his animals—or even for his family—he was a babe in the woods, generally employing the most ignorant and boastful practitioners in the community.[49]

This rural hostility to a trained professional class in veterinary science was reflected in various actions designed to inhibit its growth and maintain the existing state of affairs. An example is the vigorous opposition to state or federal regulations designed to control the quacks and nonprofessionals. Clinging to the old methods and cures, farmers contended that if the laws were passed giving the right to practice to trained veterinarians alone, a large percentage of the nonprofessional practitioners would be barred from performing their services, a situation that would create a serious problem in areas miles removed from the nearest professionals.[50]

Another impediment to the science of veterinary surgery was the national government's failure to encourage its development. The Department of Agriculture for years tended to ignore the problem of diseases—at a time when epidemics and scourges were rampant—and showed a complete apathy toward the establishment of a veterinary division. No country in the world had as many animals or took less interest in their behalf, as was demonstrated by a comparative study made in this and foreign nations of the number of veterinary colleges and the number of animals during this period.[51] For example, Prussia, with one-third as many animals in 1877 as the United States, had as many as five colleges, all maintained by the state. France gained renown for her early scientific studies in this field and was especially noted for her three superior veterinary schools, founded by royal prerogative. Even Great Britain, with only about one-half our livestock, had four such colleges. On the other hand, the United States, with two to three times as many animals as any of these countries, had not a single college of national importance, and none that was maintained by public funds.[52] There were two or three struggling private colleges in the East, but largely diploma mills. Most western states had no veterinary schools of any kind.[53]

Census reports on the number of veterinarians in the United States for the decades between 1850 and 1900 show the retarded state of the profession: 46 in 1850; 392 in 1860; 1,166 in 1870; 2,130 in 1880; 6,494 in 1890; and 8,163 in 1900.[54] This increase in numbers was more an increase in quantity than in quality, since the census figures included some who called themselves doctors, but were not trained surgeons. Furthermore, these figures do not tell the complete story, for many practitioners had migrated to America from other countries and were not educated here. For example, the census for 1870 reveals that 63.8 per cent of our veterinarians were American born, 20.4 per cent came from Great Britain, 10.5 per cent from Germany, and 5.3 per cent from various other countries.[55] Thus, more than a third of the academically trained doctors had come to the United States from other countries. Even with the Old World's contributions the profession in America was still greatly retarded in comparison with other countries; its development had been impeded by the lack of a scientific climate and by the agrarian myths, values, and ideals of the rural inhabitants.

But, by 1890, the tide had begun to turn. A growing interest in various aspects of veterinary science in the United States developed on both the state and national levels. As a result of the great plagues that swept the country in the seventies and eighties, a few veterinarians were employed to staff and supervise the state veterinary departments and experiment stations, federal sanitary commissions and special investigating committees of the Congress, although it was not until 1883 that the Veterinary Division was finally established in the Department of Agriculture to meet the urgent needs for reliable information concerning the nature and prevalence of animal diseases as well as the means of eradicating them. In that same year the Bureau of Animal Husbandry was set up—superseding the Veterinary Division—for the immediate purpose of eradicating the pleuropneumonia epidemic.[56]

During the eighties several of the universities and agricultural colleges began to develop veterinary departments as well as colleges with trained faculties, offering relatively respectable degrees, and maintaining certain basic standards for entrance and graduation. However, the private veterinary schools that were operated mainly for profit escaped control and continued for some years to carry on their low caliber type of instruction and to flood the country with poorly trained practitioners.[57] State veterinary associations, especially in the more populous states, were organized and held regular annual meetings in which they discussed not only the usual scientific papers but also the pressing problems of both educating the public and regulating the profession. One of the early annual meetings of the National Veterinary Medicine Association was held in Boston in 1878 with seventeen members present, three of whom were medical men; another meeting was assembled in Chicago in 1884 with twenty-six delegates in attendance; a very humble beginning that within a few years developed into an important learned society.[58]

By 1890 laws regulating veterinary practice had either been enacted or were being considered in various states of the nation. But instead of prohibiting all untrained practitioners from practicing, the states generally took into consideration the nationwide shortage of surgeons, and most state laws permitted individuals with a certain number of years' experience to continue their work. This was only the beginning of a long struggle for the creation of a veterinary profession, and the first step toward the recognition of a scientific basis for the treatment of livestock diseases.[59] The days of the "hoss doctor," "the cow-leech," and other varieties found in the rural communities were now numbered. Once again we witness the modification of age-old values, superstitions, and folkways by the introduction and acceptance of science and technology into the rural areas of America.

CHAPTER IV

The Bogus Butter Controversy:

Cows versus Hogs

BUTTER-MAKING is one of the most ancient household arts. For thousands of years, using many different devices, man has agitated the milk taken from animals to produce a substance that he could use in his diet after adding a sufficient amount of salt. In the earliest known method this agitation was accomplished by placing the milk or cream in a skin bag and swinging it back and forth. Later the fluid was rocked or shaken in an earthenware churn, and still later the same effect was obtained by plunging a dasher up and down in a container. This process of agitation separated from the cream a butterfat that could be worked into highly delectable food.

For generations American dairymen had made butter by hand on their farms, keeping what they needed for their tables and selling or trading the surplus nearby. The marketing area was restricted to the immediate vicinity until about the middle of the nineteenth century, when transportation and cold storage facilities were developed; these changes enlarged the marketing zone considerably. Hand in hand with this extension of the market zone went sweeping changes not only in butter production but in organizational and selling techniques; the large-scale demands for this commodity in the rapidly growing urban centers brought about the development of commission merchants and middlemen as well as exchanges and boards of trade. Moreover, foreign ideas such as co-operatively owned creameries and factories, were introduced from abroad in the early 1800's and flourished especially in the eastern states.[1]

The state of New York was probably the first to organize and extend the marketing area through application of the creamery system and the development of commercial dairying. It is generally recognized that the first cheese factories and commercial creameries were established in this area during the 1850's and 1860's, and in the course of the next two or three decades the system experienced a rapid growth. During the fifteen years following the establishment of the first creamery in New York, more than 500 establishments sprang up in different sections of the state.[2] As a result it became the leading dairy producer of the nation and consequently influenced the butter developments in other states.

Despite this rapid growth of the co-operative system, the greatest amount of butter manufacture continued to be done on the farm, with the farmer's wife selling her product directly to the villagers or to the local grocery store. In 1873 the Commissioner of Agriculture observed that the butter-makers of the nation "are for the most part working individually and without associated organization, and under great diversity, often opposition, in practice. Mismanagement in making and marketing may be said to be the rule instead of the exception." In 1899 there were in operation some 8,000 creameries in the United States, making two-fifths of a billion pounds of butter. Yet their output represented less than one-third of the total production, for over two-thirds of the total still remained in the hands of the farm dairy.[3]

While this phenomenal increase in butter production took place in the United States, France was developing a substitute destined in time to compete with butter throughout the western world. In the late 1860's a shortage of edible fats and oils spurred the search for substitutes for such common items as lard and butter. The individual who responded to this challenge was a French chemist by the name of Hippolyte Megè-Mouriès. Professor Megè-Mouriès undertook the task of producing an artificial commodity cheaper than butter yet suitable for use not only by the poorer citizens but also by the French navy. He hoped to produce such a substance from the waste products of slaughter houses.

As a scientist, Professor Megè-Mouriès set himself the goal of discovering the secret of the natural production of butterfat in the cow and imitating it artificially. He began his research by placing a number of milch cows on a restricted diet in order to determine what effect such a diet would have on the butterfat content. He observed that although the cows lost weight quite rapidly, they continued nevertheless to produce milk containing butterfat. From this he concluded that the fat in the milk was a product of the animal's own fat, and not the diet, and that this transformation was effected by a chemical process within the body itself.

Acting on this theory, Megè-Mouriès began his experiments by subjecting samples of certain fats taken from around the kidneys and intestines of beefs to artificial digestion by the use of chemical pepsin or the actual chopped-up stomachs of the animals themselves; then he put the oils secured from this process through the successive steps of heating, settling, crystallizing, and pressuring so as to secure the necessary oleo oil. After this animal liquid had been obtained, it was in turn put through a thorough churning process together with finely chopped cow's, hog's or ewe's udders along with a compound of carbonate of sodium; the latter was designed to facilitate the emulsion. The solidified substance that resulted from this second process, when salted and colored, resembled real butter in appearance, taste and in its general properties. Megè-Mouriès christened the finished commodity with the name of margarine; but in other countries, which quickly adopted it, oleomargarine became the common term.[4]

Professor Megè-Mouriès now established a factory for production of the new substance at Poissy, a suburb of Paris, in 1870, just before the outbreak of the Franco-Prussian War. The war, creating a scarcity of real butter in France, gave a further impetus to his efforts. By April, 1872, the new product was so widely used that it was officially recognized by the National Council of Health as an item of trade, with the proviso that it be labeled margarine, not butter.[5]

This artificial butter, affording a cheap spread for the many millions who could not afford the higher-priced ones, enjoyed such success that it soon was introduced abroad. In 1869 it was adopted and patented in England, and in 1873 the United States Dairy Company purchased the Megè-Mouriès patent and soon thereafter began commercial manufacture of oleomargarine in New York City. This action set in motion a great expansion of margarine production in America. A few figures will illustrate this growth. Between 1873 and 1886 the national government granted thirty-four margarine patents; by the year 1884 no less than 180 patents were applied for, though many of these were rejected. In 1874 only one American concern produced oleomargarine; by 1887 there were thirty-seven in the field. Some of the largest producers were Chicago meat-packing firms. In 1886 these factories manufactured an estimated 30 million pounds of butter substitutes. This figure came to only 3 per cent of the total butter output. By 1887, 259 wholesalers were distributing this commodity to grocery stores throughout the nation.[6]

During the two decades of this expansion significant changes were made in the process of manufacturing and in the composition of oleomargarine itself. The original Megè-Mouriès method of using pepsin or the actual stomachs and udders of calves, pigs, or ewes was gradually discontinued and new kinds of animal fats and oils came into use. The major unsolved problem was to find animal fats that contained smaller amounts of the objectionable oils, yet were firm to the touch, white in color, available in sufficient quantities and free of odor or easily deodorized.

About 1883 a breakthrough came when Chicago packers created a new commodity that they called butterine. This was made with 40 per cent of leaf lard, a "white and odorless product" which was mixed with 25 per cent creamery butter, 20 per cent oleo oil, and 15 per cent ordinary milk. When colored and salted, the result was a marketable product that gave a keen competition to both oleomargarine and dairy butter.[7] As the demand for animal fats continually increased, lard refiners gradually turned to other oils derived from common commercial plants such as cotton and peanuts. Both of these crops were plentiful in the South, and each produced a seed or nut which, properly treated and refined, was not only cheaper and less difficult to deodorize but had a much better taste than most of the rancid butter then available in the local markets.

The introduction of oleomargarine into this country as a butter substitute almost immediately provoked controversy over its composition. In length and bitterness this controversy has few parallels in our history of food production. Most of the arguments centered around the character of the ingredients used in margarine manufacture, its digestibility, tendency to transmit infectious diseases, and finally, and most importantly, its allegedly fraudulent sale as an imitation product for real butter.[8]

Of all the indictments used against oleomargarine by farmers and dairymen—and these were the groups most seriously challenged by the new product—the most damaging was the claim that the ingredients were unwholesome, dangerous, and even poisonous. The reader of any farm journal published during the period of the controversy was likely to find several exposures of "bogus butter" and the injury it did to the ancient and honorable dairy industry.[9]

These attacks focused on the claim that oleo oils were secured from animal tissue and fats cut from the kidneys and intestines of slaughtered beefs; that the manufacturers also rendered oils for their imitation butter from collected scraps of the abattoirs, butcher shops and hotels; and even on occasion from diseased and dead animals.[10] Editors ardently culled and reprinted carefully selected statements of well-known microscopists found in various scientific publications. National and state agriculture reports carried unconfirmed accounts to the effect that

oleomargarine is simply uncooked raw fat, never subjected to sufficient heat to kill the parasites which are liable to be in it, and those who eat it run the risk of trichinae from the stomachs of animals which are chopped up with the fat in making it.[11]

A certain Dr. R. V. Piper of Chicago read a paper on the theme of germs in foods before the Boston Board of Trade in 1880. In this paper he declared that he had found in oleomargarine different kinds of fungi and certain living organisms which had resisted boiling and acetic acid; he had also found some living eggs that resembled those of the tapeworm found in hogs. Another scientist related that in the course of working in the laboratory of the Bureau of Animal Industry he had performed numerous experiments on guinea pigs, inoculating them with different samples of oleomargarine; these inoculations had caused congestion and death. The inference was that death was due to an infection received from the artificial butter.[12]

The suggestion that oleomargarine could serve as a "highway through which eggs of animals" and tapeworms could find their way into the digestive system provoked a stormy debate. Oleomargarine was produced at a temperature of not more than 120 degrees F. Some chemists, public health officials, and professors, noting that a heat of 212 degrees was necessary to destroy the "myriad of germs and eggs in the animal tissue," concluded that if such living organisms entered the human stomach they soon burrowed destructively into vital organs.[13] Journals throughout the country carried terrifying microscopic pictures of tapeworms, eggs, larvae, and the like, allegedly found in margarine, enlarged many times. Scientific authorities soon were aligned in battle on one or the other side of the dispute.[14] Some even thought it advantageous to cite as many foreign scholars as possible, due to their reputation in this country.

Microscopists and professors, the scientific opposition, represented a small though influential contingent of the anti-oleomargarine crusade. Much more numerous were the farmers, and especially the dairymen who carried on a prolonged and unyielding campaign against the "bogus butter" interests, and in certain sections of the country organized themselves into typical protective societies in order to secure remedial legislation.[15] Typical of such groups was the Ohio Farmers' Protective Association with headquarters in Chagrin Falls. The society had a fairly large membership, held regular meetings, and strenuously lobbied to achieve its ends in the legislature. In its statement of purposes, the group declared that it sought "aid and assistance in righting a great wrong to the dairymen of this State." [16] Granges in various other sections of the country gave assistance to these protective societies by circulating petitions for signatures to be sent to the various state legislators in behalf of the dairy interests. The dairy organizations were almost unanimously opposed to any kind of butter substitutes. In fact, the National Dairymen's Protective Association was called into special session for the purpose of taking action against oleomargarine, butterine, and other "frauds" perpetrated upon the dairy industry.[17] Many of the Farmers' Alliances took up the struggle, at least during the period when Milton George was the fighting editor of the *Western Rural*, the principal news vehicle for this farm organization. In the 1870's and 1880's he carried on an unrelenting campaign against "food forgers," and more specifically against the large packers who manufactured a greater part of the "bogus butter" in the United States.[18]

Enemies of this poor man's butter, in addition to charging that it was unsanitary and prejudicial to health, maintained that it was fraudulently sold as genuine butter. Dairies and creameries representing the butter industry made wide use of this argument; it appealed to producers of many other commodities, alarmed by the hordes of counterfeiters who were flooding the market with spurious articles. This was truly the golden age of adulterators, and few basic commodities escaped their debasing hands.[19] Many reformers proclaimed that to prevent the multitude of adulterations and substitutions government should compel

the manufacturers to stamp the character and the ingredients of each article on the package, giving their true name. There is no objection to cotton in woolen cloth if the article is labeled and sold as cotton mixed cloth; nor is there any objection to chicory in coffee, or glucose in sugar and sirups, if they are so marked and the purchaser knows it and is willing to buy them. We should have stringent laws enacted in this country with heavy penalties for their violation. If men cannot be punished for selling cotton mix for all wool, nor for chopping coffee berries out of chicory roots, mixing glucose in sugars and sirups, adulterating butter and spices, . . . and selling the farmers Bohemian oats and Red Line wheat at fraudulent prices, the farmer should not be arrested, fined and punished for putting stones in his wool or for mixing sirups made of granulated sugar with maple tree molasses and then selling it as the pure and genuine sirup made from the sap of the sugar maple. They are all frauds and intended to swindle the purchaser.[20]

In view of the many documented charges made by the farm journals of the time it appears certain that oleomargarine was often sold as butter, and, what is more, for butter prices.

In 1885 the Pennsylvania State Board of Agriculture issued an exhaustive report on the problem of imitation butter. This report cited testimony from dealers in Philadelphia that the competition of margarine had forced the price of butter down from twelve to ten cents per pound. So attractive had the imitation commodity become that it composed about half of the total consumption of spreads.[21] According to the same witnesses, manufacturers producing butterine, margarine or suine rarely sold their products under those names; instead they sought to deceive their customers by labeling the true name of such a product "in very small letters" as BUTTERine, or by giving it a fine brand name of creamery butter.[22] Reformers claimed that abolition of such frauds would go far to placate agrarian opponents of "bogus butter."[23]

To this barrage of charges, producers and other loyal friends of oleomargarine responded with a reasoned defense. They insisted that the product was wholesome, safe and entirely pure; they sought to prove their point by citing the supporting statements of prominent chemists, microscopists, and other professional people. Producers of oleomargarine also stressed that great numbers of consumers favored the commodity because it kept much longer than dairy butter; during the long hot summers when dairy butter could be preserved only with much difficulty from melting or becoming rancid, artificial butter could easily be preserved in a more or less solid consistency and in an edible condition.[24] This quality made the new commodity particularly attractive for workers in distant mining and lumber camps, for seafarers, and also all those persons without access to refrigeration.[25]

Friends of margarine also argued that it provided the laboring classes and cheap restaurants and hotels a healthy food much less expensive than good creamery butter.[26] Butter in this period was usually classified in two main categories. One was the butter produced on the farm by the housewife; the other that which was manufactured in the newly established creameries. Oleomargarine was never regarded as a competitor of the latter, which generally sold at a premium price to upper income groups. Oleomargarine was usually sold at the local grocery stores where it came into serious competition with the cheaper and often rancid farm butter which was purchased by the working classes.[27] Defenders of oleomargarine claimed that the "bogus butter" controversy largely had arisen because these classes preferred wholesome and edible margarine to a spoiled and rancid farm butter.

Indeed, some friends of the dairy industry conceded that the inferior quality of much of the farm butter was the basis for the phenomenal success and popularity of oleomargarine. They reasoned that

if the bulk of the butter offered in the market had been of uniformly good quality, substitutes . . . could not have been successfully introduced in this country. As it is, inferior grades of butter have within a few years been, to a great extent, driven from use in their natural form, and are consequently depressed in prices. They are replaced by substitutes composed of tallow, suet, lard, oils and other material. . . .

Earnest efforts have been made to protect the butter interest . . . against . . . ruinous competition by bogus butter. The press has worked zealously to arouse the people. . . . It is to be regretted that these efforts have not always been directed and controlled by sound judgment. Often . . . charges that could not be substantiated were made . . . but they re-act as unwarranted assertions always will, against the dairy interest when the truth becomes known. . . .[28]

The farm housewife, who was frequently charged with responsibility for rancid butter, was not always to blame for these shortcomings. Such conditions as stagnant water, bad pasture, worried cows, lack of shelter from heat, and confinement of cattle in stables reeking with odors of manure and rotten straw, thwarted the efforts of the most meticulous individuals to make palatable butter. The following description of how cows and their milk were handled illuminates the butter-maker's problem:

In how many stables in this land will men to-morrow sit down to milk cows that will have just arisen from beds of warm dung—cows that have never known the refining influence of comb or brush? To the flanks of these neglected beasts manure is sticking, often an inch or two thick, as it has clung all through the winter months, and will hang until summer suns shall loosen the hair that holds the mass. Thousands of these men will squeeze a little milk from time to time into the hollows of their hands, and with it wet the teats to make them soft and pliable. Other thousands will dip grimy fingers into the foam in the milk-pails, and thus wet the teats. In either case this milk, worked downward by the hand, drips soiled with filth into the wide-mouthed pail, to flavor the general mass. . . . How can the best butter-maker in the world hope to make eatable food from milk mixed with vile matter?

How many pans of milk during the winter just past were set for the cream to rise, contiguous to, or even in rooms where the family spent the greatest part of their waking hours? How many crocks of cream have stood to "ripen" beside stoves near which steaming boots gave off the odors of unwashed feet and barnyard filth, a row of drying socks the while ornamenting the line near by? There the cat purred in content, while someone fond of pets stroked her, setting stray hairs floating through the room; where with whine or snarl the family dog fought tooth and toenail, the nimble flea. There odors of frying bacon, boiling cabbage, or onions mingle with those of damp clothes redolent of horses, hanging against the wall, and of harness, mayhap, brought in to mend or to oil. The milk freely absorbs these mingled sweets to give faithful account of each and all when the butter in which they unite has had time to gather strength. These different offenses . . . are factors in the success of the manufacturers of oleomargarine, for they . . . leaven . . . the whole lump of butter produced by hundreds of thousands of tidy house-wives throughout the length and breadth of the land who sell butter to the storekeeper.[29]

One might conclude from the above that a housewife could not produce high quality butter on the farm. Actually a good deal of such butter was made, but much of it was ruined in the hands of the country grocers before it reached the consumers.[30] Most farmwives did not have regular customers; instead they brought their butter to the country store in baskets, jars, pails, milk pans, or other receptacles and traded their product for the merchandise they desired.[31] This good butter was mixed pell-mell with poorer stuff brought in by other farm women and by peddlers employed by country grocers during the summer months when the article was in abundant supply. The butter often stood for days before the grocer attempted to match the whole lot of it by color—an almost impossible achievement in view of the many different shades. Then he packed it into whatever containers were available at the moment.[32] So long as this system of packing good and poor butter together in the same container continued, dairy women had little incentive to improve the quality of their butter.

Another obstacle to securing quality farm butter from the housewives was a psychological factor; the ordinary grocer felt obliged to pay more or less the same price for all the butter brought to his store. This practice could hardly be condoned on purely rational or economic grounds, but it had a certain logic. The grocer knew from experience that "nothing will offend a woman quicker than to tell her that her butter was not first-class."[33] If he told her that her product was too old, rancid or inferior she would sell it to another merchant and give her trade to him. Accordingly he paid farmwives the same price for their butter, whether it was fit to eat or not. The system was vicious and detrimental to the conscientious buttermaker. Often, having found that she could not secure a higher price for her good butter, she gave up the effort to excel.[34] A kind of Gresham's Law operated here: bad butter drove out good butter from the market place.

The country storekeeper's lack of facilities for keeping the butter cool and the inadequacy of refrigeration facilities on western railroads that carried the product to eastern markets were also responsible for a certain amount of the bad butter that was offered the American consumer.[35] Much of this bad butter, as we have already noted, was packed in firkins, layer upon layer of varied colors, destined for commission houses where it in turn was sold to retailers who passed it on to the poorer classes; or as a last resort, to those who sold it for soap or put it through a reclaiming process.

Tons of this "filthy stuff," with its bad odor and rank flavor, was made more palatable for the poverty-stricken masses in the great cities by the "manipulators" or "butter-magicians" who were able to reclaim or renovate it for resale. No one really knew just what methods they actually used or what "queer mixtures" resulted. The *Chicago Tribune* remarked that "the Lord only knows what the inmate of the average boarding-house has to swallow" under the names of these reclaimed butters.[36] Some of the tastier and less rancid was sold to slightly better customers, but as a rule a special selling technique was required in order to dispose of it; the butter was usually kept out of sight and instead of permitting the prospective purchaser to see the inferior product in the bulk "a sample upon the point of a knife" was brought out for him to taste or smell, in the hope that the small "unsightly chunk" would be less apt to discourage the sale.[37]

Poor butter was poor butter, but even this inferior stuff varied considerably in quality according to the section of the country from which it came. It was claimed that the poorest butter came from the newer sections of the West; this was said to be caused by the lack of ice, stagnant water, noxious grasses, filthy country stores, fly-specked washtubs, dingy cellars and tobacco-chewing attendants.[38] Given the image of dairy butter formed by the millions of eastern consumers, it was not surprising that oleomargarine, with its milder tastes and smells, gave serious competition to the dairy industry and in time became a threat to one of the basic income-producing items of the American farm.

Despite the massive evidence that much farm butter was of exceedingly poor quality, dairymen refused to consider this aspect of the problem, and inaugurated a campaign for restrictive or prohibitory legislation against the "bogus butter" companies.[39] Under pressure from farm organizations, journals and dairy associations, several of the state governments attempted to restrict the use of oleomargarine in various ways; typical legislation forbade the use of coloring matter or required that the product be labeled or branded when sold, so that the purchaser might be informed of its actual character.[40]

In some states these pressure groups were not successful. In Illinois, for example, in spite of a vigorous campaign, the great packing firms, livestock associations and vegetable oil concerns were able to prevent adoption of restrictive legislative enactments. They claimed that such legislation was detrimental to the American system, prevented competition, and placed "a bar upon progress and invention." Illinois oleomargarine producers were most successful in protecting this industry from its enemies; the Chicago Board of Trade, which was very active in its defense, lauded the product "to the skies, claiming it to be wholesome, palatable, pure, and cheap, and that its manufacture had added four dollars to the value of every bullock in the country." [41] Many hog farmers also identified themselves with the opposition to anti-oleomargarine legislation on the grounds that oleo oils produced from hogs would afford them an increase of a dollar or so per head.

In 1877 Pennsylvania and New York, the two leading dairy states in the Union, enacted laws prohibiting entirely the manufacture and sale of oleomargarine within their borders. Maryland followed suit the next year, and by 1886, when the federal regulatory law went into effect, at least half a dozen states had enacted laws of a similar nature. These enactments proved to be generally ineffective since the necessary enforcement machinery was lacking; even if available the authorities were not necessarily inclined to use it. A giant step forward in this matter was made in 1884, when New York State created a new office of Dairy Commissioner. The Commissioner was empowered to ferret out any violations of the state laws pertaining to the dairy industry and to prosecute the offenders. This innovation proved to be a step in the right direction and certain other states created similar offices.

These initial state laws, of prohibitory tendency, were not too effective as a whole. Actually what the more conservative dairy interests wanted was not prohibition but some form of regulation that would eliminate the frauds of selling colored oleomargarine for butter. They hoped thereby to assist consumers in making a fair choice between butter and the substitutes. They also believed that the public health must be safeguarded against adulteration and unsanitary products; to obtain these ends the dairymen turned to the state legislatures and the courts. In Massachusetts, for example, dairymen obtained legislation forbidding the addition of coloring matter to oleomargarine; they argued that this restriction would enable the consumer to distinguish between the substitute and the genuine article. Some states, New Hampshire, Vermont, and South Dakota, enacted laws that required all artificial butters to be tinted pink; still others required that it be "marked or branded so as to inform the purchaser of its real character." [42] Iowa made certain that it would be identified by compelling every package of "bogus butter" to be stamped OLEOMARGARINE in letters not less than three-fourths of an inch in size. A fine of not less than $20 nor more than $100, a jail sentence of not less than ten days, or both, were the penalties provided for violation of the law. [43]

Some of the state laws demanded that public institutions, restaurants or hotels serving oleomargarine must display large placards, conspicuously posted in dining rooms, to notify the patrons that they were being served imitation butter. [44] Like many other laws, this one was often evaded. One eminent editor blamed the many violations on the fact that men dislike to act as informers. Even dealers in pure butter who saw their next door neighbor selling the impure article were reluctant to have them hauled to court. [45] The congressional hearings for the 1886 enactment called attention to a typical fraud in the marketing of margarine. In 1884 this commodity was selling on the wholesale market for an average of twelve cents per pound, but the New York Commission on Public Health, reporting on its investigation into frauds in the industry, noted that some retailers were selling it "at twenty cents per pound, others are charging as high as thirty cents; and still others . . . are selling butterine at . . . thirty-five cents, and even forty-five cents, all out of the same tub." So attractive were the profits of this nefarious business that thousands of otherwise reputable grocers, market men, and dealers engaged in it. [46]

Judicial review of the new state laws, restrictive or prohibitory, discouraged prosecution of the oleomargarine interests. The Maryland and New York statutes, prohibiting the manufacture and sale of oleomargarine, were declared invalid. The courts argued that instead of protecting the consumers from imitations and frauds these laws abolished competition and thus placed a bar upon progress and invention. [47] Several cases were carried to the Supreme Court and finally, in the decision *Powell* v. *Pennsylvania*, the tribunal affirmed that the states possessed the power to prohibit the manufacture or sale of imitation butters. But with the passage of a federal law dealing with the subject in 1886, the high court reversed itself in the case of *Schollenberger* v. *Pennsylvania*. Oleomargarine was thus legally recognized as a legitimate commodity and the states were banned from prohibiting the manufacture and sale of this article; however, they could control various aspects of these two processes.[48]

We now chart the latter phase of the struggle toward federal regulation of oleomargarine. Since the few state laws were either wholly ineffective or only partially successful, the dairy interests took the issue to Congress in an effort to obtain more legislative control. It was not difficult to persuade many congressmen for the position of the dairy interests appealed to their basic prejudices; after all, was this not a struggle between rural and urban values, between industrial and agricultural institutions? Would not such infringements destroy the prerogatives of the housewife who from earliest times had been blessed with this function of butter-making? For many rural congressmen the great Chicago packing firms represented all the evils of trusts and corporations, and these diseased and filthy spreads were a threat to the very foundations of rural society. Given the rural predominance in Congress and the high level of urban-rural tension, the likelihood of a legislative victory for the dairy interests seemed strong.[49]

In the first session of the Forty-ninth Congress (1885-1886) an "act defining butter, also imposing a tax upon and regulating the manufacture, sale, importation, and exportation of oleomargarine" was introduced in both houses and during the summer of 1886 hearings were held, with extended testimony from many lay and professional witnesses. Supporters of the legislation fell into two general classes: (1) those who felt that oleomargarine was a foul and harmful product whose production and sale should be prohibited; and (2) those who would be satisfied with elimination of frauds in coloring, packaging, labeling and branding.[50] As has so often happened in the field of reform legislation, the enemies of oleomargarine began by loudly avowing their intention of completely destroying the hateful product; but when the battle was joined they discovered that compromise was necessary and finally accepted a watered-down measure.

We have already reviewed some of the arguments used to prove the dangers of oleomargarine. In the course of the hearings of 1886 prominent scientists and leaders of the dairy interests offered testimony on the pathological effects of the product.[51] Joseph H. Reall, President of the American Agricultural and Dairy Association, maintained that this substitute had defrauded millions of innocent people with a diseased imitation of butter. He also claimed that it was responsible for killing large numbers with injurious chemicals used in a vain attempt to make it "pure" and more edible. Several prominent microscopists testified that it was possible for disease germs and even the eggs of tapeworms to be transmitted to human beings through this product. Professor Daniel E. Salmon, chief of the U. S. Bureau of Animal Industry and a veterinarian of cholera epidemic fame, for example, testified that "there is reason to believe in the dissemination of both the forms of tapeworm. . . . through oleomargarine . . . but the danger of obtaining trichinae from this source is very much greater." In further statements, he made it emphatically clear that he personally would not consume this commodity under any conditions because of the risk of hog cholera and a still greater risk of tuberculosis. He alleged that the germs of both diseases were found in the fats from which it was produced.[52]

Hog cholera was such a devastating scourge during the nineteenth century that the very thought of it terrified people. To have a basic food publicized as a carrier of this disease was doubly frightening.[53] A Dr. Thomas Taylor, microscopist of the Department of Agriculture, did nothing to allay the fears of the margarine consumers when he reported to the Senate committee that one of the western agents of the Statistical Division of the United States Department of Agriculture stated by letter that he knew "large amounts of money, $30,000 at a time, had been spent within the last month for the purchase of dead hogs that died of cholera." [54] This statement implied that the fat used in the manufacture of "bogus butter" was contaminated with this contagious germ. He further claimed that he had evidence to prove that fats were also used from putrid carcasses of "a large number of sheep [that] had been drowned [in a river in the state of Missouri] and the parties were watched to see where they were taken to, and it was found they went directly to an oleomargarine factory." [55] Enemies of oleomargarine also asked if manufacturers of the product were already known to use such diseased oils, what would prevent them from rendering lards from sick or dead dogs and horses?

Proponents of the bill also stressed the need for a federal enactment, since state laws were wholly inadequate to cope with this problem. One enforcement officer in Baltimore testified that

since I have been prosecuting in Maryland I suppose we have had more than fifty—yes, one hundred—people arrested for selling oleomargarine. What is the outcome of it? The fine is paid gladly and that is all, because they make more in a week for selling it than they have to pay in fines in two weeks. We have had persons who have been indicted four times within a year. . . . Therefore we ask the Internal Revenue Bureau to take hold of it. . . .[56]

Advocates of the bill also insisted that such fraudulent and deceitful methods had practically ruined a large segment of the butter industry and especially the export trade with England. Leading commercial merchants claimed that exports of butter decreased sharply during the 1880's and that this was due to the fact that oleomargarine had increased its sales abroad by many millions of pounds. This was only a half truth. Butter exports did fall off considerably between 1880-1888 but imitation butter can hardly be blamed, since exports of the latter actually declined slightly during the period and at no time did foreign sales of oleomargarine reach a total of more than two million pounds per annum.[57] To be sure, the period 1882–1888 saw an increase in the export of oleo oils which were used in the manufacture of imitation butters in the British Isles. No doubt this contributed to the reduction of butter exports.[58]

Other developments, however, were more responsible for the decline of the butter market abroad. Ship refrigeration was perfected during this decade, making it possible for Australia and New Zealand to supply the British people with a lower-priced butter. Also the grades of butter exported to Britain were sometimes adulterated by American creameries who were purchasing oleo oils from the large packing firms and mixing it with their butter; by such a process they were able to keep within the moderate price range of the British market.[59] Such practice, however, was not well received by consumers in England.

Dairymen also claimed that imitation butter was responsible for the decline of their home butter market. It is true that the consumption of margarine during this period varied according to the fluctuation of the price of dairy butter. The *Prairie Farmer* recognized this principle as follows:[60]

When the price of butter fell so low last year that the margin of profit disappeared for all grades except gilt edged creamery, the occupation of the oleomargarinists was gone; but with the sharp advance that succeeded, came a revival of their business, which has grown and flourished, increasing in importance and magnitude until it threatens the legitimate dairy interest with great injury.

Creamery butter never had serious competition from the imitation butters, for the simple reason that as one journalist remarked, "it stands as far above it as gold above pinchbeck." But this fact was not too prominent an issue in the controversy; the real problem was the effect these artificial butters had on the middle grades of farm dairies. The question was raised whether dairymen were justified in advancing the price of their poorer grades of butter beyond the range of the lower classes, thus compelling them to turn to oleomargarine and to appeal to the national government for protection. The Illinois Department of Agriculture seemed to understand the problem and placed it in its proper perspective: [61]

With what grace can the dairymen ask government to stop the manufacture of butterine and oleomargarine—which, though cheap, are alleged to be perfectly wholesome—when the price of pure butter has been advanced beyond all sense or reason? At 40 cents, butter is beyond the reach of the vast majority of the people living in cities and towns, who can afford to pay no such price. All the laboring population, mechanics, and the salaried class generally, find the present price much too high—more than their incomes warrant paying. They must either stop consumption or use cheaper grades, most of which are mixed or compounded. In this fact will be found the secret of the vast development of the manufacture of spurious butters in the last two years. If genuine butter were, say 25 cents a pound, the people would very readily detect the spurious, and many wouldn't touch it at any price who are now compelled by stern necessity. . . .

The artificial butters were certainly competitors of the over-priced middle grades of dairy butter; but other factors than price favored the substitutes. Profit margins were usually more favorable for the retailer who handled them, and also by their very nature these spreads were more compact and contained a smaller percentage of water and animal substance, thus making them easier to keep sweet and edible for a longer period of time. This latter factor was extremely important and made them attractive to urban consumers, since dairy butter so often contained too much water and sour milk and thus could not be preserved for any length of time.

Turning to the opponents of anti-oleomargarine legislation, we find many groups who were vitally concerned in one way or another. The laboring classes, livestock industry, boards of trade, bankers, meat-packers, cheap hotels and restaurants as well as the southern producers of cottonseed and peanut oils, all shared a financial interest in the welfare of this industry. Forming a powerful combination, representatives from these various groups appeared before the congressional committees to testify. Professor Henry Morton of Stevens Institute of Technology swore that oleomargarine was pure and wholesome, thoroughly desirable and completely safe as an article of food. He also insisted that in the course of his experiments he had never found any animal tissue in the product and emphatically denied that living organisms were ever discovered within the fatty tissue of animals. Moreover, he positively denied the often repeated charge that the fat from dead animals could be used in the manufacture of this commodity, since putrefaction and the presence of odors would have set in before the fracturing process.[62]

Some prominent leaders in both Houses of Congress opposed the legislation because it levied a tax on each pound of margarine. They claimed that this would force the product out of competition with the cheaper grades of butter and would then deny the masses a desirable and edible food. They also complained vigorously of this method of destroying an item of food by the taxing arm of the government. They conceded that the government had the power to outlaw all fraudulent and harmful articles, but denied that it had the power to crush one industry in order to support another.

Business leaders and even a few prominent dairymen also opposed a tax on these artificial butters, especially so burdensome a one as the ten cents per pound initially proposed. This was considerably in excess of the amount levied upon persons engaged in other manufactures and sales of such items as liquor, beer and tobacco.[63] Henry E. Alvord, Senior Vice-President of the New York State Dairymen's Association took a position in direct opposition to that of most dairymen by stating that

prices have not declined materially, in spite of the oleomargarine and butterine competition, substitution, and adulteration. . . . Many honest and enterprising dairy-men, including, to my own knowledge, several of the largest butter-makers in the world, fail to see how their business can be possibly benefited by a direct onerous . . . tax upon a competing but equally legitimate business. Yet they do desire freedom from the unfair *advantage* which dealers, and especially small dealers, are enabled to practice by fraudulent substitution and sale.[64]

Following one of the hardest fought legislative struggles during this period, a highly modified bill "to regulate the manufacture and sale of butter substitutes" was finally passed by the Senate under the leadership of Senator Scott of Pennsylvania and by the House under the direction of Congressman Hatch of Missouri but a concurrence was obtained only after the tax was lowered from five to two cents per pound. Several prominent senators offered stiff resistance to the bill, and in the judgment of Senator Edmunds the whole idea was about as ridiculous as appealing to "Congress . . . to protect the breeder of draft horses against the breeder of mules. . . ."[65]

President Cleveland on August 2, 1886 signed the bill into law with some misgivings, reflected in the accompanying message. He was not in favor of taxation for revenue, especially if the real purpose of the tax was "to destroy, by the use of taxing power, one industry of our people for the protection and benefit of another." But, he concluded:

I do not feel called upon to interpret the motives of Congress otherwise than by the apparent character of the bill . . . and I am convinced that the taxes which it creates can not possibly destroy the open and legitimate manufacture and sale of the thing upon which it is levied. If this article has the merit which its friends claim for it, and if the people of the land, with full knowledge of its real character, desire to purchase and use it, the taxes exacted . . . will permit a fair profit to both manufacturer and dealer, . . . and if it can not endure the exhibition of its real character which will be effected by the inspection, supervision, and stamping which this bill directs, the sooner it is destroyed the better in the interest of fair dealing.[66]

Besides the small and innocuous two-cent stamp tax provision there was also a fifteen-cent levy on every pound of oleomargarine that was imported. The significant tax, however, and one that really was a burden on small concerns especially, was a license tax to be assessed on the three branches connected with the imitation butter industry; $600 was to be paid by the manufacturers, $580 by the wholesalers and $48 for each retail dealer. Combined with these financial requirements manufacturers were also compelled to mark, stamp and brand all their packages. As for the retailers, they were permitted to sell only those originally stamped; this precaution was designed to prevent misbranding at the local level. The artificial butter interests also gained by the bill: for the first time this commodity was recognized by law and was thus placed in the field of interstate commerce, where it was subject to federal regulation.[67] However, this law was not satisfactory to any of the contending parties and so the struggle continued on well into the twentieth century with further amendments and court decisions before a solution satisfactory to all was achieved.

What was the immediate effect of this anti-oleomargarine law? One immediate effect was a decline in its manufacture and distribution. This was no doubt partly due to the sudden abatement of sales as a result of a more rigorous administration of the law, and the increased cost due to the license taxes. Armour & Company estimated that the production of oleomargarine in 1886 was only about three per cent of the total production of butter, but in the following year it had dropped to nearly a third of that figure and besides this decline there was also an accompanying loss in the number of retail dealers and manufacturers, especially the smaller ones who had been dislocated by the federal tax.[68]

The act, however, was not fatal to the industry in the long run for by 1890 it had already begun to recapture some of its former markets. Dr. Harvey W. Wiley, in evaluating the effects of the 1886 measure, observed that by 1893 there was no evidence that it had restricted the use of the commodity but on the contrary had actually "increased it, by giving to the consumer a guarantee of purity." [69]

As one views the butter-oleomargarine controversy, it would appear that the difficulties confronting the dairy farmers during this period flowed principally from the lower prices resulting from their loss of exports to the British, the serious depression of the 1870's, and the competitive advantages of artificial butter in respect to the conditions of production. For generations butter-making had not only been highly competitive but decentralized at the farm level where all houswives were free to enter the field. Under conditions of household production, prices and profits were subject to the highly competitive forces of millions of butter-makers as well as the many small creameries in the eastern part of the country. Oleomargarine factories, on the other hand, were concentrated in the large meat-packing cities and tended to be large, although relatively few in number. The creamery and oleomargarine industries produced similiar products and used somewhat comparable equipment and raw materials. But the one remained decentralized, whereas the other came under the domination of large organizations of meat-packers. Here, perhaps, is the clue to the dairymen's antagonism toward the imitation butter industry; it was impossible for the housewives or the small creameries to compete with giant plants producing on a large scale and also enjoying significant advantages of labor and raw material costs. This disparity explains the outraged cries of the dairy industry and its appeal to the federal government to restrict the manufacture and sale of substitute butters.

PART TWO

Enclosure Irritations

CHAPTER V

From Rails to Barbed Wire

AMERICAN AGRICULTURE in the early nineteenth century was revolutionized by the development and adoption of innovations that differed radically from colonial methods. In fact, nearly every phase of husbandry was affected in some manner by the emerging scientific experiments and inventions. Throughout this century American farmers moved westward, penetrated the vast timberlands and plains, crossed the mountain barriers and rounded out an imperial domain. The romance of this period, replete with dramatic incidents, has somewhat obscured the prosaic aspects of agricultural experimentation that occurred parallel to this westward movement. Undramatic efforts by unknown contrivers to solve certain perplexing problems, whose outcome profoundly affected the nation's welfare and progress, have generally escaped the concern of the historian. One of those persistent and enduring problems was how to construct an effective enclosure that would meet the basic requirements of various types of agriculture. For 250 years the American agriculturist had sought a solution to this problem. A solution finally was found in the 1870's that was more satisfactory to their needs, but only after a number of other forms of enclosures proved inadequate.

Colonial ideas of enclosure were adaptations of European practices. In many areas of New England the farmers generally cooper-
ated with one another in building a common fence around the growing crops, and the wanderlust of livestock that grazed on the "great
lotts" was curbed by the many kinds of herders.[1] In other sections of
the country, and especially in the South, each planter surrounded his
cultivated fields with fences and allowed the animals to roam at will
on the open range.[2] During this early period enclosure practices
were regulated by both local customs and colonial laws which subsequently served as models for the legal codes of the western territories as each entered statehood. The early enclosure laws compelled
those who cultivated the soil to fence in their crops with a legal
barrier, or, otherwise "plant, upon theire owne perill."[3]

Between the end of the colonial period and the termination of the
Civil War, farmers east of the Mississippi developed several different types of fences. The variations and combinations that resulted
from the exercise of inventive skill may be grouped, however, into
three general types and will be discussed and evaluated in the order
of their evolvement and subsequent importance.

There were first the "dead" fences whose materials consisted of
timber, stone, or sod; second, "live" fences that were produced from
various types of hedge plants, and third, wire fences that evolved
from crude beginnings to the principal form of enclosure that has
served even to the present day. Only a nominal amount of ingenuity
was required to create most of these dead fence barriers and "perhaps not more than one in twenty" farmers had "any established
system or fixed rules" for building them.[4] Nevertheless with such a
wide range of possibilities, it would be inconceivable to imagine all
the minor variations of fence construction that developed throughout the nation during this period.

The earliest type of enclosure in America was the rail fence, later
referred to as the "relic of a lavish era of unlimited forestry."[5]
Construction followed two general forms—the "worm," "snake," or
"zig-zag" shape and the more refined straight post-and-rail. The
former, by any name, was well adapted to an early society in that it
required few tools and little skill to construct. It not only was
constructed from the timber supply that abounded wherever a fence

was to be built but its structure was so simple that it was easily repaired or removed from one field to another depending upon the needs of the cultivator at any given time.[6] These points help to explain its early use and continued popularity over a broad area. In Virginia as early as 1621 this picturesque structure was observed, and later referred to by Hugh Jones as a "worm fence" in his account of the Colony in 1724.[7] Early town records in New England contain numerous references to enclosures constructed with rails called "paling," patterned after the post-and-rail design. In the Middle Atlantic region of the country the rail, in one form or another, was the predominant type of enclosure until the depletion of the timber supply.[8] However, no particular type was used to the exclusion of all others in any area since the various ethnic backgrounds of European settlers produced diversity in stock enclosure methods as well as in other institutional practices.

Construction of a "worm" fence was a task that required considerable manual labor; rails, blocks and stakes were usually "mauled out" during the winter months.[9] In early spring after the frost had left the ground the building process began with rails of approximately ten feet in length and three to five inches thick. Since every farmer desired to have his fence "horse-high, bull-proof and pig-tight," only the straightest rails obtainable were selected. He used whatever timber was at hand; however, when a choice was possible he had a strong preference for the walnut, locust, cedar, chestnut or oak.[10]

Rail-splitting was one activity on the farm that from early times was used to indicate skill and strength, even as a yardstick to differentiate the importance of individuals within a community; if a man could "maul out" one hundred rails from hardwood trees in a single day's work he was classed by his peers as an average rail-splitter; but should he split as many as 175 or more in the same length of time he was considered eligible, as a result of such skill, to be elevated to a high position of responsibility.[11] Some men by such endeavors were successful in attaining political preferment.

Every cultivator of the soil found it necessary to devote a definite time of the year to the cutting of timber. One writer asserted that in his opinion "at least one month of the annual labor upon the farms in the western country" was devoted to building and repairing worm fences.[12] From eight to nine thousand rails were required for a mile of such fence plus the stakes; in terms of dollar value, which was determined by a number of factors, the cost per mile varied from a low of $10 to a high of $178.50 but would probably average about $50.[13] Laborers were paid from 60 to 70 cents per one hundred rails, or about a dollar a day. Considering the total financial outlay of a completed worm fence, that is, such cost factors as labor, terrain, distance of haul, available timber supply and a height of six to eight rails, the estimates varied from a few cents per rod to as high as $1.00.[14]

The task of assembling a Virginia worm fence was relatively simple, even though it required considerable energy. Wooden blocks or stones were used as supports at the corners and eight to nine rails were, as one observer related,[15]

placed horizontally above one another, as the bars of a gate; but each tier of rails, or gate as it were, instead of being on a straight line with the one next to it, is put in a different direction, so as to form an angle [like the shape of the letters V or W] sufficient to permit the ends of the rails of one tier to rest steadily on those of the next.

Timber being in plentiful supply, a pair of stakes about six feet in length were driven into the ground at each angle and tied together at the top with a withe or small yoke. A long pole, called a rider, was often laid along the top of the panels to give them additional height.[16]

Farmers who recognized the vagaries of the worm fence or lacked the necessary supply of timber to build one—a situation experienced sooner or later by all agriculturists—could adopt the post-and-rail construction. This was a more sophisticated barrier demanding certain skills but had decided advantages over worm fences; designed to follow a straight line, it required considerably less timber and space, as well as presenting fewer obstacles to the farmer in controlling the accumulation of weeds, brush, and vermin that invariably collected in and around the worm fence.[17] Thomas Fessenden, editor of the *New England Farmer*, reported in the late 1820's that the post-and-rail fences were probably "more used in New England than any other; and are, perhaps, in most cases justly preferred."[18] This style of construction rapidly gained favor in a number of other states; however, it never became popular in the South.[19]

In this, as in all other fence construction, various modifications were both useful and adaptable. General Washington introduced the innovation of building the post-and-rail fence on a ridge of dirt formed by digging a two to three foot trench or ditch, in order to economize on the number of rails; for when the ditch parallel to the fence was made use of, the fence itself needed no more than three rails, with posts only about five feet in length; but without the parallel ditch, additional rails would have to be added on higher posts in order to make the completed fence of sufficient height.[20]

A traveler in Pennsylvania, in 1770, noting a post-and-rail fence, described it as follows: [21]

Throughout the United States the cultivated lands are all inclosed, to secure them from the ravages of all kinds of cattle; which, for the greater part of the year, are left by every proprietor in the woods that are for this purpose common to them all. In the vicinity of the towns these inclosures are made with stakes, placed at the distance of ten or twelve feet from each other, and perforated with five mortises at the space of eight or nine inches; in which are fitted branches of trees unstripped of their bark, of a proper length, and about four or five inches in diameter. . . . The inclosures are generally seven feet high. . . . When they are kept in good order they last about five-and-twenty years.

This more orderly form of fence construction was without doubt superior in the particular ways already noted and gave many of the earlier cultivators an excellent second choice when they found most of the immediate timber had been used or destroyed. Nevertheless there were potential weaknesses in its construction that did reduce its utility and extensive adoption. In addition to the work necessary to split the rails, peel off the bark, as was often done, and cut the requisite size and shape of posts, expert skill was required in the process of auguring and mortising the four or five cavities in each post into which the tapered rail-ends were to be wedged. If these mortises were too large the strength of the post to sustain the barrier was reduced; if too small the rails could not enter far enough into the post to be properly joined.

Costs of constructing this type of fence varied in different sections of the country and as a result many estimates were given in contemporary literature. In New England, in the 1830's, a five-rail fence of white pine timber with chestnut posts could be built for about $300 a mile, exclusive of the setting.[22] James Worth, reporting for the Bucks County Agricultural Society in Pennsylvania in 1820, estimated that such a fence, with an additional parallel ditch and chestnut or cedar rail, would run as high as $350, including the cost of setting.[23] In New Jersey, a decade or so later when timber was getting scarcer, the cost with white oak was estimated as high as $370, including the setting; while in 1871 in the Middle West, where fencing materials were still more limited, the figure for this fence was listed at $406 per mile.[24]

Both types of "dead" fences caused a great deal of dissatisfaction wherever they were used. The principal objections that most farmers had to them may be summarized as follows: they depleted the timber supply; they were expensive both to build and to maintain; they were ineffective; they harbored weeds, brush, vermin, and snow; they occasioned neighborhood conflicts; [25] and they slowed up settlement and the cultivation of land.

The scarcity of fencing materials became a serious problem shortly after the turn of the nineteenth century, due mainly to the excessive amount of timber needed in building the worm fences so universally constructed. By 1820 the older counties in Pennsylvania, and especially the areas near large towns where wood was used for fuel, were "experiencing a shortage of timber for fencing." Farmers in Prince Georges County, Maryland, voiced similar complaints through their agricultural society.[26] In New England timber was becoming noticeably scarce even as early as 1775 when the anonymous author of the *American Husbandry* toured the region. He lamented that the New Englanders "not only cut down timber to raise their buildings and fences, but in clearing the grounds for cultivation they destroy all that comes in their way, as if they had nothing to do but to get rid of it at all events, as fast as possible." [27] In the late twenties and early thirties, farmers in many sections of New York were beginning to feel the paucity of fencing materials. In fact, so grave was this problem becoming in many parts of the nation that James Madison, in a speech delivered before the Albemarle Agricultural Society in 1819, had this to say in regard to timber: "Of all the errors in our rural economy, none is perhaps so much to be regretted, because none is so difficult to be repaired, as the injudicious and excessive destruction of timber and firewood." [28] Washington, in a letter to William Strickland in 1797 voiced the same sentiments: "I am not surprised," he said, "that our mode of fencing should be disgusting to a European eye. Happy would it have been for us, if it had appeared so in our own eyes; for no sort of fencing [Virginia Worm] is more expensive or wasteful of timber." [29]

Other eastern sections also paid the penalty for lavish use of the forests. In Delaware, cedar rails were selling at the excessive price of $8 a hundred in 1848. A New Jersey farmer observed in 1844 that the "supply of materials for the kind of fences hitherto in use" was "becoming more limited" and fencing costs were rising rapidly.[30] In 1845 farmers in certain sections of South Carolina had completely exhausted their timber supply and were compelled to purchase what they needed; in Georgia the Committee on Agriculture recommended in the same year that the Georgians try to find a substitute for the common rail fence; in Virginia the farmers had been for a number of years prior to 1850 entreating their legislative assembly to correct the evils of the fencing laws which had become so serious because of timber shortage.[31]

In time, the midwesterners also felt the loss of their timber. In 1830, a report was carried in one of the farm journals that in many parts of Kentucky and Ohio, "the timber used in the construction of these fences," was becoming so scarce that many farmers already were without the timber necessary for another "renewal of their fences." [32] In southern Illinois, at least among the oldest inhabitants, timber was disappearing at an alarming rate by 1821, and by the early forties a hue and cry was raised by many midwestern farmers that they were obliged to procure their logs many miles distant from where they were to be used.[33] Some cultivators in the same section solved their problem by buying up the available timber so that they might have enough to keep their farms "fenced for a course of years"; others claimed it was necessary to appropriate the logs, in defiance of the law, from adjacent government land.[34] However, the tedious process of reforestation appeared to be the only way to correct the mistake of the former generations. Agricultural societies and national leaders in the East recommended this plan during the twenties, and the Middle West also turned to it in the next two decades.[35]

Dissatisfaction with the cost and upkeep of these rail enclosures was well justified; careless and exaggerated estimates that emanated from countless sources on this subject prevents an accurate determination of the real cost, but it was probably high enough to constitute a serious grievance. One of the most frequent quotations cited by the agricultural press for many years was that made by Nicholas Biddle who asserted that the total cost of all the fences in Pennsylvania would reach the staggering sum of around $100,000,000 as well as an additional figure for annual maintenance that would approximate $10,000,000.[36] Other estimates varied widely in different sections of the country: for the year 1845 South Carolina reported a total value of $5,000,000; in New York it was placed at the "enormous sum of $67,000,000"; and in Ohio the total value equalled the indebtedness of the state! [37]

The cost of annual repairs and replacements ran high. Even under the best conditions, the ordinary rail fence was never known to last longer than twenty-five years and as a general rule had lost its effectiveness within a shorter period.[38] Posts, rails, and stakes were continually loosened by frosts, winds, slides, fallen trees, hunters and livestock and the ordinary deterioration that resulted from shrinkage and decay as well as loss by fires.[39] The annual expenditure of keeping a fence in repair was often exaggerated, as were other aspects of the fencing problem, and on occasions reporters, in order to emphasize it, would use patriotic themes and wrap it colorfully within its stereotypes. A reporter from New Jersey described it rather colorfully: "I will only say that a tax infinitely less exacting than this imposed by the mother country, burst out into the American Revolution, and separated the American colonies from Great Britain." [40] On a seventy-five-acre farm, according to a New Yorker, his repair bill amounted to "more than 6 per cent on the whole produce" of his land; while the Albemarle Agricultural Society estimated $100 a year for a 500-acre farm.[41] Even with vigilance and great expense farmers found it impossible to keep their fences in a state that would comply with legal requirements.[42]

The ineffectiveness of these enclosure methods was a constant problem to both owner and neighbor; hogs, sheep, cows and calves refused to accord them the proper respect. A farmer in the Middle West reported that young hogs soon "learned to work their way through or under" the rails, and once they had learned the "art of penetration" they "never forgot the habit as they grew older." Sheep also acquired the habit, usually when fences were poorly built or temporarily down.[43] These fences, even when they were well repaired, were the source of many injuries to livestock; frequently being injured in hurdling them, or having penetrated the enclosures they were often wounded or killed by a neighbor's gun, or a dog loosed upon them.[44]

To the poet or artist the rail fence was a "trellis for the vines of the woods and fields, the grape, the morning glory, the honeysuckle and the Virginia creeper"; a rural symbol of the idyllic life; the simple and genuine values of those who tended the flocks and tilled the soil. But to the farmer it was a harborer of brush, weeds, vermin and snow and a fertile source of ill will, and was a fire hazard at certain times of the year. These weaknesses were not preventable since it was impossible for a farmer to operate within about twelve feet on either side of the worm fence with oxen and cultivator. During the winter months in the northern states, snow drifted along these barricades, blocking the roads and preventing the farmer from traveling beyond his home. Insects, mice, rats, and squirrels, rabbits and even larger animals and game birds had a propensity for building homes in the hidden nooks and crannies of the worm fence. Numerous hunters periodically infested the countryside, scaling and tearing down the rails and shooting recklessly at everything that moved.[45]

The criticism that wooden fences hindered settlement and held much of the tillable land out of cultivation, was based on the fact that new settlers coming into a timberless community would naturally hesitate to settle permanently if they were compelled by law or custom to invest hundreds of dollars in enclosures.[46] Furthermore, most settlers, especially in the prairie regions, did not remain long on any one farm; if they built fences they usually had to sacrifice them when they moved to another location.[47] Edmund Ruffin wrote in 1834 that it was becoming quite difficult even to secure a tenant, let alone a buyer for a farm because of the lack, or poor condition, of the fences.[48] From New Jersey in 1844 came a report that few people contemplated "the purchase of a farm without making the state of the enclosures a paramount consideration," and three years earlier the shortage of timber for fencing was such a serious drawback in Illinois that this factor alone prevented thousands of emigrants from establishing themselves in the prairie states.[49]

In time these dissatisfactions brought about an anti-fencing sentiment on the part of many farmers throughout the nation. A few of the more progressive agricultural leaders advocated the system of "soiling," that is, the use of pens and small enclosed pastures for feeding livestock.[50] This system, according to its exponents, not only would eliminate the cost of fencing but would afford "the greatest supply of offal for conversion into manure by . . . bedding or feeding"; it would also produce a better grade of livestock, as it was quite impossible to improve a herd of animals when they were permitted to mingle with nondescript breeds in the woods or on the ranges.[51] One farmer summed up the problem of fencing in the following query: "But what is the actual benefit that we derive, after all, from fencing? The benefit of the range for our stock. And what do we gain by that? Razor-back hogs, and sway-back cattle, and sheep that dogs will hardly eat after killing."[52] On the western prairies, where fencing materials were extremely scarce, a strong resentment against fences arose. One settler from Peoria, Illinois, expressed the views of many of his neighbors in 1843, in a letter to one of the leading agricultural journals: "I have now been a resident of this country five years, and in addition to my own experience in farming here, I am backed by the opinions of seven eights [sic] of those who have emigrated to the prairies from England, that fencing upon them is just so much money thrown away." He further stated that in his judgment a "few properly trained cattle-dogs, and an agreement on this subject among the settlers" would be sufficient.[53]

With the introduction of the sawmill, other types of wooden

fences came into use. Logs were hauled to these small mills and the boards cut from them were used to construct "plank" fences.[54] Most of these were built in a straight line around the field; however, a few farmers constructed them on the old Virginia "zig-zag" pattern which demonstrates how difficult it was to modify traditional rural practices. The boards were sawed about sixteen feet in length, five to six inches in width, and four or five to a panel; posts usually ran about seven feet in length and were placed six to eight feet apart.[55] The cost for this board fence exceeded that for the rail; the boards alone cost between $8 and $10 per thousand board feet, and since farmers in the Midwest drew heavily on the pineries of Wisconsin and Michigan, transportation costs brought the total outlay of the fence to about $1 per rod.[56]

This type of fence was considered by some farmers to be superior to other wooden enclosures. The boards were straight, and as a consequence, spaces between them were not uneven, as in the case of many rail fences; and livestock were not encouraged to crawl or burrow through. They were simple in construction and easily removed when the farmer found it necessary to adjust his pattern of farming; and to those who possessed a refined sense of proportion and beauty of form, such fences enhanced the general appearance of the farm.[57] There were some shortcomings, however, besides the item of expense: they blocked the highways with snowdrifts during the winter months; they were easily blown down by heavy winds and were more easily destroyed by fires than were the rail fences.[58]

Another type of dead fence that had some popularity during this period was the one constructed with stone; this, like the rail fence, was dependent upon the supply of materials on or near the farm. It had a limited acceptance in parts of the Middle West, but was widely adopted during various periods in many New England states where it came into use as a substitute for the post-and-rail fence.[59] Its popularity in the South was never extensive, even in areas where stone was plentiful. In 1819 the Albemarle Agricultural Society lamented the fact that farmers would not use stones to construct walls but instead would haul them from the fields and strew them in heaps along the boundaries even at the expense of labor and the loss of large areas of ground.[60] Stones were not abundant in many sections of the Middle West, and those desiring to construct this kind of fence were obliged to secure them from quarries, hilltops or along the banks of rivers and streams.[61] Several patterns were used, but the best stone fences were four or five feet in height, two to three feet wide at the base and approximately eighteen inches across the top. In order to prevent crumbling and bulging they placed the larger stones at the bottom, broke the joints, and dug a ditch or furrow along the wall in order to absorb the moisture.[62]

This structure had both its advantages and disadvantages. Perhaps the most serious disadvantage was the fact that it was difficult to prevent a stone wall from crumbling as a result of freezing and thawing of the earth upon which it was built. It required an excessive amount of time and skill to construct a heavy wall that had to be shaped over hills, down slopes and across lowlands; a proficiency not often possessed by the average farmer. Therefore this barrier was primarily adaptable only to small acreages since its labor cost was high for both construction and maintenance.[63] The numerous crevices and crannies within the wall served as perfect hiding places, as well as excellent breeding dens, for noxious and predacious animals that raided the farmer's hen-coops, crops, fruits and vegetables. A factor that favored its adoption, especially in New England, notwithstanding those faulty features, was the fact that it made possible the removal of great quantities of stones existing in the cultivated fields, which hindered good farming. In ridding the cultivated fields of these encumbrances for use in building fences, it left what remained of the natural "timber standing in the woods." Also, being a straight line fence, it occupied considerably less space than the popular serpentine forms.[64]

Concluding this discussion of dead fences with one of lesser significance than the others, except in a few areas where stone and timber were scarce, is the fence constructed of blocks of sod. These fences were built almost exclusively on the prairies and large clearings where soils were deep and well bound together with long and tough grass roots.[65] This type of enclosure was erected by cutting sod in certain size blocks, laying them in rows usually about three to four feet at the base, two to three feet high and fifteen to eighteen inches across the top. In this form it followed the pattern of the stone and rail fences in that two or three rails were placed on top of the sod wall with an additional rider to give it height; at the bottom of the bank, ditches were dug to keep it dry, give it height and to keep livestock from rubbing it down.[66] Another form used only the sod without the rails. This "crossbred" fence demanded a great deal of labor to build and to maintain; and in order to reduce the cost of construction a number of sod-cutting machines were invented by western farmers during the 1840's.[67] But in spite of the labor-saving devices, as well as years of experimentation, this sod fence never came into general use, chiefly because of climate conditions which made it difficult to secure sodded walls that would not wash away or banks steep enough to restrain the animals from scaling them. Solon Robinson, in one of his letters to his western readers, summarizes the principal defects of this mode of fencing: [68]

Many attempts have been made to fence with earth and nearly all fail. Cause: the sods are piled up like laying stone wall, and in two or three years the whole fence is a pile of the softest fine manure. Others have tried to pile up earth, and sod it over with the native sods. But these rarely succeed; the grass dies, and the bank being too steep, slips down in spring, and there being no rails on top, the cattle soon form a path over [it].

I turn now to the second major category of enclosures in use during this period, the "live" or thorny hedge fence. This form of fencing emerged on the western prairies out of necessity when it was no longer possible for settlers to finance excessive costs of "dead" fence materials. Seeds for a variety of hedge plants had been introduced from foreign countries at an early date; many of the earliest hedges were grown by experienced persons who had emigrated from Europe. Their adoption was slow, however, and only a few of the leading agriculturists during the early period experimented with them.[69] The anonymous author of the *American Husbandry* in 1775 described the inertia and slowness with which the hedge was utilized in New England: [70]

[The abundance] of timber in many parts of the province is such, that they neglect planting these durable, useful, and excellent fences for the

more easy way of post and rails, or boards, which last but a few years.
. . . This is a negligence, and a want of foresight that is unpardonable:
but though the new settlers see the inconvenience of it on the lands of the
old ones, and find live hedges in many places substituted, yet do they go
on with the practice, as if it was the best in the world.

There were definite reasons why farmers were reluctant to adopt
this type of enclosure; it was a live plant and there were many things
that hindered its growth. Small animals, such as rabbits and squirrels, as well as borers, caterpillars, and worms were often injurious
to the growing twigs; cold winters often killed them before they got
started and the periodic fires that swept over the prairies played
havoc with them.[71] The hedge plant required a great deal of time
and patience to bring it to maturity, and most of the farmers in
immediate need of fences were unable to wait the necessary number
of years. "If we could grow live fences as readily as we can construct
dead ones," said a New York farmer, "there would be no hesitation
in resorting to them, however expensive. But the idea of devoting six
or seven years to bringing them to perfection, *perhaps longer than
our natural lease of life*, deters many from planting hedges, as it
does fruit and ornamental trees." [72]

Another objection to the live fence was that it could not be moved
once it grew to maturity; unlike the wooden enclosures which could
be dismantled and moved from one boundary or division line to
another, or from farm to farm, the living hedge was ill-adapted for
boundary division lines that were not to be permanent or where they
were built as cooperative ventures by landowners as was frequently
the case.[73] The hedge also required a vast amount of labor to keep it
trimmed, and where it was not attended to with diligence, it would
grow to such heights that its spreading branches would shade and
kill all crops within twenty feet of each side and also would serve as
a sanctuary for birds and all kinds of vermin, weeds, and pernicious
animals.[74]

Live fences, nevertheless, had their advocates as there were some
decided advantages to this method of enclosure. In the first place,
the initial outlay was comparatively cheap, and the total cost to
bring them to maturity was less than half the expense of a Virginia
rail fence. Once they were well established they were not easily

disturbed by the prairie winds that were so destructive to other types; in fact, many westerners attested to their genuine service as windbreaks to farm buildings. And finally, once they matured, they had an endurance beyond the lifetime of any man.[75]

During the early stages of hedge-growing the problem of finding the correct variety for the soil and climate of a particular region was a matter of trial and error. Experiments were made in many sections of the country with a number of varieties and in time certain ones were found to be more adaptable than others as barriers. Caleb Kirk, a sophisticated Delaware farmer, aided in developing the Newcastle and Cockspur hedges in that area; Benjamin Shurtleff, Josiah Quincy and Elias H. Derby experimented with the American thorn in New England; George Washington and John Taylor worked with the cedar hedge in Virginia and Jonathan B. Turner of Illinois was one of the first successfully to introduce the popular Osage Orange in the Middle West.[76]

With few exceptions the thorny hedge was ultimately considered the best substitute for a dead fence. It was produced by two general methods: planting of seeds or "haws" in the farm garden where they were to vegetate for at least two years before transplanting to the intended fence row; or, by purchasing the "quicks," as the English hedgers called the young plants, from the local nurseries.[77] Either method required much skill on the part of the farmer, and agricultural journals were surfeited with suggestions from successful hedgers. Later professional hedgers and contractors came on the scene, relieving farmers of this arduous task.[78]

To produce a hedge fence the young plants were placed in the ground in the early spring about six inches deep and six to ten inches apart. For the succeeding five or six years they were plowed and hoed, and when the young stalks were about an inch in diameter near the root, many of the experimenters performed what was known as the "plashing process"; each stalk was cut about three-fourths through a few inches above the ground; the top was then bent down and entwined with the main stock, thus closing the gaps and causing the new sprouts to shoot in an upright form to create a pig-tight fence.[79]

The Osage Orange became the most popular and the most effective of all hedges, especially on the western prairies. Its growth was fairly rapid and its thorns were long and strong with a sharpness that deterred most domestic animals.[80] Its original home was in areas of the Southwest, and by the late thirties, when the prairies were being occupied, some of its seed found its way into the North. A few early Illinois settlers experimented with it, but the credit for its success belongs to Professor Jonathan B. Turner, of Illinois College, who developed it beyond the experimental stage on his farm near Jacksonville. In 1847 he issued his first circular to the public with directions on how to successfully grow the new hedge and advertising for sale the necessary plants.[81] This advertising, however, was soon abandoned; since his interests lay primarily in the development and propagation of this hedge he arranged with a number of nurseries in Illinois to grow and distribute the plants throughout the western states. Demand grew to such proportions that representatives from midwestern nurseries were sent into the southern states during the autumn months to purchase seed; and within a few years a regular industry had developed with hundreds of bushels being shipped from the southwestern states.[82] Soon it surpassed all other kinds of fences on the western farms.

The Osage Orange had a wide influence in aiding settlement of the western lands during the forties and fifties. Without a cheap fencing material it was difficult to put land under the plow, and in most of the West other forms of fencing materials were scarce and expensive. A settler from Paris, Illinois, stated that in his opinion this hedge bid fair [83]

to accomplish the object for which it has justly been recommended, viz.: the settlement and protection of these immense prairies. . . . Thousands of acres of prairie land, lying in this country, distant from timber, have recently been entered at the Land Office, and to my knowledge, . . . entries that would not have been made for years, only for the prospect of this speedy, cheap, and lasting protection.

Cyrus Overman, one of the larger producers of the plant in Illinois, made a comparable statement concerning its influence: [84]

not only may the farming of the prairies be greatly facilitated and improved, but . . . the millions of acres, . . . yet remaining . . . in our state, for want of material to fence it, may be brought into successful cultivation by growing the fences on the soil, thus giving homes and sustenance to additional millions of population, immensely increasing the wealth and taxable property of the state, and promoting the happiness of the masses.

This same judgment was expressed in other areas west of the Mississippi and for many farmers in those vast areas it was indeed a salvation.

The last general pattern of enclosures in use during this period, and the one that preceded immediately the advent of barbed wire fencing in the 1870's, was constructed with strands of plain, smooth wire. A product of the Industrial Revolution, it was introduced into the Colonies during the Revolutionary War and was used to a very limited extent for enclosures in the eastern states. The firm of White and Hazard in Philadelphia was probably the first to be successful in substituting wire for other forms of fencing materials. In 1816 it built a wire fence on a farm near Watkins Tavern at Schuylkill Falls.[85] By the 1840's the use of this type of enclosure had spread to the prairies of Illinois.

In spite of its initial reception, however, the wire fence did not come into general use on the prairies, for it did not meet the basic requirements of a farm fence—durability and effectiveness. Iron wire was affected adversely by extreme temperatures; it snapped in cold weather and sagged in hot. As a result of this contraction and expansion it was always difficult to keep the wires at an even tension.[86] Many methods were suggested in the agricultural journals for keeping the "iron wire tight"; some recommended that stakes be set between the posts to hold up the wires; others suggested that weights be hung to take up the slack; still others recommended the windlass, which was fastened to the wire and post and with which the tension could be regulated by turning the roller one way or the other.[87] The wire was often brittle and uneven in spots, so that it broke when put under a strain. It also had a tendency to rust badly when exposed to the elements unless treated once or twice a year with a coating of oil or paint. However the introduction of galvanized wire eliminated this weakness. One of its most decided weaknesses was that livestock had absolutely no fear of it and as a consequence they either penetrated it or rubbed it down.[88] Another objection to the use of this type of fence was the fact that the wire had to be largely imported from foreign countries.

This type of fencing was usually built with from four to six parallel strands of number nine or ten wire; the posts were generally placed four or five rods apart with a stake set halfway between them and the wires were stapled to the posts or passed through bored holes and plugged with small wedges.[89] In an endeavor to confine such livestock as swine, which were the most difficult to keep enclosed in any kind of fence, farmers generally placed boards along the bottom; to restrain larger animals wooden strips frequently were fastened along the top strand to aid them in seeing the wires.[90]

Several variations appeared in constructing smooth wire fences just as they did in the other types of fences; some built them on a ridge of earth using one board between two wires; others combined the wire and picket fence, while still others constructed the regular wire fence with a rail on top to prevent animals, particularly sheep, from hurdling them. By the middle of the nineteenth century, farmers were purchasing various kinds of smooth wire patented fences built and assembled in factories to be set up in the field. An interesting variation of this fence that found limited acceptance on the western prairies was the one patented by a Mr. Arnoux of New York. It is described in the *Chicago Weekly Democrat* as follows: [91]

A model fence designed to meet the wants of our farmers where wood is scarce and expensive, and required for other purposes, has been shown us. It is the invention of Mr. Arnoux, of New York, who has been residing some time in the West. The fence consists of strips, of sheet iron, one and a half inches wide, prepared in oil, so as to resist the action of the weather and painted white. These strips are nailed to posts in the ground, two rods apart, with a perpendicular strip of board every other rod.

Another writer, in commenting on this particular patented fence, stated that the "whole cost per rod, is estimated at less than thirty cents; and it is superior to wire as it does not sag, and being painted white, cattle will see it and not run against it." [92]

The cost of constructing the ordinary smooth wire fence naturally depended upon the quality as well as the amounts of materials used, the distance from markets that the material was hauled, and the cost of labor for putting it up. The estimated cost offered by various farm journals for a mile of number nine or ten wire could be constructed in the midwestern states at a figure of about $150.00, or fifty cents per rod. But in spite of this favorable cost factor as against competing fencing materials, its other basic weaknesses prohibited any degree of acceptance, and it was not until the invention of barbed wire fencing in the 1870's that the search for an effective and economical farm fence was finally resolved.

CHAPTER VI

"No Trespassing"

IN THE history of rural America numerous irritations and conflicts among farmers resulted from their livestock and types of fences discussed in the previous chapter. Although manifestations of these "competitive, feuding relationships" were usually of minor consequence, they often provoked behavior that resulted in deep-seated patterns of ill will.[1] Conflicts over livestock represented a major cause of tension and friction in rural communities during the long process of expansion and settlement. In the value system of the farmer his animals occupied as important a position as any other real or chattel property. Disputes arising from damages done to or by livestock on the open range, in the fields, railroad right-of-ways, or the public highways, frequently blighted "the tender plant of friendship" among rural neighbors. For example, if a stockman's livestock broke through a cultivator's enclosures and trespassed upon his crops, that was an infraction liable to evoke certain hostility; if the performance continued more strenuous reactions could be expected. Infractions such as fence-burning, sheep-killing and livestock-stealing aroused deeper emotions often leading to violence, gunfire and even death.[2]

Although in most cases livestock-fencing conflicts were ameliorated without serious aftermath between neighbors, in other cases a residue of ill-feeling plagued successive generations. A wide scope of this rural phenomenon is documented by contemporary observers from various sections of the country and the following three accounts give insights into the nature and importance of this livestock problem.

A New England reporter in the latter part of the eighteenth century offers the following account:

A great part of the contentions which have taken place among neighbors in the country, . . . will be found, . . . to have originated in poor fences. . . . A principal object with every good Farmer, is the security of his crops; and when . . . his neighbor's cattle, sheep or swine, break in and destroy the fruits of his labors, . . . it will give him not a little uneasiness; and repeated inroads, . . . will bring on a coldness, and lead him, at length, to seek a redress, through the . . . medium of law. One unruly ox, horse, or sheep, has proved the ruin of all social and friendly intercourse, . . . the advantages and pleasures of which, ought not to have been hazarded for five times the value of those creatures. . . . [Such altercations] may affect those who . . . come after us: for prejudices and opinion often descend to the third and even to the fourth generation.[3]

Fifty years later an agricultural journalist in Pennsylvania expresses comparable sentiments:

Bad fences have taught our cattle to become unruly and breachy, whereby our crops and those of our neighbours have been destroyed, after the labour and expense of raising them. But a greater evil even than this is yet to be named: —bad fences have often been the means of the most unhappy disputes and downright quarrels amongst neighbours, from which have flowed assaults, batteries, lawsuits, and ill-will for life, *and after*—for the quarrel has often been entailed with the property on the son—amongst those who would otherwise have lived . . . friendly . . . all their days.[4]

In a midwestern journal a farmer points up the frustration from a more personal viewpoint:

I pronounce this [livestock-fencing] to be the leak which prevents the filling up of our cup of bliss: as things are managed in the Western

Country it is worse than a leak, it is a sore, a blotch, the source of perpetual discontent—the "fretting leprosy" of the land. Tell us how this is to be cured, . . . for in no other part of the world has the farmer so much labor to undergo in order to secure his crops. The mode of enclosing, as here practiced, and the urgent necessity there is, for the strongest fortifications, in consequence of the barbarous practice of suffering stock of all kinds to run at large, keeps the farmer poor and grovelling and ignorant;—creates the cause of more rustic quarrels than any other thing, whiskey not accepted [sic].[5]

In examining these three accounts it becomes clear that the fundamental basis for the livestock-fencing problem was the "barbarous practice of suffering stock of all kinds to run at large." This custom was a reversal of the English common law practice of requiring every farmer to enclose his animals with a legal fence. Our ancestors soon discovered that the English method was not readily adaptable here. One reason was the ever increasing number of domestic animals. Another was the fact that in the period following the first occupation of a virgin area, be it in 1620 or in 1880, the desire to utilize the open ranges and forests for livestock grazing made it seem logical to enclose only their small cultivated fields. It was far simpler and much less costly to hew down some existing trees, make them into rails, and then lay a few rods of "zig-zag" fence around the plot of land, than to enclose a much larger section for the livestock.[6]

This traditional system of fencing crops in and livestock out gave rise to incessant quarrels and feuds which in turn led to the adoption of an elaborate set of local fencing laws governing every possible type of situation encountered by cultivators and stockmen.[7]

One of the earliest colonial fencing enactments was adopted in Virginia in 1632, which required all cultivators to enclose their crops. In other words, all livestock had the right to roam at will, and those who cultivated crops had to protect their fields with some form of legal fence.[8] In case of failure to do so they could expect to suffer depredations without any recourse. Perhaps no other law in our early history had a more sweeping influence on the everyday lives of rural people. For the next 250 years it served as the parent and model for fencing laws in many of the states. Under this system, no cultivator was completely free of the depredations of roving stock, whether he lived on the very fringe of agriculture, where the stockmen ran their herds of often "half-starved and shamefully neglected" animals, or within an established community where farming and livestock interests were combined.

Abandonment of this practice was inevitable as the number of farmers increased, the cultivated areas enlarged, and uncultivated lands for grazing purposes decreased accordingly. When that transitional stage was reached the agriculturists were almost certain to reverse the fencing laws.[9] Wherever this decision was made on the local level, as was the case in some states, revision was generally easier to obtain than on the state government level, where it not only took longer but was more difficult to achieve. In either case, the change was not accomplished without considerable stress and strain, no doubt exacerbated by the fact that fencing practices and laws had too often become associated with deep emotions and traditional situations.[10] Delay in achieving legal revision tended to perpetuate those frontier conditions which irritated agricultural settlers.

In some timberless regions, where fencing materials were scarce, an intermediate step, known as the herd law, was sometimes adopted. Under this system owners of livestock were required to engage herders in order to insure protection for the growing crops.[11] With the passage of this legislation, the only alternative left for livestock interests was to conform to the majority decision or round up their herds and move beyond the farming community, where they could repeat the process all over again—a process begun countless times in the history of our pioneer communities, beginning on the Atlantic coast and continuing from one settlement to another until the final curtain was drawn on this primitive fencing system.

The problem of building and maintaining fences was a difficult and everlasting task in any community where stock was permitted to run at large. The scarcity of timber sooner or later made it more troublesome for all farmers, whether they lived in Virginia, Illinois, or the trans-Mississippi West, for wooden fences were a dreadful drain upon timber resources, and the scant reserves of the product often made it impossible to maintain good fences. By the 1840's and 1850's cultivators throughout the settled regions of the nation were feeling the scarcity of timber and were asking the all-important questions: "Where is the farmer who does not find the making and repairing of fences a heavy drawback upon his profits? And where is the man who has not bought up all the timbered land he possibly could that he might have enough to keep his farm fenced for a course of years?" [12] The scarcity of timber for fencing and other farm construction prevented whole areas of the prairie country from being settled, and caused some older lands to go out of cultivation. [13]

As a result of the paucity of fencing materials, combined with the indubitable slovenliness and laziness of many farmers, fences were often neglected until they became dilapidated wrecks. [14] Such crumbled barricades were no protection to growing crops against the onslaughts of the ever present animals of the neighborhood; besides, according to many rural observers, these "low, frail and tottering fences [permitted] cattle [to] acquire a habit of wandering," and to become as "turbulent as a gang of highwaymen." [15] Edmund Ruffin observed that the state of Virginia was so plagued in the 1830's with roving animals that it might be compared to one large commons, or to "the fabled giant in the ancient hell, whose liver is ever devoured by dogs, but never completely destroyed." [16]

Historically, the old rail fence has been a picturesque form of rustic architecture, viewed wistfully by some as a beautiful "trellis for the vines of the woods and fields," but to those who had to construct, maintain and suffer its inherent weaknesses, it was more of a constant source of neighborhood annoyance than a work of art. When animals penetrated a neglected fence and devastated growing crops, tempers might flare, and the resulting animosities might turn into permanent hostility between two neighbors, or provoke killing of the depredating livestock or even the death of one or both of the neighbors. [17] The *Prairie Farmer*, noting these "brutal conflicts" in the Midwest, remarked that nothing seemed to ruffle the neighbors' feelings so soon and generate "hard thoughts" so often "as to have our cattle, horses, and hogs ill treated by the owners of fields, who are too lazy to make strong fences." [18] In order to prevent such violence, some early fencing laws prohibited the injuring or killing of another's livestock because it happened to enter improperly upon enclosed land.

With domestic animals in ever increasing numbers running at large long after an abundance of grazing lands had disappeared, the problem inevitably grew more acute. An especially aggravating condition arose from the custom of grazing livestock, including cows, pigs, and geese, on public highways, a practice which virtually converted roads into narrow pasture lands. This custom increased the possibility of conflicts because of the difficulty of restraining hungry animals from breaking through the fences.[19] The following caustic observation indicates the attitude of farmers whose neighbor's stock used the highways as pasture:

It appears to me the man must lack one of the most essential elements of a good neighbor, who will turn his cattle into the road to filch their living from his neighbors. Cattle thus turned out, become unruly, and are every where except where they should be; and are kicked, stoned and dogged by all. . . . We have to put ourselves in battle array, and daily examine our fences, . . . or wo [sic] be to our corn fields. Who would choose that man for a neighbor who makes it a practice to keep a dozen head of cattle in the road, and half as many half-starved, lantern-jawed, pike-nosed, saw-horse breed of hogs that will go through a fence anywhere, where they can put their nose through? [20]

Townspeople also suffered from these roving herds of "cattle, sheep, hogs and web-footed poultry." From earliest colonial times all these animals abounded in both small and large towns, and, except in New England, were permitted to roam at will, with the half-starved hogs having the freest range in the streets and causing the most inconvenience. This offensive custom was frequently justified by the folk belief that these animals served as scavengers or "physicians," cleaning up the offal and garbage that, if allowed to accumulate, would lead to epidemics and plagues. But the evils of the system were innumerable and serious dissensions resulted, for the animals broke down gates, destroyed gardens and orchards, nooned under shade trees, wallowed in gutters, rooted up lawns, bred vermin of lice and fleas, and deposited their excretions everywhere.[21]

In different sections of the country, before the railroad era, the highways served as thoroughfares for great numbers of animals enroute to markets in the East. Droves of cattle from Texas came into the corn belt to be fattened before being driven on to eastern cities. Growing crops were difficult enough to maintain, but with these "lean, gaunt and starving droves" from the Southwest, herded by drovers with little concern for adjacent fields, it was doubly hazardous.[22] Farmers not only discovered that an ordinary fence would not keep many of these brutes from entering their fields, but also learned that it was next to impossible to seize and impound the mobile animals. It was difficult to obtain damages for depredations since the local overseers of township fences had a tendency to be lenient with the owners of invading stock, provided they pursued them promptly and returned them to the road.[23] Under those circumstances the cost of fencing highways ran considerably higher since it involved a tighter and stronger barrier.

A new hazard was introduced following the Civil War that precipitated conflicts between small farmers and cattlemen: the driving of diseased cattle from the Southwest to the North for fattening purposes. When it was discovered that they were infecting local cattle—as well as infesting the roads, fields, and markets— numerous struggles broke out all along the route. The farmers resorted to numerous forms of reprisals in order to protect their livestock. In Illinois a vigilance committee was organized and was called the "Texas Rangers"; its purpose was to turn back or "repel future invasions." Some farmers of more extreme views advocated the lynching of Texas cattlemen and the use of "powder and ball" tactics to protect their animals from the dreadful infection.[24]

Of the various types of animals that ran at large and grazed upon the open fields and highways, the rough and scrawny hog had the worst reputation for causing damages to crops and fences. Animals approached fences in various ways: some went under, some over, some went through. Hogs used more devious ways of getting through a fence; this fact may account for the intense feeling they generated. It is unknown whether they were actually responsible for more damages to crops than their confederates.[25] But the vagrant hog was endowed with an uncanny capacity to penetrate almost any type of farm enclosure, especially the common rail fence. Apparently it would root and burrow beneath the lower paling, then squirm through into the field. By the time a number of other hogs

had followed it through the passage, palings were more apt than not
to be loosened and the whole panel ready to topple into a mound of
twisted ruins.[26] Nothing short of a stone wall could withstand these
wild and famished animals.

No wonder the fiendish manners of these animals caused and
sometimes led to the maiming and shooting of hogs. An Illinois
reporter described a breed in his area known as the "prairie racer"
that "is a positive curse to this country. They breed like rabbits,
overrun creation, jump fences, glide between rails . . . eat and root
up crops, remaining still leaner than before, and, worst of all, keep
out better breeds." [27] Richard Parkinson, in his *Tour of America*,
related how a certain breed called the "wood swine" actually was
able to pierce the rail fence. "You may as well think of stopping a
crow," he observed, "as those hogs. They will go to a distance from
a fence, take a run, and leap through the rails three or four feet from
the ground, turning themselves sidewise." [28]

The hog's capacity for destroying both crops and fences enraged
farmers, who, sighting some of these animals in their fields, might
in "the haste and excitement of the moment . . . adopt strong
measures" and descend upon them with their dogs. These encounters were often bloody affairs attended by considerable noise and
commotion, with the dogs chewing off the intruders' ears and leaving "large gaping wounds in their sides." On other occasions, the
farmer might not rely wholly upon his dogs but get down his
long-barreled musket.[29] Such violence normally brought retaliation
from the owner of the dead animals in the form of physical attacks
or lawsuits.[30]

Yet, these stormy episodes prepared the way for solutions for
these problems. At a certain point the feuding situation became
intolerable, and in each community a majority of settlers acted to
enact corrective legislation. Typical of this process were the laws
enacted in many states requiring hogs to be enclosed, ringed or
yoked.[31]

In addition to the numerous altercations caused by animals running at large, frequent lawsuits arose from controversies over line
and divisional fences. Considerable friction could be generated over
an adjoining neighbor's share of responsibility for maintaining a

fence, by the discovery that a fence was too far over on one or the other's land, or by a neighbor's refusal to construct his section of the fence.[32] Unfortunately few neighbors took time to draw up a written memorandum when line fence agreements were initially made; this laid the basis for future misunderstandings. In one case the discovery that a fence was not located on the true boundary line caused such serious conflict between neighbors "that even the church to which they both belonged could not settle it."[33] Bill Nye was no doubt right when he once remarked that the "line fence has kept more people out of heaven than [anything except] rum." Another observer remarked that three-fourths of all the "cussin" in his community could be attributed to these fencing irritations.

An early law stipulated that a cultivator was liable "within any court of justice" if he injured or killed any livestock in the act of removing them from his field. This same law also held that the owners of these animals were responsible for damages caused to the crops provided there was a legal fence enclosing them. As a result of this and similar enactments, lawsuits for recovery of losses were common. According to one farm journal, however, not one case in twenty ever recovered anything as a result of litigation. Rarely did the owners of trespassing animals offer to make good the loss occasioned by them.[34] Most owners of invading livestock vehemently insisted that they were not liable, since the crops were not properly secured by a legal fence; consequently the owner of the field was not entitled to damages. Failure to collect damages was due not only to the laxness of township officers in enforcing the laws and awarding damages, but to hostile public opinion in many areas. As a result, plaintiffs suing for depredations "had little chance before a jury."[35]

A private settlement between contending parties was often excluded by the general atmosphere of ill will to which the fencing problem gave rise. An elderly Connecticut rustic affirmed that because of fencing hassles farmers in his community could not "sleep in peace" or "quietly enjoy the fruits of their labors"; as for himself, "the greatest sin he had to answer for was an ill-temper," developed by vain attempts to keep his fences in order and his crops secure.[36]

A farmer in a neighboring state kept a daybook in which he recorded his unhappy experiences with the fencing problem. Among his entries are the following items: $25.00 for the loss of corn destroyed by a neighbor's livestock; $5.00 loss for the wounding of a plough horse; $3.00 payment for a neighbor's hog which was killed by being "dogged"; $5.00 for lost time while attending a lawsuit over the hog, and another $5.00 for loss of his valuable dog, killed for revenge. He also recorded such deprivations as "loss of neighbor's friendship." Perhaps the most revealing entry of all was the jotting that these experiences kept him "in bad humor, fretted and crabbed nearly all summer." [37]

The custom of permitting both male and female stock to run at large had always been a source of contention in agricultural communities. Various attempts were early made to control male animals from running free with the herds; in the case of stallions rewards were offered to those who would distrain the undersized ones. In some areas, one who found "stoned horses" at large was permitted to geld or to kill them without penalties.[38] For some years an owner had no effective means of securing damages when his best cow was sired by one of the numerous scrawny undersized bulls, or his choice merino ewe by a stray buck, "whose owner allows him to ramble at large." [39] The progeny of such "miserable nondescript sires" was hardly worth raising, and, worse still, the owners were denied the opportunity of improving the quality of their herds. In time, however, state laws, carrying fines and penalties, were enacted to restrain the freedom of these "boars, bucks and bulls." One eastern state, for example, imposed a ten-dollar fine on any stray ram, the money to be paid the owner of the ewe in order to help defray the loss incurred by having an inferior offspring; in Iowa the fine was placed at a figure one-third the value of the female animal.[40]

Another aspect of the same subject was the problem of "lost, strayed or stolen" animals in every settlement. This was a serious problem, since practically all animals were free to run at large. Local newspapers from early times carried many advertisements of lost stock. For example, the *Virginia Gazette* for the years 1736–1751 carried a large number of such notices. Many years later, one issue of the *Nebraska Farmer* carried as many as twenty-three estray listings.[41]

The oft-quoted term, "lost, strayed or stolen," was not an easy one to interpret, for it was difficult to ascertain whether or not an animal was actually lost, or had strayed from its owner, or had been deliberately stolen. To differentiate between these various categories local governments and state legislatures were finally obliged to enact elaborate regulations. These laws required a person impounding an animal to follow a detailed procedure in an effort to locate its owner, but it was difficult to enforce the law. In the western states estray laws often became dead letters, since "not one-half the persons taking up estrays ever make any mention of it, but permit an estray to remain about their premises or with their herds until it 'has gained a residence.' " [42] In some cases farmers discovered their cow or horse in another's herd and insisted upon its release, only to be presented with a bill for its feed and care exceeding the value of the animal. Moreover, animals were often illegally appropriated by changing the brands and ear marks; others were secretly slaughtered for home consumption.

The stealing of domestic animals was from earliest times considered a grave offense; it provoked the deepest feelings and the most extreme measures. Yet it persisted until brought under control by public volunteer organizations or by legal enforcement of local and state governments. This achievement was a progressive and painful process that continued well into the nineteenth century.

Many lives, both human and animal, were lost in fighting this frontier menace. At times it reached such proportions that it caused struggles verging on actual warfare. In the South, the burning of buildings and fences, and terror against people in general, became so violent that it proved necessary to resort to lynch law and the Regulator movement.[43] In Iowa, one hundred years later, the lynching of horse thieves became so prevalent in parts of that state that the governor threatened to call out the militia if local officials did not control this barbarous practice. Illinois acquired notoriety about the same time for horse stealing and other crimes perpetrated by the "banditti of the prairies." [44] This phenomenon moved westward with settlement. In parts of the West gangs of thieves operated systematically, causing the rise of many protective associations. In many cases a community hit by these thieves was so aroused that summary justice was administered on captured thieves. The introduction of barbed wire fencing in the later 1870's, and the resulting enclosure of livestock, made it easier to control this form of crime since thieves preferred to operate on the open range, "where they can get at them [the stock] with a show of success." [45]

Another source of irritation was the trespassing of humans on farmers' properties. Hunters did great damage to crops, fruits, fences, trees, animals, and buildings. In many communities the love of hunting with firearms, especially by the younger men, expressed itself in a wanton practice of prowling through the meadows, along right-of-ways and in farm fields gunning *"every bird* that comes within their reach." [46] Hunting in those days was not a seasonal recreation but a pastime pursued throughout most of the year. These "fowlers and fishers," as they were sometimes called, destroyed fences by knocking down the rails with their "heavy bottoms" as they climbed over them. Young cattle-tenders, herding livestock on the highways, often deliberately destroyed adjacent buildings and grainfields. Other trespassers pilfered and carried away plants, shrubs, vegetables, anything, in fact, that was movable upon the farm. They even murdered the birds, and on occasions "beat up" and shot the owners, especially when the latter had the courage to remonstrate and order them off their premises. [47] One farmer in the East reported it "was almost impossible to raise fruit . . . unless the trees were watched night and day during the season of ripeness." [48] Others complained that their trees had been dug up, their property defaced, and that firearms were indiscriminately discharged by trespassers upon their land. [49] "Can we not get some laws passed to protect . . . ourselves and our stock from the guns of idle vagabonds who are eternally infesting our fields?" appealed a typical aggrieved farmer. "Guns are heard all over it; and if you order the scoundrels off they'll tell you 'go to hell, they'll shoot as much as they please,'. . . Is not this a glorious *free* country?— every man has a right to do as he pleases, except the owners of property. . . . Every idle loafer in the cities has the privilege of roaming over our fields with guns and dogs, and killing off all he can, caring nothing about the damage to your fences or stock." [50]

Eventually, laws were enacted to protect the farmers' land and property from unwelcome intrusions of both animals and humans.

However, the problem of fencing conflicts did not vanish completely. As the railroads penetrated westward into the prairies and plains states, farmers and cattlemen were angered by the loss of their livestock on the unfenced right-of-ways. The companies usually delayed fencing their lines to the last, not only to save the cost of materials but because there was an ancient controversy as to who was required to do the fencing—the company or the stock raiser.

During this period of the unfenced right-of-ways, western periodicals published numerous items on losses of and damages to livestock by these common carriers. Both passenger and freight trains were "in perpetual danger from cattle straying" on the tracks or congregating at certain times of the year in the cuts and banks where they could find greener grass, drier ground and shelter from the winds.[51] This resulted in a large number of deaths and injuries. A typical occurrence is described by a reporter in Dillon, Montana, during the winter of 1887: [52]

The trains have been doing heavy work among the cattle during the past few days, and it is a very common thing to see an engine's pilot covered with the hair and blood of some unlucky animal. The unfortunate beasts stand along the track where the ground is bare and where some friendly point shelters them from the wind, and the trains catch them before they can get off. The other day one engine ran into a bunch of cattle . . . throwing twelve head from the track and killing seven, and again another lot was encountered . . . and two cows were killed, making a total of nine for the trip. Of course it is hard for the trainmen to avoid killing stock, . . . but it is still harder on the owners to lose their animals, and they are certainly entitled to pay for them. There is but one way to avoid controversy in the matter—the fencing of the track— and it would seem to us that it would pay the company to do it.

Evidence of such slaughter is also found in the annual reports of the western roads. These reports cite financial losses which vividly indicate the magnitude of the problem. We find for example, that the trains of the Missouri, Kansas & Texas Railway, for the year 1876, killed 1,948 animals in the three states where it operated; along certain parts of the Union Pacific line the losses were even higher.[53] The annual reports of the Texas & Pacific Railway demonstrate that for a number of years they also had an increasing death and injury toll on their tracks; for instance, in 1876 the total loss was slightly less than $30,000, but the enormity of the burden is indeed evident with an outlay of about $129,000 for the year 1889.[54]

Human lives were also sacrificed, for train accidents caused by collisions with livestock were not uncommon. Derailments, resulting in the delay of trains, were often cited in the annual reports.[55]

The problem of assigning responsibility and liability for these losses was fought out in the state legislatures, as it had been in the East. A special problem in the West was the great herds of livestock roaming the range. These animals endangered the lives of passengers on the trains: the easiest solution for the problem was to compel the thousands of settlers along the right-of-ways to enclose their stock. The alternative was to require the railway companies to fence the track or become liable for damages to all livestock.[56]

Even with the enactment of legislation, railroads delayed enclosing their right-of-ways, claiming that the states did not have the power to regulate this matter; they insisted it was the responsibility of livestock owners to enclose their animals. A leading railway publication presented their industry's views: [57]

> The notion that a railway upon which the population of large districts of country depends for the transportation of themselves and their property—and which must run its trains rapidly in order to satisfy the public necessities—should be subordinated to the rights of a stray steer, is absurd. Indeed it is the public which are compelled to pay tribute to his . . . bovine majesty. They must pay millions of dollars in the aggregate in order that Buck and Bright may wander at their own sweet will.

Ultimately the railroads were compelled to enclose their right-of-ways with some form of legal fencing—beginning in the 1850's with the hedge in the Middle West and turning in the 1880's and 1890's to barbed and woven wire in the western states. These fencing laws were not very explicit in their basic requirements. Some demanded only that the roads maintain a "good and efficient" fence. Others held the roads liable for animals killed and injured even though the right-of-way was fenced, provided it could be shown that the company failed to exercise "ordinary care." [58] This vagueness of the laws allowed a variety of interpretation. As a result it was difficult to establish negligence or liability on the part of the companies. Lengthy lawsuits were common and claim agents were frequently busy at certain points settling accounts with the farmers and cattlemen.[59] A reporter in Illinois in 1874 related the difficulties a farmer had in securing a claim check from a railway company for damages done to livestock: [60]

At present if a farmer has the misfortune to have an animal killed by a passing train, though it may be through no fault of his, it is almost impossible for him to secure damages in any reasonable length of time, and even if he does eventually obtain pay, he is obliged to take whatever the company chooses to offer, or else resort to a litigation that will cost him more than the value of the property destroyed. . . . By all means let us have a law that shall simplify and quicken the mode of obtaining redress from these soulless corporations.

I turn now to the fencing conflicts that arose in the trans-Mississippi short-grass regions—beyond the ninety-eighth meridian—where conflicts were of larger magnitude and of greater intensity. Natural influences and the social environment had combined, as Walter P. Webb maintains in his *Great Plains*, to modify the conventional patterns of the East. What began in colonial times only as predominantly individual quarrels and annoyances on a face-to-face relationship, 250 years later, on the semi-arid lands of the West, had developed to such antagonistic proportions between "grangers," sheepmen, and cattlemen that at various times a whole region erupted into a state of warfare.[61] These competitive struggles over water, grass, and trail rights, illegal fencing, occupation of the public domain, and the like, issued from the same general source as the earlier ones; namely, the old American system of permitting animals to run at large. Not until this immense grassland was finally transformed into "farms, enclosed pastures, and fenced-in water holes," was a more cooperative and stable economy achieved.

This transition from the frontier life of the open range to its final stage of development, where no unoccupied country remained, evolved out of two distinct phases of the competitive struggle: (1)

the phase that emerged from the free grass and open range as a result of the herd laws enacted in many areas through the influence of the ever increasing number of grangers, and (2) the final stage marked by extensive use of economical and effective barbed wire fencing to enclose livestock into private pastures.[62] This latter phase was a key contribution, in spite of the many conflicts its use engendered, for it not only contributed to the downfall of the cattleman's frontier but ushered in a new chapter in livestock economy.

As ever larger numbers of agricultural settlers moved into the open range area and selected homesteads on the best government lands, cattlemen soon discovered they were seriously impeded in the movement of their herds as well as being shut off from the best grass and water holes. These competitive contacts created skirmishes where the two opposing forces met, increasing in intensity as the free grass disappeared and continuing until cattlemen, reaching the limits of their westward expansion, were obliged to settle permanently on their own lands.

The struggle for a way of life at this frontier line was a difficult one, especially for those earliest emigrant grangers. Their most serious problem was that of fencing the cultivated fields and protecting their few animals from the hazards of large herds of range cattle, particularly in areas where it was impossible to secure local fencing materials.[63] In fact, many settlers lost out in the dual struggle against a harsh natural environment and hostile cattlemen.

In due time this problem was resolved in the homesteader's favor. Two important elements worked to their advantage. In the first place, they usually had a legal claim to the land they occupied, which was often more than the cattlemen could assert; secondly, they had a flow of additional emigrants into their community who in time made it possible to form a working majority of voters which could amend the fencing laws, making it mandatory for each owner to look after his own stock either by herding or enclosing. Such a law was favorable to cultivators, since it suspended fence-building and stimulated grain-growing; on the other hand, it was ruinous to cattlemen, who must employ ever larger numbers of herders to protect people's homes and fields from the turbulent herds.[64] An account of this workable technique, utilized by the farmers against the ranchers in a western county in Nebraska, appears in one of the leading range journals: [65]

A new difficulty has arisen which promises to interfere more than ever with open range practices. A very moderate influx of settlers places them in a majority, and they seem disposed to establish regulations and invoke legal conditions favorable to their own interests. Thus the settlers in one of the extreme western counties of Nebraska . . . recently voted in favor of the herd law by a majority of two to one. It prohibits the ranging of stock upon the plains except in the charge of a herder, and makes the owners of stock responsible for damage to unfenced grain crops. . . . If the settlers should prove strong enough to secure herd laws generally it would bring the business of the open ranging of cattle to an abrupt termination.

As intended, these herding laws played havoc with the free movement of cattle because the owners were held responsible for animals "that tramped upon the grass and corn fields" as the herders attempted to thread them through the farm communities. Lawsuits were so numerous that according to the *Galveston News* "nine-tenths of all petty cases . . . which beggar our counties, grow out of the . . . depredations of stock." [66] There were on occasions such serious encounters that herders and farmers broke into "murderous conflicts" over these problems. Part of the difficulty was simply the deep-seated attitudes built up toward each other over a period of time. Cattlemen, having had priority on the range by a number of years, naturally looked upon themselves as "the grandest interest in the country," and in allowing these despicable "nesters" to flood into their midst they only were permitting a "bungling system of surface scratching called by courtesy, farming" to destroy their noble way of life. [67] This challenge they felt constrained to resist with all their power and influence. Settlers, on the other hand, did nothing to mollify the cattlemen; ensconced behind the protection of the law, they had little desire to enclose their crops, but rather, as a New Mexico editor observed, were apt to sit by and boastfully estimate "the damages they will extort from cattlemen for fancied depredations on their little patches." [68] Even where materials were suitable for fence-building, this same journalist noted, farmers did not erect fences in fall and winter months when time was available; instead, they lounged about home, or, what was worse, loafed in grogshops.

The transformation of the cattle kingdom from a free range to one of enclosed pastures was due to a number of influences. Not the least, as mentioned before, was barbed wire fencing. Alarmed and inconvenienced by an increase in homesteaders as well as the growing number of cattle companies, the nation experienced an episode of "criminal prodigality," of land grabbing and illegal enclosing, unprecedented in its history. "Whole counties have been fenced in by the cattle companies, native and foreign," reported the Commissioner of the General Land Office in 1885; and, to add insult to injury, they gave no consideration to small ranchers who had their lands illegally surrounded, forcing them to drive miles out of their way to schools, churches, post offices, and markets.[69] Letters to the Commissioners vividly reported their predicament; if they attempted to assert their rights by making gates or removing the fences they found notices posted containing intimidations and even such threats as: "The son of a bitch who opens the fence had better look out for his scalp." One letter related that if a settler should violate the signs on the fence, a cowboy "just points his Henry rifle in the direction where it will do the most good, and if someone is killed it is charged up to the Indians or the highwayman." [70]

This exclusion of people from the public domain through barbed wire fences set in motion a systematic retaliation that disturbed the peace of the whole range country. It was a competitive struggle between fence men and no-fence men, attended by bloodshed and destruction of property seldom seen in a civilized society, and in the final analysis "amounted to social upheaval whose effects ramified to all phases and aspects of Western life." [71]

A fence-cutting war erupted first in Texas and spread as far north as Montana before it was finally brought under control. People were killed, properties burned, businesses crippled, and peaceful settlers alienated from one another. In fact, this phenomenon was so widespread it "found its way to the fireside of every home" and hardly a soul was not "touched by the nippers." [72] A special dispatch from Colfax County, New Mexico, described the state of public feeling and the technique used by the cutters at the height of this hysteria: [73]

Fence cutting is going on . . . at a most destructive rate under a strong organization. An almost unbroken line of wire . . . [for] 90 miles, has been cut. . . . The cutters are not known. Should this identity be established there would be a bloody war greater in fatality than the famous county war, years ago. Some of the sufferers, . . . are very much worked up over the breaks made by the wire-fiends, and threaten to put armed men along their fences. . . . The work of the fence-cutters was as systematic as the workings of a metropolitan police force. Each man was mounted, and they were placed in squads of convenient numbers. The squads would ride up to the fences, a man would drop out at a corner and cut for the extent of one-half mile or more, up to where another fellow had begun work, then jump into the saddle and rush to the head of the line again, after the style of school boys playing leap-frog.

The use of fences to enclose public lands for livestock grazing, the fury of the fence cutters, and growing pressure in the political sphere for the redress of grievances in favor of the majority against an entrenched minority awakened responses from various departments of government. The more flagrant illegal practices and outbursts of violence were halted, and illegal fences were ordered removed.[74]

The open ranges eventually gave way to a stable rural society of enclosed farms and ranches. The competitive struggle of the past with flocks and herds running at large, yielded to an economy of improved farming and cattle breeding, attended by improved social relationships in all rural areas of the nation.

CHAPTER VII

Sheep versus Dogs

A DOMESTIC ANIMAL with an extraordinary capacity for stirring up dissension among rural neighbors was the marauding dog. From the beginning of the industry, over large sections of the country, the predatory canine had posed seemingly insoluble problems to sheep-raisers. These problems bore some resemblance to the difficulties of the fencing industry and they helped to create a great deal of conflict and turmoil; they even contributed to the economic vicissitudes of the sheep industry.

Contemporary farm literature assigned the first place among the causes of the difficulties of the sheep industry to the inherent ineptness of the animal itself in coping with the dangers commonly present in the rural environment. To be sure, other factors influenced the welfare of the industry: the state of the protective tariff, wars at home and abroad as well as industrial developments such as mechanical looms and commercial spindles. Other elements that contributed to the difficulties of the industry were disease, weather conditions and wild animals, and, of course, the human equation of imprudent handling.[1]

Given the peculiar vulnerability of the sheep to attack by predatory beasts, it is clear that areas of sparse settlement were most favorable for its raising, while the advance of civilization inevitably added to the hazards of the industry.[2] Western migration of large numbers of settlers and the ultimate rise of a farm economy exposed the industry on an ever growing scale to the evil of marauding dogs, kept by nearly every family of the constantly expanding farm, town, and city population. The problem was not only one of an ever increasing number of dogs but of the failure of communities to apply to these destructive animals the legal regulations that they established for other domestic animals.[3]

Men tended to regard predatory behavior on the part of these canines in a quite different light from the damages caused by other farm animals that ran at large. If a cow, horse, or hog had broken into a field and caused damages, there was always some possibility of holding the owner responsible for trespass. But it was otherwise with roving dogs; if they killed or wounded animals their owner was not held liable. Dogs, in short, were not placed in the same category of property as other farm animals. This situation was a carry-over from England, where domestic livestock was considered as personal property within the common law and consequently subject to liability for trespass as well as for tax assessment. But owners of dogs were neither liable for their marauding activities nor had their dogs assessed as taxable property. This latter aspect was especially significant, for it was used as a major argument in America to put off the adoption of legislation for the protection of sheep-raisers. If dogs were not property how could they be taxed? There was another difficulty in applying the law of trespass to dogs as it was applied to livestock. For example, it was possible for most farmers to enclose their cultivated fields with some form of legal fence to protect their crops from their neighbor's livestock; but in the case of roving dogs it was next to impossible to construct a barrier that would assure protection from them.[4]

Yet another aspect of the problem was the notorious loyalty of dog-owners to their curs. So strong was this attachment that owners would intemperately resist any attempts to examine or secure evidence of damage and would even swear that their dogs were home bodies who never left the farm. Under such conditions sheep-raisers had little prospect of successful appeal to the law. Since they could not fence out these marauders like other animals, the harassed sheepman had no other recourse than to take the matter into his own hands. This he often did with such deadly instruments as the rifle, the rope, and the strychnine bottle.

In earlier days the dog had justified his existence on the farm by saving life, shielding property, watching livestock, and lightening labors by providing power to operate churns, washing machines, and to draw water from wells. However, mechanization had gradually deprived the dog of these few serviceable chores and he was left to idle away his time breeding, roving, and marauding in his community.[5] An ordinary farm family owned at least one dog, which might be a mixture of any number of nondescript breeds; but many families (usually the poorest in the community) harbored more dogs than people. In the South, Negro and poor white families were accused of keeping large numbers of what were called "hunting dogs." So destructive were these animals that they often destroyed a flock of sheep before help could be summoned. In the North, one critic claimed, nine out of ten dog-owners were as worthless as their curs and could be classified as "two links from the same sausage."[6] The dogs of such owners were almost always completely neglected, half-starved and ill-treated—conditions that forced them to forage for food on small and helpless animals in the neighborhood. They spent their idle hours in attacking young calves and pigs and frequently engaged in nocturnal raids upon adjacent sheep pens, decimating the farmers' flocks; then, before midnight, they furtively stole back to the protective custody of their owners.

These incursions into the sheepfolds augmented the problems of the already overburdened sheep-raisers. The sheepman who sought to increase his flock and to upgrade his poor quality sheep—with their long legs, scrawny bodies and low grade wool—by breeding with a costly European purebred ewe or ram, had to display eternal vigilance in defending his costly investment against these dogs. A sheep-raiser summarized the frustrating and costly experiences of his group:[7]

One of the great hindrances to the more extensive ranging of sheep is the danger of loss from the ravages of dogs. Year after year we see the number of dogs, and the destruction caused by them, increasing, but no earnest action to prevent its continuance. As a consequence, many are deterred from engaging in the business, although they would gladly do so, if sure of receiving the reward after laboring for it. We can imagine better than we can describe what is likely to be a man's feelings when, on visiting his flock some morning he finds his favorite Southdowns or Merinos dead, or horribly mangled, caused by the nightly invasion of a pack of worthless curs; and it is not to be wondered at if he showers imprecations on the whole race of dogs.

What was the breed of these roving creatures and what was their approximate number? It is difficult to answer these questions for contemporary accounts were obviously biased and greatly colored. The "picturesque accounts . . . by the sheep raisers" indicted most dogs. If one could believe these accounts, all sheep communities were overrun with them. Such exaggeration of the canine population was perfectly understandable since it supported the sheep-owner's argument in favor of some form of legal control of these curs. Numerous references to dogs in the rural literature indicate that they were relatively large and powerful canines, possibly descendants of the Newfoundland, Collie or Shepherd types; but contemporary writers avoid any specific breed name and generally refer to them as a mixed variety of nondescript dogs.[8]

Anything more than a crude estimate of the population of these animals would be impossible. Rural magazines differed widely in their calculations, sometimes varying as much as one hundred per cent in their estimates. In 1850 one of the leading journals assessed the dog population for the country as a whole at approximately four million. It had arrived at this figure, the writer explained, "according to the usual rate of calculation," which was stated as follows: there was a total population in 1850 of 24 million people. Since each family averaged about six members, there must be a total of about four million families. On the basis of these data the journalist concluded that each family, rural and urban, must have at least one dog in its possession. This would give a grand total of about four million dogs in the nation in 1850.[9]

Poor Negroes or whites who hunted as a livelihood or to supplement their meager food supply were often the target of anti-canine attacks. They were accused of permitting their curs to breed freely and of making no effort to control their predatory activities. These individuals sometimes wrote spirited letters "to the Editor," defending their "lovable pets" and absolving them and themselves of any guilt. However, editors, reflecting the viewpoint of the majority of their readers, usually gave a cold reception to these apologia. Occasionally an editor printed one of the more illiterate of these letters to expose its writer to ridicule. Satire was sometimes used in the effort to brand the dog-lovers as lazy, uneducated riffraff. A letter to a leading journal, ostensibly directed against the dog-tax law under consideration in Ohio, illustrates this strategy: [10]

Mr. Bateman:-You have been saying so much lately about dogs being worthless, and doing so much mischief and ought to be taxt that Ive got mad. You needent tell me that dogs are worthless for I couldent hardly live without mine. they ketch a great deal of game, and then I made a great deal a selling pups—and then they are so healthy for children to play with, and then nobody nor nothing cant come about me to steal anything day nor nite, and if any critters gits in my lots, or if any body elses hogs comes about my door they are sure to receive bodily damage.

You think they do a great deal of mischief but they dont compared with the good they do. What if they do kill some sheep, they dont eat em all up, and then they belong to rich owners. and if they kill fokes once in a while it aint much loss for we are over run with fokes now and game has got so scarce that poor fokes cant hardly live.

And you want to have em taxt but you wont never get it done for some of the legislaters keeps dogs and they wont do it. what! make us pay twenty five cents or a doller for evry dog!! it woald ruin the state. I will take my gun and fite in blood up to my nees before ile submit to it. I reckon you want us all to sell our dogs and give you the money for your papers but I wont do it. I wouldent take no money for my dogs, and I wouldent give one pint of possums greas for all the papers yove got.

Darwin Doge
Braceville
Trumble Co., Feb. 1847.

Even as dog-lovers proclaimed the innocence of their pets accounts of wanton destruction of flocks poured into the farm journals.

These accounts depicted the stealthy, cunning nature of the marauding dogs, telling how they attacked the unwary flocks, sometimes singly, more often in packs of two to six in the dead of night.[11] Occasionally, an aggressive dog boldly attacked and chased a herdless flock in broad daylight; but the normal pattern for killing sheep conformed to the version of a contemporary poet: [12]

> *Alone, in wanton mischief he pursues,*
> *Alone in reeking blood his jaws imbrues;*
> *Chasing amain, his frighten'd victims round,*
> *Till death in wild confusion strews the ground;*
> *Then, wearied out, to kennel sneaks away,*
> *And licks his guilty paws till break of day.*

Most sheep-raisers at one time or another had the heart-rending experience of seeing marauding "dogs tearing throats and mangling the bodies of a flock of sheep." Nothing was more common in the sheep-raiser's life than to see strange dogs slinking through the grass "worrying" and "disquieting" the flocks. Occasionally expectant ewes, as a result of these experiences, miscarried while running with the flock; if such animals faltered and fell to the ground, they and their unborn lambs were usually found dead when discovered by the owner.[13]

Individual sheepmen were known to suffer losses of as many as fifty in a single attack. Much larger losses were frequently recorded in farm journals.[14] In 1877, a Nebraska farmer registered with local officials 484 sheep killed in one night; thirty more died later from their wounds and 200 suckling lambs were also lost for lack of mothers to feed them. This owner estimated his loss at ten dollars per head, since the sheep were not of the ordinary type but of the finest imported breeds.[15]

Ohio figured most frequently in accounts of losses of sheep. This was probably due to the fact that it had more sheep than any other state between 1850 and 1870 and had suffered large losses for many years. An estimate in 1863 put the number of dogs in Ohio at about 175,000 and the total sheep population at about 4,500,000; or a ratio of about one dog to every twenty-six sheep.[16] The annual value of sheep killed or wounded in that state during a number of key years was estimated as follows: in 1846, around $80,000; in 1857, over $146,000; in 1865, $150,000.[17] In 1870, however, when an apparent westward shift of the sheep population had already begun, the annual loss dropped to about $143,000.[18] Large losses of sheep also occurred in two other states. Massachusetts, for example, saw her ovine population decline in a twenty-year period by more than 260,000, and a large part of this reduction was due to the ravages of dogs. In 1862 New York reportedly lost as many as 50,000 head, representing an approximate value of $175,000 from the same cause.[19]

Farther to the west, in the state of Iowa, the Agricultural Society reported that there were in 1877 some 318,439 sheep compared to 1,598,226 ten years earlier; this tremendous reduction was blamed in part on the ravages of dogs.[20] Assessment returns on dogs in the state of Georgia for 1874 ran well ahead of the national average with a ratio of 31 dogs to every 100 sheep. These dogs managed to destroy 28,625 head, with a value of $73,852, or about nine per cent of the total sheep population. A reporter for the *Nebraska Farmer* in 1877 struck a dismal note: he claimed there were more dogs in his state than voters. According to this informant, at least ninety per cent of the agricultural correspondents in the different counties had given as their opinion that the real obstacle to a profitable sheep industry in Nebraska was the activity of marauding dogs.[21] A leading historian of the industry concluded that

a factor which must not be overlooked in the disappearance of the sheep east of the Rocky mountains was the continual loss due to dogs. Thousands of farmers who gave up small flocks in years past did so because of dogs. Men with small flocks of purebred animals which suffered from ravages of dogs . . . had good reason to discontinue the enterprise.[22]

These reports document not only the immense injury to the sheep industry but to the food supply of the nation as a whole. Estimates of value of sheep losses for the entire country varied from a low figure of around $1,000,000 for 1875 to a high of well over $3,000,000; that is, a loss of about two per cent of the total sheep population.[23] To be sure, while estimated losses remained fairly constant nationally throughout this decade of the 1870's, certain areas experienced lighter losses; this was especially noticeable after effective dog laws had been adopted and enforced in the older sheep-raising regions.[24]

It is necessary to observe that marauding dogs were not the only cause of the heavy financial losses of the industry.[25] As early as 1856 the *Prairie Farmer*, which had frequently indicted the predatory activities of the canine, observed that improvidence in feeding and sheltering, as well as gross neglect of sheep in general, had attributed to the fluctuations of the industry.[26] In many states sheep received so little attention that they were compelled to winter like other domestic animals, without grain, feed or shelter; obviously such treatment exposed them to a variety of decimating influences, including of course attack by wolves and feral dogs.[27] One observer, remarking on the poor care received by sheep stated that "for every sheep killed by dogs, at least twenty are permitted to die by starvation, want of care and similar causes, with which the owner is justly chargeable."[28] Most of this neglect was found among the small flockmasters, who had to tend their own flocks day and night, since they could not engage shepherds, as did the larger sheep-raisers.[29] As a result of their great losses, many of these small operators had to abandon the industry.

The extensive depredations of marauding dogs during this period inevitably led to efforts to solve the problem. Many panaceas—some completely impractical—were offered to small producers. These cure-alls, found dispersed throughout the agricultural publications, appear to fall into two general categories: (1) those that relied on individual action, and (2) those that required some action by a governmental agency.

Some farmers claimed to have solved the problem by placing within their flock a certain number of black cows; when a killing dog approached the sheep they allegedly scurried to the protective custody of the cattle, and this deterred the dog from attacking the sheep.[30] The assumption was that most dogs would turn tail and run from defiant-looking cows. Proponents of this plan claimed to have determined accurately the number of cattle required for such defense: not less than five cows and six one- and two-year-old steers for every 200 head of sheep. Training these cattle to play the role of defender was achieved by forcing them to move toward a tame dog held at the end of a long rope; this allegedly convinced the timid sheep that they had reliable protection from within the herd. Once a feeling of security had been instilled in the sheep, three steers with very sharp horns could be retained and the rest returned to their regular pasture. The sheep-raiser could repeat this procedure year after year using the three steers that remained with the flock to teach a younger set of steers who replaced their mentors, thus maintaining the required number.[31]

A much more drastic solution and one of great antiquity as a method of controlling the behavior of domestic animals was castration. Man had learned early in his association with animals that this operation transformed them into milder, gentler creatures. When this operation was performed on a marauding dog—usually by thrusting it head first into a barrel—the operation not only forthwith reduced the dog's roaming propensities over the countryside but also modified its quarrelsome nature toward other dogs and animals.[32] Sheepmen also discovered that for at least nine-tenths of all sheep killed and injured there was certain to be present somewhere in close proximity to the pack a female dog in heat. Such a condition, it was affirmed, caused an emotional instability among male dogs that held out the prospect of serious trouble for various small farm animals before the night was over.[33] Castration was the answer to this problem for it would help to relieve these marauding excursions; however, dog-owners did not take kindly to such operations and occasionally the castration of canines led to serious quarrels between neighbors.

Industrious and sophisticated sheepmen developed a more ingenious technique. This was a uniquely designed and constructed pen or trap similar to that which hunters used in catching wild turkeys, but the entrance was on top instead of on the bottom, so as to prevent the escape of captured dogs.[34] This novel contraption was built with four sides, about five feet high, sloping gradually in from the base to the top in order that the dogs could easily enter; once inside, however, they would find it almost impossible to scale the walls due to their inclination. One sheepman stated that if this trap were constructed properly "not even a greyhound could jump out of it." [35] Another claimed that if one built them of fence rails around ten feet high and then either placed them near the spot where a sheep had been killed or baited it with one already dead, one could expect to catch as many as seven or eight in one night. This pen could be used repeatedly, but a certain degree of caution had to be exercised. Once a dog had been enticed into it and the feat became widely heralded among the neighbors, owners of packs of dogs would certainly hasten to tie them up at night in order to prevent their capture and to save themselves the embarrassment of being charged with ownership of predatory dogs. [36]

Most rural observers agreed that such ill-fed, mistreated and neglected mongrels were almost invariably the dogs in a community which had learned the art of worrying, wounding and killing sheep. Sheepmen seeking a solution to this problem discovered that the use of simple strychnine crystals offered a perfect, made-to-order answer to their problem. Since these dogs were eternally hungry and looking for food, it was easy to entice them with a juicy morsel of meat. Advocates of strychnine suggested this prescription, and declared it to be most effective when properly administered with the appropriate bait: [37]

BEEFSTEAK . . . . . . 16 ounces
STRYCHNIA . . . . . . 4 scruples

Divide the beefsteak, or "tit bit," into sixteen parts; take a sharp knife and make an incision into each one of them, and insert one-sixteenth of the above quantity of strychnine, drop a few of the *medicated* "tit bits" around your "sheep preserves," and have a few in your coat pocket so that when you come across an ugly *cuss* of a dog . . . make his acquaintance, coax him to stay with you long enough, while you draw forth just one morsel. In the name of *mutton* let the medicine be given.

Many flockmasters felt no scruples in using this method at every opportunity in order to save the industry from its sorry plight. Such an influential figure as Horace Greeley insisted that farmers were justified in poisoning these "cut-throats," as he called them, since they were ruining the industry. "Farmers by tens of thousands," he said, "have sold off, or killed off, their flocks, mainly because they could not otherwise protect themselves against their frequent decimation by prowling curs, which were not worth the powder required to shoot them." [38] This advantageous "medicine," "so beautiful, so silent, so effective, so irresistible," was also most satisfactory from the monetary viewpoint, for it cost as little as thirty-five cents a drachm—an amount more than adequate for the above prescription.[39] Yet the saturation of fields with those "loaded" morsels of deadly meat thoroughly provoked some sensitive people, who claimed that the use of this poison violated one of man's most basic precepts, that of not taking the law into one's own hands. These compassionate individuals attempted to prohibit the direct sale of strychnine over drug counters, but to no avail.[40]

Others advocated as a "sure cure" for the dog problem the ingenious device of yoking "two stout rams to a stick four feet long and [then] tie the dog to the center, between the rams, and let them drag him about the fields" until all three were completely exhausted. This technique required more time and effort than some others, but was proclaimed the "cleverest thing known" for curing a dog that had tasted the blood of sheep.[41] Those who endorsed the use of rams for this cure not only vouched for its effectiveness but emphasized the point that it was most entertaining to the onlookers who often gathered to watch the three animals prostrate themselves.

There was a still more brutal variation of this device. If the first round of dragging failed to modify a dog's predatory habits, harsher treatment could be administered by tieing the dog's "neck and heels in a gateway and [then] race a flock of sheep over him a few times, so closely [together] that some of them must trample upon him." [42] If this traumatic experience failed to improve the dog's behavior, most sheepmen were of the opinion that the only remedy left was the skillful use of the ball and gun.

Believers in this ultimate solution wrote letters in its favor to the farm journals; they were convinced that the only good dog was a dead one. Farm families, they wrote, should give up the idea that these "traitors to wool-growing" could ever be transformed into man's best friend. The quickest, cheapest, easiest and most efficacious procedure for the long-suffering sheep-raisers was to unite and sally with a battery of firearms to kill off the outlaw canines wandering around the fields.[43] Their destruction would cause no serious loss to their owners, and would be of inestimable value to all sheep-raising communities.

A much older device for protecting sheep and the one most frequently mentioned in the ovine literature of this period, was the practice of hanging bells around the necks of certain sheep within the flock; one bell for each ten to fifteen was the usual ratio. Dogs characteristically attacked their prey under cover of night, and it was believed that the sound of bells would indicate to them the presence of human beings and frighten the dogs away. Be this so or not it was at least true that the ringing of these bells had a beneficial influence on the sheep themselves, for it served to keep them closer together in times of danger.[44]

Fencing was considered as a means of protecting sheep from dogs, but the financial outlay necessary to construct an effective barricade was too great for the ordinary flockmaster. A dog-proof enclosure of ordinary rails, boards, barbed wire or any combination of the three was expensive when built high and tight enough to enclose sheep; and its usefulness for other livestock was limited, since most of them received no such care and required no such enclosure for protection.[45] Beyond this initial cost there was always the annual process of repairing and replacing broken and fallen parts; and many farmers found this annual task too burdensome, for the result was that, within a few years, what was once an expensive enclosure ceased to be an effective barrier for the flockmaster's sheep, let alone the neighbors' dogs.[46]

Some proposed solutions bordered on the humorous or ridiculous. In an effort to arouse public sympathy for the beloved sheep, some recommended that ministers deliver periodic sermons from their pulpits on the subject; others suggested that certain ointments, possessing obnoxious smelling and tasting ingredients such as brimstone, gunpowder, tar and currier's oil, be applied to the under part of a sheep's throat where the attacking dog would be certain to "taste the awful compote." [47] Renewal of this offensive compound four or five times a year might be necessary, for the ointment often became dry and washed off. One ingenious correspondent advocated a leather collar, filled with sharp pointed nails, to be placed around the necks of the sheep.[48] Others recommended that sheepmen buy the large and stocky Cotswold, since they were too heavy to attract the pursuit of stray dogs by running away from them. It was believed that sheep usually were attacked because they ran at the sight of a dog.[49]

The idea of using certain breeds of dogs to repel the killers was broached during these experimental years. In fact, special dogs, such as the Spanish type, were occasionally imported, but because of their prohibitive cost they never became popular.[50] Some flockmasters proposed the breeding of a unique variety of dogs by the inexpensive method of allowing a well-bred pup to suckle a lambless mother ewe; this intimate relationship would presumably develop a strong bond between them, and as the pup matured it would naturally become a protector of the flock.[51] To assure the pup's absolute dedication to the fold it was necessary to separate it completely from the affectionate children in the family as well as from all other dogs. Some flockmasters were convinced that this method would insure protective guardians for their sheep; others considered it "unmitigated nonsense" to believe that one could transform a dog into a trained shepherd through association.[52]

Many small sheep-raisers contributed their panaceas to various rural journals but few gained acceptance, not only because of their impractical nature but because many flockmasters were reluctant to experiment for fear of reprisals from the neighboring citizenry if they attempted to implement them. In fact, many of these solutions were so cruel and inhumane that the authors submitted them without signing their names, presumably from fear of retaliation. As a rule, when irate sheepmen proposed the adoption of some harsh method, their project sparked a number of vitriolic rejoinders.

The upshot was that relationships between sheep-raisers and dog-owners periodically grew strained with unrestrained charges and counter-charges being hurled. Owners of sheep were often accused of deliberately killing the dogs in their communities, and as a result suffered discrimination and ostracism at the hands of their dog-loving neighbors. The sheep-raisers in turn leveled denunciations against dog-owners who allegedly condoned canine attacks against prized sheep. Editorials repeatedly charged dog-owners with pretending ignorance of the deeds of their pets, even when confronted with proof of their guilt. Some dog-owners, it was charged, displayed an excessively complacent attitude toward canine misdeeds; they allegedly held that a severe reprimand or a good thrashing would teach a dog to forbear from nocturnal raids on the neighbor's sheep pens. Dog-owners, it was further charged, lacked a sense of monetary responsibility for the crimes of their pets; they believed that having punished the marauder they were absolved of any further obligation.[53]

A major source of discord was the absence of generally accepted methods of proving the guilt or innocence of an accused dog. The problem of securing irrefutable evidence was well nigh insoluble. In order to provide satisfactory proof the accuser had to establish beyond doubt that a given dog had killed the murdered sheep; this virtually required that a dog be caught in the act; if he was found in a specially designed trap set for him, this only brought a presumption that he had killed the sheep. The dog's cunning habits of striking at night many miles away from home and returning next day to present an aspect of angelic innocence, added to the difficulty of an accuser. One cur, it was alleged, was so sly that he habitually bathed in the livestock watering trough upon his return home so as to wash away any sheep blood or other incriminating evidence of his recent foray against a farmer's flock.[54]

Some dog-owners regarded any inquiry into their dogs' movements as an invasion of private affairs, and withheld all cooperation in such matters. Occasionally a dog-owner permitted an examination of a suspected canine in an attempt to establish its guilt; as a general rule this was accomplished by giving the dog an emetic to force him to bring up any undigested food. This was done as soon as possible after the killing of the sheep in the hope that the food materials acquired from the dog's stomach would still be recognizable as mutton.[55] But the problem of conclusive proof still remained even if mutton were found, for all it proved was that the dog had eaten it but not that he had killed it, unless the food disgorged was an identifiable part of a particular sheep.

A popular method used in the effort to establish guilt was to search between the teeth of a suspected dog for small pieces of wool.

It had the advantage of being painless to the animal and quick and easy to execute, and of providing incriminating evidence that remained intact for several days, since the wool, tightly stuck within the crevices of the teeth, would survive saliva action in the mouth.[56] However, absence of this evidence did not necessarily exonerate a dog, since many dogs did not bite or wound the sheep; they merely worried them to death, or caused them to die of exhaustion or overheating.

The existence of a kind of double standard in regard to responsibility for injury done to animals or property aggravated the problem. If a farmer's hogs or sheep broke into another man's field, the law required him to make full restitution for the damages, but if a marauding dog killed or maimed a neighbor's sheep, it was almost impossible to collect payment for these losses. Protest against this double standard took the form of numerous letters directed to magazines and legislators, demanding that owners be made legally and financially responsible for their dogs, as others were for their slaves or domestic animals.[57]

Nevertheless, the dog-sheep problem persisted, and the numerous individualistic solutions advanced proved disappointing. Indeed, conditions in sheep-producing areas became gradually worse as settlement and dog populations increased, forcing large numbers of sheep-raisers finally to abandon the industry. The swelling number of canines in the rural areas was not the only factor in this decline. As settlers moved in, towns and villages grew in number and size, bringing with them more dogs until hordes of these animals infested many of the farming areas. Lacking attention or care from their owners, they roamed far and wide in the rural communities in search of food and females of their own kind. They grew so numerous and vicious that they were distinguished by the name of "town-dogs."[58]

All the blame for the disappearance of sheep in many sections should not be placed on the excess of dogs; factors contributing to the decline of the industry included disease and the high cost of fences, large pastures, and purebred stock. However, some historians of the sheep industry are of the opinion that the growing magnitude of the dog problem was responsible for the decision of small flockmasters to curtail their investments or abandon the industry altogether.[59] Some, in order to escape this canine evil of the settled communities, moved westward; this fact is amply demonstrated by the census returns: in 1840 New York had the largest sheep population, but by 1850 the center of the industry was in Ohio. This movement westward continued until, by 1880, California was in the lead, but by 1890 Texas claimed the largest number of sheep.[60]

It became obvious that if the industry were to continue in the older and more settled communities some political action to defend its interests was necessary. Several leading farm journals—whose editors had seen the handwriting on the wall for the sheep industry—laid the groundwork for this activity. Voices in the wilderness, they pleaded with state assemblies to enact legislation to check the growth of the dog population.[61] But like other problems of rural society, this too seemed to resist all efforts of compromise. Representatives of sheep-raisers and dog-owners engaged in sterile factional debate, and legislative sessions resounded with charges and counter-charges and even with threats of retaliation and violence.[62]

With monotonous regularity individual farmers and farm organizations petitioned their state governments for redress, but year after year a deaf ear was turned to these demands. The sheepmen encountered strong opposition at the ballot box, for dog-lovers and hunters combined with those who feared new taxes, to block any proposed legislation.[63] Representatives also hesitated to support dog laws for fear of becoming butts of ridicule, which would create "a hazard to their vanity or popularity." One could cite the case of Missouri's noted farm journalist, Norman J. Colman. One day in 1871, after he had made a serious effort to initiate anti-dog legislation, he approached his seat in the legislative chamber to discover that some colleague had tied a dog to it; and to make the situation even more ridiculous and humiliating, he was "laughed . . . down at every attempt" to continue his discussion of the subject.[64] In the face of such ridicule few legislators dared to vote in favor of the sheep-raisers and against the marauding cur.

Ultimately reason prevailed due to the migration of sheep westward, the campaign of the rural press and the introduction of costly purebred animals. Eastern states began in the 1850's to enact dog laws and one by one others followed suit until by 1880 some thirty-five states had enacted such measures. Typical provisions of these laws were: (1) the owner was liable to pay a specific tax, usually $1 for the male and $3 for females with a graduated tax for each additional dog; (2) each taxed dog was issued a numbered collar containing pertinent information to help separate him from stray curs who were not legally protected; (3) a fund was created from the tax receipts to pay all or in part the losses sheep-owners had suffered from the ravages of unowned or unclaimed dogs; if there was insufficient revenue in the fund to make full restitution, losses were to be paid on a pro rata basis; (4) all dog-owners were liable for payment of damages sustained by their dogs provided proof could be established; (5) a bounty of fifty cents a head was offered on all unregistered dogs; (6) owners were fined if they failed to register their dogs; and (7) all law enforcement officials who failed to execute these laws were made liable to a fine by the local magistrates.[65]

No sooner had these dog laws been enacted than some states began to weaken them with crippling interpretations and refinements. For example, one purpose of the dog tax was partially frustrated when the fee was set so low that the owners were not encouraged to avoid tax payments by destroying their excessive number of dogs.[66] Farm journals were quick to criticize local enforcement officials who often failed to collect the taxes in spite of the law, especially from shiftless owners of dogs who, it was said, were often more worthless than their guilty pack of dogs.[67] In some states officials in the towns and cities would carry out every aspect of the law while those in rural areas "treated it with magnificent scorn." Other criticisms also were leveled that the funds collected were misused and allocated for such emergencies as roads and schools rather than for the exclusive payment for injuries and deaths to sheep.[68] The bounty system—the payment of a fee for the killing of unregistered stray dogs—failed to produce an appropriate effect in most communities, for farmers were not apt to relish the idea of killing their neighbors' dogs for such a small sum. Furthermore dog-owners often escaped legal liability for damages because the language of the law made difficult the presentation of conclusive evidence; in some states, even such evidence as wool discovered in the dog's teeth was not conclusive proof.[69]

As if these inadequacies of the dog laws were not enough, some claimed that the tax was unfair, that it made the wool-growers a privileged class, for other farmers were not protected from the depredations of weevils, flies, aphides or mice. In rebuttal, sheep-raisers easily rejoined by pointing out that these evils were not the work of men but of natural forces, and that the question of guilt did not arise in such cases.[70] They also stressed that the dog laws did not afford financial aid to owners who suffered losses of sheep from natural causes. Sheep-raisers complained that some state legislatures had made a mockery of their legislative process. The Iowa Assembly, for example, had enacted in March, 1862, after several years of wrangling, an acceptable dog law only to promptly repeal it in the next session after it had been in effect for only five months. The cause of the repeal it appeared had been the many complaints from urban constituents.[71]

Finally, the *modus operandi* of these laws created a serious obstacle to the introduction of choice breeds of sheep and tended to prevent all progress and improvement in this very important branch of agriculture. Owners of small flocks of purebred animals destroyed by marauding dogs were able to recover only the price of common sheep from the local fund. These flockmasters had only two alternatives: to discontinue the high quality breeds and replace them with what the English labeled "twelve shilling *culls*," or else give up the raising of sheep completely. Many sheepmen could not afford the loss of choice Merino ewes, worth as much as $100 apiece, only to find that the county funds were exhausted or capable of paying only a petty sum for each loss.[72]

Clearly these laws had serious weaknesses and were often difficult to enforce; yet they relieved measurably the plight of the small sheep-raisers. Nebraska provides a good illustration of their beneficial effect. Previous to 1877 most farmers had considered sheep-raising a precarious undertaking because of the total lack of protection from the large number of stray dogs. During the 1877 legislative session a dog law was passed, and soon there was a noticeable decline in sheep casualties as well as an increase in the number of flocks. In fact, so beneficial was the law for the sheep industry in Nebraska that sheepmen often referred to it as their emancipation proclamation.[73]

In 1875 the Commissioner of Agriculture summarized the results of these laws from data taken from a national survey of thirty-five states troubled by marauding dogs. The statistician of the department in estimating the percentage of loss in a single year, found it to be only slightly more than two per cent, or about $1,000,000 in round figures. He also compared the position of the industry in those states which had enforceable dog laws with its situation in states which did not have them; his figures make the advantage of the first group perfectly clear: [74]

The per-centage of loss is somewhat greater in States where no efficient laws exist. For example, in the following States where no laws exist the losses were as follows: Florida, 11%; Arkansas, 6%; Georgia, 5.16%; Tennessee, 4.6%; Kansas, 3.8%; Virginia, 3.4%; and Wisconsin, 2.2%. In the protected States examples are as follows: Ohio, .4%; New York, .3%, etc.

PART THREE

Credulous Farmers

CHAPTER VIII

Tramps, Scamps and Swindlers in Arcadia

A STUDENT OF the social history of the American farmer in the late nineteenth century must be impressed by the infinite variety of humbugs developed to cheat rural people. The new industrialism thrust at the farmer a multitude of new gadgets, schemes, techniques, recipes, patents, all clamoring for his money and attention. A few of these devices were useful and were incorporated in the structure of farm life, but many were mere deceptions hawked by unscrupulous agents. This and the three following chapters will consider various aspects of this subject.

The appearance of itinerant peddlers among the farmers grew into a major problem, for they not only intruded upon their time but relieved them of their hard-earned money. The following extract from a letter to an agricultural journal reveals the seriousness of the "agent nuisance":

I should like to know what poor innocent farmers and their wives have done, that they should be annoyed by such swarms of agents. You are

importuned to subscribe for books of every kind and name, at prices
that ought to buy up a retail store. Flower roots, wine plants, patent
rights for everything under the sun, you are daily invited to buy. . . .
Some people have had their patience so exhausted by repeated sieges on
their time, in this way, that they will order every person off their premises
who looks as if he was an agent, while others bear it as one of the crosses
of this life which they cannot well avoid; others again, like myself, are
beginning to ask if there is not some remedy to be found for such
nuisances.[1]

The infinite number of contrivances, plans, devices, and get-
rich-quick schemes used by itinerant agents to cajole farmers and
their wives may be classified in two main categories: items purporting to lighten the burdens or gladden the humdrum lives of rural
people and those used in farm operations.

The burdened life of the farm woman enhanced the appeal of the
gadgets and improvements displayed by fast-talking agents. A new
churn, incubator, clothesline, washing or sewing machine held out
the prospect of reducing or easing the farm woman's endless chores.
Hence the great demand on the part of housewives for all types of
laborsaving devices. Manufacturers responded to this demand, and
by 1872 as many as eight hundred patents had been granted on the
washing machine alone.[2]

A technique frequently used to sell washers illustrates the methods used to victimize farm people. A company, whose product might
be given such a name as the "New Home Washing Machine," would
flood the countryside with circulars or dispatch agents to the farmers' homes. The circular informed a recipient that as a prominent
member of her community she had been selected for a special promotional scheme; if she sent in a small amount of money and would
be willing to show a machine to, say, five neighbors, the company
would sell her one at a greatly reduced price. When the eagerly-
awaited washer arrived on the scene, it generally was a "worthless
apparatus," of no value in eliminating the miseries of wash day.[3]

Again, an agent might call at the woman's home to inveigle her
into becoming the local agent for his machine. He would then send
her a certain number of machines with the understanding that she
was to have one free when the others had been sold. Or the agent

might assign her definite territory, such as a township, and a certain number of machines. She was to have the exclusive privilege of selling within this area. In either case, in negotiating the contract the swindler frequently had his victim sign a promissory note which he subsequently had discounted at the local bank and which she must pay before she could dispose of the machines in the community.[4] In their eagerness to get something for nothing farm wives became frequent victims of these fraudulent schemes.

No household task was more arduous than that of producing the butter supply for the family table; in addition to the problem of converting the cream to butter there was one of preserving the butter after the churning operation had been completed. Western homes were invaded by scores of agents selling patented churns. The agents and their circulars guaranteed butter from any kind of cream; some even assured the same result from sweet milk.[5] Other agents claimed to have a secret recipe or butter compound that would "coax the milk" or "make bad butter sweet." Some of these marvelous formulas did not even require cream to produce butter. The farmer's wife was informed that a certain amount of a powder placed in sweet milk would increase the quantity of butter and even prevent it from becoming rancid; the magic powder would also improve its quality and color.[6]

Housewives constantly sent inquiries to agricultural editors, asking for advice on how to turn cream to butter or information on how to prevent it from becoming rancid once it was churned. It was not difficult to sell such recipes as these described above to farm women struggling with the problem. Some imposters posed as "lecturers" who sold butter-making secrets. An Ohio correspondent reported on the activity of one of these itinerants:

There is a man in this vicinity . . . representing himself as "Ohio's gilt-edge butter maker," giving free lectures on what he pretends to know about butter making. Says he will take three gallons of milk and make more butter by his process than can be made by any one by the old process from fifteen gallons of milk, and he will set his milk alongside of theirs. Says he will wager $20 that he can do it. Said that he opened a can of his butter last fall that had been packed for eighteen years, and it was good and sweet. Said he would get from six and a half to seven pounds [of] butter from one gallon of cream, and that there would not be two spoonfuls of buttermilk to the gallon of cream.[7]

Another arduous task of the farmer's wife was to tend a flock of chickens. Poultry was an essential item on the farm and its care involved a multitude of worries and aggravations; nothing can be so exasperating and fickle as a setting hen! The housewife had a three-fold objective in raising chickens: she must see that they reproduced in ample numbers; that an adequate supply of eggs were laid for immediate consumption; and that a goodly number was preserved for winter's use. To comply with all these essential requirements demanded considerable skill on the part of the farm wife.

To aid or perhaps hinder her in the matter of hatching chickens, innumerable agents, circulars, and advertisements offered the farm woman "artificial mothers" or "hatching machines" (incubators). Many were totally useless. Of course not all incubators placed on the market lacked utility or value, but the advertising was generally misleading. In some cases the fault lay not with the machines but with the purchasers who lacked the patience and knowledge needed to operate them. An Ohio man wrote that in his area about nine-tenths "of the incubators in the market are, for practical use, about as near worthless as flying machines."[8] Another reported that so many proved impractical that nearly "every township has from one to fifty . . . now for sale, second-handed ones, that have proved to be a failure."[9]

One of the most notorious traffickers in incubators of dubious value was a J. A. Bain, who lived in New Concord, Ohio. He falsely labeled himself the Secretary of the North American Poultry Association, and his advertisements offered directions on how to build and operate the popular "Common Sense Incubator" for $2.00.[10] In one city alone he received in response eleven hundred letters requesting his booklet.[11]

Closely associated with this type of swindle was the sale of setting eggs. If a farmer's wife hoped to have a thriving and profitable flock of laying hens she must periodically introduce some new blood. Again Ohio had had the distinction of harboring some of the most conspicuous swindlers in this line. J. M. North of the city of Plymouth advertised eggs from fancy fowls and sold them at a fancy price with the "understanding that he was to have the privilege of purchasing the chickens in the fall at $5.00 each."[12] An agent in Michigan sold Plymouth Rock eggs for as high as $75 per dozen and agreed with the buyer to purchase all chickens hatched from the eggs for the enormous price of $100 apiece; another sold single rare eggs from a "Dagobertian" fowl, reputed to have originated in France; still others advertised high-priced eggs and then filled their orders with a nondescript variety that could be purchased on the market for a few cents per dozen.[13]

Other agents and circulars advertised recipes for sale with guaranteed exclusive family or township rights—recipes for the preservation of eggs as well as for almost every other perishable product on the farm. Some sold "valuable" recipes for the canning of fruit for as much as $5, and advertised that if used as directed they would "keep fresh for any length of time, without the use of sugar or heat, those fruits, vegetables, etc., that are usually canned." In one section of the Middle West over one hundred persons bought the family right to use this secret recipe, which consisted of nothing more than a half-ounce bottle of a "pinkish-buff-colored powder."[14] Other agents sold recipes for the making of soap, syrups, honey, vinegar, paints, and even perfumes.[15]

A highly touted preparation sold during this period was Ozone, put out by a firm in Cincinnati. Ozone was given advertising space in most farm journals, where its "remarkable virtues" were "spread before their readers" as a "new preservative of perishable products." It was sold in a small test package for $2.00 which was sufficient, according to the advertisement, to preserve 1,000 dozen eggs. Its promoters generally contracted with the purchaser for an exclusive right to a township or county and the sales pitch boldly promised that "a fortune awaits any man who secures control of OZONE." This compound consisted of nothing more than a powder that was to be burned in the barrel where meat was to be packed or in a vessel where other perishable foods were to be stored. A University of Michigan professor analyzed the mixture and reported in the *Ohio Farmer* that it consisted of "simply a little powdered charcoal and sulphur, with a little cinnamon to give it a pleasant odor while burning." [16] According to this report "thousands were mulcted to the tune of $2 for a 'test package' before the swindle was exposed."

This same category of chemical recipes also included numerous compounds fabricated and sold under the general term, "illuminating oils for the household." They were advertised mainly through the channels of the press and mails, but were also palmed off on rural people by traveling agents.

A great demand had developed for new types of lighting fluids by the middle of the last century because whale oil was becoming scarcer and more expensive, largely as a result of the fact that whales were being killed off at a rapid rate. One of the new substitutes was a liquid extracted by a new process from coal and shale; it became commonly known as "Coal Oil" or kerosene, and by the 1860's had become widely accepted as an illuminating fluid for farm homes.

Coal oil was decidedly superior in many ways to the tallow candle and the whale-oil lamp. On the other hand, in its early stages of development it had a tendency to explode, causing not only serious property damage but serious physical injury as well.[17] The *Rural New-Yorker*, commenting on the destructiveness of this newly developed oil, opined that it was almost as dangerous to life and property as gunpower.[18] Railroads had long been regarded as the cause of more accidents and deaths than any other agency in American life; but by the 1870's the various illuminating fluids were blamed for more deaths than the number assigned to the railways.[19]

To allay and profit upon widespread fears of explosive oils, two types of itinerant peddlers came calling on farmers during certain seasons of the year. One was humorously known as the "illuminating oil chap." This individual roamed the countryside selling recipes for as little as $2.00 to $5.00, each guaranteed to produce a compound similar to kerosene but having the advantage of selling for only about half the price per gallon. The other type of peddler was known as the "nonexplosive powder chap." He had developed a secret mixture. Put in "a pinch of his powder," and it not only rendered dangerous oils non-explosive, but prevented the lamp chimney from breaking." [20] Rural mothers not only worried about their lamps blowing up and scattering oil over the house, possibly maiming some members of their families for life, but also feared that chimneys might break, as frequently happened from minor explosions caused by the accumulation of smoke and vapors in them. The "powder chaps" were therefore able to palm off on rural people not only oil purifiers, recipes, and rectifiers, but in selling special "non-breakable" chimneys for as much as $2.85 apiece. They also sold to farmers for large sums patent-right territory of a whole community.

The "pinch of powder" agent was one who did little harm or little good; his product was usually nothing more than "common salt, colored with a little Prussian blue." He generally extracted only small sums from the rural housewife and no one had to fear for his life as a result of the substance placed in the coal oil. But the case of the recipe man was quite different; his operations not only affected the pocketbook but actually threatened the purchaser's life.[21] Most of the recipes contained as the principal ingredient large quantities of benzene, which was quite volatile and inflammable; the balance of the recipe was generally "pure nonsense" containing something that would give a pleasant color and an inviting smell. Several well known recipes were sold throughout rural America: the "Celebrated Centennial," the "Devoe's Brilliant," the "French Electric," and perhaps the most widely advertised of all was Dr. Culver's "Sun-Light Oil." [22] The following was its famous recipe which sold for only $2.00:

To make one gallon, take 3 quarts of BENZINE, 1 oz. Pulverized Alum, 1½ oz. Alcohol, 2 oz. Cream of Tartar, 2 oz. Salsoda, 1 pint of Potatoes (cut fine), 2 tablespoons of fine Salt, 2 drachms Oil of Sassafras, 4 drachms Gum Camphor. Dissolve the Alum in the Alcohol as much as possible; then add the Gum Camphor, stir for a few minutes; then add to one pint of the Benzine, stir it well for ten minutes; then add all the other ingredients, except the Benzine, stir well until it foams, then add the remainder of the Benzine; . . . ten hours time it will be fit for use. . . .[23]

A reporter who described this "Sun-Light" hoax concluded by warning: "If you will use it, make your will, insure your life, and ask your minister to get ready a sermon on the 'Mysterious Dispensations of Providence.' "

To protect users from these adulterated oils, laws were finally enacted compelling the fire test requirements to be raised and making it mandatory that they be inspected and certified; but most of these early pieces of legislation were not enforced for many years and thus provided no positive protection to the consumer.[24]

The housewife and her daughters were frequently victimized by cloth peddlers who traveled from home to home with a line of "English" broadcloth or other fabrics that they had supposedly secured abroad from bankrupt firms. Assuming a fine English accent and displaying the finest of samples, these peddlers took orders for $50 or $100 worth of such goods, secured notes from their customers, and then went off to the nearest bank where the notes were discounted. To make things worse, when the orders had been filled, the materials received were rarely as they had been represented. Most frequently they were of an inferior grade.[25]

Cloth peddlers used other swindling techniques. Some promised purchasers that a tailor would accompany the order who would make up the cloth into the garments desired. A dealer in Illinois represented himself as an heir to an English fortune, part of which was in valuable cloth which he was able to dispose of at half price.[26] There were others who merely advertised by means of the common circular in promoting their schemes; through these schemes they offered cloth at greatly reduced prices with the ruse that this was made possible because "they had been able to escape the import duties."

In Nebraska, swindlers described by one reporter as the cunning "plug hat fellows" employed another technique. They would enlist a well-known citizen of the community to assist in selling their goods. They would select a certain farmer and

employ him to accompany them about the neighborhood, and from him they learn of your standing financially. They unroll a large roll of cloth—enough they assert to make you and all your sons a good suit of clothes; they have some dress patterns that will make dresses for all the female portion of the family, and this . . . they propose to sell to you for probably $75; they do not want your cash; a note payable six months after date is good enough, and with the importunities of your children and the *apparent* cheapness of the goods, you buy; they must have your neighbor sign with you as security, and taking you in their wagon they drive over to Jones, who signs your note as surety, and, impelled by your example, in less than ten minutes is himself a purchaser and you are asked to return the compliment and sign his note as surety.[27]

For a time these cloth swindlers were moderately successful as shown by a report from Lake County, Ohio, where according to one estimate, $60,000 had been taken by dealers in bogus cloth goods in a single season.[28]

Farm wives and their children were victimized during certain times of the year and especially during periods of economic distress by a species of vagrant who frequented the countryside "like a cloud of grasshoppers." These were the tramps who on occasion threatened the safety of farm women and children, especially when the menfolk were away in town or working in the fields.[29]

In the early days of our country, novelists and poets pictured these roving characters as happy-go-lucky "Knights of the turnpike," restless, footloose, imaginative individuals who sought the freedom of the open road and the great, unfilled spaces of the West.[30] These wanderers were generally respected by rural inhabitants, who gave them food and lodging just as they would have done for any stranger coming into the community. But following the Civil War and the panic of 1873 this romantic image became clouded, especially as increasing numbers of demoralized and criminal elements left the large cities for the rural areas in search of a living or of prey. Most would not work and were entirely unlike the earlier wanderers that Walt Whitman described in his "Song of the Open Road"; many refused employment if offered. Many did not walk through the countryside but preferred to travel in boxcars on the freight trains, living in gangs and jungles and only stopping here and there long enough to secure food and steal whatever they could in villages and on adjacent farms.[31]

In 1876, when a particularly severe exodus of such elements took place, a reporter for a leading journal visited various sections of the country and returned to give his readers an excellent account of this "tramp nuisance": [32]

Of late the country has been infested with them. They are no longer simply traveling beggars, but thieves and robbers, without respect for persons or property. They appropriate to their own uses whatever they can lay hands on, and, if necessary, use violence, sometimes amounting to murder, rather than forego their plunder. . . . Farmers and others who are victims . . . are frequently obliged to arm themselves . . . and drive the wretches out of the country by force.

A cottage where the male members of the family are at work in some distant field is usually the spot selected by the tramp as the scene of his depredations.

What was the solution to this intimidation of town and farm women and children? Many reluctantly put up with it. If women-folk refused to give a tramp food or a place in the hayloft to sleep, they might be threatened with bodily harm or damage to property; if they requested the tramp to do some work at the woodpile or on the farm, he might sullenly decline. Sometimes the vagabond would reject food offered by the intimidated housewife as not being good enough; he would throw away the sandwiches and impudently demand a "square meal." [33] Sometimes the tramp related a tale of woe, of disaster at sea, or a fire, or war injury. With such tales of tribulations he might obtain from the pitying housewife the desired meal without the customary demand of repayment by a visit to the woodpile.

The eastern states were the first to deal with the vagrant problem, and their solutions were gradually adopted in the West. Some of the early vagrancy laws were severe. For example, in Pennsylvania one who went begging from house to house was subject to a year jail sentence; if he carried firearms or set fire on the highways or entered a dwelling against the will of the occupant and was convicted he was liable for a three year prison term with hard labor on the stonepiles and the making of roads. [34] Since some states were slow to deal with the tramp nuisance, towns and cities attacked the problem; some solved it rather easily by passing ordinances forcing vagrants to work attached to a ball and chain upon the streets or in adjacent stone quarries. Others adopted a system of giving employment at a small remuneration and sleeping quarters in improvised barracks—this latter method was more successful in that it deterred the loss of life and property by fire and larceny, thus helping both citizen and tramp.[35] In the final analysis, recovery from economic depression offered the best solution to this problem; in periods of prosperity rural women had little to fear from the tramp nuisance, but with the return of depression it again became a crying evil.

Even the food on the farmer's table was not immune from the swindling practices of the cheating fraternity. Since sugar was relatively scarce and high-priced in farming communities, the farmer often sought to produce some of his own sweetening material. This led to periodic hysterias for the raising of bees. Numerous frauds and humbugs soon arose to swindle the innocent bee-raiser. They ranged from the sale of exclusive county rights on a patented hive, to the sale of a "build it yourself" blueprint that would guarantee as much as "one hundred dollars . . . of . . . honey from one hive of bees in one year." Once the beginner had launched his honeybee enterprise, disappointments often followed. The hives frequently proved structural failures; and not uncommonly a royalty collector found his way to the farm to extract payments for the infringement of his patent.[36]

Musical instruments, jewelry, silverware and pictures were frequently used to exploit the pathetic desire of the rural housewife to brighten her drab existence.[37] Some firms dealt in bogus organs, juvenile-size pianos, and musical boxes. One of the most notorious companies engaged in such business was an organ concern in Washington, New Jersey, which ran large and attractive advertisements in the farm journals.[38]

Pictures of a sentimental or didactic nature sold well in rural areas, for most mothers wanted to add a little touch of the aesthetic and the spiritual to the home. A typical example was "Mama is in Heaven," of a chromolithograph sold by agents of a firm in Chicago for the excessive sum of $7.50.[39]

Writers and photographers periodically descended upon farm families, offering to take expensive pictures accompanied by laudatory accounts, all to be included in a new county history about to be published. They humbugged rural parents by "appealing to posterity"; in years to come their offspring could contemplate with tender attachment the surroundings of their youth. A county history might cost up to $100, especially if the volume contained lengthy family histories with an embellished view of each farm home.[40] It must quickly be added that these publications were not entirely devoid of value; they frequently contained information of great utility to local and regional historians.

Another form of charlatanry involved the sale of agricultural treatises. Science was being increasingly applied to various aspects of farming; consequently a craze for technical knowledge arose with the parallel rise of a corps of pseudo-scientists, self-styled professors and bogus writers who overwhelmed the farmer with "strange terms . . . taken from Liebig and Johnson of which they know not the import themselves"; with treatises on different species of domestic animals, veterinary science, chemical analyses, transmutation of seeds, terra and electroculture, not to mention such exotic subjects as brewing, tanning, farriery, photography and perfumery.[41] Many of these fascinating booklets sold for an exorbitant price and in the end proved utterly worthless.

Farmers took a deep interest in these treatises on agriculture; but the Bible was by far the best seller and provided an excellent instrument for the swindling fraternity. I have already noted that a common device of swindlers was to get the farmer's signature on some paper which the sharper would subsequently change into a negotiable note and dispose of for cash. A common ruse of the Bible-selling fraud, purporting to be an agent of some tract society, was to "present himself at a farm house about dinner time. . . . [He] accepts an invitation to dine on condition that he may be allowed to pay for his meal. The society, he says, requires that he should pay his way, . . . so he asks the farmer's signature to a form of receipt which he carries with him." Presently this piece of paper returned to the farmer in the form of a note in hand containing a sum of money filled in by the specious missionary.

Again, the agent might claim to be a student in college, preparing for the ministry. To obtain the money necessary to prosecute his studies, he was canvassing for the "People's Standard Bible," price

$5.00, and wished to negotiate an oral arrangement with a local citizen to act as distributor. In this case there was "no paper presented, no contract signed, no writing of any kind" by the "student." In fact, no Bibles were ever sold or sent. But within a short time, the "innocent" purchaser of a negotiable note for $300, accompanied by the county sheriff, appeared on the scene to demand payment from the farmer. By brow-beating and threats of suit they were frequently successful in forcing the frightened farmer to pay the note.[42] In the meantime the forger of the note, the so-called simple student, had long since disappeared from the scene.

The swindler who wished to exploit the credulity of the farmer's wife, could appeal to many emotions. Books covering many subjects were written for this market. They included standard works entitled "The Family Doctor" or "Recipe Book" and others that offered "hints for the purpose of making good housekeeping . . . more delightful"; for helping the housewife "avoid a multitude of cares and annoyances; prevent many a serious accident; remedy many troubles, and save a waste of means." Fifty cents brought through the mail any of a vast number of books, written by industrious hacks, with such titles as "Illustrated Guide," "Matrimony Made Easy," "Book of Secrets," "Secrets Disclosed," and the "Guide to Charming, Or How to Win Affections of Either Sex."[43] Agents managed to give the impression that some of these books contained titillating illustration and wonderful secrets, revelations, and discoveries for married or single people. Other agents used the mail to pose as match-makers and offered to send the deluded farm girl a picture of her prospective mate, complete with his name and even the date fixed for the marriage.

Lotteries and chances of every kind were paraded before the eyes of farm people. Buy a ticket, or subscribe to a certain poultry magazine, or contribute to a charitable organization, and you won a chance on such items as "500 GOLD WATCHES" or on more than a half million dollars worth of an incredible array of articles including rings, clocks, Bibles, albums, sewing machines, silverware, curling irons, as well as pianos, riding saddles, spring wagons, bedroom furniture and carriage horses with harness. Any one of these articles might be had for a single ticket costing only $2.00.[44]

Operators of these enterprises often hired a small upper room in some remote section of a great city or in some distant village. Here they received the letters pouring in from many thousands of people in response to the advertisements. From this office they wrote to other thousands whose names they had secured from postmasters and others, who collected them for this very purpose. To these innocent people, who hoped to get something for nothing, came ample offers of ticket schemes, fraudulent lotteries, and confidence agents.

Of all the schemes in which lots or chances were sold the lottery was the most widely used. For centuries it was the best known mode of raising money for public purposes both at home and abroad. It was a device resorted to by various institutions, among which were well-known colleges seeking to raise funds for growth, and agricultural groupings which used such incentives to induce farmers to raise improved animals or for other desirable goals.[45] In time, however, these chance devices departed from their original purposes and were debased. Promotional lottery leaders, sometimes including such prominent people as ex-governors, used the technique to develop huge enterprises that corrupted political parties, legislatures, and the press, and exploited the names of distinguished veterans in order to make fabulous profits.[46] By the 1860's and 1870's they operated not only in the southern states where the notorious Lottery Ring existed, but in other states that were willing to issue charters for such reprehensible schemes.

When the lottery idea itself was finally outlawed, operators of many of the schemes proceeded to disguise themselves under the names of societies ostensibly operating in the interest of charity, benevolence, or learning. The following are a few of the many concerns that solicited funds from farmers by selling them tickets for fifty cents while providing a gift guarantee that was supposedly "worth from 20 cents to $5.00": The Miner's Hospital Association, Soldier's Monument Association, The Grand Gift Concert and the Artist's Union.[47]

Closely associated with the above devices was the traffic in watches —especially men's watches and chains. These were sold by the tens of thousands to the poorer classes everywhere by all the means available at that time. One of the more independent editors repeatedly refused space in his journal to these unmitigated frauds, but a large proportion of the rural magazines were not equally scrupulous. Engraved gold hunting-case watches valued at $150 to $200 were offered for pathetically small sums; they were described and depicted so attractively—often with high sounding foreign names—that sales resistance became difficult.[48] Boston, New York and Cincinnati were three main operating centers, but in many cases the imposters did not even maintain an office, operating from a post office box. They disseminated vividly illustrated ornamented circulars "pretending to have on hand a great many thousands of dollars worth of watches . . . [of] bankrupt stock . . . which . . . must be sold . . . at low rates." Their original value was set at $100, but they could be secured by remitting an amount as small as 10 per cent of that figure. Some swindlers made no effort to send the respondent anything, not even a reply; they just kept the money. Others would hoax them by mailing a sundial or some ridiculous substitute for the "timekeeper" they had ordered.[49] Whatever they received, it was likely to be completely unsuited for telling the time of day.

The advent of the sewing machine in the West after the Civil War made available an important instrumentality for bilking the rural housewife. Since most of the clothes worn by farm people had to be produced in the home, sewing was one of the farm woman's most rigorous and time-consuming tasks.[50] Inevitably, she would make great sacrifices to be able to purchase a sewing machine.

Sewing machine patents had been issued to several inventors in the late forties and fifties. Following a series of long infringement suits a combination or pool of the better machines was perfected; for nearly twenty-five years these firms controlled the industry by maintaining high prices, quality of the product, and persistent vigilance through prosecutions against manufacturers who infringed their patented machines as well as consumers who purchased them.[51] Nevertheless, in spite of this monopoly, smaller firms throughout the country operated outside the patent ring; these produced a cheap machine, some pygmy in size, that sold for as little as $5.00, $10.00, and $15.00; they were often cheaply constructed and propelled by hand, and this was the type which was generally hawked in rural areas. Most of these machines were "worthless article [s] palmed off on the public, under the guise of respectability." [52]

This fraud was as widespread as any connected with domestic farm life, and for a number of years farm editors continually reported that agents were flooding the rural communities with bogus machines.[53] In 1870 a reporter from a section of Nebraska stated that there "are hundreds of cheap machines in this locality, doing the purchaser very little or no good." [54] When competition grew keener, some agents offered a "fine dress" as a premium in order to sell their machines; others sold agencies, and still others used the gift enterprise device.[55]

In the eighties, following the expiration of the patents, "gangs of sharpers" began in earnest to work the note-dodge technique on the farmers. Their plan of action was "to leave half a dozen sewing machines with a farmer, agreeing with him in writing that if he sells five of them at $50 each, he is to have the sixth for his trouble, and if the machines are not sold at the end of six months, the agent is to take them back and make no charge." The order was so constructed by the agent that portions of it could be removed, leaving the customary words of a negotiable promissory note for $250 which could be discounted at a bank.[56]

The demand for sewing machines and the amount of swindling connected with the business brought the better agricultural journals and even the granges into the field of distribution. A good example of this press activity was offered by the *American Agriculturist* which, after buying a "multitude of machines of all sorts, sizes and prices," finally found a low-priced one which it could safely offer as a premium for those who secured a certain number of subscriptions to the Journal.[57] Some of the granges in the states made arrangements with various companies whereby they could lower the price considerably by purchasing in quantity.[58] The Iowa State Grange in one year claimed a saving of $5,000 for the farmers of that state, and in Wisconsin its purchasing agent was able to sell $75 machines for as low as $28.35.[59]

A major category of mechanical humbuggery was associated with tools, devices, and implements used on the farm outside the home.

Most of the skulduggery in this field was perpetrated by traveling agents who introduced new gadgets by either selling territory to the farmer for the patented article or by selling many gadgets outright by the note-dodge technique. Their success was understandable, because the new devices had great attraction for the farmer in a period of chronic labor shortage; this shortage drove the farmer to compensate by buying the ever increasing number of technical gadgets, tools and machines available to ease his toil. One of these gadgets was the small contraption called a sickle grinder, used to hold the sickle to the grindstone while it was being sharpened. There was a brisk demand for the device. Farmers were sometimes required to pay notes of $200 or $300 for several dozen of these grinders, although at the time they signed the contract the swindling agent led them to believe that they were to be paid for when sold, a common arrangement in most of the rural states.[60] The following letter from a farmer near Bellefontaine, Ohio, describes the technique used by a certain swindler in that locality:

An agent goes to a farmer's residence and shows up a sickle grinder which he says he will give the farmer for his influence in selling to his neighbors. All that he asks is that the farmer sign a "voucher," which afterwards turns up as a note for several machines which a second man delivers. They fleeced Mr. Murdock out of $150, Mr. I. Yoder out of $210, and R. S. Oder, $200. A total of $560 in one neighborhood.[61]

Similar ruses were employed in the sale of grainbag holders and wagon tongue supporters or stiffeners. Both items were useful to the farmers, and for a time a sizeable traffic was carried on by agents who usually represented eastern firms. These devices generally sold for around $5 each. The objective of the agents was to sign up a farmer for a dozen or more of the supporters.[62] This same technique was used successfully by "oily-tongued rascals" with farm scales, saws, shotguns, and steamers; in the case of the latter, stock-raisers had been urged for many years by the agricultural press to cook or steam the feed for cattle.[63] As a result of this advocacy implement companies placed on the market patented cookers, boilers, and furnaces through the medium of traveling agents.[64]

The sale of guns was handled almost exclusively through advertisements and circulars. Through these media companies of dubious integrity placed on the market high-priced rifles, revolvers, and shotguns, offered at a "tremendous" reduction. A most notorious firm operated under the name of Chichester Rifle Company; its colorful advertisements featuring scenes of wild animals being shot by hunters using the company's guns, sometimes covered a whole page; other scenes showed the Chichester rifle quelling the savage Indian. These hunting arms sold for as little as the incredible sum of $4.50.[65] The agricultural press was tempted to accept numerous gun advertisements from the most unreliable firms, by offers of up to $1,000 for one spread. Some of the better journals refused space to such companies but less prosperous editors could not resist temptation. The publisher of the *Michigan Farmer* not only turned them down completely but he notified his readers that "We think those shot-guns are all 'loaded' and our readers had better leave them . . . alone." [66]

Traveling agents went through the countryside taking orders and selling exclusive agencies and territories for larger items such as feedmills, stump pullers, windmills, reapers, mowers, harrows, seeders, and even fences. The method used for selling most of these items was the timeworn note-dodge or shaving scheme, but in the case of fences some other ingenious practices were employed. One plan offered the farmer free of charge fifty rods of new fence as well as a sole agency for the wire if he would agree to build it along the roadway where it could be seen by his neighbors. Since fencing materials in the West were in great demand in this period, the credulous farmer promptly signed a paper to install it. In a few days a stranger arrived to collect for so many coils of fencing wire at so much a foot; the paper the farmer had signed turned out to be a legal instrument for the amount of the wire.[67] Two traveling fence swindlers in Kansas and Missouri were so effective that they took up to $50,000 out of the latter state alone.[68]

A second plan for selling fence wire in the Midwest was described by a reporter in DeKalb County, Illinois, during the late 1880's. He stated that a certain agent calls on a farmer and offers to put up an eight-wire fence at eight cents per foot. This is apparently so cheap that the farmer usually signs the contract. Then when the bill comes in, the deluded farmer finds that he has agreed to pay eight cents per foot for each particular wire, instead of that amount for the entire eight. When the scheme works right, the farmer has to surrender his farm in part payment and give his note for the balance.[69]

In summary, it can be said that a long list of mechanical devices was used to humbug the American farmer and his wife—from small articles in the home to the larger implements used on the farm. The improvement in the situation came about the close of the nineteenth century, partly due to protective laws enacted in the different states and to federal enactments which offered more protection to innocent farmers; by this time courts had also begun to hold responsible the purchasers of discounted or "shaved" notes, and bankers could no longer hide behind the "innocent" clause which previously had protected them. By this time Congress had also passed amendments to the postal laws making it increasingly more difficult for swindlers to use the mails to disseminate their bogus proposals; this was especially the case with such fraudulent devices as lotteries and gift enterprises.[70]

CHAPTER IX

Horticultural Humbugs

F ROM THE first occupation of the western lands, settlers displayed a marked interest in horticulture. The quantity and distribution of timber played a leading role in the selection of new homes in the process of settlement. Where there were ample supplies of good wood for fuel, buildings, and fences, land was not only higher in value, other things being equal, but was also preferred for settlement by frontiersmen and speculators.[1] So important was timber in the agricultural economy of the country that mad scrambles ensued when new timber-scarce sections were opened for settlement; a track of land nearest a river course or one possessing a grove of trees had the highest priority. As a matter of fact, the initial settlements in the prairie regions were made along the rivers, extending, as for example in Illinois, like ribbons far into the interior of the state.[2] When subsequent settlers were forced to the open country, they would cluster about the isolated groves like bees in a hive. In many cases these islets of trees on the broad prairies served as nuclei for whole communities.

This timber complex has often been explained by the fact that easterners coming into the western regions had been conditioned by a sylvan environment and consequently were reluctant to settle on the prairies. This psychological factor may have had some influence, but the economic effects of a scarcity of trees offers a more plausible explanation of this reluctance. Early settlers were quick to realize that without timber they must alter their traditional way of life; the ramifications of this change would reach out in a multitude of ways even to the kind, size and number of houses and barns they could build.[3] They were also well aware that shortages would affect their social realtionships; for example, without fencing materials people in a community could not adequately enclose their crops or their animals.[4] Such conditions would be a constant source of irritation between neighbors.[5] Besides, they would have no sheltering wind-breaks to protect them from prairie gales or from the blistering heat of the summer sun; and many associated a prevalence of fevers and lack of rainfall with scarcity of trees.[6] Finally, they had to consider that a timber shortage might deter new settlers from taking up land in their community. Older residents realized that the value of their farms would rise or fall depending upon the number of people they could attract to their area.[7]

As a result of these considerations there developed in the forties and fifties of the past century an extraordinary enthusiasm for tree culture that extended well into the twentieth century. In the West it grew to be a veritable mania. The objects of interest included trees suitable for fences and windbreaks as well as for orchards, shrubs, and vines. This movement also appeared in the East though on a smaller scale, for in that section there were still some natural resources that had not been entirely exploited. The tremendous demand for nursery stock, especially the orchard varieties, gave rise to the practice of tree peddling and the forms of humbuggery associated with it. The extent of this humbuggery and just how much discontent it created are difficult to determine. From the amount of publicity given it in the agricultural and horticultural press of the day, one is led to conclude that it played a certain part in the formation of the protest mentality so characteristic of the American farmer in the nineteenth century.

Extensive swindling of the farmers developed in the process of securing and planting horticultural products of the orchard variety. Farmers coming from the East or from Europe, had been reared in an environment where there was a large amount of fruit in the diet. Upon coming to the prairies they naturally looked forward to carrying on the practice of cultivating a family orchard. Many brought certain varieties of seeds with them, and even had stowed away in their scanty baggage scions of fruit trees, vines, and shrubs capable of propagation.[8] To secure further supplies of orchard trees, the farmers could raise their own seedlings which, as a rule, produced an inferior fruit, a procedure generally resorted to only in the initial stages of settlement; or they could secure improved nursery stock, either from nurseries in the East that sold through traveling agents, or from swindlers who claimed to represent these nurseries—better known as bogus-tree peddlers. The activities of these unscrupulous peddlers were responsible for most of the horticulture complaints among the farmers and fruit-growers.[9]

Much of the humbuggery in tree peddling could be traced to the slow development of local nurseries. Not only were they slow in coming into the newer areas, but because of their small size they could not effectively distribute their goods among the settlers.[10] What limited stock they grew was generally better adapted to the region than that of the tree-peddlers, but since they could not advertise their products or send salesmen into the field they did not command a very large patronage. The evidence, however, indicates that those who did depend upon the local nurseries secured a better and more reliable product and found it generally cheaper in price. Most of the business, however, was taken away from the local nurseries by larger concerns in the East selling through their legitimate agents, and by the activities of the bogus-tree peddlers.

Eastern vendors and producers, products of a more sophisticated urbanism, freely exploited the naïveté of southern and western rural people.[11] Agricultural editors constantly lamented that most farmers lacked even the primary elements of awareness and critical intelligence and were content to live an existence of "idleness, shiftlessness and indolence. . . ." [12] "Too many farmers," said the *Illinois Farmer*, "still think that reading, reflection, reasoning . . . is of no use to them. They laugh at science; call it book farming with a sneer. . . . The farmer, they think, need not know much. . . ." [13] Add to this lack of insight the fact that life on an ordinary prairie homestead was lonely, dull, and monotonous. As a result, when a stranger appeared in the yard, he was more than welcome. A tree merchant, arriving with articles for sale that might help to bring a little cheer and beauty to the solitary farm, was greeted with a special warmth. Olmsted, in his account of travels through the South, relates an experience he had with a farmer that bears out perfectly this characteristic of unsuspecting innocence. He noticed while walking about the farmyard with the man that he had planted twenty or thirty small fruit trees. When asked, "what sorts they were" the farmer replied, "I don't know—good kinds tho', I expect; I bought 'em for that at any rate." "Where did you buy them?" "I bought 'em of a feller that came a peddlin' round here last fall; he said I'd find 'em good." "What did you pay for them?" "A bit apiece." According to Olmsted this poor rustic not only paid too much but received a lot of trees that were very inferior in appearance and value.[14]

The farmers, in time, came to discern that these tree "missionaries" fell into two distinct classes: the legitimate agent who could be regarded as a genuine representative of some responsible nursery, and the tree peddlers who were neither nurserymen nor their representatives, but merely buyers and sellers who were likened "to a cyclone on account of the wreck they left behind." The problem for the farmer, of course, was to be able to distinguish between the two. This second class could be further refined into two separate groups, and they were well described by one of the outspoken journalists:

One is a rough, horny-handed man with duck overalls, who only goes out in his own and adjoining counties, seldom or never out of his State. . . . He is like the flatheaded borer, and does but little harm. . . . The other kind is the kid-glove tree peddler. He wears a plug hat, high heeled boots all "shined up," with a carpet bag full of fine fruit plates, and large whole fruit made of wax, sealed and preserved in glass jars filled with bitters. This tree peddler is your horticultural dude. He does not work at home. He goes abroad seeking whom he may devour. He wants pastures new and pastures green, for he has no county of his own, no State and probably no nursery. He goes West. He drops down on Kansas. He represents the "Home Hill" or some other great nursery in the East. His trees are borer proof. They are the Russian variety, or they are grafted on hard wood stock. Your dude tree peddler is a man of gab. His tongue is as long as your arm, as oily as a piece of bacon, and as loose as a calf's tail in fly-time. He pays his attention to your wife, and shows his wax fruit to your daughters. He knows he will sell you second-class trees that he will get from some neighboring nursery when it comes time to make his delivery.[15]

These men, as the above description attests, were well equipped to influence the innocent farmer when they appeared on his farm. They left nothing undone that might add to their effectiveness in selling their nursery stock; they drove the best as well as the fastest horses, with the finest harnesses and carriages; they had the necessary vocabulary to convey the impression that they were scientific and well-trained for their "profession"; and they were particularly alert to discover the farmers' interests and backgrounds. When they contacted a farmer who had come from New York, these ubiquitous peddlers were sure to enlarge upon the qualities of certain kinds of fruit that "Mr. New Yorker grew in his native State . . . . If the party to be victimized is from some other State, the same dodge is played off by substituting such varieties as grow well in that State." [16] They always had, no matter what the variety might be, exactly what the farmer wanted and each new season found them with specially developed plants which they could use as leads. Such a peddler might have in his possession a catalog or book of plates showing the most highly colored specimens of some reputable nursery in Rochester, New York, a concern whose name was familiar to most farmers. He might have the proper credentials, signatures, and seals, together with a sample of the bottled fruit magnified several times beyond the natural size.[17] Finally, to secure and cinch the farmer's signature to a large order and to guard against any remonstrances from the distaff side of the household, the peddler might throw in gratuitously a flowering vine, a scented grass plant, or a rosebush with a "jaw-breaker" of a name.[18] Better still, in many instances he might give away some foreign specimens, since farmers were very susceptible to imported stock with delectable appellations.[19]

Peddlers found it easy to sell farmers these novelties because of the endless number of new varieties they were always introducing. It was a period when most Americans, not merely the farmer, had an insatiable appetite for something new and out of the ordinary. This craze for novelty made it easy for tree peddlers to sell large numbers of horticultural humbugs. Few agencies existed at that time to enlighten or protect the innocent farmer from these frauds, for experimental stations were as yet institutions of the future, and many newspapers were willing to accept fraudulent advertisements to reap their rewards of lush payments.[20] On the other hand, the better journals constantly promoted protective legislation; as an example, we might cite the commendable work of the Orange Judd publications in securing the first experimental station and in exposing popular swindles all of which were of inestimable future value to the American farmer.[21] The activity of the commissioner of agriculture in procuring, propagating, and distributing new seeds and plants among the farmers, despite all of its shortcomings, offered some protection to agricultural interests.

The purchase of these bogus horticultural novelties provides an insight into the mind of the average farmer, for only the most naive mentality could have been cajoled into purchasing such offerings. A good example was the peddler's "rare varieties" of grapes.[22] Many farmers were interested in grape culture, a time when such an interest might cloud a man's reputation, thanks to the spreading influence of the temperance movement. In this conflict of motives the tree peddler found a lucrative field for exploitation. In order to increase his sales, without interfering with the moral idealism of rural Americans, he came forward with a grape stock that was so "mild" that the wine produced from its fruit was non-intoxicating.[23] Wine-making thus remained respectable, and as a result, great quantities of this bogus variety of grape were sold. Farmers were swindled with what the peddler called the "winter grape," or one that would produce a fruit which would "keep all winter," and still another that was so superior that it would "prune itself." [24]

The peddlers also offered many attractive oddities in berry and flower bushes. Most carried pictures of a strawberry that grew on bushes or small trees as large as an orange; this naturally appealed to farmers who had the backbreaking experience of picking small strawberries from traditional plants.[25] They took orders for a sweet chestnut, an ever bearing mulberry, a thornless gooseberry that bore twice a year, apples without cores or seeds and asparagus roots that matured into stalks "as large as a broom handle" in as short a time as three months.[26] They displayed pictures of many flowers, shrubs, and bulbs that heretofore had not been known for their excellence or beauty. A flower, most attractive to the uncritical eye of both rural and urban people alike, was what the peddlers called the "blue rose." One firm in New York sent itinerants to every section of the country selling this horticultural humbug at enormous prices.[27]

However, most of the swindling took place in the selling of fruit trees, and it was the consensus of the agricultural press that no other business afforded so many opportunities for cheating the credulous farmer.[28] Orange Judd, in an address before the American Association of Nurserymen, stated that in one-third of a century's experience in dealing with agricultural problems "he had heard of more swindling of the meanest kind by tree agents than by any other class, except perhaps the lightning rod operators." [29] The best trees were sold by the larger nurseries in the East and the poorest "culls" and "refuse stock" were shipped to the West and South where they found a ready market.[30] This was largely due to the fact that in the East the buyers of nursery stock would buy only the choice trees while in the other sections, as one nurseryman put it, a "worthless sort of trees can be sold at high prices if they are large enough." [31] The peddlers soon discovered that all they need do to get an order was to secure some large robust trees, and eastern concerns had plenty of them on hand, for among experienced orchardists it was the small tree that was in demand.[32]

Among the novelties carried by these tree "missionaries" was a category of "borer-proof" trees to be sold at a much higher price than the old stock names and brands had sold. They offered pear trees that were blight-proof, cranberry and cotton trees, sweet Chinese crabs, weeping peaches, and trees that would produce an apple "half sweet and half sour," to list only a few.[33] But the magic word, certain to sell any of their trees, was the word "Russian" attached to its name. For years western fruit-growers had been in search of new nursery stock that would withstand the arid and cold climate of the western states, and most of the eastern varieties had not proven to be too successful in sub-zero weather. As a result trees and plants from all parts of the earth had been imported, and a special interest attached to those from certain sections of Russia where natural conditions were somewhat comparable to those in the western states.[34] Experiments were carried on extensively at some of the agricultural colleges with these importations and some prominent pomologists, notably Professor Joseph L. Budd of the Iowa Agricultural College, gave them his ardent support.[35] In spite of the differences of opinion among the learned horticulturists, farmers in general were convinced that the Russian types were the answers to their problems. This situation opened the way for the tree peddler to humbug the farmer, simply by learning the foreign names of trees and then selling and delivering to his buyers any "hospital stock" that he was able to purchase from the nurseries.[36] It was a bonanza as long as it lasted.

Along with the tree peddlers came a second group of swindlers who called themselves tree grafters. It was not difficult for this group to sell their services to the farmers for many of the early settlers looked upon grafted fruit "as a curiosity, and . . . an innovation upon the works of nature." [37] Furthermore they usually found the trees that had been sold and planted some years before by a travelling fruit-tree agent in such a state of impaired vigor that perambulating "grafters" met with little sales resistance in presenting their questionable scions.[38] They usually traveled in groups, placing their advertisements in the local newspapers previous to their arrival. Their approach was somewhat similar to that of a tree peddler; a display of the necessary specimens of wax and bottled fruit and "exaggerated colored drawings and bombastic descriptions." A good account of their operations was given by the horticultural editor of the *Michigan Farmer*. He described this innovation upon nature as follows:

They traverse the country, and take orders to do grafting at so much apiece for all that live. When the season of grafting comes, a few workmen come along with a wagon load of scions, containing every variety that could possibly be called for, all procured from the most responsible source; and as proof of this, a catalogue of some well known nurseryman is exhibited, and, it may be, a forged bill or invoice, while the scions were most likely, cut from some of the orchards they had been grafting in. Thousands of orchards have been ruined in this way. We have now one in our possession which the previous owner had had grafted by one of these rogues, and instead of having some three or four sorts, as he ordered, he had a collection of vile rubbish, mostly natural fruit, and in some cases three or four different sorts on a tree.[39]

The third group of swindlers in this category of itinerants were the tree invigorators or restorers, the fraudulent precursors of the modern tree surgeons whose function it was to restore decayed parts of trees and invigorate them to higher production.[40] They also had cures for most of the blights and repellents for the common borers and other insect pests, as well as copyrighted and patented recipes or prescriptions for injections. Some "doctors" went so far as to guarantee certain injections that they claimed would cause fruit trees to bear every year; others had a medicine which when inserted in a hole in the trunk would invigorate "old decayed trees"; still others sold recipes which would, if placed "in the crotch of the tree," prevent the fruit from being killed by late frosts.[41] Prices for these miracle compounds varied considerably depending upon just how much the traffic would bear.

A farmer in Iowa related that one of these impostors was

traveling through [his] . . . country, swindling men out of their money by pretending to sell a receipt for destroying all kinds of insects that work on fruit trees—for restoring old decayed trees—for making them bear—to prevent the fruit from being killed by late frosts, etc.; for which he charges from a meal of victuals, or, a night's lodging up to five dollars; and so eager are the folks to get something of the kind, that there are scarcely any but what are imposed upon and swindled out of a dollar or two. He says he has been offered $20,000 for his receipt by Editors of Horticultural papers. He avoids all nurserymen, and for a good reason, for I am told he has got the most of their names down as reference.[42]

This particular group of swindlers found that most of the tree-growers were in need of their services since the farmer who purchased fruit trees from the itinerant peddler almost invariably received an inferior grade of stock to begin with, and the careless manner in which he handled his orchard, after the initial enthusiastic impulse for planting had subsided, created the need for such a craftsman.[43] With these two handicaps it was no wonder that most orchards were in continuous need of attention. One horticulturist stated that

although many trees were lost and worthless from improper treatment in the nursery, . . . yet more were lost by unskillful planting, and neglect afterwards. . . . In all my observations . . . I think I can safely say that I have not seen one orchard . . . in a hundred even tolerably managed. . . . Blown over to one side, anchored in a tough grass sod, buried up in groves of corn-stalks, torn and broken by cattle, barked and bruised by the plough, pruned with an axe—thus they perish in their youth, or become old, deformed, covered with lichens, and a prey to swarms of insects, before they have yielded their first fruits.[44]

A fourth group of swindlers dealt in the construction and maintenance of live fences; they were sometimes called professional hedgers. Their particular skill was in great demand during the middle years of the nineteenth century, not only because hedges had become the principal type of fencing on the prairies, but also because it generally took more time and patience than the ordinary farmer possessed to build and maintain a successful live fence. During the summer months they grew so luxuriantly that at least two trimmings were necessary to keep them in proper order. Few farmers could afford the time to trim them during this busy period, and, as a consequence, poor hedges were the rule rather than the exception.[45] This need gave rise to a class of professional hedgers who went about the countryside contracting with the farmers to build and maintain their hedges, some of which were actually patented; they represented companies from many states, including even the South, but according to their clients, most were not reliable.[46]

The *modus operandi* of the hedgers was to contract with the farmer to plant and maintain a hedge for four years at a stipulated sum—usually one dollar and twenty-five cents per rod—the company to secure a percentage of this amount each year after the services were rendered, generally thirty cents a rod for the first three years and thirty-five for the fourth. Some concerns would go as low as a dollar if the farmer would care for the young plants and also board the men and teams.[47]

Following the planting, in the spring of the first year, there was little for the hedgers to do but to reset the dead plants and do the trimming until the fourth year came around, when it was necessary to perform the most difficult service of all, the plashing operation. This was a process whereby the small branches near the ground had to be partly cut, then bent and intertwined in order to close the gaps. It was at this juncture that the actual swindle took place. A Kansas reporter pointed out that in his state these professional hedgers not only "roped the farmers in right and left with their Osage Orange fence," but after "collecting for three years they left the farmer with an unsightly fence—plashing undone."[48] It was in this fourth year that the farmer really needed the expert services of the hedger, but the latter, having made his easy profit without too much work, usually failed to carry out his responsibility. Professor W. A. Henry of Wisconsin, estimated that in the first three years of a contract the hedging concern netted a handsome profit of around $100 on each 160 rods of fence. By defaulting on the fourth year of the contract they left the farmer without a hedge fence and themselves without any liability.

To return to the ways of the fruit-tree peddler, once he had secured his orders the next step would be to make deliveries. It was in this stage of the transaction that most of the chicanery was practiced. The peddler's methods of operation has been described as follows:

An expert at the business will go to a nurseryman and purchase all the trees, good, bad or indifferent, on a certain plat of ground, for which the nurseryman will cut down the price to the very lowest figures, because he is getting rid of everything and having his ground cleared for other stock. So soon as this contract is closed the tree peddler puts himself and his agents into the market to sell what he has thus purchased. They are usually prepared with catalogues and books having not only a description but cuts and plantings, which they insist are correct

representations of what they are offering for sale. . . . Having made
their sale of worthless stuff at fabulous prices, . . . they hurry back to
the nursery where they have made their purchases.[49]

Back at the nursery, which often was not at all the one represented
in their catalogs and pictures, they proceeded to make up their
orders for delivery.[50] During the early years of tree peddling most of
the stock was secured from Rochester nurseries, there being as
many as twenty different concerns in and around that city. In later
years they were likely to contract for part of their stock with nurseries in the western states, especially if the peddler could find nurserymen on whom he could practice his frauds in the billing-out process.[51]

This technique of deception had the following pattern, with occasional deviations in detail to fit a particular situation. The peddler
would come in from the field with an aggregate of orders sometimes
amounting to ten or twenty thousand apple trees of different varieties. The nurseryman-accomplice being unable to furnish all the
various kind, would allow "large quantities of stock to go out under
false names" from his own billing grounds.[52] If a nurseryman were
solicitous of his own reputation he might insist on having the proper
labels put on the trees, to which the peddler would agree only to
change the tags after they had left the nursery. Again, not infrequently the peddler would buy the trees at a given nursery and
remove them to another concern where they were "heeled in . . .
with the privilege to label . . . [them] as they please, or as their
cupidity may suggest. . . ."[53] This fraud of mislabeling trees was
difficult to detect at the time of occurrence; it generally took from
three to five years before the innocent buyer discovered that he had
been victimized; by that time the peddler was out of reach and
restitution was impossible. His discovery often discouraged a farmer
to such an extent that he gave up the idea of raising fruit and
"decided not to try again."[54]

The trees were duly packed and frequently marked with the
imposing label "From Rochester Nurseries" and then conveyed long
distances from the nursery to a central point in each community
where trees had been sold. Most of them were sent by boat because

the charges were less and then unloaded at the docks where they were left exposed to the weather.

This problem of transporting by water was described by a Cincinnati observer in 1857 as follows:

The manner of shipping trees, . . . is another abuse which calls loudly for reformation. The nurseryman is too apt to send some stupid numskull to the river with a load of trees, and bills of lading in hand, which he gets signed by the clerk of a steamboat, when off he goes, leaving the bundles upon the wharf to take care of themselves, instead of giving explicit orders as to where they should be stowed; or, what would be better still, wait and see that they were put into the right place himself. As a general thing, steamboat men are . . . ignorant of the nature of a tree, . . . and, in consequence of this . . . thousands . . . of choice trees are ruined by being placed in too close proximity to the steam boiler.[55]

Before arrival of the trees at the destination, notices were mailed to the buyers that their trees would be delivered at a stated point and time. The person in charge of delivery would frequently not be the one who had sold the trees, so ignored all protests on the part of the buyer. Some farmers were shrewd enough to see that they had been swindled, and would attempt to resist payment. But this was not easy, as one victim reported, for the peddler "has made his papers to fit his designs so exactly that you are in a net from which you cannot escape." [56] Negotiable notes were taken from the farmers at the time of selling and were frequently resold to the party who was to deliver the trees, or they were "shaved" at the local bank. If the farmer refused payment for his stock the agent would threaten suit, in which case the legal costs would generally be higher than the actual bill. Furthermore, to prosecute a tree peddler, a farmer would have to prove that the trees delivered were a misrepresentation, which would take several years under growing conditions. In the face of these difficulties most farmers in the end chose to pay these bills, however unjust.[57]

The selling of trees in this manner was indeed a lucrative enterprise, resulting in high prices to the buyer and enormous profits to the seller. The preponderance of evidence attests to the fact that the peddlers' prices were from two to three times higher than those listed by responsible nurseries. With their novelties the margin was still higher.[58] The profit of the nurseryman who sold the bogus trees was usually only about twenty-five per cent, as he was anxious to clear his ground for new planting, while the tree peddler received the balance, and his profits in some cases rose as high as $6000 a season.[59] In the case of reputable nurseries, however, tree agents received a regular commission, selling their product at regular prices.

This practice extended to practically all the states. In time, however, it was confined largely to the period from the early fifties to the late eighties. By the latter date the farmers either had been educated to the ways of the peddler, or laws had been enacted regulating the nursery business. In some years during this period there was more fraud than in others, depending upon the general economic conditions in the country. Some states were troubled more than others but even those in the Great Plains areas, where trees were difficult to grow, too often heard "the cry of the tree peddler in the spring of the year."[60] Nor were the southern states exempt from these evils, for northern jobbers sold large quantities of inferior stock to be unloaded on the farmers of the South. One reporter estimated that twenty to thirty thousand dollars was taken from one county alone in 1859.[61] Certain sections of a state might be affected more than others, since peddlers usually traveled in groups of a dozen or so.[62]

The extent of fraud in any one section is difficult to establish in spite of numerous estimates made by victimized individuals, for the frame of mind of the victims did not make for very accurate statements. Perhaps the most accurate accounts, and these left much to be desired, came from Wisconsin where, due to the presence of many farmers of foreign extraction, tree peddlers were as numerous as "candidates at a town caucus." J. C. Plumb of Rock County, a prominent and respected nurseryman and fruit-tree dealer, made this observation:

For forty years I have had good honest competition from eastern and southern tree agents. . . . They have the same right of trade as we. . . . But when the business came to the proportions of organized fraud, with tens of thousands of dollars backing, the employment of hundreds of traveling salesmen to push their sales of bogus stock of fictitious values, then forbearance ceased to be a virtue. . . . For five years or more Wisconsin has been infested with several gangs of these pirates. . . . In this line probably over $100,000 have been drawn from the state by them, leaving nothing but the "ashes of disappointment". . . . I have collected evidence enough against them to damn any but the devil himself.[63]

There were several reasons why this dishonest business was allowed to continue for so many years before brought under control. In the first place, nurserymen themselves profited from it; it served as an excellent outlet to "work off" their old stock every year, and it did not seem irregular to many, since they claimed they were merely following the example of other businessmen.[64] In the second place, many nurserymen and journalists sincerely believed that "if it were not for peddlers there would be fewer orchards." These itinerants did encourage tree planting, granted that many of their trees were of inferior stock, for most farmers were gullible enough to buy from them instead of ordering directly from the responsible nurseries. Norman J. Colman, in his address before the American Association of Nurserymen, challenged the members to put their house in order, at the same time that he recognized certain benefits had arisen in the past from this particular evil. "Tree peddlers," he said, "have done much harm as well as good. They have induced hundreds of thousands to plant trees . . . and are a sort of necessary evil. . . . It is necessary to regulate the business so as to keep dishonest men under proper restraint. . . ."[65] In the third place, some of the responsibility for the continuance of these practices fell deservedly upon the shoulders of consumers, most of whom were not only ignorant of which varieties were adaptable to their climates but were grossly negligent in tending the trees once they were planted. Often their trees would die after only a season or so and the farmer would then lay the blame upon those who sold them. Furthermore, there were some peddlers who were honest to begin with and who would deliver the regular warranted stock to their buyers but if any of the trees were slightly crooked or were small in size, the farmer demanded a reduction in price.

Others farmers bargained vigorously with the peddlers; they would "jew and screw to the last penny; and by making the vender believe that competition is running very high,—that some other seller has offered trees decidedly lower" they would finally secure them at a lower price, thus obliging the peddler to make up his reductions by delivering an inferior product.[66] Agents who refrained from these practices sooner or later had to withdraw from the business if they wished to remain honest.

Numerous solutions to the problem were advanced throughout this period. Many reform proposals came from the legitimate trade itself, but the farmers were more vociferous in venting their grievances. Hardly a state or national nurserymen's convention was held without an address or resolution on the program dealing with the evils of dishonest tree agents.[67] By the late eighties the problem had become so acute that some form of action was imperative. The nursery business had acquired such an evil reputation that a marked decrease was noticeable in sales of horticultural products of all kinds. L. R. Bryant, a prominent Illinois nurseryman, in an address before the American Association, stated it was necessary to take some action, not only as a matter of dollars and cents, but as a question of moral responsibility. "The reform, if it comes at all," he said "must come from the association as a whole." [68]

Reforms by the nurserymen themselves, however, were adopted slowly, for some individuals in the trade organizations profited from the dishonest practices and were reluctant to make changes. Only after the business as a whole had fallen into very low repute did a majority willingly take action. Some of the important proposals made by the nurserymen were: (1) to disseminate sound horticultural knowledge to the buyers so that they might make sound judgments and encourage farmers to buy their stock from reliable nurseries in their own communities; (2) that every nurseryman adopt a set of copyright trade-marks, credentials, and signatures which could be furnished to their agents in the field; (3) that they make their advertisements and illustrations of fruit correspond to natural specimens, thus eliminating the "picture fruit" which were in most instances gross exaggerations; and (4) that they ask the federal government for legislation permitting them to secure letters patent for all new developments in plants in order to prevent tree peddlers from selling them without a license.[69]

These proposals were wise ones; if they had been put into effect they would have gone far toward eliminating many of the questionable practices, but they were treated as voluntary procedures and consequently proved ineffective. Stricter measures were necessary and inevitable. In some of the western states farmers and horticultural societies requested regulatory laws from their legislatures.[70] By 1886 they had been successful in securing such legislation in Kansas and Minnesota, and some other states followed at a later date.[71] With these enactments, a new day dawned for the buyers of nursery stock. This legislation outlawed the old swindling practices by subjecting the bogus-tree peddler to a fine or imprisonment, or both, and by requiring nursery firms from outside the state to post bonds guaranteeing their horticultural products.[72]

CHAPTER X

Seed Peddlers

T HE DEVELOPMENT of American agriculture as it unfolded from a pioneer subsistence level to that of a highly diversified commercial enterprise was marked by continuous change—change from old practices to new ones. One cause for this inconstancy of American agriculture was a growing need for different varieties of seeds and plants. Agriculturists in each new settlement soon found it expedient to explore and experiment, for old seeds degenerated after a few years of repeated planting and it became necessary to change in order to secure profitable results. The demand for new seeds also developed from the exigencies of the environment, for there were variations in soil, climate, and topography. Changing problems of transportation and storage and changes in dietary habits of people and animals at home and abroad also stimulated the demand for new seeds.

Agriculturists also were motivated by national interests; following the European wars of the eighteenth century the American people adopted policies of greater economic independence, and as a result new incentives arose to produce and develop agricultural products here at home. With an expanding market it was natural that different sections of the country would turn to new crops and methods. The growing economic disparity between the farmer and American industry after the Civil War also forced farmers to change if they wished to survive in the highly competitive economy of the latter half of the nineteenth century.

By 1860 there was a noticeable change in the Ohio Valley in farming practices, in place of a one-crop system the farmers had begun to diversify their plantings.[1] Wheat was moving west. This change created a demand for new and better seeds for both fields and gardens. In the effort to satisfy the ever increasing demands of western farmers for new and improved seeds, various schemes and techniques arose; some were reputable, others fraudulent.

This chapter describes some of these methods and products practiced to the detriment of farmers during the nineteenth century and more particularly in the post-Civil War period. To be sure, not all or even most seed distributors or vendors were dishonest; there were respectable seed houses in the larger cities which commanded a loyal patronage of the farmers. But, the contemporary agricultural literature provides incontrovertible evidence that swindling in the seed business was by no means uncommon. The psychological effects of these practices upon the rural mind cannot be dismissed as insignificant. True, the malpractices in the distribution of seeds were only a small part of a larger pattern of behavior which followed the westward spread of urbanism and industrialism in the North; but these malpractices added to a mass of fraudulent schemes and devices in other fields, contributed to the protest psychology that developed among the farmers in the latter half of the nineteenth century.

Farmers drew on at least five regular sources for their seeds. First, there were seed agents who traveled about the countryside, in much the same manner as bogus-tree peddlers, and frequently called at farm homes.[2] Most possessed a glib tongue and a knowledge of the rural mind. They were generally experienced in humbuggery, no doubt having been at different times vendors of patented cures, bogus jewelry, lottery tickets, farm gadgets, and patent-right devices, discussed in other sections of this book.[3] When one of these lines lost its appeal or had exhausted its possibilities, these agents took up another. Some even became notorious throughout the nation's rural communities, and their names became bywords as symbols of humbuggery.

Seeds were generally of poor quality, and the agents could buy and package them at low cost, making it profitable to peddle them in rural areas.[4] Most likely seeds were falsely labeled under some foreign name such as Hungarian corn, Egyptian wheat, Norway oats, Guinea corn, and German barley, since such labeling gave the seeds a much greater appeal than was enjoyed by seeds known to be grown locally. Each variety was advertised as having some uniquely wondrous origin. Egyptian wheat, for example, was reputed to have come from a few seeds discovered in a tomb of that country, and its great capacity to produce attributed to "the long rest it had."[5] Others were advertised as coming from Indian tribes, or as having been discovered by missionaries in some distant land.

These agents not only had an assortment of packaged seeds for ready distribution, but sold bulbs, roots, and other items in demand at that time. Most farming communities, and indeed whole sections of the country, often underwent periods of mania for a particular variety of seed or plant; for a few years it was the craze to grow mulberry trees, then it was Chinese sugar cane or Oriental sugar root, then in the thirties and forties a certain Rohan potato became immensely popular. Again it was Bohemian hulless oats and at another period it was sorghum plants.[6] The agents capitalized on these popular demands. In the late sixties the cultivation of the "Wine Plant" or rhubarb was looked upon by many as a profitable business; the juice from this plant was used in the adulteration of wine, and since there was a brisk demand for this beverage, farmers were urged by agents to begin its cultivation.[7]

A second regular source was from bogus-seed companies which operated solely by means of circulars, posters, advertisements through the mail, and the agricultural journals and local newspapers. Many were small concerns, or just individuals, operating in more or less isolated places where their nefarious practices would not be easily detected. Two companies operating from the small town of Cleveland, Tennessee, flooded the Middle West with circulars and posters advertising their "marvelous" seeds.[8] Ohio had more than her share of these establishments, not only in seed products but in a variety of articles such as eggs, poultry, incubators, and the like. The exaggerated testimonials and flamboyant advertising alone should have made the most credulous farmers wary, but many were caught in the net, only later to complain bitterly to the press. It is difficult to believe that farmers sent money to unknown concerns for samples of corn whose kernels were listed to be "as large as the average sized Chestnut"; for cotton seed, at thirty cents a seed, that was "worm-proof" and needed no machine to gin it; for watermelon seed that produced a melon weighing 125 pounds; for tomato seed that sold for $5.00 per ounce; and for certain varieties of oats at $2.00 per 1,000 seeds.[9]

The seeds were often old and low in germination, and generally were mixed with other similar varieties. A good example of this type of swindle concerned seed that was advertised as "Honey Blade Grass," the popular kind at that time. Instead of mailing their advertised variety to customers the bogus companies sent a blend of millet seed, which sold on the market for a much lower price.[10] In many cases the swindler would either retain the money and make no reply or would send the customer a circular containing such items as lottery tickets, with an explanation of how he could win a town lot, a watch, or some grand prize for a few extra dollars.[11] The following letter from one of these victims to the editor of the *Ohio Farmer* illustrates this practice:

As one of the . . . readers of *The Ohio Farmer* I claim the privilege of exposing one of your advertisers. In *The Farmer* . . . one James Wilson, of Fremont, . . . advertised seed corn for sale. I live six miles south of Fremont, and . . . I went . . . to see the gentleman, but could not find him. I then called upon his references, . . . but they knew nothing whatever of him. I then called upon the postmaster, who said a man of that name had rented a box in the office. With these facts in my possession, I communicated with you, warning you that he was a swindler, and yet you gave his advertisement another insertion in your paper. The postmaster now informs me that he has left the city and that there are some fifty money orders and registered letters in his box, which his victims can have returned to them by communicating with the postmaster . . . before Wilson calls for them.[12]

A third source of supply were seed houses selling their products through catalogs and on commission in the local stores. Since most farmers were on the lookout for bargains and new varieties of seeds, they became easy victims of these seed houses. The most reputable companies, and there were several, such as Vicks of Rochester and Ferry in Detroit, sold not only better products but ones that could be relied upon; however, they were reluctant to advertise in their catalogs any of the fantastic and fraudulent varieties so frequently promoted by the swindling profession. In order for the latter to sell questionable seeds at a handsome profit, they gave a large commission to the local merchants and hid themselves in some remote city or town where they could mix the seeds with dust or some old unreliable variety that when sown would not germinate. Old seeds were useless to the farmer; experience had shown that they lost their vitality with age. Corn seed that was three years old had only about fifty per cent germination; millet the same age had less than that amount; oats at three years was about three-fourths good, and at eight years had less than one-sixth germination. Wheat seed at three years was little over half good, and at eight and nine years old did not grow at all; rye at three years was practically valueless and barley at the same age was half to two-thirds good, but worthless at eight years. Grass seeds could not be depended upon for more than one year unless there was special care in storing.[13] Thus when the farmers bought these old seeds they not only were cheated out of their purchase money, but the ground which they had carefully prepared for the new variety was encumbered with worthless growth, while they themselves were defrauded of their labor for a year.

So vexatious did these problems become that most of the important magazines, such as the *Horticulturist* and the *Rural New-Yorker*, began a campaign against the frauds of seedsmen. The following is part of a communication contained in one of the western magazines cooperating in this reform, in regard to

the miserable stuff under the name . . . seeds, that is put up by irresponsible parties, and placed for sale in various obscure country stores, and sold to those who cannot be expected to hunt up the original offenders. These seeds are old refuse stuff, too old to grow, under true or false names as the case may be, and perhaps with a small portion of fresh seed mixed, that grow freely, to prevent detection. Often big names are given to these old or common seeds, and a price charged as big as the name.[14]

The press campaigns by these leading journals over a period of years resulted in attempts to regulate the frauds by law. The following is an excerpt from one of the prominent agricultural magazines in regard to an early bill:

The bill, we understand makes a fine of $50, or imprisonment for three months, or both, the penalty for selling seeds that are not true to the name with which they are labelled. Carry out such a law and our seedsmen would all be in prison in less than a year. Some kinds of seeds mix very readily; indeed nothing but the greatest care will prevent mixture, and this care, our seed-growers have not learned to exercise, nor will they learn it in a day. Buy at any of our seedstores, packages labelled *Long Green Cucumber*, and not one seed in a thousand will prove true. . . . Scarcely a pure specimen can be found at the seedstores. . . . This evil we hope to see corrected. . . .[15]

These evils were corrected, but not for several years. But by the late eighties judges and legislators had come to the rescue of the farmers in most of the western states and these frauds were greatly reduced.[16]

A fourth source of supply of seeds for the farmer was the newly established Department of Agriculture. Beginning in 1862 from a division in this department vast numbers of seed packets were delivered to farmers through senators, representatives, and territorial delegates in Congress. This division of government was established for the purpose of purchasing, disseminating, and experimenting with seeds and plants gathered from all parts of the world, and from the early fifties its representatives collected different varieties of seeds in Europe and sent them to farmers in America. William M. King, director of the seed department of the division, reported in 1886 that more than 4,000,000 packages were mailed out to the farmers in that year at a cost to the government of more than $100,000. This appeared as a lárge expenditure in that day, but according to the director it was a small amount in comparison to the increased production resulting to the farmers from the new and improved varieties.[17]

This large distribution of seeds by the government through the division and the large expenditures it had entailed brought sharp criticism from many of the regular seed companies. They inveighed against it as the government "seed store."[18] The attack was leveled largely against waste; too much money was being spent for the benefits received, for farmers were too often not interested in the seeds sent out to them by their congressmen; as a result they were never planted. One critic stated:

The government seed shop ought to be abolished now and forever; it is a travesty on agriculture. It simply deludes Congressmen that they are making votes among the farmers by sending little bags of seed to them. A man that has got sense enough to plant seeds, plants the kind he wants, not what other men think he wants.[19]

The evidence suggests that there was some basis for this. Many of the imported seeds were distributed without due regard for their value. Due to the periodic scarcity of these foreign importations, the division had to buy stocks from domestic companies in order to fill orders; not infrequently these seeds were of an inferior quality.[20] Moreover, the division occasionally recommended some imported variety which in the end turned out to be of no value; such recommendations gave swindlers excellent selling points for their own products and afforded them an opportunity to sell large amounts of them to the farmers.

The fifth source of the farmers' seed supply was an associational plan which was developed by local farm groups concerned with the growing and selling of different varieties of oats and, in a more limited way, with other cereals as well. Not the plan itself, but the fraudulent techniques used in its operation created considerable uproar. During the period under discussion, the farmers had increased manifold the cultivation of oats, an increase that was due to four main factors: (1) oats fitted into a pattern of rotation of crops; (2) they were a better revenue crop than other cereals, for yields were larger and prices were good; (3) there was a large increase in the number of horses and mules, which created a demand for feed; [21] and (4) they were becoming a popular food for humans in the form of oatmeal. These factors brought about such a demand for oats that a widespread system of swindling developed under this associational plan in regard to certain varieties of this particular seed.

Under this plan the *modus operandi* of distributing oats became quite uniform throughout the nation; beginning in the East it spread from county to county and state to state until it had run its course. The case of the Norway oats, distributed by a firm known as D. W. Ramsdell & Company presents the first true humbug in this field. The flamboyant treatment given to this reputedly fantastic oat in religious and agricultural journals, assigned it to a wondrous origin. Ramsdell claimed that in 1864, while a farmer in Vermont, he had been handed a single oat which had been found in a package of peas, sent from the Agricultural Bureau at Washington. "Its remarkable large and plump appearance so attracted . . . [his] attention . . . that he planted it in his garden" where it produced the remarkable yield of "*two thousand seven hundred and eighty-five grains*," or "from four to six times that of the old kind. . . ." He claimed that it had won prizes at fairs and that he had secured endorsements from agricultural societies. As a result of brash advertising the demand for his oats soared and the price rose as high as $50.00 per bushel.[22]

This firm commonly sent out agents to contact a number of farmers in a township and to organize an oat association, members of which were sold the seed at a price ranging from $5.00 to $10.00 per bushel; they in turn gave their notes for the amount payable the following year. The agent gave a bond guaranteeing to buy from the farmers at the time of the next harvest all the oats that they had raised for a certain amount per bushel, depending upon the price they had paid for the original seed. In turn the farmers promised to hold the seed after harvest and not sell it to anyone except the agents; thereby the parties could monopolize this particular variety and keep the price high.[23]

It turned out at harvest time that these oats not only were second rate in yield but rusted and lodged badly, making them difficult to harvest.[24] Farmers who joined the associations soon discovered that the agreements of the contracts were not enforceable, that the bonds given by the agents were fraudulent, and that only where it was profitable to them did they ever call at harvest time for the farmer's oats. On the occasions when these bonds were "lifted," that is, the contract was carried out, they were carried out not in good faith, but with the express purpose of false advertising to the surrounding community in order to encourage the formation of more associations. In many cases, when the agents failed to return on schedule, the farmers were left holding the bonded oats according to contract, since it was necessary to secure a release from the agents before they could sell them elsewhere. This situation aided the agents in keeping Norway oats off the market and in continuing to dupe new members with $5.00 to $10.00 seeds. Consequently, the notes given by the majority of the farmers to be held and paid for out of the following year's crop as was agreed to, were instead "shaved" at the local bank which made them payable in money at the time of maturity.[25] The farmer not only had to pay the purchaser of the note, but was left holding the oats resulting from the harvest. A western editor gives an excellent description of this swindle:

Mr. Ramsdell had oats that grew taller, produced more, weighed more to the bushel, were better for feed, and could be grown on all lands and soils between the Arctic and Antarctic circles. He sold them at $10 per bushel . . . and obligated himself to take all grown by those who purchased seed from him at $5 a bushel. He did a fair business the first year, a good business the second, and a wonderful one the third. Every one grew Norway oats. Then when harvest came and the immense crop of Norway oats began to arrive, Mr. Ramsdell was not to be found. That season the streets of Detroit were filled with teams loaded with Norway oats, for which the growers expected to get $5 per bushel. They sold finally for 50 cents, and the credit of the Norway oats was gone forever.[26]

By 1871 the Norway oats swindle was approaching its end. Farmers from New York to as far west as Iowa were up in arms and trying to get rid of their oats. One farmer in the latter state reported that in his own township alone "there are more than 3,000 bushels of so-called Norway Oats, produced from seed sold the farmers by Ramsdell & Co. Two brothers in an adjoining township have 1,500 bushels and many farmers from 200 to 300 bushels." [27] Others who had become suspicious wrote to journals asking that the editors "publicly request any person in the United States, who knows of D. W. Ramsdell's taking any oats according to contract, to communicate the fact to you for publication. By so doing you will relieve many from the agony of suspense which they are now enduring." [28] Some of these anxious farmers resorted to the courts in an attempt to recover damages; in Illinois one farmer who was stranded with eight thousand bushels of bonded seed sued the firm for $100,000. [29] This brought an end to Norway oats, and according to the *Prairie Farmer* Ramsdell was compelled to close up shop and subsequently disappeared.

In view of the prolonged success of the Norway oats fraud, it was to be expected that other seeds would be offered in much the same manner. In the early eighties comparable schemes developed for the selling of "Red Line," "Gold Dust," and "Seneca Chief" wheat, German barley, and various varieties of corn and beans, but these were more or less insignificant in comparison with the extent and influence of the humbuggery connected with Bohemian hulless or skinless oats. [30] A mania for this particular seed was so general among the western farmers that it took nearly a decade for this fraud to run its course. So many were involved in the fraud and so much money was lost on it that it might be compared to the mulberry hysteria that swept the agricultural states in the early part of the nineteenth century.

The idea of a hulless oat had been the desideratum of the American farmer for many years and it appeared and disappeared as a craze about every six years, for there seemed to be no end to the names under which it was sold. The farmers saw in the hulless type of oats the solution to the problems connected with this cereal. In the first place, an oat without a hull would make a good horse feed, since regular oats generally raised for this purpose had a tendency after repeated sowings to develop into an even larger proportion of hulls and stalks, [31] making it necessary to crack or grind them in order to secure what value there was in the grain, which resulted in extra cost as well. Most animals, after they had reached a certain age and their teeth had become defective, were unable to masticate the coarse kernels; hence, little food value was obtained. In the second place, hulless oats would naturally be desired by the oatmeal companies to eliminate much of the expense in preparing cereal for the breakfast table. These obvious needs of both farmers and manufacturers prepared the ground for swindlers to introduce their "skinless" oats to the western farmers in the late seventies of the past century.

According to the *New York Sun*, scarcely a year had passed during the last three hundred years that some itinerant peddler had not tried to swindle the farmers of Europe with "hulless oats," and for the past fifty years they had been at it in the United States. At one time it was called Boutella oats, at another, Chinese and *Avena nuda*, or naked oats, but the hulless oat finally terminated its course under the name Bohemian.[32]

In spite of the fact that as a hulless oat this particular variety had been in the country for many years under various names, it gained little general popularity until about 1878, when it was introduced as the Bohemian oat into the lake counties of Ohio by a general agent from Canada who was said to have brought in about two hundred bushels along with his scheme for selling it; from this seed all the rest was reputed to have come.[33] His plan was modeled on that used by the Norway oats distributor but on the whole was much more systematic, and, due to the novelty of this "new" variety of hulless oats, was more effective in capturing the imagination of the farmers.

The aim of the associations was to hold all these oats as a monopoly and each year the agents would have doubled the amount of seed to sell to the newly formed associations; the oats raised by the members over and above the contract were not to be used for seed; by such procedure both parties would profit. A good description of a Bohemian oat association that operated in Hardin County, Ohio, was given by one of the duped farmers in 1886; it was typical of the methods used by other groups:

Two years ago, two brothers . . . claiming to represent "The Northwestern and Central Ohio Seed Company," of Tiffin, and a man . . . from Cleveland, representing "The Henry, Williams and Crawford

Bohemian Seed Company," came into Hardin county, and . . . sold a few small lots of Bohemian oats in different parts of the county at $10 per bushel, taking the farmers' notes . . . and giving a sort of bond agreeing to sell double the amount for them the following season at $10 per bushel, less 25 per cent commission. It was generally thought that all those that bought were swindled and that the agents would never be back again, but they put in an appearance early the succeeding season . . . and hurried up the parties to get their oats ready, as they were needing them to sell, which seemed to establish the idea in the minds of many farmers that the business was all right. The agent . . . hired some leading influential farmer to go with him and point out the best . . . farmers for their victims.[34]

The following year the agent found the non-member farmers in this county anxious to buy his seed oats; by canvassing the balance of the townships he was able to sign up a large number. To this group he delivered oats grown by the parties he had sold to the previous year, but soon dropped them and shipped in other grain which he was able to buy at fifty cents per bushel, by the carload, and put his former customers off with a promise. The bonds were past due, and very few of them had been lifted, according to the contract. The notes given for the grain had been sold to banks and brokers and were due; the farmers had no other recourse than either to pay them and take their losses or be sued by the "innocent" parties who had purchased the promissory notes.

The agents had included several means of escape in their contracts. For example, when the farmers signed their notes most of them had not read them over carefully enough to realize that they were negotiable and could be sold to third parties; they were under the impression that the notes would be paid for from the crop of oats raised the following year. They also overlooked the clause in the agreement pertaining to "double the amount purchased." The contract did not read that the agent would "buy" double the amount—he no doubt had made that a verbal promise if at all—but rather that he bonded the association to "sell" double the amount; this was to be interpreted that if the agents did not take the oats the association would be responsible for selling them. In many cases the farmers organized a new association and appointed an agent "to go and beat some one else as they were beaten." [35] Such double swindling frequently led to stresses and strains within communities. Moreover, the bond given to the farmers was not genuine even though it was claimed to represent a corporation which had deposited hundreds of thousands of dollars with the auditor of the state as an indemnity "for the faithful carrying out of the terms of said bond." [36]

From Ohio this fraud spread both east and west. In the fall of 1885 agents were busy organizing associations in various parts of Pennsylvania and New York. By 1887 it was boasted by these swindlers that in the former state they had "never found a region so easily milked of cash as the Cumberland valley." [37] It was estimated that $500,000 was taken from three counties in this region alone. This had such a demoralizing effect upon business and created so much distress among the farmers that bankers began to refuse to discount any more notes.[38]

Having covered many of the counties in Ohio the agents moved to greener pastures; by 1888 they had canvassed every state as far west as Minnesota.[39] In the Department of Agriculture *Report* for 1886 the statistician stated that correspondents from twenty-five states had sent in accounts of the Bohemian oats schemes. The following states were listed along with the number of counties:

Ohio is the center, reports having been received from forty-five counties. Indiana comes next, twenty-four counties, then Michigan, sixteen counties, and Illinois, ten counties. Wisconsin, Minnesota, and Iowa report agents in a few counties, and Missouri, Kansas, Nebraska, Dakota, Tennessee and Kentucky an occasional foray. Agents have also appeared in ten counties of New York, in Pennsylvania and West Virginia. One is reported from Connecticut and one from Maine. Altogether 130 counties report the fraud, and it is thought a complete record would show 200 afflicted counties in the United States.[40]

According to the above report the success of the swindlers diminished somewhat as they moved westward, for the experiences of the farmers in the East had a tendency to filter through to those in the West, and as a result a stronger resistance was encountered. Furthermore, when an agent would make his appearance in a community, the agricultural journals, farm organizations, and newspapers were able to go into action immediately to protect the farmers. The editor of the *Ohio Farmer*, in commenting on the battle of the agricultural press against Bohemian oats, made this remark:

> We just received a letter from the *Iowa Homestead*, stating that the army of agents had just invaded the southern part of that State, and requesting us to send them some good ammunition. We sent it, and hope it will prove effective.[41]

The prominent agricultural journals as well as those of the state farmers' organizations throughout the West carried on a vigorous warfare against this swindle, and much of the success in eliminating it must be credited to them. Among the rural newspapers, however, the record was not so good; they were more susceptible to bribes and large fees for advertisements.[42] One exception to this was the Chagrin Falls *Exponent* in Ohio, whose wide-awake editor, in spite of attempts to bribe him, threats of libel, and even thrashings, was able by his exposures to drive the swindlers out of his part of the state. Much of the information that he uncovered in connection with these schemes was used later by other agencies.[43]

There were other good reasons why these schemes came to an end. This variety of oats, when compared to most of the other types, did poorly in yield and a certain percentage of the crop was not even hulless. Moreover, not only did they lodge easily but the kernels were found to be rather soft and spongy. This latter characteristic aroused the dislike of the millers. Several of the agricultural experiment farms throughout the Middle West tested these oats for a number of years, and in every report they were low in yield. In Ohio, out of twenty-eight varieties, they were one of the four lowest; in Wisconsin they were found to be the poorest of all the various kinds tested. The director of the latter station made this comment in respect to his experiment:

> We have grown the Bohemian oat for several years . . . and see nothing . . . to commend it to public favor. As the grain is without hulls it is a great novelty to farmers the first time they see it, and sharpers use it very successfully in too many cases to draw from one to five hundred

dollars from unsuspecting parties—or rather from farmers who would help along swindling schemes, but are themselves caught. If farmers are offered Bohemian oats by strangers at ten dollars a bushel, and wish to invest, let them send to the Station and we will give them the address of seedmen who will . . . supply this variety for one-fifth that sum. It is about time that this *very old* game was played out, and it would be were it not for an unfortunate combination of stupidity and cupidity which some possess.[44]

The farmers themselves gave the same opinions in reports to the press. Sometimes the yield ran as low as ten bushels per acre, whereas other varieties yielded as high as sixty and seventy. As one farmer said in expressing his views on this subject: "You are more apt to raise a crop of notes than you are a crop of oats."

Many of the farmers, at the time they signed up in these associations, had believed they could sell their surplus oats to the cereal and seed companies at high prices, but that hope soon vanished. D. M. Ferry, who was a prominent seed buyer and distributor in Detroit, explained his position in a letter to the *Michigan Farmer:*

We beg to state that *we do not deal in Bohemian Oats at all.* We do not consider them an especially desirable farm product, and the disrepute into which they have been brought through certain speculative schemes which have been worked in connection with them among the farmers of this State renders them particularly *undesirable* for any reputable house to deal in.[45]

Ferdinand Schumacker, one of the largest oatmeal manufacturers in Ohio, made a similar statement in regard to their undesirability for his purposes:

I do not want them for oatmeal even at the same price with common oats. I do not know of a mill anywhere using them for oatmeal, and I do not know of a farmer sowing them more than twice. . . . They have no standing in any of the grain markets.[46]

The concluding phase of this swindle was confined to lawsuits, court decisions, and legislative enactments. In 1886 the treasurer of the Ohio State Grange reported that the courts at that time were full of lawsuits connected with Bohemian oats contracts.[47] All during this period farmers often resisted payment and were ultimately sued by the holders of the notes; others, however, paid promptly rather "than have it go out that they had been nipped."[48] In a number of places, when the farmers discovered that they had been "taken in" by the bogus agents, they organized themselves into an anti-Bohemian oat association and assessed each member a certain fee in order to defray the expense of a suit.[49] Generally, however, they were unable to escape payment, for the notes had passed into the hands of persons who claimed in a court of law that they were unaware of the considerations for which the notes were given. Such claims were usually supported by the courts, and with this legal protection the bankers and brokers took advantage of the opportunity to reap large and lucrative profits, since the discount rates on these negotiable notes ran from 25 to 40 per cent.[50] The agents "hawked" the notes for whatever they could get for them.

The farmers had little chance of resisting payment to the bankers, but they were able successfully to prosecute the agents when they could be found. Many of these agents were not the original perpetrators of the fraud but were merely neighbors or farmers who lived in adjacent communities and had helped to organize new associations for the purpose of unloading the oats they had been left with. Under such conditions the lawsuits were between the farmers themselves.[51] Farmers could sue the organizers and collect damages on the bond of the association, for it was not in fact the incorporated company that it had been represented to be but was known to be false by the agent at the time of procuring the note. In several instances farmers were able to lay their hands on the original agents of the scheme; in Indiana one was fined and sent to the penitentiary for several years, and in Ohio another received a similar sentence in connection with forgeries of Bohemian oat notes.[52]

The financial effect of this swindle on farmers as a whole is difficult to assess; in some areas it was a real hardship, forcing farmers to mortgage their farms, while in others the farmers caught in the fraud were able to get out by passing the burden to someone else.[53] It is true that most of the farmers signed up for only one or two hundred dollars' worth of the oats when they joined the associations, but there were others who took as much as five hundred. Reports were numerous in the various agricultural journals as to the total amounts taken from the different counties. The following is a sample of the extent of this fraud: Trempealeau County, Wisconsin, $20,000; Eaton County, Michigan, $35,000; Hardin County, Ohio, $100,000.[54] In the latter state alone, which no doubt was affected the most, it was estimated that as much as $1 million was taken from the farmers by these oat schemes.

These losses brought about a pressure on the legislatures in several of the western states to put a "stop to this swindling business" in the "sale of grain, seeds, and other cereals." By 1900 several bills were either pending or laws had actually been passed to cover this problem; in Michigan the Supreme Court came to the rescue of the farmers by a decision in the case of *McNamara* v. *Gaggett*, preventing the purchaser of a note from collecting the amount.[55] The following editorial comment in regard to the Iowa law is representative of what was happening in other states:

THE IOWA LAW . . . makes not only the selling of seed at fictitious prices a criminal offense, but renders the notes given therefor void. Every State should not only speedily enact similar laws, but make them broad enough to cover all notes obtained by fraudulent representation, uncollectable. . . . This would put an end to all such forms of swindling, in the purchase of seeds, implements, or anything else.[56]

CHAPTER XI

"Lightning Rod Man"

L IGHTNING WAS a weird natural phenomenon that baffled man from his earliest beginnings. Since he did not understand it, he feared it, and for centuries employed all manner of means to protect himself and his property from its destructive effects. Among the most widely used defences against this celestial weapon, especially in the pre-lightning-rod era, were the building of large fires and the ringing of church bells or the firing of cannon, in the belief that loud noises would deflect the lightning strokes.[1]

Certainly better protective devices were necessary throughout the entire United States, for severe electrical storms occurred in all sections. In some areas they were more frequent and severe, but everywhere they caused great fright to farm dwellers. According to a Lightning Protection Institute study of 1963, isolation is an important factor in the probability of lightning striking a building; a house, barn or haystack in a rural area is more likely to be hit than buildings surrounded by taller structures in towns and cities, since the highest structure offers a degree of protection to the others.[2] Consequently farm houses were most vulnerable to lightning, and throughout rural America for generations it was the leading cause of destructive fires.[3]

Barns were especially vulnerable during certain months of the year, generally July and August, when they were "crammed with hay" hardly yet cured, or with newly harvested grain.[4] Moreover, lightning was a killer of thousands of farm animals each year, often destroying small herds by striking a tree or fence where they huddled together in times of storms.[5] Nor was man immune. The agricultural press carried occasional references to deaths caused by lightning.[6] The "Weekly Summary" news column of a New York agricultural publication contained these typical items: "Mr. ————, a respectable inhabitant of Perquiman's County (N. C.) was struck with lightning . . . and expired immediately." A certain "Mr. Piper of Danville, (Ky.) was also killed by lightning [while standing] . . . under a tree." [7]

By the mid-eighteenth century, experimenters in several countries were inquiring into the nature of this "electric fluid" and attempting to control its destructive proclivities, to deprive the "thunderclouds of their fire." Benjamin Franklin, concerned over the many fires set by lightning, began to explore its behavior and substance. After his popular kite demonstration, he had erected on his own house in Philadelphia some crude lightning conductors, the first of their kind in the United States.[8]

Franklin's discovery was hailed as satisfying a universal need.[9] Immediately he publicized his invention so well in his "Poor Richard's Almanack" that by 1756, only a few years after his discovery, a correspondent in Maryland observed that rods were being sold and installed in his state as well as in adjoining colonies.[10] Uncertain of the new contrivance's utility, he sent Franklin a sketch of a device being installed in Virginia, and posed a query to be asked by millions of rural people for generations to come:

There is a person [who] goes about *Virginia* erecting machines, of which I send you a draught, and should be obliged to any of your ingenious correspondents who would give me their opinion, whether they are like to be dangerous or useful? [11]

Installations of the lightning rod on farm buildings continued apace year after year. In some areas enthusiasm for the device became almost a mania; in other areas, people insisted that the surest way to burn down one's house was "to put a lightning rod on it." These newfangled conductors, like almost every other rural innovation, became a subject of fads and crotchets. Crèvecoeur reported from his farm in New York that not only barns and houses were being preserved from the "fire of heaven" but that housewives had adopted a modified form of conductor to increase their yield of chickens. They believed that if "while a hen is hatching, there happens a great storm, not one chicken will appear"; in order to "prevent this electrical mischief" they placed "a piece of iron in the bottom of their hens' nests in such a manner that it touches the ground." How this device operated Crèvecoeur was not able to say, but he was convinced that before the housewives adopted these iron conductors "the mischiefs occasioned in Pennsylvania and everywhere else by the thunder annually amounted to a great sum." [12]

A Scotsman making a tour through parts of the "North Provinces of America" in 1775 observed the extremely wide use of lightning rods by farmers:

They have frequent thunders in the summer and [during] harvests, with sudden showers of rain. The air is very full of lightning, which used to do frequent damage to their houses; but they have mostly all got conductors, which I need not inform you, are a spike of iron fixed upon the highest part of the building, and carried down along the side of the wall till it enters the ground. These are found by experience to attract the fire, and conduct it down to the earth, whereby most of the damage that used to be sustained that way is prevented.

Lead is also found by experience to be a conductor; so that where they have lead spouts, they generally bring the iron spike to join the lead; from thence they carry the lead into the ground, which answers all the purposes of a conductor. [13]

By the middle of the nineteenth century travelers in "York State" saw the "bristling rods" everywhere; one related that instead of a "spike of iron fixed upon the . . . building" he "once counted no less than twelve of these useless things on one house." In New England's rural areas, during the same period, the craze for rodding buildings was in full swing; but observers commented on the "hysterical

nervousness" of farmers who installed far more than were necessary. One traveler in the area was struck by the great numbers of
rods on buildings; and he mistakenly concluded that New Englanders purchased more rods than their neighbors:[14]

Any person travelling for the first time through that part of the Union,
at the present day, would set it down . . . that . . . scarcely a house
worth five hundred dollars in Connecticut or Massachusetts, which has
not, within the last half dozen years, mounted a *chevaux de frieze* of
bristling steel conductors, . . . A new neighbor . . . encountering one
of these domicils armed from top to toe with iron rods, and "presenting
arms" at every angle, at the top of every chimney, the turn of every
corner, yes, and at intervals of every half dozen feet . . . would he not
turn back with dismay. . . ?
We are at a loss to know how our shrewd neighbors of New-England
have been persuaded into such a . . . needless expenditure [for] . . .
lightning conductors on every house. . . . We have questioned and
cross-questioned, and for the life of us cannot ascertain that any greater
danger is sustained in . . . New York and Pennsylvania, where one
. . . rod answers for a whole building, than in New-England, where it
takes 50–100 points of the very sharpest description, shooting up into
the air in all directions.

Farmers who took part in the westward expansion of agriculture
felt the same anxieties and fears as easterners about the threat from
lightning to their lives and property. By the time of the Civil War
the craze for lightning rods had reached the West. Sir James Caird,
a perceptive English traveler of the 1850's, observed while riding
through the Illinois prairies that thunderstorms were so common
that every "house . . . is fitted with a lightning conductor. . . ."[15]
A Scotsman by the name of James McDonald, who traveled
through parts of Iowa in August, 1877, was greatly perturbed by
the frequency and intensity of lightning. He gave the following
vivid impression of the phenomenon:

During the nine weeks I have been wandering over this . . . boundless
domain I have seen more hail-storms, heard more thunder and seen more
lightning than would be experienced in the Old World in the course of
twenty years. I can count up on my fingers every day upon which I have
heard no thunder and seen no lightning, since the first time I gazed with

wonder at an American thunderstorm. . . . We had such a thunder-storm here last afternoon—such thunder, such lightning, such rain—that if I had had half the superstition of a Highland house-wife I would have . . . prepare[d] for the Great Day! Why do Americans insist on having everything on such a large scale? [16]

Despite their fears of lightning and the eagerness to protect them-selves against its ravages, the history of lightning rods is that of most other inventions introduced into rural communities. Many farmers opposed their adoption for a number of reasons, some real and some purely imaginary. Even such a prominent agriculturist as Solon Robinson declared that he had "not one particle of faith that any building that happened to be situated in the path of what we call a thunderbolt, ever was saved by the best . . . rod ever erected." [17]

An interesting objection, especially popular in dry areas, was that these rods had an adverse influence "by depriving the thunderclouds of their rain and thus causing drought." Thunderstorms would come up in the skies, these opponents maintained, but were "pre-vented from exploding by the lightning rods," and consequently no rain would fall.[18]

Another opposition view was based on an erroneous conception of how the lightning rod functioned; this was the idea that "lightning rods attract lightning" to buildings and that instead of themselves being secured against the "liquid fire" the rod only "serves to invite the bolt." It was claimed "there are more buildings injured by lightning that have conductors, than there are that have not, in proportion to the whole." [19] This erroneous conception did more to retard the universal acceptance of lightning rods than any other argument.[20]

Support for this faulty concept was found in the fact that occa-sionally a house, barn, or church was hit by lightning though it was well equipped with conductors. Whenever this happened in a com-munity the doubters were transformed into genuine skeptics; as a result, for a time rods became a drug on the market.[21] The skeptics were not aware that the failure of the rods was the result of defective installation. A great loss of confidence was suffered by one commu-nity in the East where a rodded church had been hit, with serious injury to several children. One individual, more curious than the rest, "made search for the cause of the disaster." He discovered that the church stood upon a solid rock formation. Although the conductors had been properly attached, the cable that ran from the rods to the ground had been placed in a drilled hole some five feet within the rock; consequently it was impossible for the cable to carry the electricity from the cloud into the ground, since it terminated in this dry hole.[22] For effective control of lightning it was absolutely necessary that the cable be embedded in moist earth. Such defective installations were responsible for much of the widespread dissatisfaction with lightning rods.[23]

On top of the general ignorance of the problems of installation many farmers were perplexed as to the kind and number of rods they should purchase. By the beginning of the nineteenth century so many different manufacturing companies and distributors had entered the business of producing and selling a wide variety of forms, styles, heights, and accessories, that the farmer frequently fell victim to the most dishonest form of humbuggery. This fraud was practiced throughout the country, but more particularly in midwestern states, where it lasted for more than a half century.[24] One of the most fraudulent types of rural hawkers ever to appear on the American scene was the Lightning Rod Man.

As if farmers had difficulty in learning from experience, the methods of these swindlers followed more or less the pattern practiced by humbugs in nursery stock, seeds, tools, and patent medicines. One young swindling apprentice drew on his own experience to describe this fraternity of sharpers: "I never understood the breadth of intellect, fertility of resource and depths of trickery displayed in the legitimate pursuit of this vocation until I obtained an inside view of [this swindling group]. . . . [Most local people] had a dread, or horror, of a lightning rod man and . . . hotels did not wish to accommodate them." [25]

They equipped themselves with the proper "riggs," garb and vocabulary and, as the *Prairie Farmer* related when the spring of the year appeared,

"the voice of the lightning rod man will be heard in the land," as he goes up and down among farmers, seeking whom he may devour. In autumn, when muttering thunders retire southward . . . the lightning "regulator" calls in his forces, his traps, his wagons and horses, disposing of the latter, or putting them out to board for the winter. . . . But as soon as the zigzag streams of light dart athwart the spring clouds, and awaken the fears of the nervous, he, like the circus man, gathers his retinue and takes possession of the field of operations decided upon . . . during the winter's leisure, with his vocabulary re-enforced by some newfangled "points," "angles," "insulators," "rods," etcetera.[26]

These loquacious itinerants had an almost sacred enthusiasm for their trade. If one was permitted to make his pitch, he could convince the most skeptical farmer that he lived in imminent danger, even though his buildings had safely stood for years without lightning rods. An unrodded farm quickly became a "harvest field for the rodders." [27] They diligently watched the local press for news items of thunderstorms, lightning strikes, fires, death notices, and the like, in order to impress their clients and increase their sales.

They were pleased to find only the women at home when they called, for it was easier to work on their anxieties.[28] They would reel off a list of fake statistics on how many women and children had been killed "last year" by this dreadful menace. If the farmer or his wife showed more fear of thunder or cyclones than of lightning, these glib talkers had just the proper kind of rod for that danger; they would sell them a "gold tipped rod that would take care of thunder," or a special type that would "scare away the cyclone." [29]

When the rodders met with too much resistance, they frequently resorted to a "persuader" that they carried with them; a "portable lightning battery" which they used to apply shocks of electricity to their victims which, suggesting the awesome power of lightning, usually secured the desired signature from the most obdurate.[30] If they found buildings already equipped, they frequently attempted to convince the farmer that his rods were ineffective and that a liberal allowance would be made on the old ones.[31] Once they had persuaded the farmer to have them installed, their next move would be to sell him an expensive kind with all the trimmings. They often displayed several types of highly ornamented forms with expensive points, glass insulators to prevent the bolt from jumping the cable, and rods that were square, twisted or triangular in shape. Sometimes they brought forward a "hollow rod" in order, as they said, "to let the fluid freely down into the ground." [32]

The climax of the humbuggery was the manipulation of the contract used to clinch the deal. A Kane County, Illinois, farmer has left a good description of how the fraud was operated in his community. He stated:

Agents of a lightning rod company are perambulating through this county. They go to a farmer and agree to rod his building for a given sum. Then they present him with a written contract, read it over to him, not as it is written, but according to the verbal agreement. The price agreed upon, we will say was $20 for rodding a barn. An employe puts up the rods, and presents a bill of $240, $20 a rod. "But," says the farmer, "you agreed to rod the barn for $20."—"The contract reads $20 per rod."—"You did not so read it."—"You must pay according to the written contract," says the employe. Now I advise every farmer to order lightning rod men off their premises and *in no case to sign your name to any paper.*[33]

Other swindling possibilities arose when an agent signed a farmer to rod his building or buildings and promised to install free a certain number of feet if the farmer would pay seventy-five cents per foot on all the *balance that was needed* beyond the number of feet stated in the contract. Such a clause in the contract could lead to wholesale abuses.[34] A farmer from Birmingham, Michigan, described one of the swindles practiced on a neighbor:

Not very long ago a slick, genteel lightning rod man called on Mr. Spear, who gave him a signed order to rod his house at a cost of not over $10, and with about sixty feet of lightning guide, and soon there appeared a gang of men who began their work of ornamentation and astonishment. They rodded the house, the kitchen, the woodshed, the little house, the pig-pen, the sow-shed, the chicken-coop, and chased an old cow clear to the back lot and tried to get a rod on her. . . . Anyhow the farm house bristles with lightning rods so that it looks like the back of a fretful porcupine.[35]

He went on to say that the farmer was unable to get the crew to cease their operations and finally was forced to settle with the agents by giving his note for $335.

These notes invariably were sold elsewhere to some "innocent" third party, a lawyer or banker who notified the farmer when the note came due, at which time the astonished farmer discovered the terms often differed markedly from those agreed upon at the time of settlement. For example, he may have bought the rods with the understanding that they would be paid for on the installment plan; or the agent may have offered a commission in the form of a number of rods to cover specific payments if the farmer would assist him in selling rods to his closest neighbor. These malpractices aroused indignation among rural people, and in many areas the victims followed the regular pattern and organized anti-lightning-rod movements to resist them.[36] But their efforts generally failed in the courts, for as usual the individuals who held the notes and demanded payment were declared innocent parties and not parties to the original transactions.[37]

Various estimates were made by leading journalists as to the extent of this swindle. Agents' profits were enormous, for they always sold many more rods than were needed at prices three to four times what the devices had cost the agents. Observers stated that a farmer could install his own rods at a cost of $4 to $6 per building or from fifty cents to one dollar per rod, depending on whether it was copper or iron; the agents, by literally studding the structure with rods, usually managed to get the figure to $50 or more.[38] One person reported from Wayne County, Indiana, that so many farmers there had succumbed to the lure of the rodders that the money thus wasted would have purchased for them subscriptions to a good agricultural journal for the remainder of their lives.[39] Another observer in Wisconsin remarked:

If we had all the money they have taken out of the pockets of Wisconsin farmers, without proper equivalent, we could put a fine library into every Grange hall in the state, and have enough left to pay the expenses of a few hundred young men up to Madison this winter to attend the short agricultural course.[40]

The *Prairie Farmer* observed that after "watching and exposing thousands of humbug operations . . . for almost a third of a century, we place the lightning rod swindle ahead, so far as the amount of money fraudulently taken from the people is concerned." [41] In Iowa, agricultural editor Clarkson of the Des Moines *Iowa State Register* observed in 1878 that the whole state was "covered by

Lightning Rod agents." [42] Farther west, and three years later, a Kansas farmer wrote an editor that the rodders had "done" so many people in this community that they "are sick and sore." [43]

Farmers also worried about just how effective these peddled rods were in protecting their houses and barns. There was considerable discussion as to whether they had been properly manufactured and made with the correct metal. Few farmers were properly informed as to the necessary size of the cable, height of the rod, number of points on the rod or how to ground it so as to give maximum protection. Few had consulted the literature on the subject although several farm journals made serious efforts to inform their readers by carrying numerous articles on lightning arresters, and some even sold pamphlets at nominal fees. [44]

Leading experts and scientific institutions of the day, such as Joseph Henry, Benjamin Silliman, Denison Olmsted, the Smithsonian Institution, the American Philosophical Society, and the leading Meteorological Societies also helped "to counteract the machinations of a great nuisance . . . called the 'lightning rod man.'" [45] Joseph Henry, a leading authority on electricity, contributed his expert advice on one important and controversial point. In one of his treatises he wrote:

The manner in which they are usually put up by the itinerant lightning rod peddlers is, to say the least, exceedingly faulty, and not infrequently probably less safe than a building would be if left wholly without them. The radical error in these peddled rods is their size, which is usually from three-eights to one-half inch, instead of three-fourths, which experience seems to have demonstrated as the smallest safe size. But, says the lightning rod man, the difference between the smaller and larger sizes is not much. [46]

Several of these authorities recommended that farmers have the rods made by their local blacksmith or buy them from the Grange, put them up themselves, and shun the swindling agents. [47]

For nearly a hundred and fifty years the ubiquitous lightning rod peddler had taken advantage of his golden opportunity to imbue his image upon the minds of country folk. "The lightning rod man" became a good conversation piece with the farmers, and even poets and writers immortalized him in their art. [48]

By the turn of the century this lightning rod humbuggery had become less of a problem, thanks to the fact that the rural population was better informed through the many agencies of education that now touched their lives. Farm institutes and agricultural colleges were reaching out to farm homes throughout the nation, informing farmers to beware of such peddlers, swindlers, and advertisers who offered them "something for nothing" at a handsome bargain. An additional factor of protection was the emergence of specialized manufacturers of lightning rods with reputations for honesty and quality. Prestigious companies of this kind attracted the patronage of an increasing number of farmers and finally drove out or compelled the adoption of higher standards by their competitors.

PART FOUR

Patent Conflicts

CHAPTER XII

The Patent Problem

T HE AMERICAN farmer of the post-Civil War period faced a host of economic and political problems; they included falling prices and rising costs and bitter controversies with railroads, banks, elevators, loan companies, and middle men. These important problems have received the attention of many historians. Historians have given less attention to a related question of a different nature, namely, the struggle against what farmers called the "outrages of the patent rights system." This and the following two chapters will trace the history of this struggle.

It is difficult to appraise the importance of patent grievances in the cause of the agrarian revolt. Certainly grievances against them were not as extensive, nor did they affect as many people, as did the railroads, for example; it is not my intention to overrate their significance. But the evils of the patent system played at least a minor role in arousing rural discontent during this period. The various protest and protective organizations that were formed to contest specific patents, and the frequent official pronouncements of the granges, alliances, and agricultural societies in the farming states offer proof of this fact.[1]

The extent of agrarian discontent over patents varied from region to region, but tended to be greater in the western states. The geographical factor had much to do with this variation; farmers who lived in sparsely settled areas, with few contacts with the larger world, were easy subjects for victimization by the patent vendors and royalty collectors. Farmers who worked hard for what they earned looked with favor upon any scheme which would allow them to make money easily. They were also more susceptible to flattery by the agents who called at their homes, and being generally honest themselves, were "slow to suspect others of dishonesty or wrong intent." [2]

Another factor in the rise of the storm over patents was the relative success western farmers had achieved in solving some other economic grievances during this period. Through cooperative political and economic efforts, they had succeeded in lowering prices and reducing the profits of merchants and manufacturers and had partially freed themselves from the bonds of the credit system.[3] With these conditions slightly ameliorated, the farmers could turn their attention to other grievances.

Certain developments in the manufacturing and selling of patented articles also influenced the rise of this protest movement. Beginning in the seventies and eighties, a large number of devices for farm use were patented by inventors throughout the country. The items were often insignificant and sold so cheaply that the inventors found it impossible to realize any money on them; in such cases they allowed the patents to lie dormant.[4] Manufacturers frequently infringed these inactive patents and put them on the market in large numbers. The patentees, seeing their inventions in general use among the farmers, would suddenly come to life and insist upon their legal rights.[5] They could either collect damages from producers for infringing their patents, which they seldom chose to do for litigation against corporations was expensive; or they could seek to collect royalty fees from the purchasers.[6] Since farmers constituted much easier targets than manufacturers, royalty agents found it expedient to descend on rural communities.

With the opening of the western lands to homesteaders following the Civil War, a need arose for many different kinds of agricultural tools and implements. This need soon produced a flood of patented inventions. In 1863 the Patent Office recorded nearly 400 agricultural patents, the number increasing to 642 by 1865 and to more than 1,800 by 1866. The flood of inventions grew at an ever accelerated pace. In 1876 the Commissioner of Patents reported that during the previous seven years a larger number of applications for patents were filed and patents granted than in all the years since the founding of the office in 1790.[7] By the 1880's practically every device or tool that the farmer had in his home or on his farm, from a "clevis to a fence post," was covered by a patent. "Let the farmer," said the editor of the *Prairie Farmer*, "take an inventory of his utensils, beginning with the wringer, the sewing machine and the reaper, and he will see that his in-door and out-door instruments of industry represent numerous inventions, bearing stamps of originality."[8]

This wide use of patented articles created a series of problems that in time threatened the existence of the whole patent system. These problems fall into three main divisions. First was the tendency, found in the patent system itself, to encourage the development of monopolies by allowing the patents on various essential articles to be controlled by a single patentee, but most generally by a group of manufacturers called a patent "ring."[9] Weaknesses in the patent law, whose provisions were quite indefinite, promoted this tendency. Old claims, or "bottom" patents as they were called, that had become inoperative and unremunerative to the inventor, were often bought up at a small fee by a patent "ring" and through manipulation of the Patent Office, or by the inadvertence of officials, reissued not on the original claim, but on a broadened or revised patent to cover subsequent improvements.[10] The law also permitted extension of a patent for a seven-year period through congressional action, if the owner could show that he had not secured adequate compensation for the benefits derived. Congressmen were usually willing to champion the cause of these patentees, and as a result, several of the more important patents were extended.[11] This practice not only kept a patent in effect for a longer period of time, but also made it possible for a "ring" to use original and enlarged claims to develop a monopoly of the article. Moreover with possession of the "bottom" patent, owners, through costly litigation, could drive out all competitors by compelling them either to sell or assign their patents, or pay a royalty fee for every article manufactured.[12] Formation of the barbed wire fencing and sewing machine patent monopolies illustrates this procedure. To the American farmer all monopolies were anathema, and he denounced monopolies on essential farm equipment and household articles as vigorously as the railroad pools.

Secondly, the farmers were irritated by the indiscriminate issue of so many patents to different people on virtually the same article, as well as the grant of patents on the most insignificant detail or variation in a manufactured product.[13] The multitude of articles thrown on the market made it difficult for a purchaser or user to keep from infringing someone's patent. Farmers had neither the time, money, nor skill "to wade through this vast labyrinth of inventions." Senator William Windom of Minnesota commented on this phase of the problem:

> I believe it is true that there is not a farmer in this country to-day who is not liable to a score of suits or more for the infringement of patents on his farming implements. There is something about his plow, his harrow, his thrasher, or his reaper, some little insignificant thing that nobody ever ought to have had a patent for, and never would upon a properly administered patent system. . . . There are a dozen things in your kitchen, in your library, your dining-room, your workshop . . . covered by some unsatisfied patent . . . [on] which you must pay or be subjected to harassing suits.[14]

A Michigan farmer put it more colorfully that no matter how or what one did he could not escape the patent system. Professor R. C. Carpenter of the same state elaborated on this point: "It is in our boots, it is in our clothes, it is in the tools we work with, in the buggy we ride in, in the harness on the horse, in the whip we strike him with. It is to be found in our fences, in our gates, in our pumps, in our kitchen, in our food, and finally in our coffin." [15]

Rural opinion held that the great number of patents resulted from laxity in administering the patent law; that sufficient care was not taken at the Patent Office to ascertain whether the inventions were really novel, and that patents were granted on trifling modifications which required no genius to originate and therefore were not entitled to protection.[16] This evil was so obvious that it led the keen student of rural life, Professor Seaman A. Knapp of the Iowa State College, to remark: "A goodly portion of the patent wrongs have grown out of the reckless methods of the Patent Office. It has been accustomed to grant most of the applicants and let the questions of infringement be fought out in the courts."[17] To leave this matter to the courts, however, was not satisfactory either, for once the patents were issued the judiciary rarely declared Patent Office actions invalid. The farmer thus found himself the victim of a strange paradox: the Patent Office issued patents freely and left the matter of their infringement to the courts, while the courts held the claims legal because they were issued by the Patent Office.

Out of this multitude of patents grew another grievance: the practice of prosecuting "innocent purchasers" for infringement. The patent laws allowed the patentee or his assignees to collect damages from manufacturers or consumers, with the option of choosing which they would sue for royalty fees. In most cases they settled upon the farmer, knowing him to be easier prey in that (1) he was not versed in patent laws, (2) he usually lived far from the federal courts, (3) he had a proverbial fear of the law, (4) he could not finance expensive suits, and (5) he was unable to engage lawyers who could "answer the sophistry of the legal men employed to collect royalty fees."[18] Aware of these weaknesses patentees deluged rural consumers with circulars and royalty collectors threatened and harassed them over such articles as sliding gates, barbed wire, clover hullers, harvesters, seeders, plows, drivewells, and others too numerous to mention.[19]

The farmer who purchased one of these articles was seldom certain that it had been properly patented or was being sold by a licensed dealer. In some cases he was purposely kept in ignorance of the facts. Frequently "moonshiners," as unlicensed producers were called, deceived purchasers by using false trademarks and license tags on their products, further complicating the problem.[20] Salesmen and peddlers who traveled about the countryside selling patented articles, assured farmers that their wares were legally patented and that they need have no fear of royalty suits. Farmers soon learned

that to be absolutely safe required an expensive trip of many miles to
secure a lawyer familiar with patent laws.[21]

When two or more patents had been granted on practically the
same article, as happened in many instances, purchasers could not
distinguish the valid from the void. Some farmers were visited by a
number of collectors, each representing a different patentee for the
same article. Such practice led one perplexed victim to remark:
"How is a farmer to know to whom to pay the royalty, even if it was
legal, with three or four applicants swarming around him, all claiming to be the legal patentees . . . ?" [22] The confusion surrounding
the question placed the farmer in a most vulnerable position. One
far-western editor remarked that it was next to impossible for the
consumer to become familiar with the intricacies of the patent problem. The innocent farmer who lived in the

interior of the country, remote from the great cities, without the abundant facilities for posting himself . . . it is the next thing to impossible
for . . . [him] to be posted as to who is the proper owner of the right to
manufacture and sell various articles he now finds in the market. . . .
The country is so large and the number of articles under patent so great
that there are not one-tenth of our farmers who know whether their
implements are patented or not.[23]

In some instances persons were sued for articles they had developed themselves or which they had borrowed from their friends and
neighbors before any patent had been granted.[24] In such situations, a
patent collector or attorney might come to the farm with cuts,
figures, and detailed specifications of the patent. The shrewd agent
often convinced the inexperienced farmer that the patent covered the
exact tool or implement in question and collected a royalty fee.[25]

This practice of collecting fees grew to such dimensions that the
rural population became suspicious of all patented articles. Some
farmers became so wary and anxious to avoid suits that they refused
to buy many articles, even those essential on the farm.[26] Senator
Samuel J. Kirkwood of Iowa described in a speech the predicament
of farmers in his state in respect to two important basic patents:

Take the so-called barb-wire being extensively used now in the State where I live for fences. . . . Those wires are sold by our dealers in the county in which I live. . . . [The farmers] cannot know whether one man's patent is good or another man's patent is good. . . . They must either buy the wire and fence their fields, or leave them unfenced where lumber cannot be had. . . . [Someday] a patentee shall come along and say to each, "Sir, pay me so much a mile . . . for the wire that you have used . . . or you must go to Des Moines . . . and defend a suit to be brought against you, the cost of which and the fees in which will themselves be more than I demand of you." The thing [that] is being done in . . . Iowa now in regard to these barb-wire fences, is [also] being done . . . in regard to what is called drivewell [s], and our people are paying day by day $10, $15, $20, when they do not know a particle more whether they owe the man a dollar or a cent . . . but paying the money just because it is cheaper to do it than to defend a suit. . . . Should they not have some protection? [27]

The number of suits brought against the farmers for infringement does not necessarily provide an accurate picture of the extent of this practice; most paid the royalty fees demanded to escape costly litigation. The total amount of fees collected is difficult to estimate, for too many statements on the subject were made by interested parties. Senator Daniel W. Voorhees of Indiana estimated that the agents representing the barbed wire fencing patents had taken from the pockets of western farmers "over six million dollars." [28] In Iowa the State Grange reported that three million dollars annually was unjustly taken from the farmers for patent royalties. [29] In Ohio it was estimated that a total of $100,000 had been extracted in royalties on the celebrated drivewell patent alone, while in Missouri whole communities had been "agitated and worried by the intolerant exactions of agents representing" the same patent. [30] The editor of the *Western Rural* wrote in 1886 that to his knowledge, "three-quarters of the readers of this article, at one time or another . . . have been mulcted for royalty on something or threatened or have expected to be threatened." [31]

Suits were brought against purchasers in agricultural states all the way from the Atlantic to the Pacific. [32] Senator Windom reported that a partnership of lawyers and agents, covering the entire state, had been formed at the Minnesota capitol to bring suits against farmers; by 1878 they had some five hundred cases filed in the St. Paul District Court alone.[33] Congressman Nathaniel C. Deering of Iowa reported in 1879 that a Chicago paper had received a dispatch from Des Moines to the effect that

upward of two hundred drive-well cases were filed in . . . one day; that in one city, near by, a single attorney is preparing papers for more than one thousand cases; and that the attorneys for the patentee of the iron barbs for wire-fences are preparing papers for upward of four thousand cases in . . . our State. Hundreds, if not thousands, of the unwary and unsuspecting farmers in my district will no doubt be compelled, by threats and intimidations, either to yield to the extortionate demands of these plunderers, and pay $10 or $20 each . . . or be dragged one hundred and fifty miles away from their homes, at great inconvenience and expense, to make defense . . . for purchasing . . . an article the entire cost of which would not. . . . exceed $3.[34]

Another grievance involved was the practice of selling rights on a patented article for a certain territory. Farmers themselves were inveigled into acting as agents for some patented device. In some cases it covered only a farm right; in others a township, county, or even a state right. This practice of swindling farmers either by selling them patented articles or territorial rights began in the eastern states, and by the 1870's and 1880's it had spread to the West where nearly every community had been victimized by one or more of these "brimstone angels" as they were often styled.[35] Agents for such farm and home articles as lightning rods, sickle grinders, churns, incubators, washing machines, beehives, and even hencoops, would prevail upon prominent farmers and their wives in a community to become their representatives or to purchase certain territorial rights.[36] These itinerate patent-peddlers were shrewd merchandizers and well trained in the art of swindling; possessing a glib tongue and mastery of all the techniques needed to influence susceptible farmers, they painted plausible pictures of "glittering wealth and princely fortunes" and assured their victims that little or no money was involved, since payments could be made after the articles had been sold. They would end their convincing arguments by furnishing a list of excellent prospects in the immediate community. The farmer usually succumbed to this mendacious salesmanship and affixed his name to the contract. A midwestern observer described the swindlers as traveling in gangs, with headquarters in Indianapolis; they dealt in all kinds of farm implements, using the patent right dodge: "The parties go to a well-to-do farmer and tell him he has been recommended as a good man to sell their machines and ask him to become their agent. He is persuaded that they sell rapidly, and that he can make a large per cent profit. . . . He is induced to sign the contract." [37]

On receiving notification that the contract had come due, the astonished farmer realized the nature and proportions of the swindle. He discovered that the agent had secured his signature to an order for a specified number of the articles and to a negotiable note for a sizeable sum of money, obtained by a clever manipulation of the contract form.[38] The note had either been concealed in the order blank or had been so craftily drawn up "that the conditions and other portions of the instrument could be cut off, leaving the ordinary words of a negotiable promissory note by themselves above the defendant's signature." [39]

This note-shaving scheme, widely employed during this period, as we have noted elsewhere with so many other swindles, was also used, for example, in connection with seeding machines. Sharpers went about obtaining notes for these implements from farmers who believed that they were becoming selling agents in return for a fee of $10, to be paid after $275 worth of the machines had been sold. A contemporary published the text of the document used: [40]

Lebanon, Me., May 1st, 1871
One year after date, I promise to pay A. Sharp, or bearer ten dollars, when I sell by order, Two Hundred and Seventy-five dollars worth   of   seeding   Machines for value received, at ten per cent. per annum, said Ten Dollars, when due, is payable at Lebanon, Me.   John Smith, Agent for A. Brown.
Witness: John Doe

Farmer John Smith, having examined this instrument, supposed it to be an obligation for only a small sum, but the swindler, A. Sharp, had drawn up the note arranged in three long lines with an intentional perpendicular spacing left between the words *or* and *bearer* in the first line. By "amputating" the paper down through this spacing he had remaining in the left piece a legal note for $275.00.[41]

Having induced a farmer to accept an agency, as specified in the original note, and having secured his signature, the sharper departed. He quickly sheared off the right-hand portion and proceeded to the nearest banker, to whom he offered to sell the note at a profitable discount. The farmer named in the note was generally a responsible person, well known in the community. As a result the note was easily saleable. When it fell due and was presented for collection, the signature was indisputable, and the horrified farmer was compelled to pay $275 instead of $10. According to the *Rural New-Yorker*, this was "one of the most infamous of all tricks of deception," and was "largely practiced throughout the country."[42]

There were several variants on this swindling game, and the sharpers shifted from one technique to another as required. Sometimes the farmer would give his note for ten or twenty dollars for an agency or patent right and the solicitor would change it to a higher figure by adding a cipher and then would "shave" it at a near-by bank; again, the farmer might agree to sell a certain number of sickle grinders, plow coulters, or stump pullers for a definite amount of money, but hardly was the ink dry on the paper when the follow-up agent called at the farm with a note for collection. When the victim protested, he discovered that the written agreement differed from the verbal assurance of the advance agent—who was miles away by this time—that payment could be made after sale. In other cases the farmer was to receive a patented article free as a commission if he sold a number of such devices for a certain sum of money. But in a few weeks, he learned that his note for the total amount was at the local bank, and the patented articles were at the railway station.[43]

Many times these notes meant ruination to the farmer, for they seldom called for less than $100 and occasionally for as much as $2,000 or more when they covered patent rights for several states.[44] In every neighborhood one or more farms were ruined financially by these swindling note-dodge practices. One editor cautioned his readers, "In nine cases out of ten a farmer will lose money if he buys 'territory' for any patent right." [45] If he did not lose money on the patent right itself, or on the agency with which he contracted, he was certain to waste valuable time traveling around the countryside selling his devices, or, as was the case in some instances, collecting fees from those who infringed his territorial rights. This meant neglect of his own farm work. Frequently, in order to come out ahead financially, farmers themselves had "to turn swindler and sell rights or false patents." This created ill will between neighbors, and especially between farmers and the bankers who purchased the notes at a heavy discount.

Farmers responded to these swindling practices with serious efforts to protect themselves. The contemporary literature discusses two major answers to the patent right swindles: education of the farmer to the ruses of the sharpers, and special legislation to eliminate the practice of getting a farmer's name upon a negotiable note by deception.

The first objective was consistently pursued by a section of the rural press. Leading journals, like the *American Agriculturist*, set the pattern. For years Orange Judd, editor of this authoritative journal, exposed frauds of every type in his "Humbug Column," and when the note-dodge swindle became a major problem he placed a notice in each issue, warning farmers to be careful of what they signed.[46] He assiduously excluded advertisements that might bring losses to his subscribers, and at times endured libel suits as a result of his bold attacks. For a number of years this journal employed a corps of investigators whose business it was to ferret out swindlers who preyed upon the farmer. In one issue he stated: "We hold it our duty not only to help the reader to make money, but to prevent him from being cheated out of it. . . . That we have saved . . . the farmers . . . *millions of dollars*, there is not the least doubt." [47]

Other crusading farm journals tried to educate the rural dweller in the ways of the swindler. The *Western Rural*, under its fiery editor Milton George, frequently published an official list of swindlers furnished him by the Post Office, and in many of its issues the "Rogue's Gallery" column carried names of those whose operations were especially directed toward farmers.[48] It published pictures and cuts of the devices these peripatetic swindlers used in obtaining signatures to so-called double action agreements, which later turned up as promissory notes. One of the farm journals made a major effort to develop skepticism and caution in the farmer, with stress on the need to be informed about the deceiving advertisements of the patent vendor and fraudulent agents of all kinds, but they were able to reach only a minority for, as the *Prairie Farmer* stated, "only about one farmer in ten takes . . . a paper." [49]

Other farmers, unable to cope with the oily-tongued swindlers, turned to the state legislature for relief. Under the existing laws dealing with negotiable notes, the farmers had to pay notes procured by fraud, for discounters and "shavers" pled they were innocent of the ways in which the agents had secured them. When court action was resorted to, judges generally upheld the claims of the note "shaver." This led to many abuses, for local bankers found these notes a profitable investment. Farmers individually and collectively appealed to their legislators for laws to hold the purchaser liable for notes that had been secured by deception. A call went forth from the Wisconsin Grange to agriculturists of that state as well as of others

to rise up in their might and compel their legislatures to protect them from these note-forging and note-shaving thieves. The farmer who buys a stolen horse does so at his own risk, and, no matter how innocent he may be of connivance at or knowledge of the theft, the horse may be taken from him by its rightful owner; but the note shaver who buys a stolen note sets up the plea of "innocent" purchaser, and under this plea the courts protect him in his connivance theft.[50]

By 1887 bills covering different aspects of this problem had been presented in many legislatures. Several of these bills were enacted. Some required that in all cases where signatures were secured to an order, agreement, or note for patent rights, the agents must indicate on the form to be signed the exact purpose to be served in the transaction; others outlawed all financial instruments, irrespective of the holders, if they had been secured by deception; still others provided that whoever purchased a negotiable note, or any form of indebtedness, must stand in all ways as the original holder.[51] In the light of these laws, the courts in several states ruled that in cases where a patent-right salesman had secured signatures "to some innocent looking papers, and has afterward altered it to the form of a note," such action was considered a fraud and the holder could not recover his loss.[52]

Abuses of the patent system had become so rife and the individual farmer so helpless in coping with them, particularly those relating to infringements and the collections of royalty fees, that an organized protest movement arose. This campaign began in those areas where such movements had developed in the past and where certain patented articles, such as the sliding gate and the clover huller, were in great demand; other areas attacked the barbed wire fencing and drivewell patents.

Agricultural journals, newspapers, granges, alliances, and farmers' associations were quick to enter the fight on behalf of the farmer. These agencies launched a two-pronged campaign: one in the courts to prevent collection of royalties and to invalidate the patents; another to persuade Congress to reform the patent laws so as to eliminate these abuses.

As a prelude to the court fights, mutual protective societies were organized in counties, states, and the nation to raise funds and employ counsel. Several important test cases, in which these organizations participated, contributed considerably to the formation of the Farmers' Alliance.[53] In a few court cases decisions were handed down setting aside the claims of the patentees; in others the farmers were not so successful.

The grangers kept up a continuous pressure on the Congress to revise the patent system. A number of state granges proposed establishment of a definite royalty fee to be paid to patentees, so that when patents were issued or renewed the payees could thereafter construct and sell improved machines and bring them into immediate use without fear of a visit from royalty collectors.[54] The granges took very seriously this proposal of securing the right to use patents, for when they launched their program of producing farm machinery they soon discovered that some of the valuable inventions were exclusively controlled by a few manufacturers. As the President of the Kansas Grange remarked:

This is the greatest barrier now in the way of our success. We are unable to obtain the right to manufacture many of the leading and most desirable farm implements, for the reason that individual manufacturers have exclusive control of the various patents. These laws must be changed so that free competition will be secured in the manufacture of all classes of goods.[55]

The National Grange at its annual convention in 1874, and at succeeding meetings, as well as the National Farmers' Alliance that succeeded it, passed resolutions calling on the Congress "to make needed changes in the patent laws, so as to prevent the indiscriminate extension and reissuing of patents; to guard against the monopoly of the same, by providing that any party shall have a right to use them by payment of a reasonable royalty."[56] In 1879 resolutions from thirty-two state granges requested Congress to revise completely the laws to protect "innocent purchasers" by enacting legislation making manufacturers and dealers wholly responsible "for infractions of patent rights."[57]

Other farm organizations got on this campaign bandwagon in 1875, for the Illinois State Farmers' Association reported in a circular that "our . . . patent and copyright laws, are perverted to build up immense fortunes at the expense of the masses of the people," and proclaimed that the time had come for action against this intolerable burden.[58] Certain third-party organizations also heard the cry of the Grangers; to attract farmers the Anti-monopoly and National (Greenback) parties in 1884 drew up platforms containing planks to regulate patents so as to prevent the formation of monopolies.[59] Even the American Prohibition Party demanded a "revision and enforcement of law concerning patents and inventions."[60]

Congressmen were also deluged with petitions. An examination of the *Congressional Record* reveals that the number of these petitions ran a close second to those pertaining to Civil War pensions. In these petitions the petitioners sought relief from the patent evils through a revision of the laws, protested against the extension of certain farm machine patents, or simply sought advice as to whether a patented device was valid and safe to purchase.[61] Several western legislatures controlled by farmers passed joint resolutions requesting relief for the "people from the oppression of patent-right monopolies," [62] and submitted them to their congressmen.

The rural press entered the fray, giving active support to the campaign; but its approach was more informal and its demands were stated in language that could not be misunderstood by legislators. Two examples, written during the height of the controversy, will suffice. The *Western Rural* wrote:

Almost every day the outrageous wrongs which our patent system inflicts upon the people are illustrated either in some chronic shape or in some new phase. The neglect of Congress to remedy these evils is a part of the exasperating do-nothing policy which distinguishes that almost perfectly useless body. As farmers we are more interested in the inauguration of patent law reform than any other class of our people.[63]

The Des Moines *Iowa State Register*, one of the most outspoken farm papers in the West, leveled a similar attack against Congress:

No State is now suffering as much perhaps as Iowa for want of protection in patents. It was to be hoped that the *average* Iowa Congressman would have remembered the dear farmer before this, but perhaps they will wake up by the next election to the importance of the farmer. If they will not, some of them might get fast on some of our barb wire fences.[64]

Rural journals not only directed attacks on Congress and the Patent Office but denounced the judges for adverse decisions with a fervor reminiscent of the railroad controversies. So abusive were some of these denunciations that one of the more moderate journals intervened in behalf of the jurists, asking the press to cease assailing the integrity of the bench, and instead "train your guns upon your senators and representatives . . . who *make* such laws." [65]

There is some evidence that a few western judges were influenced by this agrarian discontent; at least the patent "ring" appeared to feel a good deal of suspicion toward the western courts. The barbed wire patentees took considerable time to decide upon the judge to handle their cases, the particular patent to be used in test cases, and the opportune time to press the litigation. In certain instances they thought it the better part of wisdom to delay the suits, and in others they chose to settle outside of court.[66] As an indication of the anxiety created by Granger agitation, attorneys for the fencing patentees wrote in 1881, "The political agitation of demagogues in inciting the farmer, is beginning to tell upon the Court, and I very much fear . . . the effect of the political influence on the Court." [67]

Criticism of the government for its slowness in revising the patent laws prompted many congressmen to introduce bills in rapid succession covering every phase of the problem.[68] Among the supporters of this legislation were several senators, including Windom of Minnesota, Ferry of Michigan, Kirkwood of Iowa, and Voorhees of Indiana as well as a large number of House members. These measures received overwhelming support in the House, but expired in the Senate. An analysis of the House vote on some of the measures reveals the intense interest in this subject. In 1877 a bill was passed with only forty-three dissenting votes; in 1879 more than two-thirds of the members favored a bill; and in 1884 only six votes were cast against a certain measure.[69] Analysis of the geographical distribution of negative votes on the bill in 1880 reveals that out of twenty-eight dissenting votes, twenty-one were from the eastern industrial states.[70]

These bills and many others failed to receive the necessary support from a conservative Senate. Such prominent senators as Roscoe Conkling, Orville H. Platt, and George F. Hoar, saw only danger in these attempts to revise the system; they minimized its alleged evils and stressed the immense value of many patents under the existing laws to farmers.[71]

To add to the difficulties of securing favorable action in the Senate, the Patent Committee during the Forty-sixth Congress had not a single representative from the Middle West, where discontent was highest.[72] The inventors of the nation also organized themselves in opposition to change and applied pressure upon Congress.[73] Thomas A. Edison opposed the bill of 1879 in a letter to General Butler: "I am sure that this provision will not only act oppressively upon many inventors, but will strongly tend to discourage and prevent the perfection of useful inventions by those more fitted for that purpose, and most likely to accomplish it. . . . It would be very burdensome to me." [74] Newspapers and trade journals expressed the hope that they might "arrest, if possible, the unjust attacks being made on the property of inventors," and warned Granger congressmen that their continued opposition to the patent system would prevent companies from coming to their states, for businessmen would consider their property to be unsafe "in that part of the country."

Thanks to this strong opposition, the agrarian Congress failed in these efforts to correct the evils of the patent system through legislation. They learned in these struggles what they were to discover many times over in the twentieth century—that the United States Senate was seldom receptive to proposals for economic and social reform.

CHAPTER XIII

Barbed Wire Battles in Iowa

T HE STORY of fencing in the western states goes back to the earliest settlements. As immigrants from the East moved across the Mississippi River into the prairies they soon were confronted with the problem of enclosing their land. The period of unbounded pastures and free ranges, with miles of waving grass common to all, quickly came to an end. At first the early settlers had to fence out their livestock; later, when cultivation of crops prevailed, they were compelled to fence them in or otherwise move on with their herds to the open range.[1] For those who chose to enclose their livestock the supply of natural resources was extremely limited—in the case of Iowa about seventy-five per cent of the state was destitute of timber. This shortage of materials placed the cost of rails quite beyond the reach of the average homesteader; as a consequence some resorted to pine board fencing, the materials for which came from the pineries of the upper Mississippi. The cost of these materials still was too high for many of the farmers. With the introduction of Osage Orange hedge, large numbers turned to this as a solution to their fencing problems. Even though it was much cheaper as concerned the initial cost, its defects were many and most farmers soon discovered that it was not the solution.[2]

As population increased, the fencing question steadily grew more acute; by 1860 it was recognized by the farmers as one of their most perplexing problems. J. H. Wallace, in his report to the Iowa Agricultural Society in 1859, gave a vivid account of the shortage and high cost of fencing materials in Iowa. An excerpt follows:

What shall we do for fences? is a question that is asked by every intelligent stranger who visits and looks over our State. . . . In many portions of the State, the timber is about exhausted, and the efforts that are being made to produce artificial groves are so few in number and limited in extent, that we may put this down at nothing. The pineries of the upper Mississippi, vast though they be, cannot be made available for more than one-tenth of the necessity. Hedges are very tardy in their introduction, and on account of the care, skill and time requisite to perfect them, they will probably not come into general use during the present generation. We have no rocks to enclose our fields with walls; and embankments are a nuisance. In the meantime, our present fences are rotting down, and we are still waiting from year to year "for something to turn up" by which we may replace them.[3]

Something did "turn up." With the development of smooth wire in the East it was only a matter of time until farmers and practical mechanics were experimenting with some form of pricker or barb to fasten on it. Wire with thorns or barbs attached, like many other agricultural inventions, has a long history behind it. The invention seems to have had its origins in the East. William D. Hunt of New York took out a patent on a crude and quite impractical type of barbed wire as early as 1867; his example was followed the same year by L. B. Smith in Ohio; and the next year a patent was secured by Michael D. Kelly of New York.[4] These three inventors laid the foundations and furnished the "bottom" patents for this type of fencing, though none of these creations proved very practicable in actual use.

In 1873 Hunt came to Illinois to sell territory for his patent. In DeKalb County he came across a certain Charles Kennedy, who had also been experimenting with a loose barb for a single wire. Hunt sold Kennedy his patent, thus setting in motion the origin and development of the barbed wire industry in the Middle West. Numerous new patents quickly emerged in this area; presently out of this large number of patents on various forms of barbed wire two stood out as practicable, durable, and easily manufactured. Joseph F. Glidden, on his farmstead west of DeKalb, perfected a fence that determined in time the pattern for most of the barbed wire producers and consumers of the country, while Jacob Haish, a lumber dealer in the same community, developed simultaneously in his carpenter shop the "S" barb that ranked a close second for several years.[5]

Both of these patents were of the same general type, having two twisted wires; the main difference between the two consisted in the way the barbs were attached to the wires. By 1874, Isaac L. Ellwood, a hardware merchant in DeKalb, seeing the possibilities of the Glidden barb, purchased for a few hundred dollars a one-half interest in the patent, formed a partnership with the inventor, and commenced producing by hand a few tons per year. Haish reorganized his business into a small factory at the same time, and from these two small manufacturing concerns came the first successful barbed wire on a commercial scale. Two years later, a wire mill in Worcester, Massachusetts, known as the Washburn & Moen Manufacturing Company, purchased Glidden's half interest in the bottom patent and secured a reissue of it from the Patent Office. Then began the long process of development and consolidation, which terminated in the organization of the American Steel & Wire Company at the turn of the nineteenth century.

If the prairie state of Illinois first produced and manufactured practicable barbed wire fencing, Iowa was a close second. Factories sprang up in a number of the principal cities of the latter state, for the demand was far in excess of the supply. During the 1870's and 1880's Iowa had at least fifteen different factories. Some of these had the same owners but operated under different names and patents. Each producer had his own particular style of barbed wire, and two or three of them became rather famous in the development of the industry.[6]

In 1876 Washburn & Moen and their joint-owner of the Glidden patent, Isaac L. Ellwood, began a series of lawsuits against manufacturers in various parts of the country for infringement of patents.[7] The principal suit was filed in Chicago against Jacob Haish and thirteen other defendants from the Middle West; these defendants organized themselves into a protective society, called the Barbed Wire Manufacturers Union, assessing themselves one-half cent per pound on their output to defray legal expenses and to protect their buyers.[8] The legal battle that ensued was a long one, with the defendants arguing that the "bottom" patents were neither novel nor a product of inventive genius.

The defendants made every effort to prove that barbed wire fencing was used before the Hunt patent was granted and they introduced a large mass of evidence purporting to show that farmers had used barbed fencing prior to 1867. The country was combed in search of old fences; some were unearthed in Iowa and one was found as far south as Texas.[9] The trial dragged on for more than four years, since the disclosure of every pre-1867 fence compelled the plaintiffs to scurry about in search of rebutting evidence.[10]

During the period of litigation both sides loudly claimed victory through their publications and advertisements; circulars informed every farmer and railroad company in the West of the risks they ran by using wire produced by infringers of patents. It was a period of great uncertainty for dealers and consumers alike; but at last the trial closed in December of 1880 and the two judges, Thomas Drummond and Henry W. Blodgett, ended the long suspense by handing down their decision in favor of the validity of the "bottom" patents. This was the first step in the slow process of consolidation of the barbed fence industry.

This *cause célèbre* created considerable excitement in many areas of the country; a Chicago newspaper stated on the day of the decision that it had created a most profound sensation; its "sweeping nature . . . has taken the whole country by surprise. . . ."[11] Repercussions were heard from sections as far west as Montana; in light of subsequent developments, it was without doubt one of the most important patent decisions of that period.

This decision marked a turning point in the barbed wire industry. It produced consternation in many who suddenly found themselves liable for royalties. The owners of the "bottom" patents immediately capitalized on their victory by offering to issue licenses to the defendants on condition of settlement for back damages. By February 24th all the defendants in the suit, with the exception of Jacob Haish, had settled for damages and had taken out licenses.[12]

Some of the special features of these licenses were interesting from the point of view of their monopolistic tendency: (1) the licensee must operate on a definite tonnage; (2) assign all of his own patents to the combination; (3) settle for back damages on all that he had produced covering a two-year period; (4) pay a royalty of seventy-five cents a hundred on future production; (5) sell to consumers at a fixed price; and (6) each month report to the licensors the amount produced and sold, along with the names and addresses of those who purchased it.[13]

The victory of Washburn & Moen provoked strong opposition in the West to the process of consolidation. Protest was especially loud in Iowa for the state was not only a center of agrarian dissent but was one of the leading consumers of barbed wire.[14] Moreover, these farmers had been kept for some time in a state of high tension and uncertainty by circulars from patent-owners threatening damage suits against anyone handling or using infringing wire.[15] These discontented elements could count on the support of certain political leaders; they also enjoyed the sympathy of a number of newspapers which could provide outlets for their propaganda.[16] The wave of agrarian resentment in Iowa against the patent monopolists in the late seventies and early eighties was further swelled by other grievances, including severe grasshopper plagues and droughts.[17]

The first organized protest against the monopoly of the patent-owners was a meeting held by a small group of citizens in the township of Westburg in Buchanan County, Iowa, on December 20, 1878. The Independence *Conservative* carried a lengthy report of this meeting together with a number of resolutions embodying strong sentiments of "boycott" against the patent-right "sharks" and the patent system that made a man liable for royalties on articles "offered for sale in what the law calls the open market." [18]

Shortly after this initial meeting, Coken F. Clarkson, agricultural editor of the Des Moines *Iowa State Register*, began a series of articles which circulated widely; he attacked the "monopolists" as "bulldozers" and appealed to the farmers for action. In one article he reviewed the history of patent litigation to date and gave an example of what consolidation of the patents would mean in dollars and cents to the Iowa farmer. He took as an illustration the Iowa Steel Barb Company at Marshalltown, which, he stated, manufactured 300 carloads of fencing annually; a royalty fee of seventy-five cents per hundred pounds exacted from this one firm would amount to the staggering sum of $195,000, all of which would ultimately come from the farmers' pockets.[19]

Clarkson condemned the whole patent system for allowing a company to gain control of the barbed wire industry through the process of "purchasing two or three old patents," which before were worthless, by "manipulation of the Patent Office." In a characteristic vein of satire that made him popular in Iowa, he caustically remarked, "we have no doubt that the patent office . . . will soon . . . issue patents on the first practices of Adam and Eve, as being new devices." He likewise claimed that in many legal battles, the patent-owners had not pushed their suits to clear-cut conclusions, resorting instead to tricks, bribery, and profitable compromises. "By such methods," he continued, the farmers of Iowa "are left to the exclusive monopoly and extortion of Washburn & Moen." In May, 1879, he published another article, addressed directly to the patent-owners, asking them if they intended to prosecute the innocent farmers.[20]

The patent-owners made sharp retorts to these biting criticisms. Isaac L. Ellwood & Company sent its dealers a lengthy circular which indicates the low morale prevailing in the industry:

> They [opponents] have sent circulars broadcast that we dare not come to trial. They have called us swindlers, liars, Monopolists, and all kinds of low and foul names, such as only proceed from the mouths of men that have no honorable means of defence. The country has been flooded with these vile circulars, and they only show to an intelligent public the most infamous scheme to bolster up an unlawful manufacture and use [of] an inferior quality of barb wire, that they may well be compared to the mushroom stock companies that manufacture it.[21]

A year later Ellwood addressed two lengthy letters to hostile citizens of Westburg in an effort to refute their charges and to explain his position. He tried to allay the fears of the farmers, but also demanded his patent rights.

> We will as briefly as possible define our positions. . . . *We* have never in a single instance brought suit against a consumer, but instead we have laid our ax at the root of the evil namely the Manufacturers and Wholesale Dealers. Although we have received offers of large sums of money for the privilege of collecting damages from Farmers, we have steadily refused all such offers, believing that as a rule they have been deceived by the misrepresentations of irresponsible and unscrupulous parties. But now that our suits are decided, which fact we have published throughout the N.W. should any parties, . . . persist in buying and using infringing wires, we should deem it our duty to protect that which the Courts have decided is our property, and we candidly ask our Farmer friends if they would not do the same? [22]

By the first of the year 1881 feelings were running high and patent-owners and even licensees were sending broadcast increasing numbers of circulars.[23] One licensee, the Baker Wire Company of Des Moines, dispatched letters to dealers and farmers informing them that whoever handled or purchased any wire infringing the patent they controlled would be "held responsible for the violation . . . to the full extent of the law." [24] In such conditions farmers grew bewildered. Some inquired of their local papers what wire they should purchase; others became so jittery that they refused to make any purchases, while still others attempted to solve the problem by appealing to the national government for relief.[25] This chaotic state of affairs inspired the *Western Rural*, which was hardly known for its toleration of monopolies in any form, to state that the "patent office needs a thorough purification, and a good deal more industry and practically inclined brains than it has had." [26]

One group of Iowa citizens tried a new tack; they proposed an appeal for relief to the United States Supreme Court.[27] G. H. Crosby of Sheridan Center, Poweskiek County, and a number of other leaders, declared the time had come to unite their forces, collect a fighting fund, and contest the patents in the federal courts.[28] Writing in the Des Moines *Iowa State Register*, Crosby gave voice to his alarm:

It seems to me that we cannot afford to sit tamely down and be robbed without making an effort to defend ourselves. . . . A small contribution from each one will make a sufficient fund to test the question. As the matter stands every man who has a rod of barbed wire fence is liable to be called upon to pay a good round sum for infringement . . . our only way would be to allow a new suit to be brought and make a test case of it.[29]

Chester C. Cole, a prominent attorney in Des Moines, journeyed to Washington to examine the barbed wire patents. After a thorough investigation he encouraged the farmers to move ahead with a test case.[30] The protesters turned for support to Jacob Haish of DeKalb, Illinois, the most recalcitrant manufacturer as far as the patent-owners were concerned; he had been the principal defendant in the Chicago case and the only one who had refused to come to terms.[31]

In the spring of 1881 Haish leveled an attack on the "monopolists" in his *Barb Wire Regulator* that caused a stir throughout the Middle West. He became the rallying point for all farmers and dealers who opposed the consolidation. In fact, his propaganda caused such an uproar that Washburn & Moen allegedly feared "an open rebellion against them." Washburn characterized him as a "man who . . . is determined to fight, to wriggle, to scold and pull wires and issue ridiculous circulars; if necessary . . . [even] encourage Farmers Associations."[32]

An organization was needed to unite and coalesce the varied movements of revolt. On January 12, 1881, the Iowa Farmers' Alliance held its first meeting in Des Moines, concurrently with the meeting of the Iowa State Agricultural Society.[33] On the eve of the meeting a group of agricultural editors—many of whom were officials of these two organizations—were invited to the residence of Clarkson to discuss "subjects of current interest." During the course of the evening he proposed formation of an organization of farmers to fight the barbed wire monopoly.[34]

A few weeks after this gathering a call was sent out over the state to farmers, mechanics, and businessmen to attend a mass meeting at the courthouse in Des Moines. "The grasping world, combined

capital, Congress and the Legislatures should be taught the lesson
that the people are not yet ready to bear patiently unreasonable,
unjust and tyrannical oppression," wrote Clarkson. "And we have
faith to believe that this meeting will be only a commencement of
the meetings which will be held throughout this State to declare
their opinions and raise means to assert and maintain human liberty." [35]

Other heady articles followed. "Our fore-fathers had spunk
enough to cast the tea into the sea, because they were compelled to
pay unjust stamp duties on it. . . . Have any of our fathers spirit
enough not to use one pound of this wire, which has the blood of
liberty staining it?" [36]

In the same patriotic vein Professor Seaman A. Knapp of the
State College of Agriculture asserted that "it is a contest which
involves so much of liberty that if it fails the republic cannot long
endure." [37]

On the appointed day the "whole face of Iowa" was covered with
several inches of snow. The inclement weather was blamed for the
small number of delegates that attended the meeting. [38] Clarkson was
chosen president, and Benjamin F. Gue was selected as secretary.
The morning session was largely devoted to speeches and the reading of letters from such men as Jacob Haish, Jed Lake, and others.
Haish vowed that he would not capitulate and would continue to
manufacture his wire at prices the "farmers can pay, if the people
will sustain me"; he assured the meeting that all his customers
would be amply and fully protected. Lake, who was the leading
attorney in the drivewell patent case, pleaded with the farmers to
back Haish and thus save the $20,000 that it would cost them to
form a new case. [39] J. A. Hull of Boone proposed to refer the case to
General Benjamin F. Butler, who, he thought, would handle the
whole matter for not more than $2500. Hull was authorized to
contact Butler and ascertain if his services were available and what
his fees would be. [40]

In the afternoon session, Judge W. E. Miller, who secretly represented the patent-owners, delivered a speech in which he attempted
to scuttle the protest movement by promising the farmers that no
suits would be brought against those "who purchased from licensed

dealers." The delegates were less than courteous to the judge, for they suspected that he was a "mouthpiece for the trust." [41]

A certain James H. Coon, who was engaged at the time in the manufacture of barbed wire in Des Moines with two other men, John H. Given and W. L. Carpenter, was present at the meeting; his firm was even then being sued by Washburn & Moen for infringement. Coon assured the farmers that if they gave financial aid to his firm's defense, he "could supply all the farmers of Iowa" with barbed wire at one-third the regular price.[42] At the close of the meeting several resolutions were adopted; one provided for the selection of an execution committee to direct the organization.

A few weeks later this organizing committee met. They named their organization the Iowa Farmers' Protective Association; it was to be incorporated with authority to sue and be sued, to buy, sell, or manufacture barbed wire; and to assess a membership fee of one dollar per year. Any member sued "for infringement or using unlicensed wire will be given counsel in suit free of charge and where possible the Organization will become the defendant." A board of directors was appointed, with a list of officers and Chester C. Cole as their legal advisor. The capital stock was set at $100,000 to be secured by membership fees and annual dues of fifty cents; the maximum indebtedness that could be incurred at any one time was limited to $15,000 and members from adjoining states were eligible to join.[43]

On July 13th, the directors met in Des Moines to draw up a contract with the Coon concern to manufacture fencing to be furnished directly to members at seven and one-fourth cents per pound for enameled wire and eight and one-fourth cents for galvanized wire. Three-fourths of a cent was to be held in reserve for the purpose of paying royalty or damages, in case the litigation resulted adversely; this reserve was to be distributed to the members purchasing wire if their case prospered. Coon, Given, and Carpenter were to receive five-eights of a cent for manufacturing the wire and the Association was to operate without profit. Barbed wire was to be "free"; that is, no royalty was to be paid the Washburn & Moen concern.[44]

With the structure of the Association established, the next move was to get the farmers of the Northwest behind it. Appeals were sent out requesting farmers to organize locals in the various counties, select officers, raise fees, and report their work to the secretary. These appeals included the usual stock charges against the patent-owners and courts.[45]

Within a brief time the protest movement spread far and wide. Chas. F. Washburn, fearing a general rebellion among his licensees, came to Des Moines, and in the editorial office of the *Homestead* held a meeting with some of the directors of the Association to "ascertain if the interests and differences . . . could not be reconciled." [46] Having no success in securing an amicable settlement, he began distributing a series of pamphlets to the consumers as well as buying a goodly amount of advertising space in the local newspapers. One reporter noted that these pieces of literature were "placed in farmers' wagon[s] and sent directly or indirectly to every farmer in the Northwest." [47] The Association, not to be outdone, published a little monthly paper for fifteen cents a year called the *Farmers Advocate*, to "inform farmers of the monopolistic evils." [48]

Washburn's next move was to attempt to close the Coon factory as he had done in the case of many others producing unlicensed wire.[49] An injunction against the Coon concern had been asked for as early as 1879, but the case had been postponed until the fall of 1881. With the aid of the Association, Coon managed to secure another postponement from the judge until the January session; in the interim, a good deal of intrigue took place between the two litigants. Coon managed to convince the patent-owners that he was the sole owner of the patents and machinery in the factory, and he agreed to a pre-trial settlement whereby Washburn & Moen were to secure possession of the equipment for a certain price. He was to come to Des Moines from Chicago, where the arrangements had been drawn up, and deliver the machinery to a Washburn representative at an early hour of the morning.[50] Since Given and Carpenter owned a two-thirds interest in the equipment and were suspicious of their partner, they hired a detective to shadow him while he was in Chicago; when he appeared at the factory to deliver the barbing machines they were there to prevent the removal. However, after some delay Given and Carpenter finally capitulated and sold their interest in the patents and machinery for $4,000.[51] Thus ended the first chapter in the "free barbed wire factory."

Following this "betrayal" by their own people, the directors of the Association began to perfect a new arrangement with other patent-owners for barbing machinery. "Sturdy John Given was placed in charge of the factory with Carpenter as its agent and in a few months the factory was in operation again." [52] By this time the Association had become better known throughout the Middle West and as a result much of the erstwhile opposition to it, especially in Iowa, was beginning to disappear. The *Western Rural*, which at first openly advised farmers not to join the Association, was by now opening its columns in active support.[53]

The National Farmers' Alliance at first opposed the Iowa Farmers' Alliance, and naturally, the Farmers' Protective Association; but by the fall of 1881 the alliances had buried many of their differences and were holding joint meetings.[54] Furthermore certain barbed wire factories, especially the Grinnell Wire Company, whose owners found it difficult to secure a license from the patent-owners, gave their support to the Association.[55]

Realizing that a test case in the lower courts would be long and involved, the Association now turned toward the Supreme Court of the United States and again contacted General Butler to advise them as to the best procedure. He advised the farmers to make a test in the highest court through the Attorney General of the United States; he had recently interviewed this official and found him "willing to proceed against this unjust monopoly." [56]

This method of approach required that the initiative had to come from the legislature. Pressure was applied upon the legislators, and on March 10, 1882, Senator John D. Nichols of Benton County introduced in the Iowa Senate a joint resolution requesting the President of the United States to have proceedings commenced by the Attorney General "to set aside patents and reissues" now "claimed to be owned by Washburn & Moen Company." The Iowa Secretary of State was directed to send a copy of this resolution to each United States senator and representative from Iowa and they were requested to secure legislation to cancel patents issued inadvertently, or to void them for lack of novelty.[57]

The resolution maintained that these patents were not novel inventions and that the reissued ones covered more than the original patents. The petitioners furthermore averred that there was "no remedy for the public unless proceedings can be instituted," since the owners of the patents had thus far prevented the Iowa farmers from testing their validity "either by obtaining consent decrees or by default." A copy of the resolutions, as passed by both houses, was mailed to Washburn. In a few days he replied to this petition by a direct appeal to the Attorney General, stating that the claim of the legislators "is full of gross errors" and that his concern had not made illegal settlements.[58] In the end General Butler's solution proved valueless as did so many others that sprang from his inconstant mind.

By mid-summer, Washburn & Moen had brought suit against a number of producers in Iowa by asking for temporary injunctions.[59] Judge Love of the United States District Court in Des Moines refused to grant these requests, whereupon the patent-owners turned for relief to the other federal District Court in Keokuk under Judge George W. McCrary.[60] The legal firm of Wright, Cummins, and Wright was engaged by the Association as their counsel while Washburn, as his critics remarked, brought from Chicago a "whole galaxy of sleek, well-fed eastern patent lawyers." The battle was joined in dead earnest and both sides began to assemble their evidence.[61]

Albert B. Cummins was a keen lawyer and caused intense anxiety to the patent-owners; indeed, he performed so well that he was subsequently employed by the complainants in other patent litigations.[62] His experience in this litigation also prepared him as a senator for his vigorous attacks on the iron and steel schedules in the Payne-Aldrich Tariff Act.

While arguments were being presented in the suit at Keokuk a similar trial was in session in St. Louis under Judge Samuel Treat, who on June 4th held that the reissue of the bottom patents were invalid, on the grounds that they were enlargements. A few days later Judge McCrary handed down his decision at Keokuk, refusing an injunction on the same grounds—that the patents had been "illegally broadened." [63] These two decisions, coming so close together, gave rise to considerable excitement among the farmers; so much so in fact, that the directors of the Association released a report that their work was drawing to a close—they had accomplished their primary objective.

A battle had ended, but the war was not won. Washburn & Moen had another card to play; they turned to the original Glidden patent, the bellwether of them all, and began a series of suits to test its validity. Nine cases were begun in the state of Iowa, and others were initiated in other western states.[64]

Judge McCrary had meantime resigned his judgeship to become the general counsel for the Santa Fe Railway and his district was placed under Judge David J. Brewer of Kansas. To aid the Association in their suit in the latter's court, an appeal was made to the Iowa State Legislature for funds since the receipts from membership, annual fees, and royalty fees were inadequate to finance a legal battle of this proportion. By a two-thirds majority vote in both houses an appropriation of $5,000 was made to the Association.[65] The friends of the patent-owners attempted to block the appropriation through an injunction restraining the state Treasurer from paying the sum; on appeal to the state Supreme Court, however, it was ruled constitutional and the injunction was disallowed.[66]

It appeared that the Iowa farmers had the patent-owners on the run; licensees were growing rebellious under the royalty yoke and many defaulted on their payments. "Moonshiners," or unlicensed producers, took heart and circularized the trade with greater intensity. In one of their circulars they stated that the trust, now failing in the courts, was "adopting a course of intimidation and threats, in the vain hope of thereby bolstering up their tottering monopoly." [67] The patent-owners met the challenge and redoubled their efforts; agents were dispatched to warn farmers of the risks they ran; contracts were mailed to dealers in order to extract from them a promise that they would not "sell any barbed wire except that made by licensees" or "patent owners"; and their regular dealers were urged to report all unlicensed jobbers.[68]

By February, 1885, this uprising had reached such proportions that in an effort to quell the agitation all licensees were summoned to Chicago; at this meeting the patent-owners found it expedient to lower the royalty fees from thirty to twelve and one-half cents per hundred pounds so that the licensees could better compete with the western "moonshiners." [69] This rate was to remain in effect until the Glidden patent cases were decided in the western courts.

The two test cases that concerned the Iowa farmers were held in Leavenworth and Des Moines, both before Judge Brewer. In the latter part of May, 1885, he handed down his decision in the former city sustaining the original Glidden patent and on June 10th the same decision was given in Des Moines; in the latter court the Farmers' Protective Association and the Grinnell Wire Company were the two important defendants. Judge Brewer conceded the difficulty of the case, noting that Cummins and his aids had unearthed a number of "prior fences" that added considerably to its confusion and complexity. [70] In his decision he offered the following observation about the case:

This question has troubled me greatly. I am no mechanic; have no taste for mechanics; no mechanical turn of mind. And it has been very hard for me to weigh or appreciate the reasons and arguments based upon the facts and laws of mechanics, and I can only say, in concluding this branch of the case, that I have done the best I could. [71]

In spite of his confession of limited understanding of the technical aspects of the patent problem, he granted the complainants the right to collect back damages for infringement; he also allowed them to require a bond from the defendants in case an appeal was made to the higher court. After an accounting of the business of the Association, he did permit them, in his interlocutory decree, to continue manufacturing barbed wire as before, pending an appeal, by paying fifteen cents per hundred weight royalty into the court and depositing a $5,000 bond. [72]

Cummins insisted on going forward with the appeal on the strength of a new prior fence specimen that he had recently discovered. [73] A special appeal was made to the Iowa Legislature for $1,000; but by now the legislators had cooled off and it was not possible to secure the necessary two-thirds vote, although a clear majority supported the request. [74] Without this pecuniary aid it was difficult to carry on the litigation, for many of the members had dropped out along the way, and following this adverse decision many felt it useless to continue. Moreover, the reduction in price of barbed wire had achieved one of their principal aims.

When the Association began production in 1881, barbed wire was selling in Iowa for around nine to eleven cents per pound; by 1885 the price had fallen to lows of four and five cents per pound.[75] With these reduced prices it was difficult for the Association to compete with the "pool," but unless they could do so, the farmers had no particular reason for continuing to support the "free barbed wire factory." It was also getting increasingly difficult to secure smooth wire at a reasonable figure, because the Smooth Wire Pool in the East was now collaborating with the licensed barbed wire producers.[76] Furthermore, the St. Louis group of "moonshiners" under the leadership of John W. Gates, who had been for several years a source of encouragement to the Association as well as independent producers in other parts of the country, in the eighties began a new policy of cooperating with the patent-owners, leaving only a few small concerns in Iowa to carry the burden of litigation.[77]

Carpenter, however, continued his manufacture of "free" barbed wire under these adverse conditions, with his production and sales declining month by month until by April, 1887, he was compelled to close down.[78] Cummins, not easily discouraged, came to his rescue and perfected a reorganization of the concern by discontinuing the method of selling directly to the farmers; by securing a loan, supposedly from the Swan Cattle Company, he was then able to purchase the needed smooth wire.[79] Circulars were broadcast throughout the Northwest, notifying the trade of the reorganization of the company; in bold relief they emphasized the fact that they were planning to establish exclusive agencies. Their price list to dealers quoted wire under that of the patent-owners, causing an immediate stir in the enemy's camp.[80] In June, Ellwood wrote as follows to his attorney (F. W. Lehmann) in Des Moines:

The fact is friend Lehmann, I cannot help but feel that we have made a terrible mistake in not purchasing that concern when we had an opportunity to do so; I agree with you in that the time ought to be here when we would not be compelled to purchase peace, yet I feel that we have never up to the present time made a purchase of this kind but what has proved a good investment. . . . To-day the country is being flooded with that Carpenter circular and it is doing us more damage than ten such concerns are worth, or in other words it would have been cheaper for us to have bought them at $50,000 than to have had the circular issued that is being sent to the trade. What this thing will lead to, it is hard to say. . . . You will readily realize that it is a very hard matter for us . . . to hold exclusive agencies through the country on the Glidden wire when another concern can put up their royalty in Court and sell to the competitors of our agents in the different towns. . . . It seems to me that everything possible should be done to annoy this concern and to give them the hottest fight possible, and in the mean time . . . use your own good judgement to investigate this matter and find out whether we cannot yet purchase that concern . . . and get them out of the way.[81]

The patent-owners had two alternative ways of besting the rival concern; one was to try to hold the tonnage within the amount set by the court in the interlocutory decree; the other was an outright purchase. After careful consideration the patent-owners chose the latter alternative.[82] Two Washburn & Moen licensees in Iowa came up with proposals for approaching the Carpenter concern. They knew that Cummins was uneasy over the fact that his legal fees had accumulated unpaid for a number of years; they also knew that Carpenter was willing to sell his machinery for a handsome price. After a short period of negotiations the licensees were able to report to Ellwood that they had come "to an agreement in reference to the Carpenter concern."[83] The only hitch was that there was some barbed wire on hand which Ellwood would be required to purchase. Once agreement had been reached on this point, the last chapter of the "free barbed wire factory" came to an end.[84]

Patent litigation continued, however, for there still remained some small "moonshine" factories in Iowa. A small producer at Waterloo, called the Beat 'Em All Barb Wire Company, was brought to trial for infringement of the original Glidden patent before Judge Oliver P. Shiras at Dubuque in the Northern Iowa District Court, although Judge Brewer had already rendered a favorable decision on it in the Circuit Court at Des Moines. This new suit was begun to determine the validity of recent evidence of several prior fences that had just been unearthed in various parts of Iowa.[85] The defendant called in many witnesses who testified that they had seen an Alvin Morley Fence displayed at the Delhi Fair in 1859; the plaintiff introduced as many witnesses from the same section who swore not only that such a fence never existed but that the alleged inventor was feeble-minded and an inmate of an insane asylum.[86] Judge Shiras, after considerable deliberation, handed down a "voluminous decision" in which he declared that the Glidden patent was completely "void for want of novelty." [87]

The plaintiffs, in order to protect their patent monopoly and control the business until at least the expiration of the Glidden patent as well as to collect the large sums of delinquent royalty fees, appealed to the United States Supreme Court, where, after four more years of litigation, on February 29, 1892, following the expiration of the basic patent itself, Justice Henry B. Brown delivered a favorable opinion, with Justice Stephen J. Field dissenting on the grounds that there was no novelty in the invention.[88] The majority of the justices, however, reasoned that "as a general rule, though perhaps not an invariable one, if a new combination and arrangement of known elements produce a new and beneficial result, never attained before, it is evidence of invention." In spite of the fact that the Glidden patent did not indicate a wide scope of ingenuity over other such patents, and its novelty was indeed slight, it was, nevertheless, this slender difference, they reasoned, that made the barbed wire fence "a practical and commercial success." [89]

Thus ended nearly a decade of bitter and expensive litigation over a mechanical contrivance that embodied little creative inventiveness, yet possessed a tremendous utility and economic significance. Even before the final legal decision was rendered, however, many of the barbed wire patents as well as large segments of the industry had gradually been consolidated. The minor legal victory in Iowa had little actual influence in controlling prices or preventing the further combination and control of wire commodities that was to follow with the formation of the American Steel and Wire Company.

CHAPTER XIV

Victory and Defeat in the Patent Wars

THE STRUGGLE over barbed wire fencing was not the only patent controversy to rage in the rural states in the years covered by this book. The drivewell pumping device, sliding and swinging gates, and clover hullers provoked similar hotly contested patent battles. These inventions made great contributions to American agriculture; they also enabled patent-owners to amass large fortunes by collecting small royalty fees from a multitude of farmers.[1]

The drivewell invention was a product of the Civil War period. In 1861, Nelson W. Green, a young man with some West Point training, organized a volunteer regiment in his home community of Cortland, New York, and was placed in command as colonel. While encamped on the fair grounds at Cortland, he instructed another officer, Lieutenant Byron Mudge, to install a pumping device which Green had thought up in response to rumors that the rebels intended to poison the wells in areas occupied by Union armies.[2] This device was a 1½ inch galvanized pipe, having a point on one end, perforated with holes, and was driven into the ground fifteen to twenty feet by means of a wooden block and sledge hammer until the point projected into the water sand; a small pump was then attached at the surface and by pumping out some of the loose sand a reservoir was created. Its operation, then, was like that of all other suction pumps.

Shortly thereafter, Green's relations with the men of his regiment became extremely strained, largely because of his strict discipline. During one altercation he shot and wounded a captain in his regiment. This incident gave rise to intense excitement in and around Cortland, and rumors spread that there would be an attack upon the camp and Green. Thirty regimental officers applied to the general for a hearing on charges that Green "had shown by his conduct that his mind was affected." [3] Relieved of his command, he was tried by a military court and reinstated; later, however, he was again suspended, and at the end of April, 1862, his connections with the regiment came to an end.

Green's real troubles began after this fiasco; the scandal of the shooting affair and its aftermath dogged his footsteps and poisoned his relations with his neighbors. He grew so despondent that he was accused of being insane; he was harassed by civil suits over debts; and, finally, difficulties arose between him and his pastor in Cortland. Although Green was a devout Christian, his pastor had objected to the fact that Green organized a regiment on the grounds that the war was not a "peaceable act." In the sequel Green was dismissed from the congregation and as a result brought a libel suit against the pastor.[4] All these "unusual" and "extraordinary circumstances" were later cited by Green's counsel to explain his delay in applying for a patent on his drivewell device which he had earlier developed.[5]

While these "unusual circumstances" were taking Green's time, other men were taking out patents on the drivewell invention; Mudge, who had driven the first well at the fairground, constructed two or three more in the village of Cortland with the assistance of a well-digger by the name of James Suggett. After the regiment had gone off to war, Suggett made application for a patent on a pump with which to operate the wells and secured it early in 1864; while Mudge, after leaving the army in the fall of 1865, successfully applied for a patent on the process of sinking the well.[6] On hearing of these patents, Green also applied in the spring of 1866. Although more than four years had passed since he had made his invention public, after some deliberation the Patent Office declared what was termed a case of interference between the three parties. This involved case was brought before the Primary Examiners who finally decided in favor of Suggett, then before the Examiners-in-Chief, who ruled in favor of Mudge. Upon final appeal to the Commissioner of Patents Suggett was sustained in the question of the pump; Green was given the patent on the process of driving the well, which became known as the "broad claim." The decision thus gave him exclusive rights to the drivewell patent; and he clinched his case when Mudge unsuccessfully appealed to the Supreme Court of the District of Columbia.[7]

Use of the drivewell device soon spread to sections of the nation where it could be used effectively; it became especially popular in parts of the West.[8] The lack of success in some areas was due to unfavorable rock formations; in others water was not close enough to the surface of the earth.[9] The drivewell had several advantages over the older types of wells in that it could easily be put down on any part of a farm; it was inexpensive and quick to install and could be placed in any other kind of augered or digged well; it seldom was out of order; it prevented the water from becoming contaminated by surface materials; and it provided fresher and cooler water—the latter feature being very important during the hot summer months.[10] These advantages gave it a wide sale throughout the country; by 1887 it was estimated that considerably more than a million of the devices were in operation.[11]

Drivewell equipment was secured chiefly from Cowing & Company —a pump-and-well supply concern at Seneca Falls, New York —by agents and dealers who purchased county rights from the inventor.[12] Well-diggers and hardware concerns were licensed to install the wells and collect the $10 royalty fees, the usual charge for regular installations. Before long, however, many well-diggers were going about the country claiming to have an invention of their own or to represent other patentees; these men assured farmers that royalties would not be collected from them.[13] Since these wells were easily installed and equipment easily secured outside the regular licensed channels, it was difficult to prevent infringements of the patent. In 1868, the Cowing concern, aware of the fact that unlicensed wells were being installed freely, issued a series of circulars over the inventor's signature informing the public of these illicit practices. Green said:

In order to bring my invention within the ability of everyone legally to use it, . . . I have fixed the Royalty or Patent Fee, at a very low rate, and I intend that no person shall use it without a license under my Patent; to this end I have employed counsel to institute legal proceedings against all persons who shall use this invention without such license.[14]

He went on to warn that persons continuing to use the patents without paying fees, would be fined double the amount. Special agents and law firms were engaged to ferret out infringers and illicit users, but since legal and investigatory expenses proved high the inventor found it necessary to assign part-ownership of his patent to other parties who would assist him in the cost of litigation.[15]

In 1871, a short period after the assignment, litigation was begun in earnest against eastern infringers; a short time later it was initiated in the West. In 1876, the first important decision sustaining the validity of the patent was rendered in the case *Andrews* v. *Carmen* in the Circuit Court for the eastern district of New York.[16] The defense attempted to show that Green had legally abandoned his invention to the public by waiting more than two years before making application; the complainants contended that the long delay before applying for a patent was due to "trouble arising out of his indictment for shooting" and that these complications occupied all of his time between 1861, when the first drivewell was installed, and 1868, when the patent was granted. The judge considered this trouble "unusual" and "sufficient to excuse a delay." [17]

During the following year cases were begun in several western states and the patent was upheld by a Minnesota court in the case of *Andrews* v. *Wright*. This decision incited Senator Windom of that state to make a bitter attack in Congress on the patent system in general and the drivewell patent in particular.[18] In reviewing the litigation he scored the presiding New York judge, noting that

ultimately the judge decided in favor of Green's patent because of
certain "extraordinary circumstances" in his life. The Senator went
on to state that here

is a case where such vigilance was excused because through an unsuccessful attempt to commit murder the applicant became involved in so
many troubles with his regiment, troubles with his neighbors, troubles
with the grand jury, troubles with the criminal courts, with his government, with his church, and with his pastor, that he could not be expected
to find time to give notice of his pretended invention by applying for a
patent.[19]

He even suggested that the case was what was called a "friendly"
one, in which both sides, plaintiff and defendant, had connived with
each other in order to collect royalties from "innocent" farmers.

Heartened by these decisions, the patentees vigorously moved to
carry out their threats. United States marshals, armed with decrees
from the two courts, asked farmers to pay the fees or appear in
court.[20] In some counties in the Middle West as many as three
hundred individuals were sued for refusing to make payments, and
it was estimated that a total of 2,000 cases were pending in various
federal courts when the final decision came in 1887.[21] Powerless
individually to resist the collectors in some areas, the farmers organized associations to raise funds, employ counsel, and fight the matter
through the courts.[22]

Nebraska drivewell agents gave notice in the *Fremont Herald* to
all users of the patent who neglected to pay the $10 royalty fee that
they "will be liable, without notice, to suit for damages and injunctions, restraining them from use of such wells." In Dodge County
this threat called into being an organization, formed in December,
1880, whose purpose was to unite drivewell users in Nebraska and
raise funds to meet "all necessary expenses incurred in fighting the
matter to a successful end." [23]

In Iowa citizens in Winneshiek County assumed a more militant
posture and set up a group to resist all collections not only on
drivewells but on any patented article that had been purchased for
farm purposes. This Iowa group demanded that the patentee "seek

redress against the persons who have used his invention fraudulently, rather than against the person who has purchased the same
innocently." [24] In case this demand was ignored and their rights to
the "enjoyment of articles patented or otherwise, bought at fair
prices in the open market," were encroached upon, "then it becomes
us as men who know our rights to organize vigilance committees or
other effective means to defend our property by force and arms." [25]

In Minnesota the Anti-Drive-Well-Royalty Association collected
nearly $10,000. In Michigan the matter was considered of such
consequence that the state Grange undertook the defense of the
injured farmers; they engaged a Detroit law firm and all member
granges were invited to solicit a dollar from every man who had a
drivewell. [26] In Boston an organization was started by one hundred
and fifty users of the patent for the purpose of collecting testimony
and raising money to pay the costs of litigation. [27]

Western farmers were encouraged to continue their struggle with
the drivewell patent "sharks" by the successes of the St. Louis and
Minneapolis millers, who had consolidated into an organization to
fight the American Middlings Purifier Company, a joint stock concern incorporated under the laws of the District of Columbia. [28] This
company had purchased the William F. Cochrane patent for bolting
flour and had demanded fifty cents a barrel from all millers who
used the process. [29] The millers through their organization resisted
what they believed to be a fraudulent and unjust claim; they raised a
fund of about $75,000 through their state and national associations,
employed legal talent, and, after a long and bitter fight, won a
decision against the patent-owners in 1879. [30] This victory stimulated
other western farmers to combine and persevere in their fight
against the drivewell patentees.

In the early eighties, several drivewell decisions were rendered in
the lower federal courts. The patent was upheld in the Circuit
Court of Kansas, in the Indiana case of *Hine* v. *Wahl*, and in the
Circuit Court of New Jersey. [31] The Indiana case was appealed to the
Supreme Court, and in December, 1882, a decision was reached by
that tribunal in which eight justices, by an evenly split vote, sustained the patent. [32] This decision gave the patent-owners a seemingly definitive victory and an effective weapon to force collections

of their royalties. Although some farmers capitulated and paid their fees, others held out and continued the battle.

Other circuit court and Supreme Court decisions followed before the curtain was finally rung down on this patent. In the early eighties the case of *Andrews* v. *Hovey* was begun at Des Moines before Judges Shiras, Love, and Nelson; since this was a test case for identical suits in both Iowa and Minnesota, the judges agreed to consider them jointly.[33] The farmers organized and raised money to employ legal talent; they engaged the law firm of Lake and Harmon in Independence, Iowa.[34] Jed Lake, an attorney active in such patent cases, carried the burden of this suit for nine years; he introduced a great deal of pertinent new evidence, and approached the question somewhat differently than his predecessors in other drivewell cases. It was his aim to prove that the patentee was not entitled to a patent on this device because it had been public property and publicly used for some time before the patent was granted to Green. To establish this difficult point, the defense must cite an authentic case of a drivewell used prior to the date of the patent.[35] This approach ultimately won a favorable decision in the Supreme Court.

Accordingly, the countryside was combed for old pumps, pipes, wells, and recollections of people who had seen and used them along with accounts from old newspaper clippings. Books and technical magazines were searched in order to prove that the device was known several years before the patent was issued. In the case of a certain well at Independence, Iowa, Lake was able to prove that it antedated Green's. By reference to the files of three Independence newspapers as well as evidence of contemporary events the defense demonstrated that it was used by the Cricket Club, a young men's organization, which had been forced to disband when the majority of its members entered the Union Army in 1861. The May 30, 1866, issue of the *Independence Guardian* had an article describing a reservoir well created by driving a rod some twenty-two feet into the ground, and on June 6, in the same paper, a reward was offered to anyone who could pump it dry; but after several attempts, the paper reported on June 13, the "water still comes."[36]

Evidence of prior wells in other states was also introduced. E. W. Purdy of Milwaukee testified that he had driven a well by the same process as that of the patentees as early as 1850, and altogether a total of over two hundred persons were alleged to have had prior knowledge of drivewells at seventy-six different points in the United States.[37] As far west as Stockton, California, a certain Jesse A. Austin introduced this type of well in 1857 "in the sinking of a shaft by means of a two-inch auger, attached to light bars of iron; with other apparatus for pumping," on his own farm. Evidence was produced that farmers throughout the adjacent area paid him a "trifling" fee to make them a well.[38]

This evidence of prior wells was so damaging that in the spring of 1883, a few months after the Supreme Court decision in the Indiana case, Judge Shiras read the majority opinion of the Iowa Federal Court in which the complainant's bill was dismissed on the grounds that there were drivewells prior to those of the patentees.[39] Judge Love concurred in this opinion but Nelson dissented. The decision was precedent-making for two reasons. First, it was the only one in any of the lower courts that favored the defendants. Second, when the case reached the Supreme Court in 1887 it reversed its previous decision and denied the validity of the patent.[40]

This Iowa case, besides revealing abundant evidence of prior wells, threw considerable light on other aspects of the struggle. George Hovey, of Independence, who, with his two brothers was the defendant in the case, had for a number of years been putting down wells for farmers in several counties in Iowa as well as in sections of central and northern Illinois. This small concern of well-diggers had taken out a patent on a device similar to Green's, and, in order to keep from infringing his patent, listed it as a "bored" well; that is, they sought to evade the patent by boring instead of driving until they came to the water-bearing stratum; then, utilizing the advantages of the drivewell, they drove the tube downward a few feet into the water-bearing sands. They would also utilize the old wells on the farms that were no longer of any use by sinking a drivewell into them. With their techniques and devices the brothers did a thriving business, for they not only kept the names of their customers secret but they also collected no royalty fees from the farmers. At the time this firm was brought to trial some interesting facts were disclosed; when asked to produce the names of those on whose farms they had installed wells, Hovey refused, observing that the patent-owners through their agents, "would sue every man that had any wells," and he himself "would not be safe in the hands of the people"; furthermore, he said, "I do not want to be an informer." Farmers had issued warnings and threats to anyone who would inform a royalty collector, and Hovey stated that should he do so, there was no doubt that he, as well as the collectors, "would be mobbed." [41] This incident reveals how high feeling ran in some rural communities during the period of this litigation.

In the final phase of this struggle—between 1883 and 1887— there was little actual litigation, but a great deal of activity displayed by both sides. Three lower court cases were appealed to the United States Supreme Court—one from the Connecticut Circuit Court, one from Ohio, and one from Iowa; and for more than three years the attorneys in these cases gathered evidence for their final pleas. In the spring of 1887, two decisions were handed down. In the Ohio case of *Beedle* v. *Bennett* the Supreme Court decided that Green's patent had been infringed and that all users of drivewells must pay not only the royalty fee of $10 but an additional $2.03 in interest charges. Three out of eight justices dissented from this opinion. Simultaneously, in the second case, *Andrews* v. *Eames*, the court decided that the reissued patent of Green's was also valid; the same three justices disagreed. [42] This was the third decision by that tribunal in favor of the patentees.

Encouraged by these decrees from the highest court and the several favorable opinions of the lower courts, the patentees intensified their efforts to collect the royalty fees. Newspapers, especially in the East, advised the farmers "to accept the monopoly and pay the royalty." Eminent attorneys, who until that time had stood by the defendants, now told them to get out as cheaply as possible. Several leaders did settle with Andrews and left the fight to others, certain that the Supreme Court would never reverse its former decisions. [43] In spite of the gloomy perspective, some farmers continued to organize and support the cause; in the summer of 1887, meetings were held in various parts of Indiana "for the purpose of devising some plan to defeat the collection of this royalty." [44] About the same time, the president of the Ohio State Board of Agriculture called for a

November meeting of drivewell-owners in Columbus to plan a united effort against collections in that state. Eleven counties were represented, some of which already had protective organizations collecting dues and employing counsel.[45] A prominent jurist addressed the gathering, giving some legal points connected with the patent and urging the importance of organizing to fight the infringement; a committee was appointed and the following resolution adopted:

Resolved, as the opinion of this meeting, that the demands now made by parties representing the Green patent are unjust and illegal and extortionate, and we advise parties interested to form organizations in every county and unite in defraying the expense of defending any suits that may be brought to enforce such demands.[46]

In some Ohio counties there were not only more members but more suits than in others; in Union alone there were over five hundred members, two hundred and fifty-five of whom had been sued. An estimated $35,000 in royalties had been collected in Montgomery County while about $100,000 had been obtained in the entire state.[47]

Excitement ran high in Michigan following the Supreme Court decisions in favor of the patentee and even the Governor became embroiled in the controversy. A strong supporter of the Grange, he advised the farmers of his state to fight the royalty collections. This action brought attacks upon the Governor and the leaders of the state Grange from the patentee himself; in a personal letter to a prominent granger of Tekonsha, Green attempted to show that the Governor was a deluded "ignoramus."[48] Some of his caustic remarks follow:

We must exercise a little patience in behalf of a State which could elect a governor who could undertake to utter absurd law opinions in opposition to the Supreme Court of the United States. The State of Michigan is what she is because of the national supremacy behind her. Even these wonderful grangers cannot go alone without the rest of us. Your very explosive Chief Executive may not be altogether an idiot, although he talks marvelously like one. These grange magnates . . . are fishing for political favor, at the expense of the deluded farmer. . . . The wealth and general prosperity of the American people have been to a greater degree due to patents and patented improvements than to agriculture. In saying this I do not seek to belittle agriculture. This is not saying the farmers have no rights; but it will go without saying, that the farmer has no more right to use my patent, without my consent, than he has to use my horse. . . . My patent is as much property as the farmer's land or crops; and the governor of Michigan proves himself an idiot or a knave, when he says otherwise.[49]

In Illinois the patentee brought a good deal of pressure upon farmers, especially in the northwestern area where many drivewells were in use.[50] Agents were sent among the farmers to frighten them into paying the royalty; and in the southern part of Whiteside County alone "over fifty owners of driven wells" were brought to trial; but many farmers refused to make settlements. Mass meetings were held in the townships in the northern counties "for the purpose of taking united action in the matter of settling the . . . claims." [51]

The appeal of the Iowa case, *Andrews* v. *Hovey*, to the Supreme Court was still pending. Following the decisions of the spring of 1887 some farmers in Iowa dropped out, believing the cause was lost, but others remained in the fight and made even larger contributions.[52] Several leading editors encouraged them to continue support of their legal counsel, Lake and Harmon; they argued that it would save Iowa alone nearly a half million dollars if the decision were reversed.[53] In the summer of 1887, Jed Lake traveled widely through the states of Iowa, Illinois, Michigan, and New York digging up more evidence and testimony on the prior wells that he had cited in the Iowa case; in late July he went to Washington to make the final arrangements for printing the record.[54] In his argument before the high court he was able to present five witnesses who testified that the patentee had known of the public use of several of his drivewell devices for more than two years prior to his application for a patent.[55] "We proved," said Attorney Lake, "that he allowed others to use it; the other cases didn't prove it." [56]

On November 14, 1887, Justice Samuel Blatchford delivered the court's opinion affirming the appeal from the Iowa court.[57] Word was immediately flashed by wire throughout the nation of this great victory and there was immediate rejoicing by the farmers especially in the western states. The *Prairie Farmer* stopped its presses to include a victorious telegram from its Washington correspondent, for it had from ten to fifteen thousand readers interested in the outcome.[58] Iowa hailed the victory with greatest enthusiasm, for the "pluck and perseverance" of the farmers of a few counties in that state and their liberal contributions, were chiefly responsible for the outcome. The *Waterloo Reporter* immediately proposed to the legislature that it appropriate $5,000 to assist in defraying the expenses incurred by this small band of farmers, whose sacrifices and persistence had saved the people of Iowa immense sums of money.[59] A brief editorial announcement in the *Prairie Farmer* urged the farmers involved in the case to "catch every fellow who has collected any such 'royalties' before he can get out of town and make him disgorge." At Morrison, Illinois, the farmers attempted that very thing; a collector from New York and his legal staff had been doing "a thriving trade with the farmers" in that vicinity, but before they could approach him he withdrew "the balance of the money deposited with the . . . Bank of Morrison," and "left for parts unknown." [60]

In some areas farmers talked of recovering their royalties from the patentees by bringing suit, but the patentees had no intention of capitulating; they immediately gave notice that they would contest any attempt at recovery by carrying a case to the Supreme Court if necessary. However, the farmers desisted when advised by counsel to make a most searching legal investigation before they went into court to be sure that the patentees had attachable property.[61] Weary of costly litigation, the farmers decided to rest on their laurels. Meanwhile the appellants suddenly decided that they might secure a favorable opinion in a rehearing from the high court. They were heartened, according to the *Prairie Farmer*, by the "appointment of a new Judge . . . whose previous connection with monopolistic railways led to doubts as to his action in a case of this kind." But the *Prairie Farmer* was soon happy to announce that "the Supreme Court, *after an exhaustive application for a rehearing*, . . . denied the application." [62]

Some weeks after the conclusion of this controversy, editor Orange Judd offered a thoughtful and concise summary of the history of the case and its lessons:

Probably the best illustration of the evils of the present delay and uncertainty in the courts, is that of the notorious "drive well" patent. That patent . . . was nine times before the Circuit Courts in different states, sustained eight times; was sustained three times by the Supreme Court, and then . . . *more than two years after the patent had expired* the Supreme Court at a fourth hearing decided that the patent was void and ought never to have been issued! In the meantime, . . . it had cost the public thirty millions, not a cent of which can be recovered. It is safe to say that the litigation cost half a million, the printing of the record of the last case for the Supreme Court alone costing $3,500.[63]

During the seventies a patent controversy arose over a machine for threshing and cleaning clover seed, known as John C. Birdsell's invention. It was a significant improvement over previous mechanical contrivances because it combined the two processes involved in a single operation.[64] This huller-cleaner machine gained favor from the first, since it not only reduced the cost of processing clover seed by at least one half, but was a great time saver as well. Because of these advantages, combined with the fact that clover was an important crop both as a feed for animals and as a fertilizer in several of the midwestern states during this period, the patentee had no sooner begun to manufacture his invention at South Bend than a number of other producers came into the market with devices incorporating all his improvements.[65]

As a result, the story of barbed wire fencing, drivewells, and sliding gates was repeated; the patentee was eventually forced to carry on an extended and costly litigation against the manufacturers infringing his patent and to issue circulars and advertisements warning farmers against the purchase of unlicensed machines. His attack was a two-pronged one: against the infringing producer and against the "innocent" consumer.[66]

Birdsell faced a combination of concerns, however, that ultimately succeeded by legal maneuvers, price cutting, and misleading advice to the rural purchasers, in forcing him to close his factory for an extended period of time.[67] On top of these serious reverses he faced the expiration of his original patent, which required him to petition Congress for a seven-year renewal. This procedure required the patentee to demonstrate that his patent had been a definite benefit to society and that he had not received adequate compensation from it, due to circumstances beyond his control. Birdsell was able to satisfy Congress on these points and received a renewal of his patent.[68]

There followed unsuccessful efforts by the infringing companies and irate farmers to deprive Birdsell of his patent by contesting the renewal in the Supreme Court. After several court postponements and delays, the case was finally decided in June, 1874. The high tribunal sustained the original patent and Birdsell received the right to collect royalties on all machines that had been manufactured and sold by the numerous companies in the past. This privilege also granted a perpetual injunction against all concerns from continuing to manufacture his device. In case the infringing of any concerns should fail to meet its obligations to the patentee, he could seek compensation from the farmers who purchased machines from such a concern.[69] Several of the plaintiff companies, pressed to pay royalties in pursuance of the decree, sought relief in bankruptcy, thus shifting their burden to the farmer-purchasers.

Armed with the judgment of the highest court of the land, the patentee waged a vigorous campaign with circulars, advertisements, lawsuits, and royalty agents against the farmers.[70] Birdsell pressed for quick settlements in Michigan, where more hullers had been sold than in any of the states; he also dispatched royalty collectors to other sections of the country with power to compel the owners of hullers to meet their obligations.[71] Assessments were levied against all of Birdsell's machines as well as all those manufactured by nine other concerns, regardless of their age. Every individual who had ever owned a machine, no matter how often it had changed hands, was also liable.[72] In many cases the patentee could collect from one to five hundred dollars on a single huller-separator; in a few cases he could collect as much as $1,000.

The patentee's legal victory certainly brought him handsome

profits; one government source lists a figure of $1,181,576.35 for the seven-year extension period, 1872–1879.[73] A leading farm journal in Michigan stated that in 1876 Birdsell had turned out five hundred machines in his plant. These machines sold for $465 apiece. Birdsell also collected royalties from several other firms licensed to produce hullers.[74]

What is certain is that royalty fees in this period appeared excessive to the farmers concerned. Since the patentee was armed with an ironclad right to collect his fees, the farmers had few alternatives, but several solutions were suggested. One group of farmers proposed to meet with the patent-owner and arrive at some compromise of the claims. These men believed it would be folly to appeal to the Supreme Court, for they predicted that "only the lawyers will benefit." Others felt the owners should form a combination as had been done in the case of the drivewell patents, and resist the exactions of the patentee in the courts; still others advocated petitioning Congress to change the patent laws by putting an end to the collection of royalties from "innocent" purchasers.[75]

Necessity soon forced united action upon the farmers, but all in vain. Eight suits brought by the Birdsell concern against individual owners in a federal court in Michigan were decided in favor of the complainant.[76] By 1879 royalties were collected from "every person who had ever owned or worked . . . a clover thresher." [77]

Professor R. C. Carpenter offered a good summary of this patent controversy in a speech to some Michigan farmers in 1879. He said that as far as this machine was concerned

royalty was collected of every person who had ever owned or worked any other kind of a clover thresher. Perhaps not one of these men knew anything in regard to the nature of the patents owned by Birdsell; they bought and used other machines, on the supposition that they infringed the rights of no person. In many of these cases, as a matter of fact, it was not known by any person for years after they had quit threshing that every other clover machine was an infringement on Birdsell's patent. Yet on the principle that "ignorance is no excuse," even though it be an utter impossibility to learn, these men were held equally liable with the manufacturers, and forced to pay a large royalty.

The frequency of such cases of flagrant injustice has created a strong feeling which, in some places, is expressed in favor of a complete abolishment of the entire patent system.[78]

Another dispute over patent rights had to do with the "partially sliding and partially swinging gate." During this period farmers throughout the Middle West were modifying fencing laws and beginning to enclose their agricultural lands; fields were being subdivided and highways enclosed, making it necessary, if proper ingress and egress were to be practicable, to develop some simple barrier or gate.[79] Responding to this challenge, farmers, carpenters and mechanics applied their skills to the problem, and soon made available numerous forms, shapes, and styles of elementary structures for openings in fences. In fact, they were so easy to design and construct that one farmer in Michigan, where much of this controversy centered, remarked in 1878 that he personally did not "know of a farm about here but has one or more of these gates"; in most cases they carried no patent mark and were constructed by the farmer.[80]

Patents were issued, however, and two finally emerged from the sixty-four listed in the Patent Office by 1879 to monopolize the field and provoke most of the controversy.[81] One was issued to Ammi C. Teal of Girard in Macoupin County, Illinois, on December 1, 1863, and reissued July 20, 1867; the other was granted to a John C. Lee of Seville, Ohio, on October 24, 1865.[82]

Soon after these patents were issued farmers began to be harassed by infringement collectors who roved through the rural districts, attempting to collect a fee of $5 from all users of any form of sliding gate on farms of 160 acres.[83] The first evidence that farmers were being coerced to pay for the use of this device came in New York in 1866. From that time on an increasing number of anxious references to the problem appeared in the press.[84]

Since it was the home of the original patent, Illinois was early exploited by the collectors; traveling agents toured many counties, selling territorial rights to individuals which granted them the power to threaten legal action against other farmers if they refused

to pay the royalty.[85] In some sections, farmers who had no knowledge of the patent laws and their rights under them grew panicky.
One prominent editor attempted to allay their anxieties by encourag-
ing them to stand firm; "the law," he said "was not made to oppress
honest and innocent people." [86] The same journal informed farmers
that "if any person claims a patent upon a gate" the important thing
was not to be frightened by his threats and blustering manner; the
farmer should stand his ground and exercise his rights for the agent
"can't bring you into court under several months" time; the farmer
should demand to see the official patent and its date; he should not
pay the agent but instead write to the Commissioner of Patents for a
copy.[87] Such resistance to royalty fees by the farmers generally
caused the collectors to transfer their activities to more susceptible
areas, for they knew well that it would be risky to test their claims in
the courts.[88]

Farmers in other states were also pestered by collectors; one could
judge how serious the annoyance was in Iowa, Missouri, Ohio, and
especially Wisconsin by the tone of the letters sent to farm editors.
In Wisconsin feeling ran so high that in some counties local
granges combined to defy the royalty solicitors; if they yielded to
them on this point, one member remarked, the "next thing will be to
demand payment for the right to drive a fence post on more than one
side of a fence." [89]

The stiffest opposition to patent gates arose in Michigan, largely,
it seems, because both patents were ultimately purchased by parties
in that state. That considerable sums in royalties were collected
from the farmers during the seventies is suggested by the fact that
in Livingston County alone up to $5,000 was collected.[90]

The State Grange rose up in arms and mobilized hundreds of
farmers into what they named the Farmers Mutual Defense Association. Its headquarters was located in Ypsilanti. A tightly-knit organization, assessing a $2 membership fee, enabled it to wage a vigor-
ous court battle against the two patents.[91] In federal court they
proceeded to prove that this invention was not novel and had been in
public use several years prior to the date of the first patent. Farmers
from different sections of the state willingly testified that they had
seen and used the gate long before a patent was obtained. So over-

whelming was the evidence, that in the fall of 1879 a decision was rendered against the patentees, thus bringing to a successful conclusion another major controversy with the patent system.[92]

These controversies make clear that the operations of the patent system generated considerable discontent among American farmers, especially in the western states. These controversies cover two aspects of the problem: those connected with territorial rights, and, more importantly, those dealing with infringements. At a time when farmers were attempting to compensate for high labor costs by buying increasing amounts of machinery, tools, and accessories they found themselves embroiled in constant conflict with the patent-owners, and, due to the nature of patent laws, there was continual harassment by royalty collectors and patent-right agents. To remedy these evils, they sent hundreds of petitions to their congressmen to amend, or to abolish the patent system; they called on the President to set aside certain specific patents; they organized special associations to raise funds and to employ counsel in order to annul the patents in the courts.

Farmers had some success in securing favorable decisions in the federal courts; as a result they were able to free themselves from royalty payments on certain major patents. It should also be noted that by 1900 an increasing number of patents on farm equipment had expired and entered the public domain; in these cases infringement and collection of royalty fees were no longer problems. The farmer was also relieved of these burdens through a process of consolidation of industries manufacturing farm machinery; the ownership and control of such patents tended to concentrate in the hands of larger manufacturers rather than in those of the individual inventors. Under these new conditions farmers were freed from harassment, since producers now could license their patents and dealers and collect royalties not from the farmers, but from their licensees.

Notes

NOTES: *Chapter One*

1. *New England Farmer* (Boston), I (January 4, 1823), 180. Most inventions and new ideas did not come from tradition-bound rural communities. One prominent editor observed: "Of all the great labor-saving machinery introduced into agriculture during the last forty years, not two per cent of it has been invented by those raised and engaged upon the farm." *National Live-Stock Journal* (Chicago), XV (January, 1884), 1–2.

2. *New England Farmer*, I (December 21, 1822), 164–65. Scottish farmers exhibited a similar prejudice against new implements on the advent of threshing machines; farmers objected to them on the grounds that the "mechanical wind" was not "God's wind." Others refused to change the axle-tree when the employment of three horses instead of two was introduced. *British Farmer's Magazine* (London), X (July, 1841), 228.

3. James F. W. Johnston, *Notes on North America: Agricultural, Economical and Social* (2 vols.; Edinburgh: Blackwood and Sons, 1851), I, 135; *Boston Weekly Messenger*, VII (March 5, 1818), 341.

4. *Homestead* (Hartford), II (July 2, 1856), 653.

5. *Ibid.*, II (March 12, 1857), 393.

6. *Ibid.*,‖II (July 2, 9, 1857), 653, 672.

7. *Northwestern Farmer and Horticultural Journal* (Dubuque), III (May, 1859), 165; *Farmers' Library and Monthly Journal of Agriculture* (New York), I (July, 1845), 1–2. Other excuses offered besides the lack of time were that the idea had not been "adopted previously by their sapient sires," or that it "originated in transatlantic climes" and thus savored a little too much of "foreignism." *New England Farmer*, XXI (August 17, 1842), 49; *Homestead*, III (June 24, 1858), 641.

8. *Cultivator* (Albany), new series, I (November, 1853), 353; *Boston Weekly Messenger*, VII (March 5, 1818), 341.

9. Curtis P. Nettels, *The Roots of American Civilization* (New York: Appleton-Century-Crofts, Inc., 1938), pp. 494–95.

10. *Virginia Gazette* (Williamsburg), July 28, 1738; *Farmers' Library and Monthly Journal of Agriculture*, II (April, 1847), 487; Peter Neilson, *Recollections of a Six Years' Residence in the United States of America* (Glasgow: D. Robertson, 1830), p. 192; *New England Farmer*, new series, VI (June, 1854), 291; *Cultivator*, IX (April, July, 1842), 63, 110; *American Veterinary Journal* (Boston), III (September, 1858), 276–77; *Medical Repository* (New York), III (1800), 257; new series, II (1810), 185; III (1812), 377–82.

11. Nettels, *Roots of American Civilization*, pp. 494–95.

12. For a discussion of this subject from various points of view in agricultural farm journals, see the references listed by Albert L. Demaree, *The American Agricultural Press, 1819–1860* (New York: Columbia University Press, 1941), pp. 48–49 and Richard Bardolph, *Agricultural Literature and the Early Illinois Farmer* (Urbana: University of Illinois Press, 1948), pp. 113–14.

13. *American Farmer* (Baltimore), I (May 28, 1819), 68.

14. *New England Farmer*, I (August 10, 1822) (May 23, 1823), 11, 339; IV (March 3, 1826), 249; XVII (August 8, 1838), 35; *Farmers' Library and Monthly Journal of Agriculture*, I (May, 1846), 547–52; II (April, 1847), 487; *Cultivator*, IV (March, 1847), 88; V (May, 1848), 157–58; new series, VIII (March, 1860), 136; Herbert A. Kellar (ed.), *Solon Robinson: Pioneer and Agriculturist* ("Indiana Historical Collections," XXI–XXII [Indianapolis: Indiana Historical Bureau, 1936]), p. 90; *Cultivator and Country Gentleman* (Albany), L (July 7, 1887), 537; R. S. Elliott, *Notes Taken in Sixty Years* (St. Louis: Brentano Bros., 1883), p. 86. Some believed that the only time of the moon to kill bushes and the like was during a two-day period in August, at which time neighbors would assemble with their scythes and work furiously. *New England Farmer*, XXII (August 21, 1844), 59; XXIII (August 7, 1844), 46. See Chapter III, p. 41.

15. *New England Farmer*, II (August 10, 1822), 11; VI (December 14, 1827), 168; XIV (August 26, 1835), 57; XXI (March 22, 1843), 302; XXIII (January 8, 1845), 219; *American Farmer*, I (January 7, 1820), 327–28; *Cultivator*, V (December, 1838), 173; new series, II (September, 1855), 276; *National Live-Stock Journal*, XVI (January, 1885), 32; Carl R. Woodward, *The Development of Agriculture in New Jersey, 1640–1880* (New Brunswick: Rutgers University Press, 1927), p. 64; James W. Whitaker, "A Venture in Jack Stock," *Agricultural History*, XXXVIII (October, 1964), 218; Clifton Johnson, *What They Say in New England and Other American Folklore*, ed. by Carl Withers (New York: Columbia University Press, 1963), pp. 143–48.

16. John B. Bordley, *Essays and Notes on Husbandry and Rural Affairs* (Philadelphia: Thomas Dobson, 1799), pp. 200–04, 223; *Plough Boy* (Albany), III (October 27, 1821), 173; *Annual Register of Rural Affairs* (Albany), II (1858–1860), 110–11; *Homestead*, II (June 11, 1857), 602; *Western Stock Journal and Farmer* (Cedar Rapids, Iowa), X (October, 1880), 220; *Farmer's Journal* (Cedar Rapids, Iowa), IV (August, 1875), 17.

17. *Valley Farmer* (St. Louis), II (December, 1850), 382; IK Marvel [pseud.], *My Farm of Edgewood: A Country Book* (New York: C. Scribner, 1863), p. 276.

18. *The American Farmer's Hand-Book* (Boston: R. Worthington, 1880), pp. vii–viii (Italics mine); *Rural New-Yorker* (New York), XLI (June 3, 1882), 371.

19. Western Farmer and Wisconsin Grange, *Bulletin* (Madison), IV (December 5, 1885), 11; Iowa State Grange, *Proceedings* (Des Moines ?), No. 18, pp. 33–34; *Farmers' Review* (Chicago), XIX (August 22, 1888), 530; *American Agriculturist* (New York), XIX (November, 1860), 345; XXXIII (August, 1874), 285; XXXIV (September, 1875), 330; XXXVII (December, 1878), 457; XXXVIII (February, September, 1879), 50, 333; *National Live-Stock Journal*, VIII (September, 1877), 376.

20. *Farmer's Journal*, IV (March, 1875), 37; *Cultivator and Country Gentleman*, XLIX (November 6, 1884), 924.

21. Vernon Carstensen, "The Genesis of an Agricultural Experiment Station," *Agricultural History*, XXIV (January, 1960), 13–20; Gould P. Colman, "Pioneering in Agricultural Education: Cornell University, 1867–1890," *Agricultural History*, XXXVI (October, 1962), 200–206; Roy V. Scott, "Early Agricultural Education in Minnesota: The Institute Phase," *Agricultural History*, XXXVII (January, 1963), 21–34.

22. Bardolph, *Agricultural Literature and the Early Illinois Farmer*, pp. 67–89.

23. Demaree, *The American Agricultural Press*, pp. 196–230.

24. Samuel P. Hays, *The Response to Industrialism: 1885–1914* (Chicago: University of Chicago Press, 1957), pp. 1–3; Solon J. Buck, *The Granger Movement, 1870–1880* (Cambridge: Harvard University Press, 1913), pp. 286–87; Irwin Unger, *The Greenback Era* (Princeton: Princeton University Press, 1964), pp. 201–02, 202 n.

NOTES: *Chapter Two*

1. *Veterinarian: A Monthly Journal of Veterinary Science* (London), IV (May, 1831), 268–69; Edward Lisle, *Observations in Husbandry*, ed. by Thomas Lisle (London: J. Hughes, 1757), pp. 267, 273; John Lawrence, *A General Treatise on Cattle, the Ox, the Sheep and the Swine* (London:

Symonds ?, 1805), p. 17; Mabel E. Seebohm, *The Evolution of the English Farm* (London: Allen & Unwin, 1952), pp. 232, 268.

2. Some cattlemen claimed they could determine the age of an animal by its horns, since they contained certain characteristics that were a reliable

index of growth: "At three years of age the tip of the horn dropped off and at about the same time, a ridge or ring of thicker horn, is seen above . . . the root; and a new one appears on each successive year; so that if you count these ridges . . . and add two to them, you will have the age of the beast." *Veterinarian,* IV (May, 1831), 268–69. So widespread was the belief in these "tell-tale wrinkles" that in order to deceive buyers of oxen dealers often had them "rasped out of their horns." *Dwight's American Magazine and Family Newspaper* (New York), III (March 27, 1847), 207; Marvel [pseud.], *My Farm of Edgewood,* p. 106.

3. *American Farmer* (Baltimore), I (December 31, 1819), 315; III (February 22, 1822), 378. Since some farmers secured their animals in the stalls "with a cord round the horns," they held these appendages to be necessary. *Moore's Rural New-Yorker* (Rochester), XXIX (March 14, 1874), 171.

4. *Western Stock Journal and Farmer* (Cedar Rapids, Iowa), VIII (December, 1878), 135; XI (June, 1881), 129; *Hoard's Dairyman* (Fort Atkinson, Wisconsin), XVII (December 31, 1886), 6; XVIII (October 28, 1887), 4; *Ohio Farmer* (Cleveland), LXXI (May 14, 1887), 317.

5. Ohio State Board of Agriculture, *Report* (Columbus, 1889), pp. 129–33; *Breeder's Gazette* (Chicago), XV (January 2, 1889), 8.

6. Philadelphia Society for Promoting Agriculture, *Memoirs,* I (1808), 25–26; *Philadelphia Medical and Physical Journal,* I (November, 1804), 77–79; *Plough Boy* (Albany), II (September 9, 1820), 114; *Country Gentleman* (Albany), IX (September 17, 1857), 188. The horn's construction served as a thermometer for the early doctors who believed that it had a thinness at its base, and that by placing the hand there they could judge the extent of fever. *Veterinarian,* IV (May, 1831), 266.

7. *Farmers' Review* (Chicago), VIII (June 15, 1882), 376; Wisconsin State Agricultural Society, *Transactions* (Madison, 1887), pp. 271, 284, 287; *National Live-Stock Journal* (Chicago), IV (January 3, 1888), 10.

8. Ohio State Board of Agriculture, *Report* (1889), pp. 129–33; *Breeder's Gazette,* XV (January 30, 1889), 117. An authority at the University of Wisconsin estimated that more farmers were killed in a single year by bulls than by railway trains in rural areas. Wisconsin State Agricultural Society, *Transactions,* XXVI (1887), 284–87. A reporter stated that vicious bulls and hooking cows were responsible for the loss of 200 human lives and 200,000 cattle in a single year; the number of calves lost through abortions was impossible to determine. *Rural New-Yorker* (New York), XLV (August 7, 1886), 517; Iowa State Agricultural Society, *Report* (Des Moines, 1888), p. 29.

9. *Western Stock Journal and Farmer,* XI (June, 1881), 129; Ohio State Board of Agriculture, *Report* (1882), pp. 512–20. Wounds inflicted on cattle by goring each other were often reported in veterinary columns. *New England Farmer* (Boston), I (February 22, 1823), 232; XII (April 23, 1834), 325; *American Agriculturist* (New York), XLIV (January, 1885), 11.

10. *Western Stock Journal and Farmer,* XI (June, 1881), 129; *Cultivator and Country Gentleman* (Albany), L (November 3, 1885), 840; *American Farmer,* II (August 11, 1820), 158.

11. Wisconsin Agricultural Experiment Station, *Report* (Madison, 1886), pp. 19–21.

12. Ohio State Board of Agriculture, *Report* (1882), pp. 512–20; *Breeder's Gazette,* XIII (February 29, 1888), 208–209; Iowa State Agricultural Society, *Report* (1888), p. 29.

13. *Western Stock Journal and Farmer,* XI (July, 1881), 157–58; *Henry County News* (Geneseo, Illinois), November 5, 12, 1885. Horns were no serious problem when cattle were driven to market, but when loaded into railway cars, "as we pack herring in a barrel," and hauled from the "Mississippi River to the Seaboard they naturally suffer[ed] from the injuries of horns." *Western Stock Journal and Farmer,* VIII (December, 1878), 135. In an attempt to eliminate inhuman treatment in transit, a new type of "parlor stock car" was

created to lessen injuries and reduce frequency of unloading for food and water. *Ibid.*, XI (July, 1881), 157–58. A cowman relates in his reminiscences that even before loading, steers were sometimes brutalized by cutting one horn from each animal's head with an ax in order to mesh them closer together in the car. Angie Debo (ed.), *The Cowman's Southwest, being the Reminiscences of Oliver Nelson . . . 1878–1893* (Glendale: A. H. Clark & Company, 1953), pp. 73, 167.

14. *American Agriculturist*, XXXVIII (December, 1878), 468; *National Live-Stock Journal*, XV (March, 1884), 120. According to an English report for the 1881 crossing, 8,721 were thrown overboard, 498 were landed dead, while 472 arrived so injured and exhausted they had to be killed, making a total loss of 9,691 in the space of twelve months. *Farmers' Review* IX (August 3, 1882), 70.

15. *Rural New-Yorker*, XLVII (January 14, 1888), 20.

16. When the practice of removing horns first appeared in the British Isles, and later in the United States, the terminology varied in the two countries and for a period of time each determined its own usage. Should it be dis- or de-horning? After considerable debate in the journals, the Webster Publishing Company was asked for its expert opinion. Webster advised dropping the useless "s" and substituting "e" for "i" in the Latin prefix. However, English breeders insisted on retaining the original form because they did not wish to "yield the Shakespearean usage to American English." *Breeder's Gazette*, XI (March 10, 17, 1887), 372–73, 414; XIII (May 9, 1888), 465; *Prairie Farmer* (Chicago), LX (March 17, 1888), 171; Heman H. Haaff, *Haaff's Practical Dehorner, or Every Man His Own Dehorner* (Chicago: Clark & Longley & Company, 1888), p. 95.

17. *Rural New-Yorker*, XLI (December 9, 1882), 836; *Cultivator and Country Gentleman*, XL (June 10, 1875), 360.

18. *Cultivator* new series, I (February, 1844), 48; *Breeder's Gazette*, XI (April 4, 1887), 336.

19. *New England Farmer*, XXII (February 7, 1844), 254–55; *Cultivator*, new series, I (April, 1844), 108.

20. *Rural New-Yorker*, XLI (February 18, 1882), 107; Ohio State Board of Agriculture, *Report* (1889), pp. 129–33. *American Agriculturist*, XLVI (February, 1886), 50–51.

21. *Western Stock Journal and Farmer*, XI (October, 1881), 221; Ohio State Board of Agriculture, *Report* (1889), pp. 129–33. Polled cattle were unpopular for other reasons: stockmen had the notion that animals without the power of defense would huddle together and perspire excessively; this, they believed, led to respiratory diseases and loss of flesh. Buyers of cattle for fattening purposes passed up hornless animals on the grounds they could not defend themselves at the feeding ricks. *Farmers' Review*, XX (October 23, November 13, 27, 1889), 726, 780, 822.

22. *Western Stock Journal and Farmer*, XI (June, 1881), 129.

23. *Ibid.*, (February, 1881), 30–31. Where both horned and hornless animals were fed, housed or shipped together, horns presented a real menace. But hornless cattle fed alone at the ricks would drink, stand and huddle like sheep, making it possible to increase their number by one-third to one-half. They would herd without danger to each other, to cowboys, or their horses. *Farmer* (St. Paul), II (January 13, December 22, 1887), 23, 815; *American Agriculturist*, XLVI (February, 1886), 50–51. It was estimated that mulley cows afforded a saving of one-fourth the hay in the winter season, one-tenth the corn, one-half the lumber for sheds, and the many calves lost theretofore by abortion. All these savings in the aggregate would mean an increase of profits from 20 to 25 per cent. *Rural New-Yorker*, XLV (August 7, 1886), 517; Iowa State Agricultural Society, *Report* (1888), p. 29; *Western Stock Journal and Farmer*, XI (July, 1881), 157–58. Some horn fanciers insisted that polled cattle could still strike terrific blows with their heads and were by no means safe; removing the horns from a bull's head, they claimed, was no guarantee of docility. *Ohio Farmer* (Cleveland), LXXI

(April 16, 1887), 253; *Rural New-Yorker*, XLV (August 14, 1886), 318–19; *Breeder's Gazette*, XIII (May 9, 1888), 463–64.

24. *National Live-Stock Journal*, XV (May, 1884), 214; *Prairie Farmer*, LIX (March 12, 1887), 163; LX (July 14, 1888), 450; *Breeder's Gazette*, XII (November 17, 1887), 787; XV (January 16, February 6, March 6, 1889), 62, 145, 258.

25. In New York State by 1895 enthusiasm to remove horns had reached such proportions that prizes were offered for the best essay on how to perform the operation. *Rural New-Yorker*, LIV (December 28, 1895), 866.

26. This caustic compound is widely used today, and the removal of adult horns with saws of different types is still one of the routine methods. Jules J. Haberman, *The Farmer's Veterinary Handbook* (New York: Prentice-Hall, 1953), pp. 31–32.

27. Philadelphia Society for Promoting Agriculture, *Memoirs* I (1808), 25–26. A southern livestock editor reported that the practice was performed in his area by "one sweep of a strong, sharp pocket-knife" which forever after left the calf completely hornless. *Farmers' Review*, XVI (January 6, 1886), 5.

28. *Cultivator*, new series, I (July, 1844), 227; *American Agriculturist*, XXXVIII (November, 1879), 481. Scotland had an earlier procedure, called "doddiefying," performed just before cattle were housed in their winter quarters. The district veterinary surgeon contracted with the larger stock-raisers to poll the calves at so much per annum. *Breeder's Gazette*, XI (February 17, 1887), 247. In New Zealand horns were removed simultaneously with the branding of calves; both operations were effected with a red-hot iron. *Ibid.*

29. *Prairie Farmer*, LXI (March 23, 30, 1889), 179, 197; *Breeder's Gazette*, XV (February 13, 1889), 172–74.

30. *Farmers' Review*, XX (July 10, 1889), 478; *Rural Affairs* (Albany), V (1867–1869), 223; Robert Wallace, *Farm Live Stock of Great Britain* (5th ed. rev., assisted by J. A. Scott Watson; Edinburgh: Oliver & Boyd, 1923), pp. 303–5.

31. Rosamond Bayne-Powell, *English Country Life in the Eighteenth Century* (London: J. Murray, 1935), p. 138; *New England Farmer*, XI (July 25, 1832), 16; *American Agriculturist*, XXV (January, 1866), 13.

32. *Homestead* (Hartford), I (November 8, 1855), 124; IV (March 10, July 21, 1859), 397, 700; *Cultivator*, new series, I (January, 1853), 37; *Breeder's Gazette*, X (September 2, 1886), 249; XI (February 10, 1887), 207. Lopped horns could be rearranged by attaching to them at night a weight and pulley that was removed during the day. By keeping it fairly tight, horns could be refashioned in about six months' time. *New England Farrier* (3rd ed., Woodstock, Vermont, David Watson, 1824), p. 59; *Working Farmer* (New York), IV (December, 1852), 251.

33. *Veterinary Journal and Annals of Comparative Pathology* (London), III (September, 1876), 223; *Agricultural Gazette* (London), XXIX (April 22, May 20, 27, 1889), 370–71, 468, 489; *Rural New-Yorker*, XXXVI (September 14, 1878), 584.

34. Of the opinions rendered by twenty judges upon this subject in the lower courts, sixteen declared the practice legal; four pronounced it illegal. Cornell University Agricultural Experiment Station, *Bulletin 54* (Ithaca, 1893), 119. The legality of this practice was tested in several suits both in Ireland and Scotland and in all these cases, after many farmers and professional witnesses had given conflicting opinions on its cruelty, the right to dehorn was given judicial approval. *Agricultural Gazette*, XXXII (July 14, 1890), 33. Cattle-raisers in Australia were vitally interested in these cases. Their horned cattle had never known handling by men from the time they were branded as calves until they were rounded up for slaughter; in the process of getting these half-wild beasts into railway cars, cattle boats and stockyards, horns often became lethal weapons, ruining valuable stockhorses and killing their riders. *Ibid.*, XXXII (September 1, 1890), 199.

35. Donald P. Seymour, "A History of the Practice of Dehorning Cattle, 1885–1900" (unpublished Master's thesis,

History Department, Northern Illinois University, 1963), pp. 1–61.

36. *Geneseo Republic* (Geneseo, Illinois), January 29, 1886.

37. *Prairie Farmer*, LVIII (January 30, 1886), 68; *Hoard's Dairyman*, XVI (January 29, 1886), 3.

38. Seymour, "Dehorning Cattle, 1885–1900," pp. 18–36; *Portrait and Biographical Album of Henry County, Illinois* (Chicago: Biographical Publishing Company, 1885), pp. 651–53.

39. Seymour, "Dehorning Cattle, 1885–1900," pp. 18–36.

40. Haaff, *Haaff's Practical Dehorner*, pp. 46, 88–90; *Prairie Farmer*, LXI (March 9, 1889), 148–49. By 1887 dehorning had become a rural profession; practitioners traveled the countryside with patented tools and chutes, "topping off the horns at 15 cents a head." Some traveled widely and attracted crowds compared in size to those of the camp meeting period. A few dehorners became prominent. E. P. C. Webster of Marysville, Kansas, for example, covered several states and averaged about 100 animals per day. One dehorner stated that he had dehorned 3,552 cattle in slightly more than four months. Haaff claimed he was personally acquainted with at least ten dehorners who had removed tens of thousands; one had processed about 40,000 animals. Fees varied "from fifteen to twenty-five cents a head" usually depending upon such factors as the number in the herd, location, and special circumstances. *Farmer*, II (November 24, December 22, 1887), 741, 806; III (April 19, 1888), 263; Ohio State Board of Agriculture, *Report* (1889), p. 133; Haaff, *Haaff's Practical Dehorner*, pp. 34, 38, 46. Dehorners became so plentiful that the service was performed for ridiculously low fees. In some cases, as many as 100 cows were dehorned for as little as $5.00. Dehorners frequently placed posters in conspicuous spots; they offered to remove the horns for a few cents per head and in a more humane manner than others. *Breeder's Gazette*, XIV (August 29, 1888), 196–97; *Prairie Farmer*, LXI (February 16, October 19, 1889), 100, 680; Haaff, *Haaff's Practical Dehorner*, pp. 34, 38–39, 46, 88–90.

41. For a discussion of these crazes and some of their contributions to American agriculture, see Arthur H. Cole, "Agricultural Crazes, A Neglected Chapter in American History," *American Economic Review*, XVI (December, 1926), 622–39.

42. *Henry County News*, November 5, 12, 1885; February 4, 1886; *Geneseo Republic*, January 29, 1886.

43. *Chicago Tribune*, January 24, 28, 30, 1886; *Henry County News*, January 28, 1886.

44. *Henry County News*, January 28, February 4, 1886; *Geneseo Republic*, January 29, 1886.

45. *Geneseo Republic*, January 29, 1886; *Farmers' Review*, XVI (January 27, February 3, 10, 1886), 56, 72, 84–85.

46. Letters of protest against the practice poured into the metropolitan papers; one lengthy article signed by seven doctors, four of whom were veterinarians, strongly opposed this cruelty. *Chicago Tribune*, January 28, 30, 1886, pp. 6, 7.

47. *Farmers' Review*, XVI (February 3, 1886), 72; *Henry County News*, February 4, 1886.

48. *Rural New-Yorker*, XLVII (January 14, August 14, 1888), 20, 525; *National Live-Stock Journal*, IV (May 15, June 5, 1888), 311, 360.

49. *Farmer*, III (March 29, 1888), 199.

50. *Breeder's Gazette*, XV (June 12, 1889), 622; *Agricultural Gazette*, XXIX (May 20, 1889), 468; XXXII (July 14, 1890), 33.

51. *National Live-Stock Journal*, XVIII (September, 1887), 315–17; *Hoard's Dairyman*, XVIII (October 28, 1887), 4; *Farmer*, IV (July 12, 1888), 20; *Ohio Farmer*, LXXIII (May 12, 1888), 308.

52. *Breeder's Gazette*, XIV (September 5, October 17, November 7, 1888), 219, 384 ff., 468.

53. *Ibid.*, (October 17, November 7, 1888), 384 ff., 468.

54. *Ibid.*, (November 28, 1888), 552.

55. Haaff, *Haaff's Practical Dehorner*, p. 7.

56. *Northwestern Farmer and Breeder* (Fargo, North Dakota), VI (March, 1888), 48; *Jersey Bulletin* (Indianapolis), VI (January 5, 1887), 5; *Hoard's Dairyman*, XIX (April 13, 1888), 1; Wisconsin State Agricul-

tural Society, *Transactions,* XXVII (1888), 257–69. Dr. Horne claimed that dehorning would expose the brain and rot or deform the head to such an extent as to cause death. *Prairie Farmer,* LX (June 2, 1888), 359. He had manifested this same tendency for exaggeration a decade earlier when he described the newly-introduced barbed wire fencing as the "most dangerous and cruel fence ever invented. . . . a murderous, treacherous snare . . . [that] inflicts much suffering upon our domestic animals." *American Agriculturist,* XXXIX (June, 1880), 222–23; *Vick's Monthly Magazine* (Rochester), IV (March, 1881), 90.

57. *Farmers' Review,* XX (November 13, 1889), 780; *Northwestern Farmer and Breeder,* VI (March, 1888), 48. There was a belief that dehorning milk cows would reduce the flow of milk, change the butter fat content and even transform the butter color. *Rural New-Yorker,* XLVII (June 2, 23, 1888), 365, 412; *Breeder's Gazette,* XIV (November 7, 1888), 468.

58. *Hoard's Dairyman,* XVII (December 31, 1886), 6; *American Agriculturist,* XLVI (June, 1887), 245; XLVII (October, 1888), 412; *Cultivator and Country Gentleman,* L (January 20, 1887), 58; Iowa State Improved Stock-Breeders' Association, *Proceedings* (Des Moines, 1888), pp. 94–98.

59. *Hoard's Dairyman,* XVII (December 31, 1886), 6.

60. *Breeder's Gazette,* XI (February 10, 1887), 210; XV (February 13, 1889), 172–73.

61. *Farmer,* III (April 19, 1888), 263.

62. *Hoard's Dairyman,* XIX (April 13, 1888), 1.

63. *Prairie Farmer,* LX (August 4, 1888), 498. Appealing to feminine sensitivity, Dr. Horne pleaded with farm women to help him "put down this piece of brutality." *Jersey Bulletin,* VI (January 5, 1887), 5.

64. Wisconsin Agricultural Experiment Station, *Report* (1886), pp. 19–21.

65. *Farmer,* I (December 23, 1886), 523; II (January 1, 1887), 39; *Farmers' Review,* XVIII (January 12, 1887), 20; *Hoard's Dairyman,* XVII (December 10, 1886), 2.

66. *Hoard's Dairyman,* XVII (December 10, 1886), 2.

67. Wisconsin Agricultural Experiment Station, *Report* (1886), pp. 19–21.

68. *Ibid.* (1887), pp. 142–58.

69. U. S. Department of Agriculture, *Report* (Washington, Government Printing Office, 1892), p. 121; *House Executive Documents,* No. I, Pt. 7, 51 Cong. 1st Session (1889–1890), 526–27.

70. Ontario Commission on the Dehorning of Cattle, *Report* (Toronto: Warwick & Sons, 1892), pp. 9–23, 29.

71. *Ibid.*

72. *Ibid.*

73. The widespread opposition to dehorning in the United States and Canada on humanitarian grounds contrasts strangely with the prevalence in Anglo-Saxon tradition of brutal practices with animals that served no such essential need as did dehorning. Examples include docking and nicking of horses' tails for the purpose of giving the latest style of curve and elevation to suit the "morbid fancy of the horse dealer"; "bishoping" an older horse's teeth with a file so as to misrepresent its true age; or the intolerable practices of firing, blistering, drugging, and purging sick animals. Perhaps the worst cruelty to cattle was leaving them to fend for themselves in subzero weather without shelter or provisions. Many animals were severely mistreated for sheer entertainment; bulls and bears were inhumanly baited and goaded at public spectacles; horses were raced beyond their endurance for great distances; roosters and ganders were often used as objects of torture, and contests in which great weights or loads were hauled by pairs of oxen or horses for wagers or prizes frequently taxed the animals beyond their strength and capacity. David Mushet, *The Wrongs of the Animal World* (London: Hatchard & Son, 1839), *passim; New Sporting Magazine* (London), II (October, November, December, 1831), 3, 57–58, 133–36; James Carver, *The Farrier's Magazine* (Philadelphia: Littell & Henry, 1818), p. 43; *American Veterinary Journal* (Boston), I (February, 1852), 168; new series, III (August, 1858), 237–38; *Veterinary Record and Transactions of the Veterinary*

Medical Association (London), II (July, 1846), 247; *Rural Affairs*, I (1855–1857), 120; *Cincinnatus* (Cin-

cinnati), II (March, 1857), 134–35.
74. Ontario Commission on the Dehorning of Cattle, *Report, passim.*

NOTES: *Chapter Three*

1. *Northwestern Farmer and Horticultural Journal* (Dubuque), IV (July, 1859), 213–14; *National Live-Stock Journal* (Chicago), V (July, 1859), 255; *Nebraska Farmer* (Lincoln), new series, II (May, 1878), 79–80.
2. *Cultivator and Country Gentleman* (Albany), XLVIII (June 14, 1883), 478; *Breeder's Gazette* (Chicago), I (March 30, 1882), 455. Animals were injured and killed in large numbers on unfenced railroad rights of way during this period. See this author's "The Fencing of Western Railways," *Agricultural History*, XIX (July, 1945), 163.
3. *Valley Farmer* (St. Louis), XI (December, 1859), 372; Iowa State Agricultural Society, *Report* (1873), (Des Moines, 1874), p. 20; (1874), pp. 234–35; *National Live-Stock Journal*, I (September, 1870), 2.
4. *American Stock-Journal and Farmers' and Stock-Breeders' Advertiser* (Parkesburg, Pa.), IV (January, 1869), 3; *National Live-Stock Journal*, III (November, 1872), 390; *Scientific American* (New York), new series, XXVII (August 10, 1872), 83. Some farmers "allow the shoes to be worn just as long as they will stay on; often letting a poor horse do hard work with three, two or even one shoe on." *Nebraska Farmer*, new series, IV (May, 1880), 115.
5. *Western Farmer* (Madison), new series, VI (March 5, 1887), 153; *Medical Counselor* (Columbus, Ohio), II (February 16, 1856), 154–55; *Homestead* (Hartford), IV (February 3, 1859), 317.
6. *National Live-Stock Journal*, I (January, 1871), 137; *Prairie Farmer* (Chicago), new series, XXI (February 15, 1868), 100; *Rural New-Yorker* (New York), XXXVII (May 11, 1878), 295; *Farmers' Review* (Chicago), XI (September 13, 1883), 166. Blacksmiths were en-

dowed with a certain mystique; in some parts of the country they not only were horse-doctors but were even licensed to prescribe medicine for human beings and were considered just as capable as practitioners more "liberally educated." *Southern Quarterly Review* (Charleston, S. C.), IV (October, 1843), 474–75.
7. *National Live-Stock Journal*, X (September, 1879), 378; *Nebraska Farmer*, new series, II (May, 1878), 79–80. Sheep with grubs in the head would often have wires inserted into their nostrils in order to dislodge the parasites, or they would be shut up in a tight room for many hours, in the expectation that the foul air and heat would drive out the grubs. Iowa State Agricultural Society, *Report* (1874), pp. 234–35.
8. *American Stock-Journal and Farmers' and Stock-Breeders' Advertiser*, II (January, 1867), 15–16.
9. *Ibid.*; *Nebraska Farmer*, I (April, 1860), 77.
10. *Rural New-Yorker*, XXXVII (June 15, 1878), 375; *American Agriculturist* (New York), XL (July, 1881), 271; *Southern Cultivator* (Augusta, Ga.), XVI (August, 1858), 244; XIX (March, 1861), 96.
11. *Northwestern Farmer and Horticultural Journal*, VI (June, 1861), 203; *American Agriculturist*, XXXIX (January, 1880), 6–7. One of these peripatetic spavin-melters guaranteed cures for $10 with one-half "down" and the balance at a later date. *American Veterinary Journal* (Boston), new series, II (November, 1857), 341. In firing for founder, the frog of the foot was cleaned, turpentine applied, and then ignited. *Nebraska Farmer*, I (November, 1859), 29.
12. *Cultivator* (Albany), new series, V (February, 1857), 55; VI (April, 1858), 128; *Rural New-Yorker*, XXXVII (June 15, 1878), 375.

13. *Rural New-Yorker*, XXXVII (June 15, 1878), 375; *Country Gentleman* (Albany), X (July 9, 1857), 28.

14. *Cultivator*, new series, IV (May, 1856), 152; *American Stock-Journal and Farmers' and Stock-Breeders' Advertiser*, IV (June, 1869), 168; *American Veterinary Journal*, new series, II (November, 1857), 334, 341.

15. *American Stockman and Farmer* (Chicago), III (February 3, 1881), 2; *American Stock-Journal and Farmers' and Stock-Breeders' Advertiser*, IV (June, 1869), 168; VI (August, 1871), 241. In the spring, when fat and overfed, horses often were given as much as five drachmas of Barbadoes Aloes in the form of a ball or drench. *Michigan Farmer* (Detroit), new series, II (April 1, 1871), 104.

16. *Western Rural* (Chicago), XXIII (December 5, 1885), 773, 781; *Prairie Farmer*, new series, XVIII (December 1, 1866), 356; *Ohio Farmer* (Cleveland), LXX (September 25, 1886), 199. "Soot and Salt" were two common ingredients in these concoctions. Both were free and plentiful. Iowa State College Staff, *A Century of Farming in Iowa, 1846–1946* (Ames: Iowa State University Press, 1946), p. 340.

17. *Western Farmer*, new series, VI (March 5, 1887), 153; *Moore's Rural New-Yorker* (Rochester), XXXVI (July 7, 1877), 7.

18. Lewis C. Gray, *History of Agriculture in the Southern United States to 1860* (2 vols.; Washington: Carnegie Institution, 1933), II, 845. A Nebraska reporter stated that bleeding cattle in the spring, either from the "neck, vein or cutting their tails" was common in his community. *Nebraska Farmer*, II (December, 1861), 188.

19. *American Stock-Journal and Farmers' and Stock-Breeders' Advertiser*, II (May, December, 1867), 139, 364.

20. *National Live-Stock Journal*, X (June, 1879), 260; XI (February, 1880), 52–53; *Rural New-Yorker*, XXXVII (August 24, 1878), 539.

21. *National Live-Stock Journal*, XII (April, 1881), 157; *Nebraska Farmer*, new series, II (March, 1878), 36–37; *Rural New-Yorker*, XXXVII (June 15, 1878), 375.

22. *American Veterinary Review* (New York), VIII (January, 1885), 485–86.

23. *Ibid.*, (January, 1885), 454–56.

24. It was not only quack veterinarians who practiced this fraud but "even regular graduates . . . are often found laying claim to titles to which they have no right, and acting altogether in the most unprofessional manner." *National Live-Stock Journal*, IX (January, 1878), 2. Diplomas were not the only documents doctored and sold; pedigrees were also falsified and peddled for a handsome fee. *Northwestern Farmer and Horticultural Journal*, III (August, 1858), 258.

25. *Western Rural*, XXII (August 16, 1884), 523; *Prairie Farmer*, new series, XXI (February 15, 1868), 100.

26. *Ibid.; American Agriculturist*, XXXIX (October, 1880), 418–19. One Philadelphia diploma mill was closed in 1877 and the professor in charge at the time was fined $2,000 and sent to prison for nine months. *American Veterinary Review*, I (November, 1877), 301–303. In the case of medical schools, the situation was even worse. Diplomas were sold by the thousands by colleges located mainly in Philadelphia and Cincinnati. *Hearth and Home* (New York), V (April 20, 1872), 324; *Bistoury* (Elmira, N. Y.), VII (October, 1871), 295–96.

27. *National Live-Stock Journal*, VII (June, 1876), 250.

28. James H. Young, *The Toadstool Millionaires* (Princeton: Princeton University Press, 1961); Stewart H. Holbrook, *The Golden Age of Quackery* (New York: Macmillan, 1959).

29. *Michigan Farmer*, new series, XIII (October 24, 1882), 4; *Ohio Farmer*, LXX (September 25, 1886), 199; *American Agriculturist*, XXXIX (October, 1880), 418–19.

30. *Prairie Farmer*, LI (February 28, 1880), 68; *Western Rural*, XXIII (December 5, 1885), 773, 781. It was reported that more than 1,000 cures for colic alone were in existence. *Bistoury*, VIII (April, 1872), 15.

31. *National Live-Stock Journal*, XII (April, 1881), 157; *Western Rural*, XXIII (September 26, 1885), 613.

32. *National Live-Stock Journal*, V (July, 1874), 255; VI (November, 1875),

436; *Nebraska Farmer*, new series, II (May, 1878), 79–80.

33. *Ohio Farmer*, LXX (September 25, 1886), 199; *National Live-Stock Journal*, XII (June, 1881), 263; *American Agriculturist*, XXXIX (May, 1880), 176.

34. *American Stockman and Farmer*, III (January 20, 1881), 7; *National Live-Stock Journal*, XI (December, 1880), 530–31; XII (January, 1881), 28–29; Stanley V. Deming, "Nineteenth Century Hog Cholera: Its History and Social Effects," (unpublished Master's thesis, History Department, Northern Illinois University, 1965), pp. 50–65.

35. *American Agriculturist*, XXI (March, 1862), 69; *National Live-Stock Journal*, XI (December, 1880), 531.

36. *Orange Judd Farmer* (Chicago), V (February 23, 1889), 114.

37. *Michigan Farmer*, new series, II (November 25, 1871), 370. So ineffective were cholera cures that the Nebraska legislature in 1878 was urged to offer $10,000 reward for a proven remedy. *Nebraska Farmer*, new series, IV (December, 1880), 285.

38. *National Live-Stock Journal*, XII (June, 1881), 233; *Western Home* (Chicago), III (January, 1870), Supplement; *American Agriculturist*, XLIV (August, 1885), 342.

39. *Nebraska Farmer*, new series, I (January, 1877), 6; II (January, 1878), 2; *National Live-Stock Journal*, I (March, 1871), 213; XIII (October, 1882), 447; *Cultivator and Country Gentleman*, L (April 9, 1885), 313.

40. *Nebraska Farmer*, new series, IV (June, 1880), 149.

41. *National Live-Stock Journal*, XII (June, 1881), 233; *Western Stock Journal and Farmer* (Cedar Rapids, Ia.), XI (January, 1881), 19.

42. *Prairie Farmer*, new series, XVIII (December 1, 1867), 356; *Farmer* (St. Paul), II (December 15, 1887), 791. Fees for early untrained horsedoctors ranged from $1 to $2 per trip to the farm. Wisconsin State Agricultural Society, *Transactions* (Madison, 1874), XI (1873), 343.

43. *Western Rural*, XXII (May 17, 1884), 312; *Western Stock Journal and Farmer*, VIII (October, 1878), 90–92.

44. *Moore's Rural New-Yorker*, XXXIV (October 28, 1875), 281.

45. *The Veterinarian* (London), I (January, February, October, 1828), 26–28, 37–43, 410–11; Sir Frederick Smith, *The Early History of Veterinary Literature and Its British Development* (4 vols.; London: Baillière & Company, 1919–1933), IV, 15–33; Orlando C. Bradley, *History of the Edinburgh Veterinary College* (Edinburgh: Oliver & Boyd, 1923), pp. 6 ff.

46. *New England Farmer* (Boston), XVII (August 8, 1838), 35; XIX (February 10, 1841), 250–51; *Library and Monthly Journal of Agriculture* (New York), I (May, 1846), 547–52; II (April, 1847), 487; *Cultivator*, new series, VIII (April, 1860), 136; *Prairie Farmer*, IX (February, 1849), 58; *Farmer's Journal* (Cedar Rapids, Ia.), I (May, 1872), 5. See Everett M. Rogers, "Agricultural Magic and Technological Change" (paper read before the Ohio Valley Sociological Society, May 3, 1958, in Cincinnati, Ohio). See Introduction, Chapter I, pp. 7–8.

47. One authority in this field has reported 467 different signs and superstitions found in American rural communities. One-fourth referred to climate and weather, while the majority pertained to plants and animals. Carl C. Taylor, *Rural Sociology* (New York: Harper & Brothers, 1933), p. 145.

48. *Rural New-Yorker*, XXXVII (August 24, 1878), 538–39; *National Live-Stock Journal*, VI (December, 1875), 463; VII (June, 1876), 243–44.

49. *Medical Counselor*, II (February 16, 1856), 154–55; *Western Rural*, XXIV (January 2, 1886), 8.

50. *Western Rural*, XXII (July 16, 1884), 523; XXIV (July 17, 1886), 461; *American Stock-Journal and Farmers' and Stock-Breeders' Advertiser*, II (May, 1867), tiser, II (May, 1867), 100.

51. *Rural New-Yorker*, XXXVII (December 14, 1878), 796; *National Live-Stock Journal*, IX (January, 1878), 2.

52. *Moore's Rural New-Yorker*, XXXVI (January 20, 1877), 44. Canada had a veterinary college patterned after English veterinary schools, and it attracted a number of students from the United States. *National Live-Stock*

Journal, VII (June, 1876), 243; *Farmers' Review* XI (September 13, 1883), 166.

53. *Colman's Rural World* (St. Louis), XXXVI (January 25, 1883), 5; *American Veterinary Review,* X (May, 1886), 87–89.

54. *Journal of American Veterinary Medicine Association* (Ithaca), new series, XXVII (May, 1929), 915–17.

55. *Ibid.* The 46 veterinarians listed in the 1850 census were distributed as follows: New York, 20; Ohio, 8; Massachusetts, 5; Indiana, 5; Illinois, 4; Virginia, 2; Vermont, 1; and the District of Columbia, 1.

56. *American Veterinary Review,* III (December, 1879), 373–78; Kansas State Board of Agriculture, *First Quarterly Report* (Topeka, 1885), pp. 82–84; United States Department of Agriculture, *Yearbook* (1956), p. 2.

57. *American Veterinary Review,* VIII (January, 1885), 454–56; *American Agriculturist,* XXIX (November, 1870), 405; XXXVII (October, 1878), 378; *Nebraska Farmer,* new series, IV (June, 1880), 140.

58. *American Veterinary Review,* II (May, 1878), 89–90; *Journal of Comparative Medicine and Surgery* (New York), VIII (October, 1887), 393–94; *Prairie Farmer,* LIX (November 26, 1887), 768.

59. *Western Rural,* XXII (April 19, 1884), 252; *Prairie Farmer,* LIX (June 4, 1887), 364; United States Department of Agriculture, *Yearbook* (1897), pp. 236–58. By 1890, laws regulating the practice of veterinary science had been enacted in New York, Wisconsin, New Jersey, and Pennsylvania. Bert W. Bierer, *A Short History of Veterinary Medicine in America* (East Lansing: Michigan State University Press, 1955), pp. 86–87.

NOTES: *Chapter Four*

1. Edward S. Guthrie, *The Book of Butter: A Text on the Nature, Manufacture and Marketing of the Product* (1st. ed.; New York: Macmillan Company, 1920), pp. 1–6.

2. United States Department of Agriculture, *Yearbook* (Washington, Government Printing Office, 1900) (1899), pp. 384–86; Edward Wiest, *The Butter Industry in the United States* ("Columbia University Studies in History, Economics, and Public Law," Vol. LXIX ² [New York: Columbia University Press, 1916]), pp. 11–13, 20, 126–29.

3. United States Commissioner of Agriculture, *Report* (Washington: Government Printing Office, 1874) (1873), p. 247; United States Department of Agriculture, *Yearbook* (1899), pp. 400–401; William R. Pabst, *Butter and Oleomargarine: An Analysis of Competing Commodities* ("Columbia University Studies in History, Economics, and Public Law," No. 427 [New York: Columbia University Press, 1937]), pp. 11–15, 18, 20–21.

4. *National Live-Stock Journal* (Chicago), I (December, 1870), 115; United States Commissioner of Internal Revenue, *Report* (Washington: Government Printing Office, 1886–1887), pp. cli–cliii; *Popular Science Monthly* (New York), VI (November, 1874), 122–23; XIV (December, 1878), 249–50.

5. By 1872 a *Société Anonyme Alimentation* was organized with a capitalization of 800,000 francs for the purpose of using the Megè-Mouriès discoveries. Two factories were opened in Paris and Nancy—the one in Paris producing 120,000 pounds daily by 1882. Soon thereafter other factories were established in Munich, Frankfort, Dresden, Berlin, Vienna, etc. *Kansas City Review of Science and Industry,* VI (September, 1882), 317.

6. Wiest, *The Butter Industry,* pp. 216–21; Pabst, *Butter and Oleomargarine,* pp. 18–20, 31.

7. *Senate Miscellaneous Documents,* No. 131, 49 Congress, 1st Session, (1885–1886), p. 104; *Prairie Farmer*

(Chicago), LVI (April 5, 1884), 213; Iowa State Agricultural Society, *Report* (Des Moines, 1881) (1880), pp. 20–21; *Colman's Rural World* (St. Louis), XXXVIII (May 14, 1885), 159.

8. *Bistoury* (Elmira, N. Y.), IX (January, 1874), 206.

9. *Moore's Rural New-Yorker* (Rochester), XXXIV (December 23, 1876), 412; *Rural New-Yorker* (New York), XXXVII (December 7, 1878), 778; *Nebraska Farmer* (Lincoln), new series, I (April, 1877), 8; *Prairie Farmer*, LV (May 5, 1883), 277; *Ohio Farmer* (Cleveland), LXVIII (November 14, 1885), 312.

10. *Cultivator and Country Gentleman* (Albany), L (January 22, 1885), 77; *Farmers' Review* (Chicago), VI (March 3, 1881), 129; *Western Rural* (Chicago), XXII (April 19, 1884), 251; XXIV (January 9, 1886), 27.

11. Illinois Department of Agriculture, *Transactions* (Springfield, 1881), p. 354; *Western Rural*, XX (March 18, 1882), 81. A leading editor stated that oleomargarine was a combination of filth, dead animals, and waste fat all thrown together, rendered and sold by its producers; and wherever it was manufactured one could detect a smell and stench beyond description as well as the accompanying pile of bones and meat scraps piled high around the building. *Cultivator and Country Gentleman*, L (January 22, 1885), 77. Another reporter, no doubt prejudiced, insisted that during epidemics of hog cholera the dead ones were gathered up from farm to farm and delivered on railroad cars to the large packers in Chicago. *Western Stock Journal and Farmer*, XII (February, 1882), 38; Illinois Department of Agriculture, *Transactions*, XVIII (1880), 354. Bogus butter opponents included a number of physicians who attributed certain outbreaks of cholera in Chicago to it since it was made from contaminated and unrefined lard. *Farmers' Review*, VI (March 3, 1881), 129.

12. Illinois Department of Agriculture, *Transactions*, XVIII (1880), 354; United States Department of Agriculture, *Yearbook* (1895), pp. 449–50.

13. The controversy over purity between butter and oleomargarine finally centered on the sources of fat from which they were produced; butter interests claimed that the cream came directly from the *glands* in the udder, while oleo interests claimed that oils came from such fats as lard, tallow or suet in the *tissues* of the cow. Upon the differences between these two sources rested much of the heated argument as to whether or not disease germs and larvae could be transmitted to the human stomach. To butter proponents *secreted* fat was cleaner and safer than *deposited* or *stored* fat. *Rural New-Yorker*, XXXVII (December 7, 1878), 778.

14. *Western Rural*, XXII (December 13, 1884), 800; XXIV (April 24, 1886), 267; *Popular Science Monthly*, XIV (December, 1878), 249; *National Live-Stock Journal*, X (August, 1879), 350–51; XI (May, 1880), 208–209; *Nebraska Farmer*, new series, I (April, 1877), 8.

15. A few journalists and scientists attempted to be objective in this controversy. Professor Wiley in the Bureau of Chemistry sought opinions of various chemists and microscopists and in his published report stated that "about nine out of ten . . . who have expressed themselves declare a belief that properly made oleomargarine is unobjectionable and wholesome." *Western Farmer* (Madison), new series, VI (April 9, 1887), 225; United States Department of Agriculture, *Yearbook* (1895), p. 447.

16. *Ohio Farmer*, LXVIII (November 14, 1885), 309; *Chagrin Falls Exponent* (Ohio), December 17, 1885; January 14, February 25, 1886.

17. *Western Rural*, XIX (December 17, 1881), 405; XXII (February 2, 1884), 75; *Ohio Farmer*, LXVIII (December 19, 1885), 392; LXIX (January 30, 1886), 72. Petitions from citizens from many dairy states were mailed to Congressmen protesting certain evils of oleomargarine. *Congressional Record*, 45 Congress, 2nd Session (1878–1879), pp. 3642–43.

18. *Western Rural*, XVIII (November 20, December 4, 1880), 372, 388.

19. *Scientific American* (New York), new series, XXVI (February, 3, 1872), 89; *Horticulturist* (Albany), XVII

(July, 1862), 342–44; *Leslie's Illustrated Weekly Newspaper* (New York), LV (February 3, 1883), 387.
20. *Ohio Farmer*, LXX (November 6, 1886), 291.
21. *Ibid.*, LXVIII (July 18, November 21, 1885), 40, 322.
22. Wisconsin State Agricultural Society, *Transactions* (Madison, 1880), XVIII (1879–1880), 180; *Farmers' Review*, XII (April 17, 1884), 289.
23. *Rural New-Yorker*, XXXVII (February 16, 1878), 108; XXXV (March 17, 1877), 166; *National Live-Stock Journal*, VI (July, 1875), 274; *Farmer* (St. Paul), I (June 3, 1886), 55; II (December 22, 1887), 808–809. Large producers operated mostly in Chicago, but exporters were concentrated in Boston and New York. Complaints were made that this latter group was shipping oleomargarine abroad mislabeled as butter, causing foreign buyers of butter from the United States to reduce their purchases. Many foreign countries protested this deception, for they had prohibited the sale of colored margarine and attempted to rigorously enforce their laws. *American Stockman and Farmer* (Chicago), III (February 17, 1881), 8–9; *Coleman's Rural World*, XXXIV (October 6, 1881), 319; *American Agriculturist* (New York), XLIV (March, 1885), 106.
24. *Colman's Rural World*, XXXVIII (May 14, 1885), 159.
25. Wiest, *The Butter Industry*, pp. 216–18, 239.
26. *National Live-Stock Journal*, IX (February, 1878), 73; *Farmer*, II (January 13, 1887), 22.
27. *Western Stock Journal and Farmer* (Cedar Rapids, Iowa), IX (March, 1879), 43; Ohio State Board of Agriculture, *Report* (Columbus, 1885), XXXIX (1884), 444.
28. *Prairie Farmer*, LVII (April 18, 1885), 24.
29. *Ibid.*; *Northwestern Farmer and Horticultural Journal* (Dubuque), III (November, 1858), 365; *Farmer's Journal* (Cedar Rapids, Iowa), III (November, 1874), 171; Guthrie, *The Book of Butter*, p. 161.
30. *American Stockman and Farmer*, III (February 10, 1881), 6.
31. *National Live-Stock Journal*, IX (February, 1878), 73; *Western Stock*

Journal and Farmer, XI (August, 1881), 197.
32. *National Live-Stock Journal*, III (February, 1872), 59; IX (February, 1878), 73.
33. *Rural New-Yorker*, XXXVII (February 16, 1878), 108. In order to avoid a loss, grocers tried to sell the better grades for a higher price and then "lose on the poorest"; as a result, makers of good butter lost unless they could locate select clients willing to pay premium prices for a good product. *Ibid.* Really good butter-makers were scarce, but they were usually discovered. Their butter was often singled out by the local grocers and funneled upward to the leading commission merchants in distant cities. *American Stockman and Farmer*, III (February 10, 1881), 6.
34. *Michigan Farmer*, new series, IV (September 16, 1873), 273; *American Agriculturist*, XIX (June, 1860), 175. The loss of the better producers apparently did not affect the total output, for by 1884 the farm dairies were making at least 80% of the nation's butter supply. Ohio State Board of Agriculture, *Report*, XXXIX (1884), 444.
35. *Prairie Farmer*, L (June 7, 1879), 181.
36. *Chicago Tribune*, September 26, 1879, p. 12; *Nebraska Farmer*, new series, IV (December, 1880), 285. Restoring and preserving butter became a regular industry during the heyday of rancid butter, and some of the formulas were considered of such value that patents were issued on them. *National Live-Stock Journal*, X (May, August, 1879), 215, 350–51. Renovated butter was mainly the residue of that not consumed locally. It was collected from, or shipped by, the storekeepers to these renovating firms, in whose plants it was melted at a certain temperature, causing the impurities to rise, after which they were skimmed off so that the pure oil that remained was used. It was then churned with fresh milk, colored and salted. Some companies were accused of using certain chemicals in the process; however, the patent was usually obtained on the method used to eliminate faulty odors. *Ohio Farmer*, LXXI (June 4, 1887), 365. Some

producers were so deft in their product packaging and labeling that they could sell it as creamery butter without detection. *Ibid.;* Wiest, *The Butter Industry,* pp. 16, 132, 229–30.

37. *Michigan Farmer,* new series, IV (September 16, 1893), 273; *American Stockman and Farmer,* III (February 10, 1881), 6.

38. *National Live-Stock Journal,* III (February, 1872), 59; *Western Stock Journal and Farmer,* XI (February, 1881), 31; *Western Rural,* XXIII (December 5, 1885), 779.

39. United States Commissioner of Agriculture, *Report* (1879), p. 77.

40. *Nebraska Farmer,* new series, IV (December, 1880), 285; *Farmers' Review,* VI (May 12, 1881), 289; *Ohio Farmer,* LXVIII (December 19, 1885), 392; *National Live-Stock Journal,* XI (May, 1880), 208–209. The Iowa Grange was so opposed to oleomargarine producers that it recommended criminal penalties for individuals who failed to brand it by its true name. *Proceedings* (Des Moines ?) No. 16 (1885), p. 16; No. 18 (1887), p. 10; No. 20 (1889), p. 27. The Ohio Grange also moved against the "bogus butter" interests by drawing up petitions and circulating them in the counties throughout the state for farmers to sign. These petitions requested legislation to protect them from this "illegal practice." *Ohio Farmer,* LXVIII (November 14, December 19, 1885), 309, 392.

41. *Ibid.,* LXIX (May 22, 1886), 348; *Western Rural,* XXIII (October 24, November 28, 1885), 677, 763.

42. *Prairie Farmer,* LVII (August 8, 1885), 501; *Western Rural,* XXVII (May 25, 1889), 331; Wiest, *The Butter Industry,* pp. 239–41.

43. *American Agriculturist,* XXXIX (April, 1880), 132.

44. *Scientific American,* LXIX (July 15, 1893), 34.

45. *Colman's Rural World,* XXXVIII (February 12, 1885), 52.

46. *Senate Miscellaneous Document,* No. 131, 49 Congress, 1st Session (1885–1886), pp. 1–274; Wiest, *The Butter Industry,* pp. 234–35.

47. *Prairie Farmer,* LVI (July 19, 1884), 452; *American Agriculturist,* XLIV (August, 1885), 327; *Ohio Farmer,* LXVIII (July 4, 1885), 8. The re-

peal of the New York law created a furor throughout the butter-producing states since this state was the largest consumer of this product. Dairy farmers were urged to unite with those in the Empire State and fight the issue through to the Supreme Court. *American Agriculturist,* XLVI (July, 1887), 292; Pabst, *Butter and Oleomargarine,* pp. 29–30.

48. *American Agriculturist,* XLVII (June, 1888), 266; Wiest, *The Butter Industry,* p. 241.

49. The butter-makers regarded Philip Armour as their principal enemy. They claimed Armour was not only the largest manufacturer of "hog butter" but was also responsible for preventing restrictive legislation in some of the states. *Ohio Farmer,* LXX (July 24, 1886), 53; *Western Rural,* XXIV (February 27, 1886), 139. Manufacturing plants, according to the Internal Revenue Office, were located in the following cities: Chicago had 11 factories; New York, Providence (R. I.), Cleveland, and Philadelphia had 3 each; Denver, Brooklyn, and Pawtucket (R. I.), had 2 each; and 8 other cities had one each. There were 259 wholesale dealers in the major cities. *Ohio Farmer,* LXXI (June 18, 1887), 400. In percentages, distribution of the output was as follows: Chicago packers produced about one-third of the total; the larger independents another third; and the smaller ones the remainder. Pabst, *Butter and Oleomargarine,* pp. 20–21, 27–28.

50. *Political Science Quarterly* (Boston), II (December, 1887), 545–47; *Cong. Rec.,* 49 Cong. 1st Sess. (1885–1886), XVII, *passim.*

51. For the complete testimony before the Senate Committee on Agriculture and Forestry covering the manufacture and sale of imitation dairy products, see *Senate Miscellaneous Documents,* No. 131, 49 Congress, 1st Session (1885–1886), pp. 1–274.

52. *Ibid.,* pp. 215–17.

53. See Stanley Deming, "Nineteenth Century Hog Cholera: Its History and Social Effects," pp. 1–77.

54. *Senate Miscellaneous Documents,* 131, 49 Congress, 1st Session (1885–1886), p. 45.

55. *Ibid.,* pp. 45–46. It was also claimed that the Treasury Department had re-

ceived information that soap grease was produced from deceased hogs, formerly kept in the distilleries for the purpose of eating up the swill. *Ibid.*, p. 46.

56. *Ibid.*, p. 11.

,57. *Statistical Abstracts of the United States* (Washington: Government Printing Office, 1889) (1888), p. 105.

58. *Ibid.*

59. *Senate Miscellaneous Documents*, No. 131, 49 Congress, 1st Session (1885–1886), p. 203.

60. *Prairie Farmer*, LI (April 10, 1880), 117; *American Agriculturist*, XL (September, 1881), 350–51.

61. *Transactions*, XIX (1881), 417.

62. *Senate Miscellaneous Documents*, No. 131, 49 Congress, 1st Session (1885–1886), pp. 47 ff.

63. *Ibid.*, p. 191.

64. *Ibid.*, pp. 267–68.

65. *Farmer*, I (July 22, August 26, 1886), 165, 246; *Michigan Farmer*, new series, XVII (August 3, 1886), 7. Much credit was given the American Agricultural and Dairy Association for its work in supporting this measure. It reported that more than $7,000 was raised under the able leadership of Joseph H. Reall; part of this money came from his own pocket. *Farmer*, I (August 26, 1886), 246; *Western Farmer and Wisconsin State Grange, Bulletin*, V (August 21, 1886), 7. The bill passed the House quickly, but Senate passage proved more difficult. Initially it had a close call when a single vote saved it from going to the unfavorable Finance Committee. It passed only after the tax had been lowered from ten to two cents per pound. *Ohio Farmer*, LXX (August 21, 1886), 120.

66. James D. Richardson (ed.), *A Compilation of the Messages and Papers of the Presidents, 1789–1908* (11 vols.; Washington, D. C.: Bureau of National Literature and Art, 1908), VIII, 407–9.

67. *Ohio Farmer*, LXX (August 21, 1886), 120; United States Department of Agriculture, Bureau of Chemistry, *Bulletin*, No. 13, Pt. I, "Foods and Food Adulterants" (Washington: Government Printing Office, 1887), pp. 5–24. For scientific testimony see pp. 16–35; for the law, see Gilman G. Udell, *Laws Relating to Agriculture* (Washington: Government Printing Office, 1958), pp. 376-78.

68. Pabst, *Butter and Oleomargarine*, p. 31. For a concise study of oleomargarine in the nineteenth and twentieth centuries see Eric E. Lampard, *Rise of the Dairy Industry in Wisconsin: A Study of Agricultural Change, 1820–1920* (Madison: State Historical Society of Wisconsin, 1963), pp. 257–66.

69. *Scientific American*, LXXI (July 21, 1894), 39; Oscar E. Anderson, *The Health of a Nation: Harvey W. Wiley and the Fight for Pure Food* (Chicago: University of Chicago Press, 1958), p. 194. It did decline, however, in some states due to certain regulatory measures. For example, in Minnesota there were 4,000,000 pounds shipped into the state in 1884, but in a few years, due to the enactment of the state and federal laws, it had been reduced as much as two-thirds. Edward V. Robinson, *Early Economic Conditions and the Development of Agriculture in Minnesota* (Minneapolis: University of Minnesota Press, 1915), p. 113.

NOTES: *Chapter Five*

1. Newell L. Sims, *The Rural Community, Ancient and Modern* (Chicago: Charles Scribner's Sons, 1920), pp. 94–99; William B. Weeden, *Economic and Social History of New England, 1620–1789* (2 vols.; Boston: Houghton, Mifflin & Company, 1890), I, 51–62; Isabel M. Calder, *The New Haven Colony* (New Haven: Yale University Press, 1934), pp. 152–54; Percy W. Bidwell, "Rural Economy in New England at the Be-

ginning of the Nineteenth Century,"
Connecticut Academy of Arts and Sciences, *Transactions*, XX (April,
1916), 321–22. Dutch settlers
along the Hudson River farmed in
common; "each and every one is
obliged and bound to make and kepe
his owne fence." Sims, *Rural Community*, pp. 80–94.

2. Hugh Jones, *The Present State of
Virginia*, ed. by Richard L. Morton
(Chapel Hill: University of North
Carolina Press, 1956), pp. 76–77;
Philip A. Bruce, *Economic History of
Virginia in the Seventeenth Century*
(2 vols.; New York: Macmillan &
Company, 1896), I, 316–18; Lewis C.
Gray, *History of Agriculture*, I, 146–
47, 149, 200; Ernest L. Bogart and
Charles M. Thompson, *Readings in
the Economic History of the United
States* (New York: Longmans, Green
& Company, 1916), pp. 35–36, 41.

3. Walter W. Hening (ed.), *Statutes at
Large; being a Collection of all the
Laws of Virginia, 1619–1792* (13
vols.; Richmond: n.p., 1809–1823), I,
176, 199, 332; Alexander J. Dallas
(ed.), *Laws of the Commonwealth of
Pennsylvania, 1781–1801* (4 vols.;
Philadelphia and Lancaster: Hall &
Seller, 1793–1801), II, 188–89;
Ransom H. Tyler, *A Treatise on the
Law of Boundaries and Fences* (Al-
bany: W. Gould & Son, 1874), pp.
361–504; Theodore C. Pease (ed.),
"Laws of the Northwest Territory,
1788–1800," Illinois State Historical
Library, *Collections* (Springfield,
1925), XVII, 46–51, 235, 347–50.

4. *Farmers' Register* (Shellbanks, Petersburg, Virginia), VIII (January
31, 1840), 23.

5. Charles L. Flint, *The American
Farmer* (2 vols.; Hartford: R. H.
Clark & Company, 1882), I, 563.

6. *American Farmer* (Baltimore), I
(March 24, 1820), 412; Percy W.
Bidwell and John I. Falconer, *History
of Agriculture in the Northern United
States, 1620–1860* (Washington,
D. C.: Carnegie Institution, 1925), p.
121; Bruce, *Economic History of Vir-
ginia*, I, 316–18.

7. Jones, *Present State of Virginia*, pp.
76–77; Bruce, *Economic History of
Virginia*, I, 316–18.

8. *New England Farmer* (Boston), VII
(April 24, 1829), 318; X (March 7,

1832), 270; Weeden, *Economic and
Social History*, I, 51–62; Bidwell
and Falconer, *History of Agriculture
in the Northern United States*, pp. 21,
121.

9. Cyrus Bryant to Sarah Bryant,
Princeton, Illinois, April 1, 1833, in
the Bureau County Historical Society,
Princeton, Illinois; John C.
Fitzpatrick (ed.), *The Diaries of
George Washington, 1748–1799* (4
vols.; New York: Houghton, Mifflin &
Company, 1925), III, 166, 286,
289; Ulrich B. Phillips, *American
Negro Slavery* (New York: D. Apple-
ton & Company, 1918), pp. 207–208,
231. Splitting was done with wooden
wedges or "gluts" as they were called
by the backwoodsman. Daniel Drake,
Pioneer Life in Kentucky, ed. by
Charles D. Drake (Cincinnati:
R. Clarke & Company, 1870), pp. 67,
70.

10. Felix Flügel and Harold U. Faulkner
(eds.), *Readings in the Economic and
Social History of the United States*
(New York: Harper & Brothers,
1929), pp. 137–38; *American
Farmer*, IV (May 10, 1822), 49–50.

11. Drake, *Pioneer Life in Kentucky*, p.
70; Timothy Flint, *The History and
Geography of the Mississippi Valley*
(2 vols.; Cincinnati: E. H. Flint &
L. R. Lincoln, 1832), I, 184–87,
190–92. Southern fence-building was
not performed exclusively by male
slaves; some slave-owners delegated
fence-building tasks of a lighter nature to slave women. Fitzpatrick, *Diaries of George Washington*, III,
171, 199, 205, 294; Gray, *History of
Agriculture in the Southern United
States*, I, 553–54.

12. Sir James Caird, *Prairie Farming in
America* (London: Longman, Brown,
Green, Longmans & Roberts, 1859),
p. 15; Fitzpatrick, *Diaries of George
Washington*, III, 166, 286, 289, 293;
American Farmer, I (February 4,
1820), 358–59. A settler on the Des
Plaines River near Chicago, made 75
daily recordings in his "Day-Book"
pertaining to cutting, drawing and
laying of rails between January 1 and
June 14, 1836. Many entries repre-
sented only a few hours' work per day.
Augustus H. Conant, "Day-Book"
(Des Plaines, Illinois: 1836–1853),

in the Chicago Historical Society Library.

13. *American Farmer*, I (March 10, 1820), 396; *Southern Agriculturist* (Charleston), new series, V (July, 1845), 257; *Prairie Farmer* (Chicago), III (February, 1843), 44; Henry W. Ellsworth, *Valley of the Upper Wabash, Indiana* (New York: Pratt, Robinson & Company, 1838), pp. 50–51.

14. *New England Farmer*, XX (November 10, 1841), 148; *Prairie Farmer*, III (February, 1843), 44. In the West, rails were accepted at general stores in payment of bills at figures ranging from 37 to 55 cents per hundred. John Edgar's, "Account-Book" (Kaskaskia, Illinois Territory, 1810), p. 14; William Morrison's, "Account-Book" (Kaskaskia, 1817), p. 4, both in the Chicago Historical Society Library.

15. Flügel and Faulkner, *Readings in the Economic and Social History of the United States*, pp. 309, 393.

16. *Ibid.*, pp. 137–38; *American Farmer*, II (August 11, 1820), 158; Ulrich B. Phillips (ed.), *Plantation and Frontier Documents: 1649–1863.* (In *Documentary History of American Industrial Society*, I–II [Cleveland: Arthur H. Clark & Company, 1909]), II, 276.

17. It was estimated that only about one-half the amount of timber was necessary for this type and only about one-sixth to one-third the land space. *Prairie Farmer*, V (March, 1845), 80; Flint, *American Farmer*, I, 563; Flügel and Faulkner, *Readings in the Economic and Social History of the United States*, p. 309.

18. VII (April 24, 1829), 318; Bidwell and Falconer, *History of Agriculture in the Northern United States*, p. 21.

19. *American Agriculturist* (New York), III (June, 1844), 180; Gray, *History of Agriculture in the Southern United States*, I, 540.

20. Fitzpatrick, *Diaries of George Washington*, III, 199, 204, 289; William Oliver, *Eight Months in Illinois, With Information to Emigrants* (Chicago: W. M. Hill, 1924), pp. 239–41. In Illinois, Morris Birkbeck taught early settlers the English technique of combining ditch, bank and rail into a fence. C. Dewitt Hardy, "The Influ-

ence of Morris Birkbeck in Illinois, 1817–1825," (unpublished Master's thesis, History Department, Northwestern University, 1934), pp. 33–35.

21. Flügel and Faulkner, *Readings in the Economic and Social History of the United States*, pp. 137–38.

22. *New England Farmer*, IX (February 4, 1831), 228.

23. *American Farmer*, III (August 10, 1821), 160.

24. United States Commissioner of Agriculture, *Report* (Government Printing Office, 1872) (1871), p. 509; *American Agriculturist*, XV (June, 1856), 129.

25. *American Agriculturist*, XLV (July, 1886), 279.

26. *American Farmer*, I (July 9, 1819), 115; III (October 26, 1821), 243; *Agricultural Museum* (Georgetown, D. C.), II (April, May, 1812), 298–300, 339–44.

27. *American Husbandry* (2 vols.; London: J. Bew, 1775), I, 83; Bogart and Thompson, *Readings in the Economic History of the United States*, pp. 34–35. William Strickland reported in the early 1800's that timber in New England had actually doubled in value "within ten years." Bidwell, "Rural Economy in New England at the Beginning of the Nineteenth Century," p. 335 n.

28. *American Farmer*, I (September 3, 1819), 179; *Farmers' Register*, I (April, 1834), 659.

29. Everett E. Edwards, "Washington, Jefferson, Lincoln and Agriculture," United States Department of Agriculture, Bureau of Agricultural Economics, *Bulletin* (United States Government Printing Office, November, 1937), p. 35.

30. *American Agriculturist*, III (June, 1844), 180; *Farmer's Cabinet and American Herd-Book* (Philadelphia), VII (January, 1843), 184.

31. *Southern Agriculturist*, new series, V (July, 1845), 257–59; VI (April, 1846), 145; *Farmers' Register*, II (December, 1834), 399; VIII (August 31, 1840), 504; X (November 30, 1842), 501, 513. It was suggested in 1834 that if the Virginia Assembly failed to heed the many petitions, a convention would be called by farmers, to meet in Petersburg or Richmond, to protest the

fencing injustices. *Ibid.*, I (May. 1834), 753.

32. *Western Agriculturist and Practical Farmer's Guide* (Cincinnati: Hamilton County, Ohio Agricultural Society, Robinson & Fairbanks, 1830), p. 55.

33. *Edwardsville Spectator* (Illinois), March 27, 1821; *Illinois Gazette* (Shawneetown), May 5, 1821; *Ohio Cultivator*, VI (February 1, 1850), 35.

34. *Prairie Farmer*, VII (February, 1847), 58; Oliver, *Eight Months in Illinois*, p. 240.

35. *American Farmer*, I (August 27, 1819), 172; *Prairie Farmer*, IV (March, 1844), 71, 79–80.

36. *Farmer's Monthly Visitor* (Concord, N. H.), IX (April, 1847), 58; *Ohio Cultivator*, V (May 15, 1849), 153; *Rural Affairs* (Albany), II (1858–1860), 271–82.

37. *Southern Agriculturist*, new series, V (July, 1845), 257; *American Agriculturist*, IV (February, 1845), 45; *Ohio Cultivator*, I (April 1, 1845), 63. The South Carolina state geologist estimated that the cost of fences in a ten-year period equaled the annual value of all the stock they were intended to enclose. Thomas N. Carver, (comp.), *Selected Readings in Rural Economics* (Boston: Ginn & Company, 1916), pp. 292–93. Edmund Ruffin, not known for a tendency for understatement, reported that the amount expended in Virginia was more than the total cost of a 90 days' session of the legislature, the support of public education, and of all roads and canals in the state. *Farmers' Register*, I (March, 1834), 634–635 n. Norman J. Colman's estimate was much higher than the New York figure; he appraised the value in 1871 as somewhere between $150,000,000 and $200,000,000. *Colman's Rural World* (St. Louis), XXVI (August 5, 1871), 241.

38. Flügel and Faulkner, *Readings in the Economic and Social History of the United States*, pp. 137–38; *New England Farmer*, VII (April 24, 1829), 318; Oliver, *Eight Months in Illinois*, pp. 239–40.

39. *American Farmer*, I (March 17, 1820), 403; III (August 24, 1821), 170, 172. It was averred that many

"top rails [are] broken by the heavy bottoms of lazy gunners who get over the middle of a length of fence, instead of [at] the post." *New England Farmer*, IX (February 4, 1831), 228. There were numerous suggestions for preserving posts from decay: one should dip them in ocean water, or deposit salt in a bored hole near the base. Another method was to reverse their position from the way they had grown as trees. *Ibid.*, VII (April 24, 1829), 318; IX (December 31, 1830), 191; *Homestead* (Hartford), III (July 22, 1858), 699.

40. *American Agriculturist*, IX (May, 1850), 155. The Ohio State Board of Agriculture reported that using a figure of 80 cents per rod and one mile of fence to every forty acres, the building and repairing of fences in that state would cost more than $115,000,000. *Homestead*, II (October 2, 1856), 27–28.

41. *New England Farmer*, VII (April 10, 1829), 200; *American Farmer*, I (February 4, 1820), 358–59; New York State Board of Agriculture, *Memoirs* (Albany), I (1821–1822), 9–10.

42. Bogart and Thompson, *Readings in the Economic History of the United States*, p. 220; *American Husbandry*, I, 74.

43. *Prairie Farmer*, VI (March, 1846), 90; VII (April, 1847), 115; *New England Farmer*, VII (April 24, 1829), 318; XI (April 10, 1833), 310. Hogs were a constant source of trouble, for few rail fences could keep them in or out. As a result, many states prohibited them from running at large. *Farmers' Register*, X (November 30, 1842), 502, 514; *Agricultural Museum*, II (February, 1812), 269–72.

44. *Western Agriculturist and Practical Farmer's Guide*, pp. 52–54; *New England Farmer*, XI (January 30, 1833), 226; XII (September 25, 1833), 83.

45. *Country Gentleman*, IX (January 8, February 12, March 19, 1857), 34 n, 35, 120, 194; XII (November 4, 1858), 288; *Rural Affairs*, II (1858–1860), 271–82; *Homestead*, I (February 14, 1856), 323; *New England Farmer*, XI (January 30, 1833), 226.

46. *Farmers' Register*, VIII (August 31, 1840), 505; *American Agriculturist*, II (December, 1843), 370; III (June, 1844), 180.

47. Cornelius Swartwout to Robert Swartwout, Quincy, Illinois, September 11, 1837 in the Swartwout Papers, Chicago Historical Society Library; *American Quarterly Journal of Agriculture and Science* (Albany), II (October, 1845), 348–50.

48. *American Agriculturist*, III (June, 1844), 180.

49. *Union Agriculturist and Western Prairie Farmer* (Chicago), I (May, 1841), 34; *Cultivator* (Albany), IX (March, 1842), 42; *Farmers' Register*, I (March, 1834), 633.

50. *Southern Agriculturist*, new series, V (August, 1845), 312–13; *Moore's Rural New-Yorker* (Rochester), XVII (July 28, 1866), 238; Gray, *History of Agriculture in the Southern United States*, I, 146, 200.

51. Avery O. Craven, *Soil Exhaustion as a Factor in the Agricultural History of Virginia and Maryland, 1606–1860* (Urbana: University of Illinois Press, 1925), pp. 101–102. The idea of "soiling" was highly recommended by leaders in both the North and South as a solution to soil exhaustion and also to the fencing problem. *Ibid.; Farmers' Register*, II (December, 1843), 399; William Drowne, *Compendium of Agriculture; or, The Farmer's Guide* (Providence: Field & Maxcy, 1824), p. 172.

52. *American Agriculturist*, V (February, 1846), 48.

53. *Ibid.*, II (December, 1843), 370; IV (June, 1845), 173–74; *Prairie Farmer*, VII (February, 1847), 58; Herbert A. Kellar (ed.), *Solon Robinson: Pioneer and Agriculturist*, XXI, 320–21, 337–39, 364 n, 365–66.

54. Edmund Dana, *Geographical Sketches of the Western Country* (Cincinnati: Reynolds & Company, 1819), p. 142. In scattered sections of the country a few farmers even built fences with pickets, stumps and brush; the latter produced by throwing up a ridge of earth about a foot high into which stakes were driven and brush woven between them. John Spurrier, *The Practical Farmer* (Wilmington, Delaware: Brynberg & Andrews, 1793), p. 261; Dixon R. Fox, "The

Old Farm," *New York History*, XIX (January, 1938), 22; *Prairie Farmer*, VI (March, 1846), 91.

55. *Prairie Farmer*, VI (March, 1846), 90; *Western Journal of Agriculture, Manufactures, Mechanic Arts, etc.* (St. Louis), III (February, March, 1850), 339–40, 405–406.

56. *Ohio Cultivator*, VI (February 1, 1850), 35; *Prairie Farmer*, VI (March, 1846), 90. Prices for board fences varied considerably; in some areas they were two to three times greater than the worm fence. *Cultivator*, IX (October, 1842), 154.

57. Flint, *The American Farmer*, I, 564; *Southern Agriculturist*, new series, V (December, 1845), 368–69.

58. *Cultivator*, IX (June, 1842), 95; *New England Farmer*, XII (June 25, 1834), 402; *Prairie Farmer*, VI (November, 1846), 336; *Nebraska Farmer*, new series, III (December 17, 1873), 35; *Junction City Union* (Kansas), May 8, 1880.

59. Bidwell, "Rural Economy in New England at the Beginning of the Nineteenth Century," pp. 321–22, 336 n. Professor George W. Pierson of Yale University, in a letter to the author, posed the question of why the early New England settlers constructed so many stone wall fences and so few stone houses. In point of fact, the early settlers did not use stone for fences in that early period for two reasons: (1) stones required more skill and a higher cost in handling than was the case with timber, and (2) stone fences were not only difficult to keep in a horizontal position but were ineffective on rolling or marshy lands. The post-and-rail fence was the ideal enclosure for this area even though there was a growing scarcity of timber. It was not until the early part of the nineteenth century that stone walls became the general pattern of fencing. *New England Farmer*, VII (April 10, 1829), 200; IX (February 4, 1831), 228; X (March 7, 1832), 270; Peter Neilson, *Recollections of a Six Years' Residence*, p. 107; *American Agriculturist*, IV (June, 1845), 173–74.

60. *American Farmer*, I (February 4, 1820), 358–59. On some farms these piles occupied as much as "a fourth or fifth of a cultivated field." *Ibid.*

61. *Edwardsville Spectator*, August 7,

1819; William Bek (trans.), "Gott-
fried Duden's 'Report,' 1824–1827,"
Missouri Historical Review, XII (January, 1918), 84.

62. *New England Farmer*, VI (September
7, 1827), 55; *Cultivator*, III (August,
1836), 106–107; *Prairie Farmer*, VI
(May, 1846), 140–41.

63. Flint, *The American Farmer*, I,
565; *American Farmer*, I (March 24,
1820), 412; II (August 11, 1820),
158. It took considerable skill to build
these walls; in time there emerged the
professional stone-wall-layer. *Cultivator*, VII (January, 1840), 18; *American Farmer* (March 10, 1820), 395.
Four rods were considered a good
day's work for one man paid between fifty cents and a dollar a rod.
Prairie Farmer, VI (May, 1846),
140; *Homestead*, II (October 2,
1856), 27–28; IV (December 15,
1859), 1036–1037.

64. New York State Board of Agriculture,
Memoirs, I (1821–1822), 9–10;
*Farmers' Library and Monthly Jour-
nal of Agriculture* (New York), I
(September, 1845), 326; Bidwell,
"Rural Economy in New England at
the Beginning of the Nineteenth Cen-
tury," pp. 321–22.

65. *Union Agriculturist and Western
Prairie Farmer*, II (February, April,
1842), 16, 35; *Prairie Farmer*, VI
(March, 1846), 91, 95; *American
Agriculturist*, IX (May, 1850), 155.

66. *Cultivator*, III (August, 1836), 106;
Prairie Farmer, V (August, 1845),
190; VI (March, 1846), 91, 95; Ellsworth, *Valley of the Upper Wabash*,
pp. 50–51.

67. *Prairie Farmer*, V (August, 1845),
190. When built by hand labor, a sod
and ditch fence with riders cost about
one-fourth the amount of a stone wall,
or around 25 to 30 cents per rod.
Cultivator, III (August, 1836), 106;
William Kingdom, Jr., *America and
the British Colonies* (London: G. and
W. B. Whittaker, 1820), p. 63.

68. *Cultivator*, IX (March, 1842), 42;
*Union Agriculturist and Western
Prairie Farmer*, I (February, 1841),
12.

69. *American Farmer*, I (January 21,
1820), 337; *Cultivator*, IV (January,
1838), 176, 181; Paul L. Haworth,
George Washington: Farmer (Indianapolis: Bobbs-Merrill   Company,
1915), p. 163.

70. Vol. I, pp. 74–75. Professor Fox relates that some early New York settlers considered hedges unsafe as they
"exuded a mysterious poison that
brought on epidemics." *New York
History*, XIX (January, 1938), 22.

71. *New England Farmer*, VIII (December 11, 1829), 164; *American
Farmer*, I (October 8, 1819), 221.

72. *Cultivator*, IV (October, 1837),
126–27. Interest in hedge growing
was stimulated by premiums offered
at fairs by agricultural societies.
These usually ranged from $20 to
$30. *New England Farmer*, XII (Jan-
uary 29, 1834), 227; XIX (July 15,
1840), 9; *Ohio Cultivator*, XI
(March 15, 1855), 85.

73. *American Agriculturist*, IX (May,
October, 1850), 155, 298; *New England Farmer*, VII (October 10,
1829), 200; *American Farmer*, V
(October 24, 1823), 244.

74. *American Farmer*, I (August 27,
1819), 172; *Farmers' Library and
Monthly Journal of Agriculture*, I
(September, 1845), 325–26; *Prairie
Farmer*, VIII (May, 1848), 145, 147.
Thorny hedges were nuisances when
planted along roadways; the sharp
thorns would catch the clothing and
even "pierce through thick [shoe]
leather, . . . and often cause serious
lameness to cattle and sheep" if trimmings were not carefully collected
and burned. *Western Stock Journal
and Farmer* (Cedar Rapids, Iowa),
VIII (March, 1878), 228.

75. *Ohio Cultivator*, VI (February 1,
1850), 35; *Farmers' Library and
Monthly Journal of Agriculture*, I
(September, 1845), 325–26; *Nebraska Farmer*, new series, I (November, 1877), 2.

76. *American Farmer*, I (June 25, 1819),
100; II (June 2, 16, July 7, 1820),
76, 93, 118; *New England Farmer*, X
(May 9, 1832), 339; XXI (May 17,
1843), 364; John Taylor, *Arator,
Being a Series of Agricultural Essays,
Practical and Political* (4th ed. rev.;
Petersburg, Virginia: J. M. Carter,
1818), pp. 156–57.

77. *American Farmer*, I (September 24,
1819), 204; (January 28, 1820),
350–51; II (April 14, May 12,
1820), 20–21, 53; *New England*

Farmer, III (August 18, 1824), 33–34; VIII (December 11, 1829), 164.

78. New York State Board of Agriculture, *Memoirs*, III (1825–1826), 368–72; *Ohio Cultivator*, II (November 1, 1846), 166–67.

79. *American Farmer*, I (January 21, 1820), 337; *Illinois Farmer* (Springfield), I (March, 1856), 70. "Quicks" could be purchased from nurseries at prices between $1.50 to $5 per thousand; the requirement being about 17,000 per mile. *Prairie Farmer*, VIII (May, August, 1848), 148, 168, 242.

80. *Ohio Cultivator*, V (January 1, 1849), 6.

81. *Prairie Farmer*, V (December, 1845), 284; *Cincinnatus* (Cincinnati), III (October, 1858), 437–38; Mary T. Carriel, *Life of Jonathan Baldwin Turner* (Jacksonville?, Illinois: privately printed, 1911), pp. 65–69; Mary L. Rice, "The Role of the Osage Orange Hedge in the Occupation of the Great Plains" (unpublished Master's thesis, History Department, University of Illinois, 1937), pp. 1–81.

82. *Ibid.*, Walter P. Webb, *The Great Plains* (Boston: Ginn & Company, 1931), pp. 290–95. Adoption of the hedge was so widespread that upright mowers, cultivators and drills had to be perfected in order for farmers to care for the many miles of this fence. *Western Journal of Agriculture, Manufactures, Mechanic Arts, etc.*, III (1850), 191; Paul W. Gates, "Large Scale Farming in Illinois, 1850–1870," *Agricultural History*, VI (January, 1932), 18. By 1878 this type of fence exceeded all other forms combined in the western states; in some Kansas counties it was preferred over all others in a ratio of two to one, measured in actual miles of fence. Other types followed in this order: board, wire; stone and rail. Kansas State Board of Agriculture, *Biennial Report* (Topeka), I (1877–1878), 526–27; *The Kansas Monthly* (Lawrence), II (February, 1879), 31. The situation was different in Indiana, where in 1880 a statistical survey was made of the 341,201 miles of fences. At that time the Virginia worm exceeded its nearest competitor, the board and plank, by at least one hun-

dred to one. The others were ranked in the following order: hedge, post-in-rail, smooth and barbed wire, and far down in importance was the stone fence. *American Stockman and Farmer* (Chicago), III (January 20, 1881), 1.

83. *Prairie Farmer*, XII (December, 1852), 523.

84. *Ibid.*, XV (November, 1855), 342; Illinois State Agricultural Society, *Transactions* (Springfield, 1855), I (1853–1854), 412–23.

85. *Niles Weekly Register* (Baltimore), II (March 7, 1812), 9–10; *Agricultural Museum*, II (February, 1812), 266–69; Philadelphia Society for Promoting Agriculture, *Memoirs*, IV (1818), 3–8, 229–30.

86. *American Agriculturist*, IV (August, 1845), 242; VIII (August, 1849), 255–56; Illinois State Agricultural Society, *Transactions* (1855–1856), pp. 425–32. This problem of temperature became so acute by 1850 that some agricultural agencies declared this fencing material wholly inadequate. *Ohio Cultivator*, V (May 1, 1849), 131; VI (February 1, 1850), 34. Fires that raged on the prairies not only destroyed trees and board fences, but made wire enclosures ineffective; once fires had moved through an area, the oil coatings of the wires were burned off and the temper was removed, leaving them susceptible to rust and falling into disrepair during severe atmospheric changes. *Breeder's Gazette* (Chicago), V (April 24, 1884), 632; *Nebraska Farmer*, new series, I (August, 1877), 2; *Western Manufacturer* (Chicago), VII (September 15, 1879), 105.

87. *Wool Grower and Magazine of Agriculture and Horticulture* (Buffalo, Rochester), I (August, September, 1849), 73–75, 88–89; III (November, 1851), 126; *American Agriculturist*, XVI (October, 1857), 228.

88. *Prairie Farmer*, V (September, 1845), 227; X (April, 1850), 112–113, 117; *Ohio Cultivator*, V (May 1, 1849), 131. These wires held no terror for domestic animals, but since they were difficult to see at a distance or on dark days large numbers of wild fowl, such as prairie chickens, were killed in flight by col-

liding with them. *Prairie Farmer*, VII (February, 1847), 68.
89. *Ohio Cultivator*, V (May 1, 1849), 131; *Genesee Farmer* (Rochester), IX (February, March, May, October, 1848), 55, 76, 132, 244.
90. *American Agriculturist*, VIII (January, March, 1849), 14, 95; *Ohio Cultivator*, V (May 1, 1849), 131.
91. November 7, 1848; *Western Journal*

of *Agriculture, Manufactures, Mechanic Arts*, I (December, 1848), 690.
92. *Ohio Cultivator*, V (May 1, 1849), 131; VI (February 1, 1850), 34; *Prairie Farmer*, VII (February, 1847), 68; *Western Journal of Agriculture, Manufactures, Mechanic Arts*, II (April, 1849), 265; III (March, 1850), 404–406.

NOTES: *Chapter Six*

1. Horace Miner, *Culture and Agriculture, An Anthropological Study of a Corn Belt County* (Ann Arbor: University of Michigan Press, 1949), pp. 8–9, 75.
2. *Prairie Farmer* (Chicago), V (April, 1845), 85; *Farmers' Library and Monthly Journal of Agriculture* (New York), I (September, 1845), 20 n.
3. John Dabney, *Address to Farmers* (Salem, Mass.: J. Dabney, 1796), pp. 40–41.
4. *Farmers' Cabinet and American Herd-Book* (Philadelphia), VI (September, 1841), 59.
5. *Western Agriculturist and Practical Farmer's Guide*, pp. 52–54; *Prairie Farmer*, VII (February, 1847), 58; *American Agriculturist* (New York), IV (February, 1845), 44–45.
6. Ransom H. Tyler, *A Treatise on the Law of Boundaries and Fences*, pp. 468–69; Lewis C. Gray, *History of Agriculture in the Southern United States*, II, 843.
7. Gray, *History of Agriculture in the Southern United States*, I, 140–43; Alexander J. Dallas (ed.), *Laws of the Commonwealth of Pennsylvania*, II, 188–89.
8. Walter W. Hening (ed.), *Statutes At Large*, I, 176, 199, 332; Dallas, *Laws of the Commonwealth of Pennsylvania*, II, 188–89.
9. *Prairie Farmer*, LV (August 11, 1883), 505; *Southern Planter and Farmer* (Richmond), new series, V (January, 1871), 52–55.
10. Virginia provides a good example of this time lag. The 1632 law remained in effect in spite of opposi-

tion until the post-Civil War period, when, due to scarcity of timber and wide devastation, it was finally amended. *Farmers' Register* (Shellbanks and Petersburg, Virginia), II (October, 1834), 311; VIII (August 31, 1840), 504; *Southern Planter and Farmer*, new series, V (January, 1871), 52–55.
11. Bidwell and Falconer, *History of Agriculture in the Northern United States*, pp. 55, 268–69, 387, 392. The use of children as herders often disturbed neighbors who feared that the children were being denied an education and that they developed shiftless habits. One writer stated: "I regard this herding as a school for tramps. The young boys become more and more indolent and insulting. . . and a few years of such life graduates them into successful tramps, loafers and ruffians." *Ohio Farmer* (Cleveland), LXI (July 1, 1882), 440. Other observers, however, thought "parents would be delighted to have them [the children] watch the flocks and herds either for their board alone or for . . . a few cents a day . . . and if a child could weave baskets or braid straw hats, . . . it might make days thus spent quite profitable . . . [and] to the farmer the expense of perhaps miles of fence, would be spared." *Homestead* (Hartford), I (February 14, 1856), 323.
12. *Prairie Farmer*, VII (February, 1847), 58; *Michigan Farmer* (Detroit), new series, IX (July 29, 1879), 1.
13. Mary L. Rice, "The Role of the Osage

Orange Hedge in the Occupation of the Great Plains," Ch. I.

14. *Ohio Cultivator* (Columbus), I (April, 1845), 63.
15. *New England Farmer* (Boston), XI (April 10, 1833), 310.
16. *Farmers' Register*, II (December, 1834), 399.
17. *Prairie Farmer*, V (April, 1845), 85; *Farmers' Library and Monthly Journal of Agriculture*, I (September, 1845), 20 n; *Illinois Farmer* (Springfield), VII (May, 1862), 147.
18. *Prairie Farmer*, V (April, 1845), 85.
19. *Western Agriculturist and Practical Farmer's Guide*, pp. 52–54; *Working Farmer* (New York), III (January, 1852), 249; Horace Greeley, *What I Know of Farming* (New York: The Tribune Association, 1871), pp. 219 ff.
20. *Cultivator* (Albany), VIII (August, 1841), 135. Such annoyances provoked the wrath of individuals who had land on both sides of the highways. When passing in and out with loads of hay and grain, they "must get down and open and shut two gates everytime to keep out somebody's stock." Des Moines, *Iowa State Register*, January 5, 1881; *Country Gentleman* (Albany), X (September 17, 1857), 194. Roving animals caused accidents and even death to those traveling on public highways. Ferocious bulls were known to attack individuals and hogs to frighten horses into running away, "killing riders and breaking bones." *Ibid.; New England Farmer*, XXI (June 7, 1843), 389.
21. *American Museum; or Repository of Ancient and Modern Fugitive Pieces* (Philadelphia), IV (August, 1788), 133; *The Aesculapian Register* (Philadelphia), I (July 1, 1824), 21; *The Country Gentleman's Companion* (2 vols.; London: n.p., 1753), I, 165.
22. *Indiana Farmer* (Indianapolis), VII (April, 1858), 28–29; *Homestead*, IV (October 28, 1858), 94.
23. *American Agriculturist*, XVI (January, 1857), 4; *Moore's Rural New-Yorker*, XXXV (June 2, 1877), 348; Jacob H. Beuscher, *Law and the Farmer* (New York: Springer Publishing Co., 1953), p. 349. In some communities, when individuals injured stray livestock they could expect threats and even retaliatory acts

against their property. *American Farmer* (Baltimore), III (June 15, 1821) 92–93; *Country Gentleman*, X (September 17, 1857), 194.

24. Margaret B. Bogue, *Patterns from the Sod* ("Collections of the Illinois State Historical Library," Land Series, Vol. XXXIV[1] [Springfield: Illinois State Historical Library, 1959]), pp. 49, 59–67; Ernest W. Osgood, *The Day of the Cattleman* (Chicago: University of Chicago Press, 1929), pp. 31, 164.
25. *Prairie Farmer*, VII (January, April, 1847), 21, 115–16; Iowa State Agricultural Society, *Report* (Des Moines, 1874), (1873), 24–25.
26. *National Live-Stock Journal*, V (January, 1874), 26; *Farmers' Register*, I (November, 1833), 338. Jumping sheep were a nuisance and difficult to restrain. A deterrent was to "carefully cut one of the sinews which passes through their hind fetlocks." To prevent hogs from rooting, one "cut the two sinews to which their snouts hang while they were still young." J. Hector St. John de Crèvecœur, *Sketches of Eighteenth-Century America*, edited by Henri L. Bourdin and others (New Haven: Yale University Press, 1925), pp. 81–82.
27. *Union Agriculturist and Western Prairie Farmer*, I (June, 1841), 44.
28. *A Tour in America in 1798, 1799, and 1800* (2 vols.; London: J. Harding, 1805), I, 290–91.
29. *Prairie Farmer*, V (April, 1845), 85; VII (April, 1847), 115–16. The custom of "dogging" the neighbor's stock was an early practice; one of the first laws passed in Virginia held the offender liable in "any court of justice within the Collony." Hening (ed.), *Statutes at Large*, I, 244.
30. Lincoln at one time represented a client in a suit, *Byrne v. Stout*, involving a runaway hog that had been impounded. The animal had either strayed or was "coaxed" away. Lincoln sought to prove the latter and obtained a $3 judgment. However, the Illinois Supreme Court ultimately found that the animal had not been taken or "coaxed" in the eyes of the law. John P. Frank, *Lincoln as a Lawyer* (Urbana: University of Illinois Press, 1961), p. 44.
31. *Farmers' Register*, X (November 30, 1842), 502, 514 n, 515; Bidwell and

Falconer, *History of Agriculture in the Northern United States*, p. 22; *National Live-Stock Journal*, V (March 1874), 99.

32. *Cultivator*, new series, VIII (February, 1851), 66–67; *New England Farmer*, XVI (December 27, 1837), 196; *Rural New-Yorker* (New York), XLI (October 7, 1882), 687.

33. *American Cotton Planter* (Montgomery), I (April, 1853), 118; *American Garden and Floral Cabinet* (New York), new series, X (September, 1889), 287.

34. *Farmers' Review* (Chicago), VIII (January 26, 1882), 54.

35. Gray, *History of Agriculture in the Southern United States*, II, 843. Landowners were often advised "to let trespasses pass unpunished rather than to seek redress," as it was not only considered less vexatious but far more profitable since a lawsuit would generally cost "several times more [than] the value of the property supposed to have been destroyed." *American Farmer*, III (June 15, 1821), 92–93. If the plaintiff brought suit for damages, he subjected himself to many uncertainties and inconveniences: there was always the possibility that his fences would not meet the legal requirements as a barrier and in that case he would suffer the loss of court costs and fees; if he won there was the probability of insolvency of the defendant. If the plaintiff was compelled to impound the trespassing animals upon his own land—and that was usually the case, for few public pounds were maintained except perhaps in larger cities—then he became responsible for their welfare; as distrainer he was not legally privileged to sell the animals if their owner saw fit to be obstinate, but he must satisfactorily feed and care for them until replevied, or compensation was made for the damages done. *Ibid.* Some plaintiffs, however, were not so easily persuaded. Driven by an intense anger to "put the law" on the offender, they refused to accept an amicable settlement of the trespass and demanded a court trial. *Henry County News* (Geneseo, Illinois), February 16, 1882.

36. *New England Farmer*, VII (April 24, 1829), 318; XV (September 14,

1836), 76; XVI (December 27, 1837), 196.

37. *Ibid.*, XI (January 30, 1833), 226.

38. *American Farmer*, III (June 15, 1821), 92–93; *Prairie Farmer*, VI (July, 1846), 226; VI (January, 1847), 21; Gray, *History of Agriculture in the Southern United States*, I, 203. Some states allowed the distrainer to collect a fee for performance of the castration from the stallion's owner when he appeared to claim the animal. This law provoked numerous lawsuits as well as a few "cutting scrapes." Thomas Clark, *The Rampaging Frontier* (Indianapolis: Bobbs-Merrill Company, 1939), pp. 226–27.

39. *Homestead*, IV (August 4, 1859), 731; *Farmer's Journal* (Cedar Rapids, Iowa), II August, November, 1873), 122, 164. An illustration of the harmful possibilities of this practice was reported by a correspondent who related that a "coarse native . . . mongrel buck" got into an adjacent pasture consisting of a valuable flock of Merino sheep. Before he was discovered, a "get" of more than 30 worthless lambs made their appearance the next spring. *Cultivator*, new series, III (May, 1846), 157–58.

40. *Western Stock Journal and Farmer* (Cedar Rapids, Iowa), VII (March, 1877), 195; X (May, July, 1880), 106, 150–51; *American Agriculturist*, XXX (November, 1871), 408.

41. *Nebraska Farmer* (Lincoln), new series, IV (January, 1880), 19. For criticisms of the estray laws see *Ibid.*, new series, I (February, 1877), 2; IV (January, December, 1880), 4, 285.

42. *Ibid.*, new series, I (February, 1877), 2; IV (December, 1880), 285.

43. Gray, *History of Agriculture in the Southern United States*, I, 143–44. At different times in North Carolina the penalties were whipping, nailing to the pillory by the ears, cropping the ears, branding on the cheeks, and death without benefit of clergy. *Ibid.*; *Virginia Gazette* (Williamsburg), October 29, 1736.

44. *Prairie Farmer*, VI (September, 1846), 269; *Homestead*, II (August 13, 1857), 755–56; Earl W. Hayter, "Wanderings in the West in 1839," Illinois State Historical Society, *Journal*, XXXIII (December, 1940), 403–

404. The extent of horse-stealing is well documented by the large number of references under the entry "Horses Stolen," in the index of Reuben G. Thwaites (ed.), *Early Western Travels, 1748–1848* (32 vols.; Cleveland: Arthur H. Clark & Company, 1904–1907), XXXI, Index, 277.

45. *Breeder's Gazette* (Chicago), IV (September 13, 1883), 329; Osgood, *The Day of the Cattleman*, p. 157.

46. *New England Farmer*, IX (May 11, 1831), 337–38; XXII (September 20, 1843), 93; *Homestead*, II (June 18, 1857), 622.

47. *Country Gentleman*, IX (February 12, March 19, April 2, 1857), 120, 194, 225; *Cultivator and Country Gentleman*, XL (February 4, 1875), 67; XLIX (March 20, 1884), 238. By the 1820's and 1830's in the East, and later in the West, remonstrances against slaughtering of unprotected song and insectivorous birds were numerous; it was becoming apparent to reflective farmers that they were losing one of their most important assets. On "almost every pleasant day, and more numerously on holidays," city dwellers invaded the countryside to see who could bag the largest number of birds. With guns, dogs and nets they snared or shot everything in their paths until rural dwellers protested to their legislators for laws to "spare the birds." *Horticulturist and Journal of Rural Art and Rural Taste* (Albany), VI (April, 1851), 157; *Prairie Farmer*, LX (October 6, 1888), 640; *Working Farmer*, II (September, 1850), 138; *Nebraska Farmer*, new series, I (January, 1877), 7.

48. Fruit-, flower- and vegetable-stealing, mostly by young people from nearby towns, was a widespread activity throughout rural America at various stages of its development. It was a form of depredation that ordinarily went unpunished, since most local citizens felt that this type of plundering was not a theft but a boyish trick or prank, or something akin to a youthful frolic. *Genesee Farmer* (Rochester), II (January 14, May 12, June 30, July 28, August 4, 1832), 12, 150, 202, 235, 241. Since fruit-growers could not prosecute for this type of larceny and trespass, it had a re-

tarding influence on development of the industry. Many observers objected to such depredations, claiming that it offered young boys their first lessons in pilfering and developed thievish propensities. One editor insisted that many a horse thief commenced his career in crime by robbing an orchard. In time, some of the leading editors, such as Andrew J. Downing, campaigned to secure protection against this evil; but to curb such a persistent folkway was not easy and the practice went unrestrained for years. Occasionally a community was aroused by the shooting of a young culprit or by the lamentable effects of a hidden dose of tartar emetic, which, properly placed in the stolen fruit, would "lay a fellow out limber for a while." *Cultivator*, new series, V (June, 1848), 183; *Horticulturist*, V (September, 1850), 151; XV (October, 1860), 479–81; *Western Horticultural Review* (Cincinnati), I (1850–1851), 168–69; *Prairie Farmer*, XIII (April, 1853), 146.

49. *Western Rural* (Chicago), XXIV (October 2, 1886), 631; *Cultivator and Country Gentleman*, XL (February 4, 1875), 67.

50. *Ohio Cultivator*, VI (January 1, 1850), 9.

51. *Cheyenne Democratic Leader* (Wyoming), April 3, 1884. Not only did cattle stray onto the tracks, but trains often stampeded them into the moving cars. *Ibid.*, June 30, 1887; *Galveston News* (Texas), April 19, 1882.

52. *Dillion Examiner* (Montana Territory), quoted in *National Live-Stock Journal*, XVIII (January, 1887), 37.

53. Missouri, Kansas and Texas Railway Company, *Report* (1876), p. 94; *Cheyenne Democratic Leader*, April 3, 1884. During the period 1884–1890 the Union Pacific Railway's outlay for stock killed on its right-of-way increased from $97,790.83 to $286,878.35. *Reports* (1884), p. 118; (1890), p. 98. On one occasion, in Missouri, a passenger train killed as many as 25 head of cattle in a single run. *National Live-Stock Journal*, I (December 30, 1884), 47.

54. Texas and Pacific Railway Company, *Reports* (1878), pp. 25, 29, 32–33; (1889), pp. 13–14, 29.

55. Atchison, Topeka and Santa Fe Railroad Company, *Report* (1880), pp. 10, 12; *Railroad Gazette* (Chicago), new series, IX (August 17, October 19, 1877), 373, 463; XIII (January 7, 1881), 9.

56. William W. Thornton, *The Law of Railroad Fences and Private Crossings, etc.* (Indianapolis: Bowen-Merrill Company, 1892), pp. 22–26.

57. *Railway Age* (Chicago), IX (February 21, 1884), 116; *Nebraska Farmer*, new series, IV (October, 1880), 241. On some larger ranges in the West, cattlemen opposed fencing of railroads because it prevented roaming of cattle from one range to another. The Texas & Pacific found many resentful cattlemen who were "so handy with the nippers" that the wire was cut as fast as the road could be fenced. *Cheyenne Democratic Leader*, April 3, 1884; *Breeder's Gazette*, X (October 21, 1886), 603.

58. See Ransom H. Tyler, *A Treatise on the Law of Boundaries and Fences*, *passim*.

59. *Breeder's Gazette*, X (October 21, 1886), 603. Payments were supposed to be a "fair market price," but in Missouri a "double liability" was imposed upon the carriers. Washburn & Moen Manufacturing Company, *Fence Laws* (Worcester, Mass.: Washburn & Moen, 1880), No. 21.

60. *Creston Times* (Illinois), January 31, 1874. Nebraska farmers had the same problem: how could they get the companies to pay what animals were worth? They objected to "beef" prices being paid for family milk cows and thoroughbreds. The companies operated as follows: the section-boss reported the killings to the paymaster at a cheaper price than the market value. The owners drove six to ten miles to the railway station, only to find a check considerably lower than the amount they were entitled to. If they refused to accept, they were advised to write headquarters, which delayed the settlement indefinitely. Outraged by this practice, the farmers proposed to form an association to compel the companies to fence or pay the regular price. *Nebraska Farmer*, new series, IV (October, December, 1880), 241, 285.

61. *Rocky Mountain Husbandman* (White Sulphur Springs, Montana Territory), VI (January 29, 1880) *passim; Cerrillos Comet* (New Mexico Territory), February 24, 1882. In the eighties, regular war was waged against the sheepmen by cattle interests. Cowboys were armed and casualties were high in both sheep and men. *Cheyenne Democratic Leader*, March 27, 1884, December 31, 1885; Charles Michelson, "The War for the Range," *Munsey's Magazine*, XXVIII (December, 1902), 380–82. Cattlemen circulated stories that sheep poisoned the soil and killed the grass; such beliefs made it possible to secure legislation discriminating against them. *Texas Live Stock Journal* (Ft. Worth), VIII (July 28, 1888), 5.

62. Earl W. Hayter, "Barbed wire Fencing—A Prairie Invention," *Agricultural History*, XIII (October, 1939), 189–207.

63. I. H. Miller to Secretary of the Interior, Henry M. Teller, La Junta, Colorado, November 16, 1883, in the General Land Office, Letter No. 108683. Homesteaders not only had trouble settling on the land but were hard pressed at times to preserve even their homes. Sometimes cattle from the Texas trail were turned upon them for the purpose of tearing down their sod shanties. *Senate Executive Documents*, No. 127, 48 Congress, 1st Session (1883–1884), pp. 3–6, 10.

64. *Burke's Texas Rural Almanac and Immigrants' Handbook* (Houston), V (1885), 150.

65. *Breeder's Gazette*, XII (September 8, 1887), 383.

66. *Galveston News*, July 18, 1873, quoted in Walter P. Webb, *The Great Plains*, p. 289; *Cheyenne Democratic Leader*, January 17, 1884.

67. *Gringo and Greaser* (Manzano, New Mexico Territory), February 15, 1884.

68. *Ibid.*

69. *Cheyenne Democratic Leader*, December 10, 1885; *Senate Executive Documents*, No. 127, 48 Congress, 1st Session (1883–1884), pp. 12, 13, 22, 143; James Jenkins, et al., to Henry M. Teller, Pratt County, Kansas, May 26, 1883, in the General Land Office, Letter No. 50211.

70. *Senate Executive Documents*, 127, 48 Congress, 1st Session (1883–1884),

p. 22; *House Executive Documents*, 119, 48 Congress, 1st Session (1883–1884), p. 2.
71. Webb, *Great Plains*, p. 313.
72. *Galveston News*, November 28, December 3, 5, 7, 13, 23, 1883; *Prose and Poetry of the Live Stock Industry* (Denver, Kansas City: National Livestock Historical Association, 1904), pp. 684–85; Louis Pelzer, *The Cattlemen's Frontier* (Glendale, California: Arthur H. Clark & Company, 1936), pp. 173–91. So serious was this mania that a special session of the Texas legislature was convened.

While it was deliberating, a member was notified that more than a mile of his fence had just been destroyed by the cutters. *Fort Worth Daily Gazette*, January 19, 1884, cited in James K. Greer (ed.), *A Texas Ranger and Frontiersman* (Dallas: Southwest Press, 1932), p. 225.
73. *Iron Age and Metallurgical Review* (New York), XXXV (January 22, 1885), 31.
74. *Cheyenne Democratic Leader*, August 13, 1885, January 21, 1886; *Galveston News*, September 1, 1885.

NOTES: *Chapter Seven*

1. *Western Stock Journal and Farmer* (Cedar Rapids, Iowa), X (February, 1880), 32; *Wool Grower and Magazine of Agriculture* (Buffalo, Rochester), III (May, 1851), 27–28; *Farmer's Journal* (Cedar Rapids, Iowa), I (June, 1872), 6.
2. Frank W. Taussig, *Some Aspects of the Tariff Question* (Cambridge: Harvard University Press, 1915), p. 309.
3. *Horticulturist* (Albany), VII (April, 1852), 161; *American Agriculturist* (New York), XXVI (May, 1867), 175; United States Commissioner of Agriculture, *Report* (1865) (Washington: Government Printing Office, 1866), p. 73.
4. *Ohio Cultivator* (Columbus), I (May 15, 1845), 75; VIII (May 1, 1852), 135; *Michigan Farmer* (Detroit), new series, IV (August 19, 1873), 244; Iowa State Agricultural Society, *Report* (Des Moines, 1888) (1887), pp. 59–60.
5. *New England Farmer* (Boston), XII (April 2, 1834), 304; *American Agriculturist*, XXI (August, 1862), 228; *Cultivator and Country Gentleman* (Albany), XXXIII (March 11, 1869), 197.
6. United States Commissioner of Agriculture, *Report* (1868), pp. 42–43; *Breeder's Gazette* (Chicago), XII (October 30, 1887), 1010; *Western Stock Journal and Farmer*, X (May, 1880), 106. Many curs roamed the

countryside at will, killing any living thing that came within their range. Their habit of robbing hens' nests and raiding chicken houses was one consequence of their uncontrolled mobility. On occasions they carried the kill back to their masters to be consumed by the family, making it possible for dog and owner alike to "feed on the public." Farmers sometimes attempted to control this depredation by placing strychnine in nest eggs. *Southern Planter and Farmer* (Richmond), new series, V (March, 1871), 139; *Southern Cultivator* (Augusta), XVIII (May, 1860), 165–66; *Rural New-Yorker* (New York), XL (February 26, 1881), 131.
7. *American Stock-Journal and Farmers' and Stock-Breeders' Advertiser* (Parkesburg, Pa.), II (March, 1867), 87. Wolves were even greater threats than dogs to domestic animals in the newer settlements. They took a heavy toll not only of sheep, but of calves, colts and even young pigs. The only recourse livestock-producers had was to appeal to local governments to offer a bounty for each scalp. As industry developed in the East and moved across the country, the bounty system was used to control this and similar predators. Eliphalet and Phinehas Merrill (comps.), *Gazetteer of the State of New Hampshire* (Exeter: C. Norris & Company, 1817), p. 17;

Herbert Kellar (ed.), *Solon Robinson: Pioneer Agriculturist*, II, p. 75; *Prairie Farmer* (Chicago), XI (February 15, 1851), 81; *Cheyenne Democratic Leader* (Wyoming), January 15, 1885; *Fort Benton River Press* (Montana), December 17, 1884.

8. John G. Wells and others, *The Grange Illustrated; or, Patron's Hand-Book* (New York: Grange Publishing Company, 1874), p. 53.

9. *American Stock-Journal and Farmers' and Stock-Breeders' Advertiser*, II (September, 1867), 271. An analysis of one county in Iowa in 1875 revealed these facts in respect to the people-sheep-dog ratio: there were 7,546 people, 6,119 sheep and 1,420 dogs, or a proportion of one dog to about four and one-half sheep and slightly more than one dog to five people. The council minutes for May, 1888, in one small town of this county reveal an entry of $8 paid to the marshal for killing eight unlicensed dogs. A later entry shows the price reduced to fifty cents per dog. Clair B. Heyer, "Prairie Town: The Founding of a Small Iowa Farming Community in the 1880's," (unpublished seminar paper, History Department, Northern Illinois University, 1965).

10. *Ohio Cultivator*, III (February 15, 1847), 30.

11. *Homestead* (Hartford), III (July 28, 1858), 720; *Nebraska Farmer* (Lincoln), new series, I (February, 1877), 2, 5; *Western Stock Journal and Farmer*, X (February, 1880), 37; *National Live-Stock Journal* (Chicago), VI (June, 1875), 236.

12. *The Plough, the Loom and the Anvil* (Philadelphia), I (March, 1849), 542.

13. *National Live-Stock Journal*, XI (February, 1880), 77; XVIII (December, 1887), 411.

14. *Cultivator* (Albany), IV (July, 1847), 214.

15. *Nebraska Farmer*, new series, I (February, 1877), 2, 5.

16. *Prairie Farmer*, new series, XV (January 7, 1865), 1–2; *Valley Farmer* (St. Louis), XI (December, 1859), 374.

17. *National Live-Stock Journal*, IV (December, 1873), 424; *Nebraska Farmer*, IV (January, 1880), 15.

18. *The Plough, the Loom and the Anvil*, I (March, 1849), 542–43; Ohio State Board of Agriculture, *Report* (Columbus, 1859) XIII (1858), 619; *Prairie Farmer*, new series XV (January 7, 1865), 1–2; *National Live-Stock Journal*, IV (December, 1873), 424.

19. *American Agriculturist*, XX (February, June, 1861), 57, 166; United States Commissioner of Agriculture, *Report* (1863), pp. 452–53.

20. *Western Stock Journal and Farmer*, VIII (May, 1878), 263; *Nebraska Farmer*, III (March, 1862), 44. Losses in Illinois followed the same pattern; between 1876 and 1879 they more than doubled, rising from a dollar value of $30,578 to $65,384. Illinois Department of Agriculture, *Transactions* (Springfield, 1880), XVII (1879), 546–47.

21. *Nebraska Farmer*, new series, I (February, 1877), 5–6; III (December, 1879), 285; *Western Stock Journal and Farmer*, VIII (May, 1878), 263.

22. Lewis G. Connor, *A Brief History of the Sheep Industry in the United States* (Washington: Government Printing Office, 1921), pp. 148–49.

23. *American Stock-Journal and Farmers' and Stock-Breeders' Advertiser*, II (February, 1867), 47; *National Live-Stock Journal*, VI (March, 1875), 105.

24. *National Live-Stock Journal*, VI (March, 1875), 105.

25. *Farmer's Journal*, I (June, 1872), 6; *Southern Cultivator*, III (July, 1845), 105; *Working Farmer*, VII (April, 1855), 58.

26. *Prairie Farmer*, XVI (October 2, 1856), 157.

27. *National Live-Stock Journal*, III (November 29, 1887), 767; *Nebraska Farmer*, new series, IV (January, 1880), 15. Sheep-killing dogs in certain parts of the West were reported as having feral habits. In Colorado, in 1880, sheepmen were so harassed by bands of dogs who ran wild, killing sheep and young calves, that they agitated for vigilance committees to end the menace. Edward N. Wentworth and Charles W. Towne, *Shepherd's Empire* (Norman: University of Oklahoma Press, 1945), p. 227.

28. *Wool Grower and Magazine of Agriculture*, III (May, 1851), 27–28.

29. Connor, *Brief History of the Sheep Industry*, pp. 148–49; Cornelius O. Cathey, *Agricultural Developments in North Carolina, 1783–1860* (Chapel Hill: University of North Carolina Press, 1956), p. 179.

30. *Prairie Farmer*, new series, XIX (June 29, 1867), 427; *National Live-Stock Journal*, V (January, 1874), 26; Philadelphia Society for Promoting Agriculture, *Memoirs*, I (1808), 3; *American Farmer* (Baltimore), III (June 8, 1821), 87.

31. *Boston Cultivator*, VIII (January 17, 1846), 17; *Prairie Farmer*, new series, XIX (June 29, 1867), 427. Some flockmasters questioned the advisability of placing horned steers among sheep for protective purposes. They feared the sharp horns of the steers would not only damage the sheep physically but would pull much of the wool from their backs. *Boston Cultivator*, VIII (March 14, 1846), 82.

32. *National Live-Stock Journal*, XII (May, 1881), 211; *Country Gentleman* (Albany), XXI (April 30, 1863), 284.

33. *Country Gentleman*, XXVII (April 19, 1866), 253.

34. *Prairie Farmer*, new series, VIII (November 14, 1861), 321.

35. *Western Stock Journal and Farmer*, XI (September, 1881), 199; Solon Robinson (ed.), *Facts for Farmers, Also for the Family Circle* (2 vols.; New York: Johnson and Ward, 1865), I, 255–58.

36. *Cultivator and Country Gentleman*, XXX (July 4, 1867), 12; *Prairie Farmer*, new series, VIII (November 14, 1861), 321.

37. *Homestead*, III (July 22, 1858), 701. Opposition to dogs in the eastern sheep-raising areas was so strong that "poisoning clubs" were advocated as one way to cope with the problem. *Ibid.*, II (April 30, 1857), 508–509. An advertisement placed in a South Carolina newspaper announced that a certain farmer had "baited *one hundred and nineteen* spots on his farm with pieces of meat heavily charged with strychnine." This individual warned "all owners of hounds, . . . or dogs generally, that to assist this poison . . . he had placed between each two pieces of

meat an 'unfernal machine' which explodes with unerring aim at the sight of one of the canine species." *Ibid.*, IV (October 14, 1858), 61.

38. Horace Greeley, *What I Know of Farming*, pp. 203–204.

39. *Prairie Farmer*, XII (July, 1852), 311; *Farmers' Review* (Chicago), VIII (February 2, 1882), 71.

40. *Country Gentleman*, XXV (February 2, 23, 1865), 88, 123. Professional veterinarians objected to the selling of these deadly drugs over the counter and attempts were made to secure legislation compelling druggists to register names, residences and intentions of buyers, but to no avail. *American Veterinary Journal* (Boston), II (February, 1857), 44–45.

41. *Prairie Farmer*, new series, XIV (December 10, 1864), 372; *Cultivator*, IV (July, 1837), 80–81. Scotch rams, reputed to be good jumpers, were recommended as the best type for this feat. *Cultivator and Country Gentleman*, XXXIII (May 20, 1869), 401. Some farmers tried to hinder the dog from running by buckling "a strap around . . . [its] neck with a light chain attached, long enough to reach to his hind feet, where it is fastened to a . . . billet of hard wood. . . . It is impossible for him to run with such a clog at his heels." *American Agriculturist*, XXIV (November, 1865), 339.

42. *Prairie Farmer*, new series, XIV (December 10, 1864), 372; *American Agriculturist*, XXVIII (March, 1869), 85.

43. *Nebraska Farmer*, III (March, 1862), 44; *National Live-Stock Journal*, V (March, 1874), 99; XI (February, 1880), 77.

44. *Prairie Farmer*, XXI (May 31, 1860), 340; *American Stock-Journal and Farmers' and Stock-Breeders' Advertiser*, III (June, 1868), 165.

45. *The Plough, the Loom and the Anvil*, I (January, 1849), 443–45; *American Agriculturist*, XLIV (January, 1885), 16.

46. *The Agriculturist* (Nashville), IV (January, 1843), 6–7; *The Plough, the Loom and the Anvil*, I (January, 1849), 443–45.

47. Iowa State Agricultural Society, *Report* (1870), pp. 16–18; *Medical Repository* (New York), new series, VI

(May–July, 1808), 66. Gouverneur
Morris, son of the Revolutionary
leader, offered the pessimistic view
that he who hoped to save some of his
sheep for the table would have to take
"them into his own bedroom every
night." Keller, *Solon Robinson*, II,
438.

48. Philadelphia Society for Promoting
Agriculture, *Memoirs*, III (1814),
366.

49. *Western Stock Journal and Farmer*,
XI (December, 1881), 271.

50. *Ibid.*, XII (February, 1882), 35;
Moore's Rural New-Yorker (Rochester), XXXIII (May 20, 1876), 332.
In spite of the controversy few Spanish
dogs were imported for the simple
reason that the advertised price of $50
for an adult and $20 for a pair of pups
was too costly. *Country Gentleman*,
VII (February 14, 1856), 112; *Boston
Cultivator*, VIII (January 17, 1846),
17.

51. *Prairie Farmer*, IX (October, 1849),
303; *Nebraska Farmer*, new series, I
(April, 1877), 13; *Homestead*, III
(August 5, 1858), 736–37.

52. *Prairie Farmer*, IX (October, 1849),
303; *Homestead*, III (August 5,
1858), 736–37.

53. *Southern Cultivator*, XVIII (May,
1860), 165–66. Another rural bard
composed a lengthy poem on the
roaming dogs in New York State.
Country Gentleman, XXI (April 23,
1863), 269.

54. *Western Journal* (Adel, Iowa), I
(October 29, 1863), 4; *Michigan
Farmer*, new series, IV (August 19,
1873), 244; Edward N. Wentworth,
America's Sheep Trails (Ames: Iowa
State College Press, 1948), p. 487.

55. *Ohio Cultivator*, I (October 1, 1845),
147; *Country Gentleman*, XXII (September 10, 1863), 172; *Nebraska
Farmer*, new series, I (February,
1877), 16.

56. *American Agriculturist*, XXII (July,
1863), 197.

57. Complaints of a different nature were
made in respect to dogs allowed to
run at large. They abused this freedom, howling at and frightening every
passer-by, biting children and tearing
their clothes. Moreover, there was
always the danger of communicating
rabies to both man and beast. *Western
Stock Journal and Farmer*, X (Novem-

ber, 1880), 244–45; Iowa State Agricultural Society, *Report* (1887), pp.
59–60; *New England Farmer*, XIII
(September 24, 1834), 84.

58. Iowa State Agricultural Society, *Report* (1870), pp. 16–18; *National
Live-Stock Journal*, XI (July, 1880),
321, 323; Marvel, *My Farm of Edgewood: A Country Book*, pp. 255–56.

59. Connor, *A Brief History of the Sheep
Industry*, pp. 148–49; Cathey, *Agricultural Development in North Carolina*, pp. 36, 179; Paul Gates, *The
Farmer's Age: Agriculture, 1815–
1860* (New York: Holt, Rinehart
and Winston, 1960), p. 226.

60. Taussig, *Aspects of the Tariff Question*, pp. 308–309.

61. Ohio State Board of Agriculture, *Report* (1849), p. 18; *Southern Agriculturist* (Laurensville, S. C.), I
(October, 1853), 312; *New England
Farmer*, IV (September 16, 1825),
62 n; *American Agriculturist*, XXIV
(February, 1865), 42–43; *Prairie
Farmer*, XXII (November 29, 1860),
337.

62. *National Live-Stock Journal*, VI
(March, 1875), 103.

63. Wentworth, *America's Sheep Trails*,
pp. 487–88. One editor angrily described the unseemly behavior of the
Illinois legislature when attempts were
made to deal with the dog menace.
Such attempts usually had the result
of "provoking the mirth and calling
forth the facetiousness of the average
legislator, and the 'curling up' of the
friends of the measure. While a dog
law was under discussion [this past
winter] in the Senate . . . a pettifogger
. . . who . . . represents an agricultural constituency—moved that the bill
be amended so as to require 'all owners
of dogs to use a collar with the name
of the dog inscribed thereon,' and
other . . . Senators laughed at this
low attempt at wit, and consigned the
bill to the tomb that enshrines the
hundreds of its predecessors." *National Live-Stock Journal*, VI (March,
1875), 103. It was claimed that lawyers constituted the principal opposition to dog laws, because the depredations of dogs secured them numerous
lawsuits. *Ibid.*

64. *Ibid.*, IV (February, 1873), 59;
George F. Lemmer, *Norman J. Colman and Colman's Rural World*

("University of Missouri Studies," Vol. XXV, No. 3 [Columbia: University of Missouri Press, 1953]), pp. 42–43. A Virginia legislator had a similar experience when he attempted to secure legislation in his Assembly. In a speech entitled, "Vive Le Mouton," he pleaded with his colleagues to abate this nuisance with a sensible law; they "laughed him down" with the objection that any member who would entertain the question would be driven from office by his constituency. *Southern Agriculturist*, I (October, 1853), 312.

65. *Cultivator*, VII (July, 1850), 249; *American Agriculturist*, XIX (May, July, 1860), 141–42, 205; XXIV (February, 1865), 42–43; *Prairie Farmer*, new series, IX (February 8, 1862), 84; *Nebraska Farmer*, new series, I (March, 1877), 9.

66. *American Agriculturist*, XXIV (February, 1865), 42–43; *Country Gentleman*, XXVI (October 19, 1865), 256; *Ohio Cultivator*, I (February 1, 1845), 18.

67. *Country Gentleman*, XXI (June 11, 1863), 385; *Wool Grower and Magazine of Agriculture*, II (June, 1850), 36; *Homestead*, I (April 3, 1856), 436. These laws were often made dead letters by the "culpable neglect of the assessors"; in fact, resolutions sometimes were passed demanding they carry out the law and threatening punishment if they failed to do so. *Rural New-Yorker*, XL (February 26, 1881), 131. It was difficult to get the assessors to list the dogs; they were also delinquent in killing those for whom the tax had not been paid. *Country Gentleman*, XXIV (November 16,

1864), 315; XXVI (October 19, 1865), 256.

68. *Prairie Farmer*, new series, IX (February 15, 1862), 98; *Ohio Cultivator*, I (February 1, 1845), 18; VI (April 1, 1850), 97–98. If any surplus accrued beyond the damages paid to losers of sheep, the money was to be given to the poor relief fund or the public schools. Maine State Board of Agriculture, *Report* (Augusta, 1876), XX (1875), 150; *Country Gentleman*, XXI (January 29, 1863), 80.

69. *Rural New-Yorker*, XL (February 26, 1881), 131; *National Live-Stock Journal*, XII (November, 1881), 496–97; *American Agriculturist* XIX (May, 1860), 141–42; XXII (July, 1863), 197.

70. *Country Gentleman*, XXII (November 19, 1863), 333.

71. *Farmer's Journal*, II (May, 1873), 75. In Minnesota, lawmakers, after temporizing between 1862–1879, finally gave to sheepmen an effective law permitting a tax on all dogs. It created a revenue fund "*sufficient to pay for the depredations of the canine race.*" Merrill E. Jarchow, *The Earth Brought Forth. . . .* (St. Paul: Minnesota Historical Society, 1949), pp. 194, 259.

72. *Ohio Cultivator*, I (February 1, 1845), 18; *Michigan Farmer*, new series, IV (December 9, 1873), 370; Robinson, *Facts for Farmers*, I, 255–58.

73. *Nebraska Farmer*, new series, I (February, March, 1877), 2, 5–6; 3.

74. *National Live-Stock Journal*, VI (March, 1875), 105.

NOTES: *Chapter Eight*

1. *Moore's Rural New-Yorker* (Rochester), XVII (May 5, 1866), 141.

2. *Hearth and Home* (New York), IV (April 13, 1872), 286; *Horticulturist* (Albany), XVII (November, 1862), 499–502; *Cultivator and Country Gentleman* (Albany), XL (January 21, 1875), 39.

3. *American Agriculturist* (New York), XXXIX (April, 1880), 132; XLI (June, 1882), 240; *Prairie Farmer* (Chicago), L (September 6, 1879), 284; *Western Rural* (Chicago), XVII (October 25, 1879), 340; XXII (July 26, 1884), 469.

4. Hollow-clothesline-wire agents did a

thriving business by using the same fraudulent technique. They would secure an order for so many thousand feet and give an agency in return; later the order would appear as a negotiable note of hand. *Michigan Farmer* (Detroit), new series, XI (January 27, 1880), 7; *Prairie Farmer*, LI (February 28, 1880), 68.

5. *Michigan Farmer*, new series, I (June 11, 1859), 189; *Western Farmer* (Madison), IV (August 17, 1872), 260; V (August 30, 1873), 2; *Farmer* (St. Paul), II (August 11, 1887), 502.

6. *Prairie Farmer*, LI (February 14, 1880), 55; *American Agriculturist*, XXVIII (April, 1869), 123; XXXV (January, 1876), 7. A bogus company in St. Johns, Michigan, sent circulars offering a secret butter additive compound, price $3.00, which would be sufficient to produce 300 pounds of butter. The company used the name of Dr. E. A. Hilgard, a famous agricultural scientist of Leipsic, Germany, changing one initial in the name. *Western Rural*, XVIII (November 13, December 11, 1880), 364, 396.

7. *Ohio Farmer* (Cleveland), LXIII (April 14, 1883), 269; *Des Moines, Iowa State Register*, May 10, 1878. Another of these fellows visited an Ohio community where he sold township rights for $100, or a county for $1,000. The purchaser in turn was to sell rights for $5 per milch cow. *Ohio Farmer*, LXXI (May 28, 1887), 356.

8. *Ibid.*, LXIX (February 20, 1886), 123; *Farmer's Journal* (Cedar Rapids, Iowa), I (November, 1872), 14.

9. *Ohio Farmer*, LXX (November 13, 1886), 311.

10. *Ibid.*, LXV (May 31, 1884), 379; *Colman's Rural World* (St. Louis), XXXVII (June 12, 1884), 186. If a poultry-raiser made his own, it was usually not only inadequate but very likely infringed upon some prominent incubator already patented; in that case he was liable to get into trouble with the patentees. *Prairie Farmer*, LVI (June 14, 1884), 375.

11. *Colman's Rural World*, XXXVI (February 15, 1883), 7; *Western Rural*, XX (May 13, 1882), 152; *Rural Affairs* (Albany), VIII (1876–1878), 300–301.

12. *Moore's Rural New-Yorker*, XXIII (May 13, 1871), 304; *Cultivator and Country Gentleman*, XXXVI (June 1, 1871), 345. It was often necessary to buy eggs for eating purposes as well as for hatching, since chickens on the farms were proverbially poor layers. So difficult was it to get them to lay that innumerable conditioning powders were prepared and advertised guaranteeing, if used, larger egg yields. *Prairie Farmer*, LIV (September 2, 1882), 12. Poultry concerns often sold farm women eggs that had a low rate of hatch; the few that did produce a chick rarely had little resemblance to those that were ordered. *Moore's Rural New-Yorker*, XXX (August 15, 1874), 108. Some agents deliberately kept down the hatch of their high-priced eggs by immersing them in hot water, thus preventing the breed from becoming too common and the price too low. *Cultivator and Country Gentleman*, XL (May 13, 1875), 295.

13. *Michigan Farmer*, new series, XVII (April 20, 1886), 4; *Cultivator and Country Gentleman*, XL (May 13, 1875), 295; *Homestead* (Hartford), I (March 6, 1856), 371.

14. *American Agriculturist*, XLIV (October, 1885), 431; *Ohio Farmer*, LXVIII (August 15, 1885), 104.

15. *Michigan Farmer*, new series, I (August 6, 1859), 255; *Illinois Farmer* (Springfield), IX (June, 1864), 176; *Prairie Farmer*, XLI (June 18, 1870), 185; LIV (September 2, 1882), 12; *Western Stock Journal and Farmer* (Cedar Rapids), XI (October, 1881), 232. In a single volume of the *New England Farmer*, in 1823, there were at least 79 different references to "Receipts" that pertained to preparing, preventing and preserving something.

16. *Ohio Farmer*, LXI (January 7, 1882), 8; *American; A National Journal* (Philadelphia), II (August 13, 1881), 288; *Western Stock Journal and Farmer*, XII (January, 1882), 17.

17. *Nebraska Farmer*, new series, I (February, 1877), 7; *Bistoury, A Quarterly Medical Journal . . .* (Elmira, N. Y.), VII (April, 1871), 219; Phineas T. Barnum, *Swindlers of Amer-*

ica (New York: J. S. Ogilvie, 1903), p. 5.

18. *Moore's Rural New-Yorker*, XXXIII (March 25, 1876), 200; XXXVI (September 1, 1877), 138; *American Agriculturist*, XXIX (May, July, 1870), 167, 245.

19. *DeKalb County News* (Illinois), May 17, 1871; *American Agriculturist*, XXIX (April, August, 1870), 126, 288.

20. *Farmers' Review* (Chicago), VII (September 29, 1881), 204; *American Agriculturist*, XXXIV (February, 1875), 46; XXXVII (August, 1878), 288; *Rural Affairs*, V (1867–1869), 227.

21. *American Agriculturist*, XXIX (April, 1870), 145; XXXIV (February, 1875), 46.

22. *Methodist* (New York), XV (April 11, 1874), 2; *Bistoury*, VII (April, 1871), 219; *Western Rural*, XXIV (January 2, 1886), 5; *American Agriculturist*, XXVIII (February, 1869), 42; XXXVIII (January, 1879), 8. These companies generally had their recipes endorsed by individuals who were often listed as prominent professors in medical colleges. *Ibid.*, XXXI (January, 1872), 39; XXXV (April, 1876), 126–27; XXXVIII (January, 1879), 8.

23. *American Agriculturist*, XXIX (April, 1870), 145. In one recipe, four parts of castor oil were used with one part turpentine. Its producer boasted that it would not smoke, crust on the wick, smell or congeal in the coldest weather. *Union Agriculturist and Western Prairie Farmer* (Chicago), I (June, 1841), 46.

24. *Michigan Farmer*, new series, IV (October 14, 1873), 309; *Moore's Rural New-Yorker*, XXXIII (March 25, 1876), 200.

25. *Michigan Farmer*, new series, IV (November 4, 1873), 332; XV (May 6, 1884), 4; Des Moines, *Iowa State Register*, April 13, 1877; *Colman's Rural World*, XXXVI (November 1, 1883), 4. This type of peddler was often pesky and bold, pushing himself and his wares into the homes. A case in Henry County, Illinois, ended in a physical encounter with the farmer who actually drove the intruder from the house and "kicked the goods into the yard." *Henry County News* (Geneseo, Illinois), June 12, 1879.

26. *Chicago Daily Democrat*, September 19, 1855, p. 2; *Western Farmer*, V (March 15, 1873), 4; *Prairie Farmer*, XLIX (February 2, 1878), 36.

27. *Nebraska Farmer*, new series, II (March, 1878), 36.

28. *Michigan Farmer*, new series, V (February 6, 1874), 44; *Western Stock Journal and Farmer*, VIII (September, 1878), 51; X (May, 1880), 106–107. Grocery frauds were also not uncommon. The trick used was to sell "choice groceries . . . at half price, which, after being delivered and paid for, proved to be anything but the articles ordered." *National Live-Stock Journal*, IV (August 21, 1888), 532.

29. *American Agriculturist*, XLIII (January, 1884), 20; *Prairie Farmer*, LX (February 4, 1888), 70; Robert Hunter, *Poverty* (New York: Macmillan Company, 1907), pp. 106–39.

30. John D. Seelye, "The American Tramp: A Version of the Picaresque," *American Quarterly*, XV (Winter, 1963), 535–53; Josiah Flynt Willard (Josiah Flynt, pseud.), *Tramping with Tramps; Studies and Sketches of Vagabond Life* (New York: Century Co., 1899), pp. 55–58.

31. *Henry County News*, September 4, 1879; March 25, 1880; December 31, 1885.

32. *Harper's Weekly* (New York), XX (September 2, 1876) 718–19, 720.

33. Sometimes trespassers were so brazen and wives so helpless that they were advised to learn how to use a shotgun. A Nebraska editor advocated equipping all homes with this weapon, so that when the tramp "threatens to mash things if she doesn't set out a square meal," the housewife could really pepper him. One gun company responded by producing what they called a "Tramps' Terror" for just this purpose. *Western Stock Journal and Farmer*, VI (June, 1876), 192; VIII (September, 1878), 65; *Nebraska Farmer*, new series, III (December, 1879), 289. In some sections of the West they plagued the countryside to such an extent by stealing, burning barns, pillaging schoolhouses, destroying ma-

chines and terrifying women that the Grange finally called for laws to force them into labor camps. *Moore's Rural New-Yorker*, XXXV (June 16, 1877) 380; *Rural New-Yorker* (New York), XXXVII (July 13, 1878), 444; *Chicago Tribune*, December 22, 1880, p. 12. Tramps were not entirely to blame for refusing to work on some farms. Professor Seaman A. Knapp observed that it would be impossible to work for many farmers, because they were mean, intolerant, completely lacking in intelligence, honesty and thrift and had themselves "been kicked from one kind of business to another till they dropped down to a piece of land and, because it held them up they thought they were farmers." *Western Stock Journal and Farmer*, XI (March, 1881), 51; *Farmer's Journal* (Cedar Rapids, Iowa), III (May, 1874), 72.

34. *Chicago Tribune*, December 6, 1879, p. 5; Des Moines, *Iowa State Register*, May 11, July 20, 1877; *Henry County News*, May 22, 29, 1879; *Moore's Rural New-Yorker*, XXXV (June 16, 1877), 380.

35. *Nebraska Farmer*, new series, II (June, 1878), 88; *Henry County News*, September 4, 1879; March 25, 1880.

36. *Prairie Farmer*, LIX (March 26, 1887), 203; *Farmers' Review*, VI (January 27, 1881), 51; *Moore's Rural New-Yorker*, XXIII (May 20, 1871), 316. By 1870 there were literally hundreds of patents granted on beehives, with pictures and diagrams carried in the farm journals, all boasting of their merits and the prizes they had won at the fairs. *Working Farmer* (New York), V (June, 1853), 95; *Rural Affairs*, VIII (1876–1878), 300–301; *American Agriculturist*, XXXV (July, 1876), 274. If the enthusiast for honey was not interested in bee-raising, he could easily make it from recipes sold by impostors who guaranteed a product "superior to bees' honey." One victim claimed that for his $5 to $10 investment he was able to create nothing "more like honey than poor molasses." *Homestead*, I (March 20, 1856), 411; *Michigan Farmer*, new series, I (August 6, 1859), 255.

37. *American Agriculturist*, XXIX (May,

1870), 166–67; XLI (November, 1882), 483; *Prairie Farmer*, XLI (November 12, 1870), 357. Farm women were able to save handsome amounts by purchasing many of these items through their local granges. George Cerny, "Cooperation in the Midwest in the Granger Era, 1869–1875," *Agricultural History*, XXXVII (October, 1963), 188, 194, 196.

38. *Colman's Rural World*, XXXVI (March 22, 1883), 8; Wisconsin State Grange, *Bulletin* (Madison), IV (September, 1878), 7; Phineas T. Barnum, *Swindlers of America*, p. 17.

39. *Western Home* (Chicago), III (February, 1870), 30; *Nebraska Farmer*, I (September, 1860), 144; *American Agriculturist*, XXXIV (May, 1875), 170.

40. *Western Stock Journal and Farmer*, VIII (July, 1878), 12–13. In Wisconsin a Chicago historical concern was denounced by the state Grange and all farmers were warned not to buy their humbug books. *Western Rural*, XVIII (April 10, 1880), 117. A common book swindle that attracted school children around Christmas time was one that sold for $20 and was free to any child who would send in twenty cents and "the shortest verse in the Old Testament." In many schools all the pupils replied to this advertisement but no books ever appeared. *Henry County News*, December 3, 1885. Other concerns offered premiums to an individual for a list of names and for finding the word "grandmother" or "wife" in the Bible. *Western Rural*, XXII (November 29, December 6, 1884), 764, 777.

41. *Cultivator* (Albany), new series, I (January, February, October, December, 1853), 35–36, 49–50, 307, 367; *Country Gentleman* (Albany), III (March 23, June 22, 1854), 186, 392; *Western Rural*, XVIII (April 10, 1880), 117.

42. *Ohio Farmer*, LXI (February 18, 1882), 112; LXIX (April 10, 1886), 245. So-called temperance lecturers also preyed upon rural women. A "nondescript adventurer could thrust his red nose and bleared eyes into the presence of a company of ladies, and by relating . . . how he once rolled in gutters and mauled his family

around, enlist their sympathies and melt the tears" and finally depart from them with a "handsome roll of bills in his pockets,—which bills soon found a . . . till of some distant barkeeper's saloon." *Henry County News*, December 4, 1879.

43. *National Live-Stock Journal*, VIII (January, 1877), 2; *Nebraska Farmer*, I (July, 1860), 111; *Ohio Farmer*, LVIII (November 20, 1880), 333; John Marquart, *600 Miscellaneous Valuable Receipts, Worth Their Weight in Gold* (Lebanon, Pa.: C. Henry, 1860); Henry T. Williams [pseud.], *Household Hints and Recipes* (New York: published by the author, 1880); William T. Henderson, *A Book of Curious Facts of General Interest Relating to Almost Everything*, comp. Don Lemon and ed. Henry Williams (pseud.) (New York: New Amsterdam Book Company, 1903). Obscene literature for the young of both sexes, promising to reveal many secrets, was available through the mail. *Farmer's Stock Journal*, VI (July, 1876), 4.

44. *Moore's Rural New-Yorker*, XXX (July 18, 1874), 54; *DeKalb County News*, October 18, November 1, 1871; *Michigan Farmer*, new series, V (May 12, 1874), 148; *Farmers' Review*, IV (February 12, 1880), 110.

45. *Farmer's Weekly Museum* (Walpole, N. H.), V (October 30, 1797), 1; *American Farmer* (Baltimore), IV (January 17, 1823), 335–36; *Homestead*, III (July 8, 1858), 667.

46. *Chicago Tribune*, November 29, 1879, p. 3; *Western Rural*, XVIII (January 31, 1880), 36; XXIII (March 7, 1885), 152. In order to increase sales the leaders would place forged names of endorsements in their advertising literature of prominent city mayors, clergy, generals and congressmen. *American Agriculturist*, XXXI (July, September, 1872), 245, 325; C. Vann Woodward, *Origins of the New South, 1877–1913* (Baton Rouge: Louisiana State University Press, 1951), p. 13.

47. *Chicago Times*, May 18, 1868, pp. 5, 8; Phineas T. Barnum, *The Humbugs of the World* (London: John Camden Hotten Co., 1866), pp. 129–31; *American Agriculturist*, XXXII (April,

1873), 125; XXXIV (January, 1875), 6. One of these enterprises in San Francisco sold 200,000 tickets for $5 each in behalf of a Library Association; the final drawing revealed where the money went: of the $1,000,000 received, $375,000 went to the Library, $125,000 to the advertisers, 628 individuals got $500,000, and 199,372 ticket holders received nothing. *Ibid.*, XXIX (December, 1870), 446–47.

48. Many watch concerns sold their bogus merchandise by the circular method. Others bought large blocks of advertising space in journals, but the advertisers often could not be located for the collection of fees. *Bistoury*, VII (April, 1871), 231; *American Agriculturist*, XXIX (May, June, 1870), 167, 206.

49. *Country Gentleman*, XXVII (May 24, 1866), 337; *Cultivator and Country Gentleman*, XXXVII (June 20, 1872), 392; *Nebraska Farmer*, new series, II (May, 1878), 104.

50. Interest in sewing machines was demonstrated at the local fairs where women were attracted in great numbers. Agents were kept busy showing machines and taking orders. *Illinois Farmer*, VIII (December, 1863), 362; *Nebraska Farmer*, new series, III (October, 1879), 238. These machines were so highly prized by western women with large families that persons known to be coming out from the East were urged to bring one with them. Sewing machines were looked upon as lifesavers since they lightened the labor of a "toiling mother" and thus saved her from the clutches of "consumption and an early grave." *California Wine, Wool and Stock Journal* (San Francisco), II (September, 1864), 143. Manufacturers claimed that their invention would free women from slavery to the needle and spare them at least two hours per day of "wearisome labors." It was a divine gift from heaven and a true "answer to the prayers of suffering thousands." *New England Farmer* (Boston), new series, VI (May, 1854), 235; *Ohio Farmer* (Cleveland, VI (March 14, 1857), 41.

51. Opposition to this monopoly was vigorous during the period of the patents. Agricultural journals brought great

pressure on Congress to prevent extension of the patents and personal attacks were especially severe against Isaac Singer, not only for his immense wealth but for the "vulgar magnificence" of his living as exemplified by his divorces, illegitimate children and castles in Europe. It was alleged that he left an estate valued at $13,000,000 to be divided among some sixty heirs. *Prairie Farmer*, XLVI (October 30, 1875), 348; *Hearth and Home* (New York), IV (December 14, 1872), 915; Floyd L. Vaughan, *The United States Patent System* (Norman: University of Oklahoma Press, 1956), p. 41.

52. *American Agriculturist*, XXVI (January, 1867), 8; XXX (May, 1871), 166; *Wisconsin Farmer* (Madison), XX (January 11, 1868), 12.

53. *Michigan Farmer*, XV (December, 1857), 376–77; XVI (March, 1858), 81; *Northwestern Farmer and Horticultural Journal* (Dubuque, Iowa), III (July, 1858), 247; *Moore's Rural New-Yorker*, X (November 26, 1859), 382.

54. *Prairie Farmer*, XLI (November 5, 1870), 348.

55. *American Agriculturist*, XXIX (May, 1870), 167; XXX (May, 1871), 166; *Michigan Farmer*, new series, II (January 7, 1871), 2.

56. *Prairie Farmer*, LV (July 28, 1883), 472. See Chapter XII, p. 219.

57. *American Agriculturist*, XXXI (March, 1872), 88.

58. *Prairie Farmer*, XLIV (December 13, 1873), 396; XLV (July 25, 1874), 236; *Michigan Farmer*, new series, VI (March 23, 1875), 95.

59. National and State Granges, *Abstract of Proceedings* (Des Moines, 1873), IV (1872), 20; Iowa State Grange, *Proceedings* (Des Moines, 1874), IV (1873), 20; Wisconsin State Grange, *Bulletin*, (Madison), I (May, 1875), 4.

60. *Michigan Farmer*, new series, XIII (February 21, 1882), 4; XV (February, 19, 1884), 4; *Western Rural*, XX (March 25, 1882), 93; *American Agriculturist*, XLI (January, 1882), 5.

61. *Ohio Farmer*, LXIX (March 20, 1886), 193.

62. *Cultivator and Country Gentleman*, XLIII (October 24, 1878), 680; *Michigan Farmer*, new series, XI

(May 25, 1880), 4; XII (December 13, 1881), 4; *Farmers' Review*, I (April 26, 1883), 268.

63. Richard Bardolph, *Agricultural Literature and the Early Illinois Farmer*, p. 129.

64. *Michigan Farmer*, new series, XV (August 5, 1884), 4; XVI (March 3, 1885), 4.

65. *Nebraska Farmer*, new series, IV (January, 1880), 18, 28; *American Agriculturist*, XXXIX (August, 1880), 298; *Western Rural*, XVIII (February 21, 1880), 60.

66. *Michigan Farmer*, new series, XV (February 5, 1884), 4; *American Agriculturist*, XXIX (March, 1870), 86; XLI (November, 1882), 483.

67. *Farmers' Review*, XX (July 17, 1889), 491; *Nebraska Farmer*, new series, III (May, 1879), 108; IV (January, 1880), 9; *National Live-Stock Journal*, IV (September 18, 1888), 596.

68. *Prairie Farmer*, XLIII (May 11, 1872), 144; *American Agriculturist*, XXXVI (September, 1877), 327; *Michigan Farmer*, new series, XIV (November 13, 1883), 5. The *Fort Dodge Messenger* (Kansas) related that a gang of fence swindlers had defrauded a number of persons in that community. The victims threatened to give the spoilers a good coat of tar and feathers, or stretch them up on the nearest tree. *National Live-Stock Journal*, IV (September 18, 1888), 596.

69. Sycamore, *True Republican* (Illinois), January 4, 1890; *DeKalb Chronicle*, May 31, 1890; *Michigan Farmer*, new series, XIV (November 13, 1883), 5.

70. *Congressional Record*, 49 Congress, 1st Session, XVII (1885–1886), 135, 770, 3140; Western Farmer and Wisconsin State Grange, *Bulletin* (Madison), V (November 27, 1886), 2; *Orange Judd Farmer* (Chicago), V (April 20, 1889), 241. The post office barred lottery literature from the mails, sent special agents in pursuit of the swindlers, and periodically issued the press lists of persons conducting schemes to defraud. *Michigan Farmer*, new series, XI (February 10, 1880), 7; *Farmers' Review*, IV (February 12, 1880), 110; *American Agriculturist*, XXIX (July, 1870), 245; *Western Rural*, XXI (July 14, 1883), 226.

NOTES: *Chapter Nine*

1. Cornelius Swartwout to Robert Swartwout, Quincy, Illinois, September 9, 1837, in the Swartwout Manuscripts, Chicago Historical Society Library; *Union Agriculturist and Western Prairie Farmer* (Chicago), I (March, 1841), 34. Some settlers believed that such natural growth was not only an economic resource but that it contributed a sense of beauty, a design of the creator as well as a moral influence upon man's life. *Western Journal of Agriculture, Manufactures, Mechanic Arts,* . . . (St. Louis), I (January, 1848), 39–46.

2. William V. Pooley, *The Settlement of Illinois, 1830–1850* (Madison, 1908). Reprinted from *Bulletin*, University of Wisconsin, History Series, I, *passim*.

3. Illinois State Agricultural Society, *Transactions* (Springfield, 1865), V (1861–64), 692–93; *Prairie Farmer* (Chicago), VII (February, 1847), 58.

4. *Prairie Farmer*, VII (February, April, 1847), 58, 116; *Michigan Farmer* (Detroit), new series, IX (July 29, 1879), 1.

5. *Prairie Farmer*, V (April, 1845), 85; VII (January, 1847), 21; *Illinois Farmer* (Springfield), VII (May, 1862), 146–47; *Farmers' Register* (Petersburg, Virginia), II (October, 1834), 311.

6. *Illinois Farmer*, I (February, November, 1856), 28, 252–53; II (January, March, 1857), 19, 72; Indiana Horticultural Society, *Transactions* (Indianapolis, 1875) (1874), pp. 86–89.

7. *Union Agriculturist and Western Prairie Farmer*, I (May, 1841), 34.

8. George Churchill to Swift Eldred, Madison County, Illinois, Warren Center, September 9, 1818, in the Illinois State Historical Society *Journal* (Springfield, 1918–1919), XI, 66.

9. *Ohio Cultivator* (Columbus), XII (November 1, 1856), 330; *Wisconsin and Iowa Farmer and Northwestern Cultivator* (Janesville, Wisconsin), VII (September, 1855), 274.

10. *Illinois Farmer*, II (January, 1857),

3–4; Indiana Horticultural Society, *Transactions* (1872), pp. 103–105. Even as late as the 1880's a western editor observed that "the extension of nurseries in the West has not kept pace with the settlement and improvement of the country." *Western Farmer* (Madison), new series, II (March 31, 1883), 1.

11. Earl W. Hayter, "Mechanical Humbuggery Among the Western Farmers, 1860–1890," *Michigan Farmer*, XXXIV (March, 1950), 1–18.

12. *Illinois Farmer*, I (November, 1856), 260; II (April, 1857), 75–77; *Southern Cultivator* (Augusta, Georgia), XVIII (March, 1860), 94. One critic observed that too many farmers "reject the instruction and experience of all those who have the results of their labors and knowledge recorded in a book." Then he added that the farmer "works too much and thinks too little." Iowa State Horticultural Society, *Proceedings* (Des Moines, 1873), VII (1872), 108; *Working Farmer* (New York), VIII (April, 1856), 31. See Chapter I, pp. 6–7.

13. *Illinois Farmer*, II (April, 1857), 75–77.

14. Frederick L. Olmsted, *The Cotton Kingdom* (New York: Knopf & Company, 1953), pp. 350–51. Edited and with introduction by Arthur M. Schlesinger, Sr.

15. *Western Rural* (Chicago), XXI (August 4, 1883), 249; *Cincinnatus* (Cincinnati), II (March, 1857), 118–24; *American Agriculturist* (New York), XXXIX (October, 1880), 419.

16. *Wisconsin Farmer* (Madison), XII (November, 1860), 339; *Michigan Farmer*, new series, II (January 14, 1871), 11.

17. *Prairie Farmer*, L (July 5, 1879), 210; *Ohio Cultivator*, XI (July 1, 1855), 202; *Michigan Farmer*, XIII (August, 1855), 245–46. One anecdote told of a vendor who showed a farmer the large plums in his glass container. By accident he dropped and broke the bottle, reducing the size of the fruit to that of a "gooseberry."

American Agriculturist, XLVI (May, 1887), 233.

18. *Prairie Farmer*, LVIII (August 7, 1886), 505; *Cultivator and Country Gentleman* (Albany), XLI (February 24, 1876), 119; *Horticulturist* (Albany), XXIX (July, 1874), 221. Peddlers, in order to expedite their sales, often employed a second party by buying "up some one in each town to go with them and recommend them." *Wisconsin and Iowa Farmer and Northwestern Cultivator*, VII (September, 1855), 274.

19. *Nebraska Farmer* (Lincoln), new series, III (March, October, 1879), 53, 58, 242–43; IV (July, 1880), 166–67; *Homestead* (Hartford), I (February 14, 1856), 330; *Western Stock Journal and Farmer* (Cedar Rapids, Iowa), X (May, 1880), 106.

20. *Ohio Cultivator*, XI (July 1, 1855), 202; *Working Farmer*, VI (December, 1854), 238–39; *Southern Cultivator*, XVII (August, October, 1859), 245, 320; XVIII (January, 1860), 27–28.

21. *Horticulturist*, XXVI (February, 1871), 45–46. Victimized farmers wrote to farm editors demanding that these peddlers be exposed. In subsequent issues other subscribers related their experiences and told how they had outwitted these scamps. *Colman's Rural World* (St. Louis), XXXVI (November 1, 1883), 5; *American Agriculturist*, XXXIX (March, 1880), 116.

22. *Illinois Farmer*, IX (March, 1864), 76–77; *Nebraska Farmer* (Lincoln), new series, III (October, 1879), 242–43.

23. Indiana Horticultural Society, *Transactions* (1871), pp. 181–84.

24. *Prairie Farmer*, XLVIII (May 5, 1877), 138; LII (February 26, 1881), 66; Des Moines, *Iowa State Register*, April 13, 1877. For years the *Horticulturist* campaigned against these humbug grapevines but to no avail, for few farmers ever read this knowledgeable magazine. VI (December, 1851), 575; VII (February, 1852), 88.

25. *Illinois Farmer*, III (June, 1858), 88; VII (April, 1862), 117–18; *Western Stock Journal and Farmer*, VIII (September, 1878), 51.

26. *American Agriculturist*, XXXVII (June, 1878), 208; XLV (June, 1886), 267; *Prairie Farmer*, VIII (June, 1848), 199; LI (July 3, 1880), 209. One farmer complained to a vendor that the gooseberry bushes he sold him last year bore currants. "Nothing wrong about that," said the vendor, "that sort always bear currants the first season." *Cultivator and Country Gentleman*, XLIII (February 21, 1878), 118.

27. *Hearth and Home* (New York), V (April 27, 1872), 329; *American Garden and Floral Cabinet* (New York), new series, XI (September, 1890), 557; *Michigan Farmer*, new series, XV (February 21, 1878), 4.

28. *Cultivator and Country Gentleman*, XXXI (March 5, 1868), 168; XXXIII (May 20, 1869), 394; *Horticulturist*, XXV (May, 1870), 150–51; XXVI (February, 1871), 45–46; American Association of Nurserymen, *Proceedings* (Rochester ?, 1881), V (1880), 27.

29. American Association of Nurserymen, *Proceedings*, XII (1887), 98.

30. *Moore's Rural New-Yorker* (Rochester), IV (November 5, 1853), 367; *Cultivator*, new series, I (February, 1853), 59; II (March, 1854), 92; *Southern Cultivator*, XVIII (March, 1860), 94.

31. Indiana Horticultural Society, *Transactions* (1871), pp. 181–84; *American Agriculturist*, XLI (August, 1882), 320; *Western Farmer and Gardner* (Cincinnati), V (April, 1845), 213.

32. *Vick's Monthly Magazine* (Rochester), II (October, 1879), 300–301; *Western Agriculturist* (Quincy, Chicago), XI (November, 1879), 6.

33. *Cultivator*, new series, II (May, 1854), 155; *Western Farmer and Wisconsin Grange, Bulletin* (Madison), IV (November 21, 1885), 6; *Prairie Farmer*, LI (July 3, 1880), 209; LII (February 26, 1881), 66; LIX (October 29, 1887), 695.

34. *Illinois Farmer*, II (November, 1857), 252–53; American Association of Nurserymen, *Proceedings*, VII (1882), 44.

35. *Farmer* (St. Paul), II (November 17, 1887), 726–27; III (May 3, 1888), 273; IV (August 23, 1888), 113.

36. Western Farmer and Wisconsin Grange, *Bulletin*, IV (October 3, 1885), 6; *Western Farmer*, new se-

ries, II (February 3, 1883), 4; *Michigan Farmer*, new series, XIV (November 20, 1883), 4. Some horticultural societies refused to recommend the Russian apples and carried on a vigorous campaign exposing the "traveling chaps" who sold them. Iowa State Horticultural Society, *Proceedings* (Des Moines, 1880), XIV (1879), 283–84.

37. Indiana Horticultural Society, *Transactions* (1872), p. 108; *Horticulturist*, III (March, 1849), 437. Among the many varieties of humbugs in grafting, there were always a few perennial ones "rescued from drowning," as the *Prairie Farmer* called it. There were "the insertion of apple grafts in a potato before planting in the earth, which insures their growth," and a host of others, which, when grafted or budded on to certain exotic branches, would produce a fruit without stones. *Cultivator*, new series, V (October, 1848), 310; *Horticulturist*, III (March, 1849), 437. Another among more than forty popular grafting humbugs was a grapevine branch pushed through a bored hole of a walnut tree still retaining its connection with the parent stem. Within a few months' time it became united with the tree; then the branch could be cut off and it would still continue to grow and produce grapes. *Ibid.*

38. *Homestead* (Hartford), I (February 14, 1856), 329.

39. *Michigan Farmer*, XIII (August, 1855), 246; *Ohio Cultivator*, III (March 15, 1847), 44.

40. *Wisconsin Farmer*, new series, I (March 13, 1869), 84; *Western Stock Journal and Farmer*, X (February, 1880), 36; *National Live-Stock Journal* (Chicago), III (January, 1872), 2. Some early invigorators were compounds of animal dung and human urine mixed to the consistency of paint; about the end of March they anointed their weak, infected trees with this weird mixture. *Agricultural Museum* (Georgetown, D. C.), II (November, 1811), 137.

41. Philadelphia Society for Promoting Agriculture, *Memoirs*, I (1808), 85, 323; *Boston Weekly Messenger*, VII (May 2, 1818), 614; VIII (May 27, 1819), 532; *New England Farmer* (Boston), IV (June 23, 1826), 382;

Illinois Farmer, IV (October 1, 1859), 345; *Prairie Farmer*, XL (January 23, June 5, 1869), 27, 178; *Farmers' Library and Monthly Journal of Agriculture* (New York), I (July, 1845), 92 n. Frauds were extensive in sales of fertilizers and especially recipes to "restore fertility to worn out land, bring orchards into bearing, drive away insects, save labor, produce great crops, and do wonders generally for the farmer." *American Agriculturist*, XXX (January, 1871), 6; XXXVIII (January, 1879), 8; *Southern Cultivator*, XVIII (January, 1860), 27–28.

42. *Northwestern Farmer and Horticultural Journal* (Dubuque, Iowa), III (May, 1859), 165; VI (June, 1862), 203.

43. *Cultivator and Country Gentleman*, XLIV (November 27, 1879), 758–59.

44. *Illinois Farmer*, I (November, 1856), 254.

45. Rice, "The Role of the Osage Orange in the Occupation of the Great Plains," pp. 1–81.

46. *Southern Planter and Farmer* (Richmond), new series, II (September, 1868), 536; *Nebraska Farmer*, new series, IV (October, 1880), 250; *Ohio Cultivator*, X (April 1, 1854), 104. A Great Western Hedge Company contracted to plant hedges by new and improved methods with no down payment. In their contract, however, they had a way of trimming off that part which held them responsible after the planting, leaving only a promissory note. This they sold at a discount. *Nebraska Farmer*, new series, IV (October, 1880), 250.

47. *Ohio Farmer* (Cleveland), LXI (February 18, 1882), 110; LXX (November 20, 1886), 326; *Western Farmer*, new series, VII (October 13, 1888), 641. Some contractors were more interested in signing farmers to contracts to grow plants. For example, paying $1 per thousand, they would promise to take all plants raised from a bushel of seed that farmers would buy from them for $50. To make offers attractive, farmers were told they could expect at least 200,000 plants for sale, or about $200 net profit per acre from their land. *Prairie Farmer*, XLIII (October

26, 1872), 338; XLIV (February 1, 1873), 34.

48. *Ibid.*, LIX (October 29, 1887), 695; *Nebraska Farmer*, new series, IV (October, 1880), 250. In Michigan this contracting system was such a "dead failure" that hedging companies found it necessary to bring suits against many farmers who refused to make their payments. *Michigan Farmer*, new series, XIX (December 22, 1888), 5.

49. *Western Rural*, XVI (October 5, 1878), 315; *Wisconsin and Iowa Farmer and Northwestern Cultivator*, VII (September, 1855), 274.

50. *Michigan Farmer*, new series, II (January 14, 1871), 11; *Wisconsin Farmer*, XII (November, 1860), 339. In some cases nurseries were paid certain sums for the use of their names and catalogs, the peddler reserving the right to purchase his stock wherever he pleased. *Prairie Farmer*, LIX (October 22, 1887), 684.

51. *Michigan Farmer*, new series, II (January 14, 1871), 11; *Illinois Farmer*, VII (April, 1862), 117–18. Rochester was the horticultural capital of the country, as evidenced by the fact that in the fall of 1853, 800,000 trees were shipped from its nurseries to various parts of the nation. *Moore's Rural New-Yorker*, IV (November 5, 1853), 367. Certain nurseries in Dayton, Ohio, became notorious for their association with tree-peddlers; others assisted them by listing trees "at a very material reduction"; and still others permitted stock from European nurseries to be funnelled through their yards. *Western Rural*, XVIII (May 29, June 5, 1880), 169, 179; *Orange Judd Farmer* (Chicago), V (June 15, 1889), 374; *American Agriculturist*, XXXIX (March, 1880), 116.

52. *Orange Judd Farmer*, IV (October 31, 1888), 231; *Michigan Farmer*, new series, II (January 14, 1871), 11.

53. American Association of Nurserymen, *Proceedings*, VIII (1883), 12; *American Agriculturist*, XXXIII (November, 1874), 405.

54. *Prairie Farmer*, LI (February 28, 1880), 66; *Cultivator and Country Gentleman*, XLIV (July 24, 1879), 470; *Moore's Rural New-Yorker*, XL (January 29, 1881), 68.

55. *Cincinnatus* (Cincinnati), II (March, 1857), 118–24; *Illinois Farmer*, II (September, 1857), 211; VII (April, 1862), 117–118; *Rural Affairs* (Albany), II (1858–1860), 331–32. An observer reported that in the fall of the year there could be "seen at most of the railroad stations piles of Rochester trees," but by the time of their arrival they were so "dried and withered that there was not one chance in a hundred of their ever growing." *Illinois Farmer*, III (December, 1858), 190; *Cultivator and Country Gentleman*, XLI (February 24, 1876), 119.

56. *Illinois Farmer*, IV (May, 1859), 269; *Valley Farmer* II (July, 1859), 218–19.

57. *Cultivator and Country Gentleman*, XLI (February 24, 1876), 119; *Ohio Cultivator*, XII (November 1, 1856), 330.

58. *Illinois Farmer*, II (January, 1857), 14; *Cultivator and Country Gentleman*, LII (September 15, 1887), 713.

59. *Illinois Farmer*, II (September, 1857), 197–98; VII (April, 1862), 117–18; *Wisconsin and Iowa Farmer and Northwestern Cultivator*, VII (September, 1855), 274.

60. *Prairie Farmer*, LVII (January 24, 1885), 54; LVIII (May 1, 1886), 280; *Western Rural*, XXIV (May 1, 1886), 274. By the time this evil had run its course in the western and plains states, peddlers were practicing their art as far west as California. *National Live-Stock Journal*, IV (June 26, 1888), 402.

61. *Southern Cultivator*, XVIII (March, 1860), 94; *Southern Planter and Farmer*, new series, V (March, 1871), 181.

62. Des Moines, *Iowa State Register*, April 20, 1877.

63. *Western Farmer*, new series, VI (March 19, 1887), 185; *Western Farmer and Wisconsin State Grange, Bulletin*, V (October 30, 1886), 5. Peddling of fruit trees reached such proportions that one nursery alone in Troy, Ohio, had no less than 200 persons living off the bogus tree business, and in Wisconsin these agents were so prevalent that the Grange, through its county and state representatives, went into the handling of nursery stock. Wisconsin State Grange,

Bulletin (Madison), I (January, 1875), 2–3.

64. *American Agriculturist*, XLIII (June, 1884), 273; XLV (February, 1886), 50; *Valley Farmer*, II (July, 1859), 218–19.
65. American Association of Nurserymen, *Proceedings*, VIII (1883), 12; *Prairie Farmer*, LVI (June 28, 1884), 406.
66. *Cincinnatus*, II (March, 1857), 118–24; *Western Agriculturist*, XI (November, 1879), 6; *Vick's Monthly Magazine*, II (October, 1879), 300–301; Iowa State Horticultural Society, *Proceedings*, XIV (1879), 283–84.
67. *Western Rural*, XVII (July 5, 12, 1879), 213, 221; XVIII (June 26, 1880), 203; Illinois State Horticultural Society, *Transactions* (Chicago, 1867), XI (1866), 63; American Association of Nurserymen, *Proceedings*, V (1880), 24.
68. *Orange Judd Farmer*, IV (October 13, 1888), 231.
69. American Association of Nurserymen, *Proceedings*, V (1880), 24–28; XI (1886), 34–35; *Farmers' Review*, IV (June 24, 1880), 402; *Country Gentleman*, XXXIII (February 25, 1869), 158.
70. *Vick's Monthly Magazine*, X (February, 1887), 53; Indiana Horticultural Society, *Transactions* (1884), p. 22; *Orange Judd Farmer*, V (January 26, 1889), 55.
71. Minnesota State Horticultural Society, *Report* (St. Paul, 1888), XV (1887), 400–401; XVI (1888), 79–81; Ohio State Horticultural Society, *Report* (Wooster?, 1886), III (1885), 127; *Farmers' Review*, XX (October 30, 1889), 743; *Farmer*, III (February 9, 1888), 88; *Orange Judd Farmer*, V (January 26, 1889), 55.
72. *Farmer*, II (March 24, November 3, 1887), 180, 693.

NOTES: *Chapter Ten*

1. Percy W. Bidwell and John L. Falconer, *History of Agriculture in the Northern United States*, pp. 330–33.
2. *Ohio Cultivator* (Columbus), XII (November 1, 1856), 330.
3. *American Agriculturist* (New York), XXXIV (April, 1875), 127; *Western Rural* (Chicago), XVI (December 28, 1878), 409; XVIII (March 13, 1880), 84.
4. In one Pennsylvania county alone an agent sold $1,000 worth of bogus seeds. *American Agriculturist*, XLIV (August, 1885), 347. Agents also sold large amounts of these inferior seeds at various fairs. *Prairie Farmer* (Chicago), LVI (December 20, 1884), 812.
5. *Illinois Farmer* (Springfield), II (July, 1857), 155.
6. *Cultivator* (Albany), VI (July, 1839), 91; *Southern Agriculturist* (Charleston), new series, II (January, 1841), 26–27.
7. *Moore's Rural New-Yorker* (Rochester), XVII (March 17, April 7, 1866), 87, 111; *Southern Agricultur-* ist, new series I (February, 1853), 51.
8. *American Agriculturist*, XXXV (June, 1876), 207; XLI (April, 1882), 145; Des Moines, *Iowa State Register*, January 25, 1878.
9. *Farmers' Review* (Chicago), IV (June 24, 1880), 402; *Michigan Farmer* (Detroit), new series, XVII (January 12, 1886), 4; *American Agriculturist*, XXXV (June, 1876), 207.
10. *Illinois Farmer*, IV (October 1, 1859), 345; *Homestead* (Hartford), IV (February 10, March 31, 1859), 344, 349, 443; *Farmer's Stock Journal* (Cedar Rapids, Iowa), VI (July, 1876), 4.
11. *American Agriculturist*, XXXI (July, 1872), 245.
12. *Ohio Farmer* (Cleveland), LXV (May 17, 1884), 348.
13. *Ibid.*, LXX (December 11, 1886), 376–77.
14. *Illinois Farmer*, VIII (January, 1863), 52; *Horticulturist* (Albany), XVII (November, 1862), 499–502.

15. *Moore's Rural New-Yorker*, X (February 5, 1859), 46. By 1887 many western states had begun to enact laws designed to "punish and prevent fraud in the sale of grain, seeds and other cereals." *Michigan Farmer*, new series, XVIII (January 10, 1887), 4; *Orange Judd Farmer* (Chicago), IV (December 1, 1888), 337.

16. *Western Rural*, XXVI (February 18, May 5, 1888), 108, 284; *Michigan Farmer*, new series, XIX (February 6, 1888), 4; *Orange Judd Farmer*, V (April 20, 1889), 241.

17. *Ohio Farmer*, LXX (December 11, 1886), 376–77.

18. Earl D. Ross, "The United States Department of Agriculture during the Commissionership," *Agricultural History*, XX (July, 1946), 133, 140, 142 n. Some critics believed that reckless distribution of these exotic seeds, fruits, and vines from all parts of the world was not only an abuse of public funds but had a tendency to inspire an excessive enthusiasm, creating a perfect climate for the development of humbuggery. *Horticulturist*, XVII (May, 1862), 230.

19. *Ohio Farmer*, LXX (July 10, 1886), 28.

20. *Ibid.*, LXXII (July 23, 1887), 56.

21. Robert L. Jones, "The Horse and Mule Industry in Ohio to 1865," *Mississippi Valley Historical Review*, XXXIII (June, 1946), 61–88.

22. *Western Home* (Chicago), III (January, April, 1870), 14–15, 3 (Supplement); *Working Farmer* (New York), III (August, 1851), 136; *Cultivator and Country Gentleman* (Albany), XXXIII (January 21, February 18, 25, March 25, May 20, 1869), 59, 138, 159, 239, 399.

23. *Western Farmer* (Madison), II (November 5, 1870), 345; *Moore's Rural New-Yorker*, XXIII (March 18, 1871), 176.

24. *Moore's Rural New-Yorker*, XXIII (May 20, 1871), 314.

25. *Ibid.*, XXIII (March 25, 1871), 187.

26. *Michigan Farmer*, new series, XVI (January 6, 1885), 4.

27. *Moore's Rural New-Yorker*, XXIII (March 25, 1871), 187.

28. *Ibid.* (April 15, 1871), 234.

29. *Michigan Farmer*, new series, II (March 4, 1871), 68.

30. *Ohio Farmer*, LXVIII (July 11, 1885), 25; *Western Farmer and Wisconsin State Grange, Bulletin* (Madison), V (March 27, November 27, 1886), 7, 2; *Michigan Farmer*, new series, XVI (April 7, October 20, 1885), 4, 1; XVII (June 8, July 27, 1886), 4; 1, 5. This fraud was most prominently connected with Bohemian oats, but in some areas was used with other cereals. By 1888, after it had nearly run its course in other states, it returned to life in California with what was known as Seneca wheat. *National Live-Stock Journal* (Chicago), IV (September 18, 1888), 593.

31. *Ohio Farmer*, LXIX (March 20, 1886), 187.

32. *Western Rural*, XVII (January 11, 1879), 9; *Moore's Rural New-Yorker*, XXX (July 11, October 17, 1874), 26, 250; XXXI (April 10, 1875), 240; *Genesee Farmer* (Rochester), II (February 4, 1832), 33–34; IV (October 18, 1834), 335. A "Skinless Oat" attracted some attention in New England and was fed as fodder to horses and cows. Promoters of the "Skinless Oat" also claimed that by boiling the kernels for four hours and serving them with butter and sugar they were made palatable to humans. *New England Farmer* (Boston), XV (October 12, 26, 1836), 110, 126.

33. *Western Rural*, XVI (November 2, 1878), 348.

34. *Ohio Farmer*, LXIX (March 27, 1886), 206–207.

35. *Michigan Farmer*, new series, XVI (November 3, 1885), 1; XVII (December 21, 1886), 4; *Chagrin Falls Exponent* (Ohio), December 10, 1885; January 14, 1886.

36. *Michigan Farmer*, new series, XVIII (March 21, 1887), 4; *American Agriculturist*, XLV (March, 1886), 123. The bond was attractive and highly decorated with a "big red seal" and a "bold signature of a secretary." *Michigan Farmer*, new series, XVIII (February 7, 1887), 4.

37. *Western Farmer*, VI (June 4, 1887), 360; *Ohio Farmer*, LXVIII (December 12, 1885), 377.

38. *Cultivator and Country Gentleman*, LII (July 7, 1887), 525.

39. *Western Rural*, XVII (January 25, 1879), 29; *Nebraska Farmer* (Lincoln), I (February, 1877), 23; IV

(March, 1880), 55; Des Moines, *Iowa State Register*, January 25, 1878.

40. *Ohio Farmer*, LXIX (April 10, 1886), 245; *Farmer* (St. Paul), II (March 10, 1887), 156.
41. *Ohio Farmer*, LXIX (February 20, 1886), 124.
42. *Michigan Farmer*, new series, XVI (January 6, 1885), 4; *Ohio Farmer*, LXXI (January 1, 1887), 9; *National Live-Stock Journal*, IV (July 3, 1888), 419.
43. *Cultivator and Country Gentler..an*, L (November 26, December 10, 31, 1885), 963, 992, 1053; *Chagrin Falls Exponent*, November 25, December 2, 1886.
44. Wisconsin Agricultural Experiment Station, *Report* (Madison, 1887), IV (1886), 11–13; Ohio Agricultural Experiment Station, *Report* (Wooster, 1887), V (1886), 66–67.
45. *Michigan Farmer*, new series, XVI (November 3, 1885), 1.
46. Western Farmer and Wisconsin State Grange, *Bulletin*, V (March 27, 1886), 7; *Ohio Farmer*, LXVIII (September 26, 1885), 201. The Buckeye Oatmeal Mills paid one cent per pound or about fifty cents per bushel for these oats and furnished "good, pure, clean seed for $2 per bushel, including sacks." *Ibid.*, XLVII (January 31, 1885), 72.
47. Western Farmer and Wisconsin State Grange, *Bulletin*, V (March 27, 1886), 7.
48. *Michigan Farmer*, new series, XVI (September 22, 1885), 4.
49. *Ibid.*, XVII (May 11, 1886), 4; *Ohio Farmer*, LXVIII (July 11, 1885), 19;

LXIX (March 27, 1886), 206–207.
50. *Chagrin Falls Exponent*, November 25, 1886; *Ohio Farmer*, LXIX (March 27, 1886), 206–207. Farmers became antagonistic toward the lawyers, claiming they were reaping a handsome profit from this swindle and were not eager to stop it. *Michigan Farmer*, new series, XVIII (June 27, 1887), 1; *Ohio Farmer*, LXVIII (November 7, 1885), 296.
51. *Ohio Farmer*, LXIX (March 27, 1886), 206–207.
52. *Cultivator and Country Gentleman*, L (November 26, 1885), 963; *Ohio Farmer*, LXXI (April 9, 1887), 240; *Chagrin Falls Exponent*, November 12, 1885.
53. *Michigan Farmer*, new series, XVI (February 17, 1885), 4; XVII (February 23, August 31, 1886), 4, 4.
54. *Western Rural*, XVIII (May 8, 1880), 145; *Farmer*, II (March 10, 1887), 156. It was estimated that one oat company alone took as much as $100,000 from Missouri farmers; of this amount, a single bank in Springfield held $17,000 in farmers' notes. *American Agriculturist*, XLVII (January, March, 1888), 32, 127.
55. *Michigan Farmer*, new series, XIX (February 6, 1888), 4; *Prairie Farmer* (Chicago), LX (February 11, 1888), 93; LXI (June 1, 1889), 352; *American Agriculturist*, XLVII (March, 1888), 127.
56. *Orange Judd Farmer*, IV (December 1, 1888), 337; V (April 20, 1889), 241; *Farmers' Review*, XIX (February 8, 1888), 82; XX (April 24, 1889), 299.

NOTES: *Chapter Eleven*

1. Henry W. Spang, *A Practical Treatise on Lightning Protection* (Philadelphia: Claxton, Remsen and Haffelfinger, 1877), p. 69; *New England Farmer* (Boston), new series, VI (September, 1854), 405–406.
2. "Lightning Facts and Figures," Lightning Protection Institute, *Report* (Chicago, n.p., 1963), pp. 5–6. This study provides significant data on the geographical incidence of lightning storms. The average number of annual electrical storms for any given area is forty, New England having the longest and most severe ones. There is a range from forty to eighty strikes per year within the average square mile of the United States and

from one to two strikes for each thunderstorm that would come within a half-mile of anyone's home.

3. *Farmers' Monthly Visitor* (Concord, N. H.), I (August 20, 1839), 124; *New England Farmer*, IV (June 2, 1826), 357; *Ohio Cultivator* (Columbus), III (July 1, 1847), 98; *Farmers' Review* (Chicago), VII (August 4, 1881), 72–73.

4. *New England Farmer*, IV (June 2, 1826), 357; new series, X (December, 1858), 560–61; *Prairie Farmer* (Chicago), LIX (May 14, 1887), 317; *Farmers' Monthly Visitor*, II (June 30, 1840), 85; Solon Robinson (ed.), *Facts For Farmers; Also for the Family Circle*, I, 342–47. One editor, summarizing the destruction caused by a thunderstorm as reported in a few local journals, found that 17 barns, several houses, and several lives were destroyed. *Farmers' Monthly Visitor*, I (August 20, 1839), 124. Vulnerability was thought to be due to the copious evaporation and "exhalations which arise from a barn filled with hay and grain . . . [that] form a column of rarefied air which reach[es] to a great height in the atmosphere. This column is a direct attractor and conductor of the electrical fluid." *New England Farmer*, IV (June 2, 1826), 357; *American Journal of Science and Arts* (New Haven), III (1821), 345–47; XI (1826), 359–62; *Genesee Farmer* (Rochester), II (September 8, 1832), 284–85.

5. *Boston Weekly Messenger*, VIII (August 12, 26, September 23, 1819), 703, 705, 754, 797; *Southern Cultivator* (Augusta, Georgia), XII (September, 1854), 279; *Prairie Farmer*, VII (September, 1847), 295; VIII (June, 1848), 196; *Henry County News* (Geneseo, Illinois), August 17, 1882; *Western Stock Journal and Farmer* (Cedar Rapids, Iowa), VI (September, 1876), 68; *Michigan Farmer* (Detroit), new series I (August 13, 1870), 531. When barbed wire was widely used in the West, casualties ran large during electrical storms. *Texas Live-Stock Journal* (Ft. Worth), VIII (September 10, 1887), 10; *Breeder's Gazette* (Chicago), V (May 29, 1884), 840.

6. *Cultivator* (Albany), VIII (May,

1841), 92; *Southern Cultivator*, XII (September, 1854), 279; *Prairie Farmer*, VIII (June, 1848), 196. Out of man's fear of this mysterious phenomenon grew many folk-beliefs containing an abundance of advice as to how to conduct oneself in an electrical storm, what devices to use for protection, and remedies for those stricken. For example, when in the house, the nearer you place yourself in the middle of the room the better, but never stand close to a fireplace or near a wall. "When you are not in a house avoid flying to the cover of the woods, . . . for safety." "If stricken by lightning let gentle shocks of electricity be made to pass through the chest and let blisters be applied to the breast." *American Museum; or, Universal Magazine* (Philadelphia), II (August, 1787), 163. An English scientist created a lightning rod in the form of a steel walking cane that could be drawn "out at each end [to a length of] . . . eight or nine feet" to be used during an electric storm. *New England Farmer*, II (September 13, 1823), 54. Umbrellas having a metal stem had an iron chain attached to the lower part which when dragged on the ground, served as a conductor. Spang, *A Practical Treatise on Lightning Protection*, p. 69. Many believed that certain diseases, such as palsy, yaws and even paralysis were cured by lightning; some even averred that they had been resuscitated from death by its power. *Philadelphia Medical Museum*, I (1804), 420–24; *American Journal of Science and Arts*, III (1821), 100–102. Others, struck by lightning, were saved from certain death by "pouring cold water freely over them." *New England Farmer*, XV (July 5, 1837), 411; XVI (July 19, August 9, 1837), 11, 40. Some farmers believed that lightning was more apt to kill livestock than humans, leaving the latter only stunned or in a state of shock. When animals were herded together it was thought that those on the periphery were in greater danger than those within the herd or flock. *National Live-Stock Journal* (Chicago), XIII (July, 1882), 300.

7. *Plough Boy* (Albany), III (July 21, 1821), 63.

8. Carl Van Doren, *Benjamin Franklin* (New York: Viking Press, 1938), pp. 160–70; George J. Symons (ed.), *Lightning Rod Conference Report* (London: E. & F. N. Spon, 1882), pp. 120–27.

9. Both ships at sea and in harbors were frequently damaged; hence, in line with "Franklin's science," rods were affixed at the highest point of the vessel with a ground wire terminating in the water. *Gentleman's Magazine* (London), XXI (January 1751), 39; XXII (May, 1752), 229; *Farmers' Cabinet and American Herd-Book* (Philadelphia), XII (September, 1847), 59.

10. *Gentleman's Magazine*, XXVI (January, 1756), 32–33.

11. *Ibid.*

12. St. John de Crèvecœur, *Letters from an American Farmer and Sketches of Eighteenth-Century America* (New York: New American Library, 1963), pp. 299–300.

13. Patrick M'Robert, *A Tour Through Part of the North Provinces of North America . . . in the Years 1774–1775*, edited by Carl Bridenbaugh (Philadelphia: Historical Society of Pennsylvania, 1935), p. 38.

14. *Horticulturist* (Albany), VII (May, 1852), 203–204.

15. Sir James Caird, *Prairie Farming in America*, p. 61.

16. *Western Stock Journal and Farmer*, VI (August, 1876), 32.

17. Robinson, *Facts for Farmers*, I, 342–47. In a column, "Odds And Ends From An Odd End," he advised his readers that "growing trees near a building are the best and cheapest conductors ever put up." Herbert A. Kellar, (ed.), *Solon Robinson: Pioneer And Agriculturist*, II, 95.

18. *American Magazine of Useful and Entertaining Knowledge* (Boston), II (July, 1836), 442; American Academy of Arts and Sciences, *Memoirs* (Boston), II (1804), 99.

19. *New England Farmer*, II (October 4, 1823), 77; *Prairie Farmer*, XII (October, 1852), 465; Robinson, *Facts for Farmers*, I, 342–47.

20. *New England Farmer*, new series, VI (September, 1854), 405–406; Robinson, *Facts for Farmers*, I, 342–47; *Farmers' Review*, IV (June 3, 1880), 360.

21. *New England Farmer*, new series, VI (September, November, 1854), 405–406, 506.

22. *Ibid.*

23. *Prairie Farmer*, XIII (October, 1853), 372; XL (July 17, 1869), 225; XLVI (September 18, 1875), 297; *Cultivator and Country Gentleman* (Albany), XXXI (March 26, 1868), 228–29; *American Agriculturist* (New York), XLII (November, 1883), 511; XLV (July, 1886), 307; *Nebraska Farmer* (Lincoln), new series, I (October, December, 1877), 10, 4. Increasing the power of conduction by a permanent moisture connection with the earth was so difficult to achieve that even experts arrived at different techniques, such as the use of water pipes, family wells, and charcoal buried at the terminus of the cable. *American Journal of Science and Arts*, IX (1825), 331–36; *Farmers' Cabinet and American Herd-Book*, XI (December, 1846), 142; *Michigan Farmer*, new series, I (June 25, 1870), 477; Anthony F. M. Willich, *The Domestic Encyclopedia; or, A Dictionary of Facts and Useful Knowledge*, ed. J. Mease (5 vols.; Philadelphia: Robert Carr, 1803–1804), II, pp. 193–95.

24. *American Agriculturist*, XLVI (November, 1887), 487; *Prairie Farmer*, LVII (June 20, 1885), 392; Spang, *Treatise on Lightning Protection*, pp. ix–x, 173–74.

25. James S. Weldon, *Twenty Years a Fakir* (Omaha: Gate City Book & Novelty Co., 1899), pp. 25–27.

26. *American Agriculturist*, XLIII (April, 1884), 157; *Moore's Rural New-Yorker* (Rochester), XXXV (June 23, 1877), 393; *Farmers' Review*, V (July 29, 1880), 73; VIII (May 18, 1882), 313; *Illinois Farmer* (Springfield), IX (September, 1864), 276.

27. *American Agriculturist*, XXXVIII (May, 1879), 175; XXXIX (August, 1880), 298; *Nebraska Farmer*, new series, II (March, 1878), 36.

28. *American Agriculturist*, XXXIII (August, 1874), 285; XXXVIII (May, 1879), 174; XXXIX (August, 1880), 298.

29. *Michigan Farmer*, new series, XIX (March 24, 1888), 4; *Prairie Farmer*, XLVI (June 19, 1875), 196.

30. *American Agriculturist*, XLVI (January, 1887), 37; Des Moines, *Iowa State Register*, January 4, May 10, July 5, 1878; *Western Rural* (Chicago), XX (July 1, 1882), 208; Wisconsin State Grange, *Bulletin* (Madison), I (January, 1875), 3. In order to protect farmers from these impostors an agricultural editor of the *Iowa State Register* reproduced facsimiles of contracts issued by lightning rod companies. Des Moines, *Iowa State Register*, July 5, 1878.

31. *Cultivator*, new series, III (March, September, 1855), 74, 287–88; *Nebraska Farmer*, new series, II (March, 1878), 36; IV (August, September, 1880), 188, 222.

32. *Cultivator*, new series, V (August, October, 1857), 240, 300; *Farmers' Review*, XX (May 22, July 24, 1889), 374, 508.

33. *Orange Judd Farmer* (Chicago), V (May 25, 1889), 326; *American Agriculturist*, XLV (May, 1886), 225; *Western Rural*, XV (June 2, 1877), 172. Rodders often issued deceptive insurance policies to those who purchased rods as guarantees that they were properly installed. *Michigan Farmer*, new series, XVII (November 2, 1886), 4; Des Moines, *Iowa State Register*, January 4, 1878.

34. *Cultivator*, new series, V (August, 1857), 240; *American Agriculturist*, XXXIII (August, 1874), 285; Chicago, *Inter-Ocean*, May 4, 1895, p. 4. It was determined by experts that a single rod eight feet high would protect a circular space with a radius double the height of the rod, or a total of thirty-two feet. If a barn was 100 feet long, three eight-foot rods would offer ample security. *Farmers' Review*, XX (July 24, 1889), 508; Joseph Henry, "Directions for Constructing Lightning Rods," *Smithsonian Miscellaneous Collections* (Library of the Smithsonian Institution, Washington, D. C.), Vol. X (1871), No. 237, pp. 1–3. In Europe many believed that the higher the rod the greater its efficacy; thus, one heavy, tapered shaft often extended as high as thirty feet above the roof. *American Journal of Science and Arts*, IX (June, 1825), 331–36.

35. *Michigan Farmer*, new series, XVII (April 20, 1886), 4; *Moore's Rural New-Yorker*, XXXV (June 23, 1877), 393; *Cultivator and Country Gentleman*, XXXVI (November 23, 1871), 744–45.

36. *American Agriculturist*, XXXVIII (May, 1879), 175; Des Moines, *Iowa State Register*, April 13, 1877; *Farmers' Review*, X (June 14, 1883), 382. The editor of the *Nebraska Farmer*, supporting this protest movement, made a strong plea to state legislators to enact a law prohibiting itinerants from flooding the countryside with their rural swindles. *Nebraska Farmer*, new series, IV (August, 1880), 190.

37. It was indeed a lucrative enterprise; one firm alone bought up as much as $17,000 of these "shaved" notes. *Cultivator and Country Gentleman*, XXXVI (November 23, 1871), 744–45.

38. *Prairie Farmer*, LVII (June 20, 1885), 392; LIX (May 14, 1887), 317; LXI (June 8, 1889), 369; *Rural Affairs* (Albany), III (1861–1863), 185–86, 270.

39. *American Agriculturist*, XXXVIII (August, 1879), 291.

40. *Western Farmer and Wisconsin State Grange*, *Bulletin* (Madison), IV (November 7, 1885), 2. In several counties of Illinois it was estimated that the loss from frauds ran as high as $10,000 to $15,000 per county. One farmer had a bill for $526, another for $491, and a third for $327. *Farmers' Review*, X (June 14, 1883), 382; *Michigan Farmer*, new series, XV (April 1, 1884), 4.

41. *Prairie Farmer*, LVII (June 20, 1885), 392.

42. Des Moines, *Iowa State Register*, July 5, 1878. See other Iowa papers: *Shellsburg Record*, June 24, 1876; *Osceola Sentinel*, July 6, 1876; *Atlantic Telegraph*, August 9, 1876.

43. *Farmers' Review*, VI (June 2, 1881), 345.

44. *Genesee Farmer*, II (September 8, 22, 29, 1832), 284–85, 299, 308–309; *American Agriculturist*, XXXIX (August, 1880), 327.

45. Joseph Henry, "Directions for Constructing Lightning Rods," pp. 1–3; *American Journal of Science and Arts*, IX (June, 1825), 331–36; *New England Farmer*, XXV (July 23, 1845), 26–27; new series, X (September, 1858), 432; *Ohio Cultivator*,

III (June 1, 1847), 83; *Nebraska Farmer*, I (October, 1859), 3; *Moore's Rural New-Yorker*, XXIX (February 7, 1874), 93; *Rural New-Yorker* (New York), XLI (June 3, 1882), 371.

46. *Wisconsin Farmer* (Madison), XII (August, 1860), 229–30; *New England Farmer*, II (October 4, 1823), 77; *Michigan Farmer*, new series, I (July 25, 1870), 477; *Ohio Farmer* (Cleveland), LXIII (April 21, 1883), 292.

47. *American Agriculturist*, XLV (July, 1886), 307; *Farmer's Journal* (Cedar Rapids, Iowa), II (November, 1873), 163; *Rural Affairs*, I (1855–1857), 112–14, 332; IV (1864–1866), 232.

48. *Ohio Farmer*, LXXI (February 12, 1887), 106. A ten-verse ballad, written by Will Carleton called "The Lightning-Rod Dispenser," tells of the rodder's tenacity, agreeability, and versatility. *Farmers' Review*, VI (March 10, 1881), 152; *Henry County News*, May 22, 1879. This boundless versatility was illustrated by the claims of a rodder who had developed a rod to "fool the lightning." He told his clients that his invention would train the "lightning so as to have it come down from the Heavens and light on one end of a crooked [forked] rod, and peaceably depart from the other end, returning again to the place from whence it came." *Western Stock Journal and Farmer*, IX (November, 1879), 246. Herman Melville gave an excellent description of the many facets of this itinerant in his short story, "The Lightning Rod Man." Jay Leyda (ed.), *The Complete Stories of Herman Melville* (New York: Random House, 1949), pp. 213–21.

NOTES: *Chapter Twelve*

1. Solon J. Buck, *The Granger Movement*, pp. 18–19, 118–20.

2. *American Agriculturist* (New York), XXXIII (August, December, 1874), 285, 446; *Cultivator and Country Gentleman* (Albany), XXXVI (July 20, 27, 1871), 457, 477.

3. Buck, *Granger Movement*, p. 278.

4. *Congressional Record*, 46 Congress, 3 Session (1881), pp. 1973–74; *Prairie Farmer* (Chicago), LI (March 20, 1880), 92.

5. *Michigan Farmer* (Detroit), XII (November 1, 1881), 1; *Western Rural* (Chicago), XXII (September 13, 1884), 588.

6. Michigan State Board of Agriculture, *Report* (Lansing, 1880), XVIII (1879), 216; *Cong. Record*, 46 Cong. 3 Sess. (1881), pp. 1972–73.

7. *Cong. Record*, 45 Cong. 3 Sess. (1878), pp. 307, 1372; *Michigan Farmer*, II (January 7, 1871), 1.

8. *Prairie Farmer*, XLV (December 9, 1874), 401.

9. Herman C. Nixon, "The Populist Movement in Iowa," *Iowa Journal of History and Politics*, XXIV (January, 1926), 16–19.

10. "Arguments Before the Committee on Patents," *Senate Miscellaneous Documents*, No. 50, 45 Cong., 2 Sess. (1877–1878), pp. 13 ff., 362–63; *Prairie Farmer*, XLIV (September 20, 1873), 297; Buck, *Granger Movement*, pp. 118–19.

11. Some of these extensions were secured, according to the rural critics, by patentees who influenced senators to attach riders to important bills just before adjournment. *Prairie Farmer*, XLV (February 28, 1874), 67.

12. *Western Rural*, XIV (September 23, 1876), 309; Michigan State Grange, *Proceedings* (Kalamazoo, 1876), III (1875), 42.

13. It was claimed that 20 patents were issued on an ordinary coal stove, 647 on a corn planter, 378 on a corn sheller and 6,211 on the different parts of a plow. *Cong. Record*, 45 Cong., 3 Sess. (1878–1879), pp. 269, 1372; *American Agriculturist*, XXXV (July, 1876), 274; XLI (August, 1882), 346.

14. *Cong. Record*, 45 Cong. 3 Sess. (1878–1879), pp. 271.

15. Michigan State Board of Agriculture, *Report*, XVIII (1879), 215.
16. *Western Rural*, XI (November 8, 1873), 354; *American Agriculturist*, XXXIV (June, 1875), 211.
17. Des Moines, *Iowa State Register*, February 9, 1881.
18. *Western Rural*, XXII (April 19, 1884), 248; Des Moines, *Iowa State Register*, January 21, 1879.
19. Des Moines, *Iowa State Register*, January 21, March 19, 1879, August 24, 1881; Janesville (Wis.), *Daily Recorder*, December 19, 1880; *Farmers' Review* (Chicago), IV (May 27, 1880), 344.
20. *Industrial World and Iron Worker* (Chicago), XXII (July 5, 1884), 21–22.
21. *Cong. Record*, 46 Cong., 3 Sess. (1881), p. 1974; *Prairie Farmer*, XLVIII (June 9, 1877), 180.
22. *National Live-Stock Journal* (Chicago), III (July 12, 1887), 435.
23. *Rocky Mountain Husbandman* (White Sulphur Springs, Mont. Terr.), VIII (June 8, 1882), 2.
24. *Western Rural*, XIX (February 12, 1881), 52; XXVI (March 24, 1888), 181.
25. Michigan State Board of Agriculture, *Report*, XVIII (1879), 221–20; XXV (1886), 17.
26. *Cong. Record*. 45 Cong., 3 Sess. (1878), p. 270.
27. Des Moines, *Iowa State Register*, January 21, 1879; *Cong. Record*, 45 Cong., 3 Sess. (1878), p. 270.
28. *Cong. Record*, 46 Cong., 3 Sess. (1881), p. 1973.
29. Iowa State Grange, *Proceedings* (Des Moines ?, 1874), IV (1873), 44–45.
30. *National Live-Stock Journal*, III (November 22, 1887), 738–39; *Age of Steel* (St. Louis), LXII (November 26, 1887), 5.
31. *Western Rural*, XXIV (January 2, 1886), 8. Not only were royalties themselves irritating but in each suit costs ran from two to three hundred dollars. *Cong. Record*, 46 Cong., 3 Sess. (1881), pp. 1974, 2072.
32. *Western Rural*, XXI (October 13, 1883), 361; *American Agriculturist*, XLII (May, July, 1883), 221, 346; *Farm Implement News* (Chicago), VIII (October, 1887), 20.
33. *Cong. Record*, 45 Cong., 3 Sess. (1878), p. 303.

34. *Ibid.* (1879), 1371.
35. *American Agriculturist*, XXXVII (September, 1878), 328; *Colman's Rural World* (St. Louis), XXXVII (June 5, 1884), 169; *Moore's Rural New-Yorker* (Rochester), XVII (October 6, 1866), 318.
36. Wisconsin State Grange, *Bulletin* (Madison), VII (October 17, 1881), 1; *Michigan Farmer*, new series, XV (March 4, 1884), 4; *Prairie Farmer*, LI (January 24, February 28, 1880), 17, 68; *Ohio Farmer* (Cleveland), LXIX (April 10, 1886), 245.
37. *Michigan Farmer*, new series, XII (August 16, 1881), 4.
38. *Orange Judd Farmer* (Chicago), IV (December 1, 1888), 337; *Prairie Farmer*, LIV (September 28, 1882), 14.
39. Wisconsin State Grange, *Bulletin*, VII (October 17, 1881), 1; *Cultivator and Country Gentleman*, XXXVI (May 18, 1871), 313. Agents often secured signatures on blanks that they could later fill in above the names of signees, changing them to legal promissory notes. Farmers were also deceived into signing a paper folded in such manner as to show no reading matter to the signee. When opened, the document proved to be a "note of hand." *American Agriculturist*, XLV (July, 1886), 307; XLVI (October, 1887), 445. Testimonies and recommendations, along with simple cards signed for receiving samples or gift articles, frequently turned out to be notes and orders for patented devices. *Michigan Farmer*, new series, IX (October 14, 1878), 1; XI (January 1, 1880), 7; *Western Rural*, XX (March 25, 1882), 93; *American Agriculturist*, XLI (January, October, 1882), 5, 401. See Chapter VIII, pp. 145–54.
40. *Moore's Rural New-Yorker*, XXIII (June 10, 1871), 368; *Cultivator and Country Gentleman*, XXXVI (May 18, 1871), 313.
41. *Cultivator and Country Gentleman*, XXXVI (May 18, 1871), 313; Wisconsin State Grange, *Bulletin*, VII (October 17, 1881), 1.
42. *Moore's Rural New-Yorker*, XXIII (June 10, 1871), 368.
43. *Western Farmer* (Madison), V (August 30, 1873), 2; *Orange Judd Farmer*, IV (December 1, 1888),

337; *Michigan Farmer*, new series, XV (May 20, 1884), 4; *American Agriculturist*, XXXVIII (August, 1879), 291; XLI (January, 1882), 5. The commission fraud with churns, washers and wringers was practiced extensively on the farmers' wives. *Western Rural*, XXII (July 26, 1884), 469; *Prairie Farmer*, L (September 6, 1879), 284. See Chapter XI, p. 205.

44. *Michigan Farmer*, new series, XII (March 8, 1881), 8; *Western Farmer*, V (May 31, 1873), 4. Accurate figures on these swindles were difficult to obtain, since many of the victimized farmers were ashamed and took their "loss in silence." *Prairie Farmer*, XLIII (May 11, 1872), 144.

45. *Western Farmer*, V (May 31, 1873), 4; *Prairie Farmer*, XLIV (October 4, 1873), 313.

46. *American Agriculturist*, XXXIII (August, 1874), 285; XXXVII (April, 1878), 126; XXXVIII (February, 1879), 50; XLI (October, 1882), 401. Papers exposing swindlers were presented at meetings of local agricultural societies. Poems satirizing the humbugs and peddlers were also read. *Nebraska Farmer* (Lincoln), new series, I (September, 1877), 15; *Ohio Farmer*, LXXI (February 12, 1887), 106; *Michigan Farmer*, new series, XIII (February 14, 1882), 4.

47. *Hearth and Home* (New York), IV (April 20, 1872), 321; *American Agriculturist*, XXXIV (January, 1875), 5–6. It was estimated that Orange Judd had received "over one quarter of a million . . . letters . . . reciting attempts at swindling by sharpers who send out books and circulars through the mails." A personal libel suit against Judd by a prominent quack doctor in New York City in 1872 gave him recognition throughout the nation. Once he was publicly thanked by the United States Post Office for his courageous campaign in behalf of the credulous rural people. *Hearth and Home*, IV (April 20, 1872), 324.

48. *Western Rural*, XVIII (February 14, March 13, 1880), 52, 84; XX (April 1, 1882), 102; XXII (August 16, 1884), 516.

49. *Prairie Farmer*, LV (July 28, 1883), 472; LVII (June 20, 1885), 392;

Farmers' Review, XVI (April 11, 1886), 88.

50. Western Farmer and Wisconsin State Grange, *Bulletin* (Madison), V (November 27, 1886), 2.

51. *Michigan Farmer*, new series, XVII (May 4, 1886), 4; *Western Rural*, XXV (February 5, 1887), 88; *National Live-Stock Journal*, IV (November 6, 1888), 705–706.

52. Wisconsin State Grange, *Bulletin*, VII (October 17, 1881), 1; *Prairie Farmer*, LV (April 7, 1883), 217. In one section the number of victims grew so large that a convention was called at the state capitol where hundreds of them met, formed a combination and contributed funds in order to employ counsel. As a result they "succeeded in bringing the holders of the notes into a compromise for a partial payment." *Orange Judd Farmer*, IV (December 1, 1888), 337.

53. *Western Rural*, XIX (January 29, April 2, September 3, October 15, 1881), 36, 105, 284, 329; Keokuk (Ia.), *Gate City*, February 24, November 30, 1880, June 30, 1881; Herman C. Nixon, "The Economic Basis of the Populist Movement in Iowa," *Iowa Journal of History and Politics*, XXI (July, 1923), 385.

54. Iowa State Grange, *Proceedings*, IV (1873), 44–45; Michigan State Grange, *Proceedings*, III (1875), 42; Kansas State Grange, *Proceedings* (Topeka, 1881), VIII (1880), 8; *Nebraska Farmer*, new series, IV (January, 1880), 10.

55. Kansas State Grange, *Proceedings*, III (1875), 4–5.

56. *Michigan Farmer*, new series, VI (March 9, 1875), 80; *Nebraska Farmer*, new series, IV (January, 1880), 10; *Western Stock Journal and Farmer* (Cedar Rapids, Ia.), XI (May, November, 1881), 104, 255. At their convention in Chicago in 1881 the National Alliance took a strong position demanding protection of both patentee and user. "We demand such changes . . . as will give patentees a remedy for the infringement of their claims from the sellers of patents only, and not from their users," who almost invariably are "innocent purchasers of rights which they are made to believe are valid."

Included was the proposition that "All persons should be allowed to make patented articles, on payment of a royalty of a per cent of the price of the article; the royalty to be the same on all patents." N. B. Ashby, *The Riddle of the Sphinx* (Des Moines: Industrial Publishing Company, 1890), p. 409.

57. National Grange, *Proceedings* (Washington, D. C., 1880), XIII (1879), 120–21; *Farmers' Review*, V (December 2, 1880), 352. In the same year Butler presented a petition to Congress from the National Grange; the petition spoke for 32 state granges. *Cong. Record*, 46 Cong. 2 Sess. (1879), p. 102.

58. *Michigan Farmer*, new series, VII (January 2, 1876), 4.

59. *Prairie Farmer*, LV (July 14, 1883), 441; *Western Rural*, XIX (October 15, 1881), 329; XXIV (March 6, 1886), 149; Des Moines, *Iowa State Register*, April 6, 1881; Edward Stanwood, *A History of the Presidency* (2 vols.; Boston: Houghton, Mifflin & Company, 1928), I, 421–27, 441. The People's Party in 1892 included a patent plank. *Ibid.*, p. 514.

60. Stanwood, *History of the Presidency*, I, 421–27, 441, 514.

61. *Cong. Record*, 45 Cong. 2 Sess. (1879), p. 1171; Des Moines, *Iowa State Register*, March 12, April 2, 1884; *Michigan Farmer*, new series, XIII (April 11, November 21, 1882), 1, 4. In the third session of the Forty-sixth Congress, approximately 155 petitions were received; of all the states heard from, Michigan, Ohio and Missouri had the highest number, in that order. 46 Cong. 3 Sess. (1880–1881), pp. 372–73.

62. *Cong. Record*, 45 Cong. 2 Sess. (1878), pp. 429, 2837; 46 Cong. 2 Sess. (1880), p. 1919; *Prairie Farmer*, LI (May 8, 1880), 145; Des Moines, *Iowa State Register*, March 12, April 2, 1884.

63. *Western Rural*, XXII (September 13, 1884), 588.

64. Des Moines, *Iowa State Register*, February 23, 1881.

65. *National Live-Stock Journal*, XII (May, 1881), 233–34.

66. Isaac L. Ellwood to Charles G. Washburn, DeKalb, Illinois, December 2, 1887, March 21, 24, 1888, January 10, 1889 in the American Steel & Wire Company Collection, Baker Library, Harvard University. See Ch. XIII, p. 236, note 40.

67. Benjamin F. Thurston to Ellwood, Chicago, Illinois, April 29, 1881 in the Ellwood Collection, Archives, University of Wyoming.

68. In a session of Congress many bills were introduced to amend the patent laws in order to relieve farmers of their evil effects. *Cong. Record*, 46 Cong., 2 Sess. (1879–1880), pp. 110, 171, 220, 462, 518, 537, 768–69, 789, 1230, 1495, 1919, 2731, 4333, 4402; *Western Manufacturer* (Chicago), XIV (May 31, 1886), 94.

69. *Prairie Farmer*, XLVIII (December 8, 1877), 388; *Cong. Record*, 46 Cong., 2 Sess. (1880), pp. 768–69; 47 Cong., 1 Sess. (1882), p. 3955; *Michigan Farmer*, new series, XV (March 4, 1884), 4.

70. *Cong. Record*, 46 Cong., 2 Sess. (1880), pp. 768–69.

71. *Ibid.*, 46 Cong., 3 Sess. (1881), p. 2072; 47 Cong., 1 Sess. (1882), p. 3954.

72. *Cong. Record*, 46 Cong., 1 Sess. (1879), p. 15.

73. By 1884 most of the industrial states had organized groups affiliated with the National Association of American Inventors, who appealed to the two major political parties for a plank to protect their interests, but both declined "for fear of losing farmers' votes." *Western Rural*, XXII (October 18, 1884), 668; *Western Manufacturer*, XII (October 31, 1884), 194; Des Moines, *Iowa State Register*, July 30, 1884.

74. Thomas A. Edison to Butler, Menlo Park, N. J., February 17, 1879. Butler Papers, in the Library of Congress Manuscript Division.

NOTES: *Chapter Thirteen*

1. Ransom H. Tyler, *A Treatise on the Law of Boundaries and Fences*, pp. 468–71; John A. Hopkins, *Economic History of the Production of Beef Cattle In Iowa* (Iowa City: State Historical Society of Iowa, 1928), p. 75.

2. Iowa State Agricultural Society, *Report* (Des Moines, 1863), IX (1862), 260–62. Besides the cost of construction there was the expense of repair and replacement. In 1860 a reporter for this publication stated that the "annual cost of keeping up the Fences of our State, and interest on the investment, exceeds the annual sales of Cattle and Hogs, by over $138,000." The weaknesses of the hedge fence were many: prairie fires were disastrous to the young plants; small animals as well as larger ones such as sheep ate the bark and leaves; they served as nurseries for weeds and vermin as well as harboring the snow in the winter; and when full grown they cast a shade that ruined a sizeable strip for cultivation. *Ibid.*, IV (1857), 226–32, 322, 357, 404; V (1858), 10; VII (1860), 110–19; *Western Rural* (Chicago), VII (April 22, 1869), 126; XIII (June 5, July 31, 1875), 177, 241; XIV (April 15, 1876), 121; XV (April 14, 1877), 118.

3. *Ibid.*, VI (1859), 9–10.

4. *Washburn & Moen Manufacturing Company* v. *Jacob Haish, Complainants Record* (Chicago, 1880), pp. 16, 66 in the American Steel & Wire Company collection, Baker Library, Harvard University. Most of the Isaac L. Ellwood, Joseph Glidden and Jacob Haish materials are in the University of Wyoming Archives.

5. *Creston Times* (Illinois), November 7, 1874; Sycamore, *True Republican* (Illinois), December 5, 1874; July 31, August 4, September 25, 1875; May 27, 1876. My examination of the 394 patents listed by the American Steel & Wire Company in its three-volume set of reproductions of "Early Barbed Wire Specimens" (pp. 1–433) revealed that 176, or nearly half of the total, were issued to Illinois inventors. Iowa was credited with 47. These specimens were photographed at Worcester, Massachusetts, and are now in my collection at the University of Wyoming.

6. Des Moines, *Iowa State Register*, March 19, 1879, February 17, April 13, August 3, 1881; May 9, 1883; *The History of Polk County, Iowa* (Des Moines: Union Historical Company, 1880), p. 716; Keokuk, *Gate City* (Ia.), January 5, 1884.

7. Ellwood to H. B. Sanborn, DeKalb, Illinois, November 16, 1876; Sycamore, *True Republican*, November 15, 1876; January 17, 1877.

8. Sycamore, *True Republican*, March 15, 1879; *Haish Barb Wire Regulator* (DeKalb), III (January, 1879), 4; Coburn & Thatcher to Thos. H. Dodge, Chicago, February 15, 1877.

9. Ellwood stated that more than 10,000 pages of testimony were collected in this one trial. Ellwood to R. R. Plane, DeKalb, February 5, 1879.

10. Eleven different prior fences were unearthed; the one from Austin, Texas alone had as many as twenty depositions allowed for each side. *Washburn & Moen* v. *Jacob Haish, Complainants Record* (1880), pp. 598–604.

11. *Chicago Tribune*, December 16, 22, 1880, pp. 9, 12. Its influence was partially due to the fact that "Judge Drummond had repeatedly, during the trial and motions, expressed himself as decidedly adverse to the broad claim. . . . What has happened to change the opinion . . . by the learned Judge, is what staggers the public." *Ibid.*, December 22, 1880, p. 12. For this decision see *10 Josiah H. Bissell* (Chicago: Callaghan & Company, 1883), pp. 65–89.

12. *Iron Age and Metallurgical Review* (New York), XXVII (January 3, 1881), 20; *Chicago Industrial World and Commercial Advertiser*, XVI (January 13, 1881), 6; *Age of Steel* (St. Louis), XLIX (February 5, 1881), 117. During the year 1881

thirty-three licensees settled for damages totaling $334,642.05. Washburn & Moen, "Letter Book" (Worcester, 1881), pp. 246, 298.

13. *Ohio Steel Barb Fence Company* v. *Washburn & Moen, Defendants Record* (Chicago, 1885), pp. 184, 188–92, 194.

14. Herman C. Nixon, "The Populist Movement in Iowa," p. 3; Fred E. Haynes, *Third Party Movements Since the Civil War* (Iowa City: Iowa State Historical Society, 1916), pp. 311, 448. An examination of Jacob Haish's account books for the period 1879–1893 disclosed that Iowa farmers were his largest consumers. Sanborn testified during the litigation that the Glidden barbed fence was sold in largest amounts in the following states: Iowa, Illinois, Texas and California. *Washburn & Moen* v. *Haish, Complainants Rebuttal*, p. 1.

15. Synder & Manoth to Jacob Haish, Brooklyn, Iowa, September 5, 1878. The Haish "Scrap-Book" contains diverse collections of circulars sent him by his dealers who had received them from other concerns. These were items showing evidence of prior fences and court decisions some of which were nothing more than slanderous remarks calling their competitors "foul names." The majority of these publications were primarily meant to frighten and intimidate dealers and consumers.

16. The agricultural editors of several leading papers in the state were also prominent leaders in this protest movement. Des Moines, *Iowa State Register*, January 12, 1881.

17. *Western Rural*, XIII (June 26, 1875), 201; XV (September 1, 1877), 276; Henry Wallace, *Uncle Henry's Own Story of His Life* (3 vols.; Des Moines: Wallace Publishing Company, 1917–1919), III, 25–28.

18. Sycamore, *True Republican*, January 4, 1879; *Haish Barb Wire Regulator*, III (June, 1879), 8.

19. Sycamore, *True Republican*, April 9, 1879; Des Moines, *Iowa State Register*, January 19, 1881.

20. Sycamore, *True Republican*, April 9, 1879; *Western Stock Journal and Farmer* (Cedar Rapids, Iowa), IX (February, June, 1879), 34, 126–27;

Des Moines, *Iowa State Register*, February 4, May 21, August 27, 1879.

21. DeKalb, Illinois, February 5, 1879; *Burlington Hawk-Eye* (Iowa), April 27, 1879.

22. Ellwood to Walrath & Sons, DeKalb, February 5, 1879.

23. A total of 22,000 copies of the Chicago *Inter-Ocean*, containing the 1880 decision, were mailed to the trade by Ellwood and a licensee in Chicago. Sycamore, *True Republican*, December 22, 1880.

24. *Iron Age and Metallurgical Review*, XXVII (April 14, 1881), 17, 19; Des Moines, *Iowa State Register*, January 13, March 2, 30, 1881.

25. *Western Stock Journal and Farmer*, XI (February, 1881), 27. Attacks upon the patent system grew to such proportions that Thomas Edison was drawn into the controversy. He made a direct appeal to Benjamin F. Butler, then a prominent patent attorney, to use his political influence to protect the system. Edison to Butler, Menlo Park, N. J., February 17, 1879, in the Butler Papers. See Ch. XII, p. 226.

26. XIX (July 16, 1881), 225; Des Moines, *Iowa State Register*, January 13, March 2, 1881; Keokuk, *Gate City*, November 30, 1880; January 25, June 30, 1881.

27. Des Moines, *Iowa State Register*, February 23, March 2, 1881. Most newspapers throughout the West denounced the patent system and many proposed to abolish it. *Janesville Daily Recorder*, December 19, 1880; *Rocky Mountain Husbandman* (White Sulphur Springs, Montana Territory), VIII (June 8, 1882), *passim*.

28. See Senate and House *Miscellaneous Documents*, 45 Congress, 2 Session (1877–1878). "Arguments Before the Committee on Patents."

29. Des Moines, *Iowa State Register*, February 23, 1881.

30. Chester C. Cole to Coker F. Clarkson, Washington, D. C., March 29, 1881.

31. Haish had secured a large amount of testimony in the Chicago suit and the farmers felt that this would save them a sizeable sum of money. Des Moines, *Iowa State Register*, March 9, 1881.

32. Washburn to Ellwood, Worcester, April 28, June 11, 1881; Benj. F.

Thurston to Washburn, Chicago, April 29, 1881; Sycamore, *True Republican*, October 21, 1882. Exactly what the Chicago decision meant in respect to Jacob Haish was not fully understood for a time. Rumors were current that he had been given some unwritten preferred treatment. There is evidence that after a period of squabbling, a reciprocal agreement was signed whereby he assigned his patents to the Washburn & Moen Company and Isaac L. Ellwood for stipulated royalties and in turn was permitted to continue manufacturing a certain tonnage of his own patent on which he was to pay royalties to them; in the final analysis one amount was to offset the other. *Age of Steel*, LIII (June 9, 1883), 605. The Patent Pool was more than compensated, for they were anxious to come to terms with this noisy and provocative Dutchman who, they believed, could stir up all kinds of dissension among the licensees as well as the farmers. He was one of the earliest inventors and manufacturers and had become very popular with the farmers, especially as a result of anti-monopolistic remarks that he broadcast through his rustic *Barb Wire Regulator*. Yet, at no time was he ready personally to join the opposition trying to break up the monopoly. Some years after this Chicago decision he began the manufacture of certain pieces of farm equipment and in time also became well known for his gasoline engine and manure spreader, both bearing the red Chanticleer as their trade-mark.

33. Des Moines, *Iowa State Register*, January 12, 13, 1881.
34. *Ibid.*, January 12, 1881. Included in this group were such prominent names as James Wilson, Seaman A. Knapp, Lorenzo S. Coffin, Benjamin F. Gue, President Adonigah S. Welch of the Agricultural College, Henry Wallace, Professor Joseph L. Budd, and others. See Wallace, *Uncle Henry's Own Story of His Life*, III, 25–28; Des Moines, *Iowa State Register*, March 23, 1881.
35. Des Moines, *Iowa State Register*, March 23, 1881; *Western Rural*, XIX (April 2, 1881), 105.
36. Des Moines, *Iowa State Register*, March 2, April 27, 1881. Clarkson's

attacks were not left unnoticed. One of the more conservative editors refused to subscribe to the denunciations of the patent system as a whole: "We think," he said, "it time that those with cool heads should withhold fuel from a flame that threatens injury to many and no good to any. . . . There is no gain in . . . denunciation . . . [of] our patent law for to it we owe in a large degree the unparalleled advancement of the last half century. It has given us the mower for the scythe, the reaper for the cradle, the steam engine and palace car for the team and stage coach, the sewing machine for the slavish needle. . . . Just reflect upon all the advantages given to us by the patent system." *Western Stock Journal and Farmer*, XI (May, 1881), 108.
37. *Chicago Industrial World and Commercial Advertiser*, XVI (June 9, 1881), 6.
38. The number present varied with the reporters. A fairly accurate estimate was no doubt somewhere between 80 and 150. Des Moines, *Iowa State Register*, April 3, 6, 1881; *Chicago Industrial World and Commercial Advertiser*, XVI (April 7, 1881), 6.
39. *Iron Age and Metallurgical Review*, XXVII (April 14, 1881), 14, 17, 19.
40. Des Moines, *Iowa State Register*, April 3, 1881. Butler replied to Hull's inquiry by stating that he was "ready and willing for a very moderate fee to fight the barbed wire case through the Supreme Court." Des Moines, *Iowa State Register*, April 22, May 11, 1881. He was probably solicited on the basis of experience in handling the telephone and cream separator patent suits as well as being somewhat of a favorite politically with some of the Iowa farm leaders. On a number of occasions he had been appealed to by them for help to curb the railroads, and in 1884 he was nominated for President by James B. Weaver. O. D. Bennett to Butler, Washington, D. C., April 11, 18, 1884; George Crilly to Butler, Barnum Station, Iowa, January 24, 1879; H. B. Hamblin to Butler, Primghar, Iowa, March 2, 16, 1885; Fred E. Haynes, *James Baird Weaver* (Iowa City: Iowa State Historical Society, 1919), p. 215. Butler was never en-

gaged save in an advisory capacity and this was probably due to the fact that Haish never appealed his case from the District Court in Chicago; without this appeal another case would have to go through the lower court. Those who controlled the basic patents and their reissues, however, had a wide range of latitude to maneuver the process of litigation. They could bring infringers into court when expedient and when it seemed certain that the case would be handled by a friendly judge. Moreover, most of the litigation was connected with infringements of reissued patents and rarely was the original challenged. They could carry on a long term infringement suit without bringing the original into question, and slow up or accelerate a suit, as they saw fit. If damaging evidence were unearthed they could slacken their efforts; if the reverse occured, they could vigorously prosecute. They watched with a keen eye the effects on prices and production any infringements might have; when a revolt arose among the licensed or independent producers, as happened, then it was time to act. They sent out agents to spy on "moonshiners"; they issued threats, offered compromises, and bought off certain leaders and their concerns. But when licensees were relatively peaceful and royalties were paid on time it was usually quiet in the courts. This advance-and-delay tactic was often used successfully, and it was not until 1888 that the original Glidden patent was finally denied by Judge Shiras. Ellwood to Washburn, De-Kalb, June 23, 1881; Haish to Washburn, DeKalb, August 18, 1881; Des Moines, *Iowa State Register*, August 17, 1881.

41. The farmers' suspicions were borne out as he was in the employ of the patent-owners. Following this meeting he sent elaborate critical characterizations of the several leaders at the meeting to Washburn. See Iowa Farmers' Protective Association Papers in the Baker Library, Harvard University.

42. Des Moines, *Iowa State Register*, April 3, July 13, December 28, 1881; *Western Rural*, XX (January 14, 1882), 12.

43. See Articles II and XI in the Des Moines, *Iowa State Register*, May 25, 1881. Four of these officers were prominent citizens in Iowa and one served as full time Secretary of the concern in Des Moines. *Ibid.*, July 6, October 12, November 9, 1881.

44. *Ibid.*, July 13, August 3, 24, September 14, 1881; Cyrenus Cole, *A History of the People of Iowa* (Cedar Rapids: Torch Press, 1921), pp. 428–29.

45. *Chicago Industrial World and Commercial Advertiser*, XVII (September 1, 1881), 5–6; Des Moines, *Iowa State Register*, June 1, 1881.

46. Sycamore, *True Republican*, May 25, 1881; Keokuk, *Gate City*, May 31, 1881.

47. *Chicago Industrial World and Commercial Advertiser*, XVII (September 1, 1881), 5–6; Des Moines, *Iowa State Register*, June 18, 1884; *Western Rural*, XXIV (June 26, 1886), 408.

48. *Western Rural*, XX (February 25, 1882), 60; Des Moines, *Iowa State Register*, November 9, 1881.

49. One troubleshooter during the 1880's revealed some years later that he had "closed up 139 factories in the States of Illinois, Iowa, Nebraska, and Missouri without bringing a single suit." Reminiscences of Jerome W. Millington in the Washburn & Moen Collection.

50. Des Moines, *Iowa State Register*, October 26, December 28, 1881; *Age of Steel*, LI (January 7, 1882), 9; Following this episode with the Association, Coon was finally influenced to become an employee of the patent-owners. F. W. Lehmann to Thos. Dodge, Des Moines, October 31, 1883.

51. *Ibid.*

52. Keokuk, *Gate City*, January 17, 1882.

53. XIX (July 16, 1881), 225; XXII (January 12, 1884), 24. By 1884 Milton George, founder of the first Alliance and editor of the *Western Rural*, was giving his undivided support and personal contributions to the association. *Ibid.*, XXII (January 12, 1884), 24.

54. *Ibid.*, XIX (September 3, 1881), 284; Des Moines, *Iowa State Register*, September 14, 1881.

55. Josiah B. Grinnell maintained friendly relations with Washburn even as

Grinnell was attempting to secure a license for his factory; in fact, he had entertained Washburn in his home on various occasions. By 1883, however, the Grinnell Company broke with the patent ring, sided with the farmers and was selling "moonshine" Glidden wire throughout the West. C. S. Martin to Ellwood, Hopkins, Missouri, October 8, 1883; Grinnell to Washburn, Grinnell, Iowa, May 21, 1881.

56. Des Moines, *Iowa State Register*, March 11, 1882.

57. *Chicago Industrial World and Commercial Advertiser*, XVIII (March 16, 1882), 5. A few weeks earlier the Legislature tabled a resolution making it a misdemeanor for any owner of patents to send out secret agents to spy on the consumers. *Ibid.*, XVIII (January 26, 1882), 6.

58. Sycamore, *True Republican*, April 5, 1882.

59. Des Moines, *Iowa State Register*, June 14, 1882.

60. Judge Love did allow the complainants a $5,000 bond from the association and this amount was subscribed by Des Moines bankers. Keokuk, *Gate City*, January 24, 1883.

61. Des Moines, *Iowa State Register*, November 1, 1882; Keokuk, *Gate City*, January 9, 1884.

62. C. K. Offield to Thos. Dodge, Chicago, February 15, 1883; John W. Gates to John Lambert, Pittsburg, August 9, 1893.

63. *Chicago Industrial World and Commercial Advertiser*, XXII (February 28, March 13, 1884), 5, 7; *Western Manufacturer* (Chicago), XII (March 31, 1884), 47; Keokuk, *Gate City*, June 12, 1883. With these favorable decisions some licensees threatened to "no longer submit to the demands of the . . . [monopoly] but . . . [rather] remove their respective manufactories from Illinois where they are within the jurisdiction of . . . Judge Blodgett . . . to Missouri, [where] the Federal Courts . . . are presided over by Judge Treat." *Age of Steel*, LIV (November 17, 1883), 536.

64. At one time there were as many as 55 cases at various stages of development in Iowa, Missouri, Kansas, Nebraska and Minnesota. *Chicago*

Industrial World and Commercial Advertiser, XXII (March 13, June 5, 1884), 7, 21; Keokuk, *Gate City*, January 9, 1884.

65. Receipts from membership, annual fees and royalties were as follows: in 1882, $1,142.33 and in 1883, $4,632.77. The association probably never had more than 3,000 paying members. *Ibid.*, January 24, 1883.

66. *Iron Age and Metallurgical Review*, XXXIV (November 6, 1884), 28, 30; Des Moines, *Iowa State Register*, March 12, April 2, 1884.

67. *Western Manufacturer*, XII (October 31, November 29, 1884), 186, 210; *Age of Steel*, LV (April 5, 12, 1884), 427, 461.

68. Deering & Monroe to Ellwood, Osceola, Iowa, August 4, 1883; *Midland Industrial Gazette* (St. Louis), XIX (April 17, 1884), *passim; Chicago Industrial World and Commercial Advertiser*, XXIV (June 18, 1885), 21. These spies or traveling investigators were detested by "moonshiners" and occasionally were treated rather roughly; in fact, Jerome W. Millington claimed that while he was "looking in on" the activities of John W. Gates, the latter had him severely manhandled. The event made national news. Washburn, in a personal letter to Ellwood, made this comment on the significance of the incident: "You must remember the whole country is in a very excited condition, nobody knows, what use may be made of Gates' recent performance in knocking down and dragging out poor Millington in St. Louis." Worcester, March 11, 1884.

69. Minutes of the Barbed Wire Manufacturers' Meeting (Chicago), February 3, 4, 1885; *Chicago Industrial World and Commercial Advertiser*, XXIV (May 14, June 18, 1885), 5, 21.

70. Des Moines, *Iowa State Register*, May 13, 1885; *Chicago Industrial World and Commercial Advertiser*, XXIV (May 14, June 18, 1885), 5, 21. The Pembroke E. Freeman fence was dug up on his farm in Hickory Grove township by officers of the Farmers' Association and used in the various suits. *Western Stock Journal and Farmer*, XI (September, 1881), 207.

71. 24 *Federal Reporter*, p. 25.

72. *Chicago Industrial World and Commercial Advertiser*, XXIV (June 18, 1885), 21. An accounting showed a production for the period September, 1883 to May, 1885 of 38 tons per month or 456 tons per year. Washburn to Ellwood, Worcester, July 7, 1887.

73. Washburn to Ellwood, Worcester, October 21, 1885.

74. Des Moines, *Iowa State Register*, May 5, 1886.

75. *Iron Age and Metallurgical Review*, XXVII (April 14, 1881), 17, 19; *Western Rural*, XXIII (June 6, 1885), 359; Cole, *History of Iowa*, pp. 428–29; Benjamin F. Gue, *History of Iowa From the Earliest Times to the Beginning of the Twentieth Century* (4 vols.; New York: Century History Company, 1903), III, 102–103.

76. *Age of Steel*, LX (November 20, 1886), 20; *Iron Age and Metallurgical Review*, XXXVI (August 6, 1885), 28. Henry Wallace, reminiscing on these early days, related how the association secured its wire; it "was bought at wholesale by a merchant who was friendly to us, put in his warehouse, and after night transferred to our factory, not far distant." Wallace, *Uncle Henry's Own Story*, III, 25–28.

77. *Iron Age and Metallurgical Review*, XXXVI (December 17, 1885), 24–25; *Age of Steel*, LIX (March 6, 1886), 22.

78. For the period October, 1885, to March, 1887, he averaged about 18 tons per month compared with 38 for the period 1883–1885. Lehmann to Washburn, Des Moines, April 27, 1887. For the six months, November, 1886 to March, 1887, he produced "less than 75 tons." Washburn to Ellwood, Worcester, April 29, 1887.

79. Lehmann to Washburn, Des Moines, April 27, 1887; Ellwood to Washburn, DeKalb, May 19, 1887.

80. Ellwood to Washburn, DeKalb, May 19, 1887.

81. Ellwood to Lehmann, DeKalb, June 13, 1887.

82. Ellwood to Washburn, DeKalb, June 6, 1887.

83. *Organization and Proceedings of the Board of Directors of the Baker Wire Company* (Des Moines, 1883–1884), p. 10. Baker was compensated with a 1,000 ton increase in his license for this service. Washburn to Ellwood, Worcester, October 18, 1887.

84. Ellwood to Lehmann, DeKalb, November 28, 1887; Ellwood to Washburn, DeKalb, March 22, 1888; Ellwood to H. B. Cragin, DeKalb, March 22, 1888.

85. *Western Manufacturer*, XIII (May 30, 1885), 94; *Dubuque Daily Herald* (Ia.), January 6, 1888; *St. Louis Republican*, February 2, 1888; *St. Louis Post-Dispatch*, February 2, 1888.

86. *Age of Steel*, LXIII (January 14, 1888), 5. Nearly 300 witnesses were examined with some 10,000 pages of testimony. Patent-owners, in order to further discredit the inventor, presented other patents of his, such as a "traveling cow pen," thinking it would show what an impractical and "hair brained fellow he was." *Dubuque Daily Herald*, January 6, 1888; *Farmer* (St. Paul), III (January 12, 1888), 20. There was only one exhibit of barbed wire—an old rusty piece about 12 inches in length containing two barbs. *Age of Steel*, LXIII (January 14, 1888), 5.

87. Des Moines, *Iowa State Register*, January 6, 1888; *Farmer*, III (January 12, 1888), 20; *Iron Age and Metallurgical Review*, XLI (January 26, 1888), 149–50. Attorneys for the plaintiffs were provoked at Judge Shiras for placing so much importance upon these old rusty prior fences, and one of them remarked: "If this Judge thinks he can, by this performance, advance himself in judicial promotion he has made a great mistake, as, when the entire facts are shown to any party of high standing or influence, it will condemn him in the eyes of all decent men." C. K. Offield to Washburn & Moen Mfg. Co., Chicago, January 6, 1888.

88. Patentees had little reason to fear that the Shiras decision would destroy their monopoly, since it applied only to a few counties in Iowa; as for price effects, it could make no material difference, for they had been declining for some years, and consolidation and mechanization were advancing rapidly under the leadership of the patent ring with closer and closer mar-

gins of profit on the manufactured product. *Chicago Industrial World and Commercial Advertiser*, XXX (January 19, 26, 1888), 21; *Age of Steel*, LXIII (January 14, 1888), 5; *National Live-Stock Journal* (Chicago), IV (January 10, 1888), 21;

Farmers' Review (Chicago), XIX (January 11, 1888), *passim*.
89. 143 *United States Reports* (Rochester, New York: Lawyers Cooperative Publishing Company, 1919), pp. 275–93.

NOTES: *Chapter Fourteen*

1. Solon J. Buck, *The Granger Movement*, pp. 118–19.
2. 123 United States Supreme Court, *Records and Briefs* (Washington, D. C.), I, 298–99; 1 *Federal Cases* (St. Paul: West Publishing Co., 1894), pp. 874–75; Nelson W. Green, *The American Driven Well* (Seneca Falls, N. Y.: Pew & Holton, 1869), p. 4.
3. 123 U.S.S.C., *Records and Briefs*, I, 339–40.
4. *Ibid.*, pp. 339–40, 354 ff.
5. 1 *Federal Cases*, p. 876.
6. 103 *United States Reports*, p. 660; Cowing & Company, *The American Driven Well* (New York: Bradstreet Press, 1868), pp. 8–9.
7. Green's patent No. 73,425 was granted on January 14, 1868. It was reissued May 9, 1871 as No. 4,372. By 1880 there were some 150 different patents granted on drivewell points and other instruments connected with the device. *Scientific American* (New York), new series, XLII (March 13, 1880), 161; 1 *Federal Cases*, pp. 868, 875. Green, along with William D. Hunt, who was one of the inventors of barbed wire, both came from the same general area of New York. *Glidden Barb Fence Journal* (DeKalb, Worcester), II (1880), 2; 1 *Federal Cases*, p. 876.
8. 122 *United States Reports*, p. 48; *Farmers' Review* (Chicago), XVIII (November 30, 1887), 760. Many fire departments, railroads and industries secured their water supply by this device. *Scientific American*, new series, XLII (March 13, 1880), 161; XLVI (June 10, 1882), 363; *Railroad Gazette* (Chicago), new series, XVIII (December 17, 1886), 863.

9. *Cultivator and Country Gentleman*, (Albany) XXXIV (July 8, 1869), 13; *Ohio Farmer*, LII (December 15, 1877), 386.
10. *Cultivator and Country Gentleman*, XXXIV (July 8, 15, 29, 1869), 13, 32, 73; *Ohio Farmer* (Cleveland), LII (December 29, 1877), 402. This device was also recommended by those who wished to dig a well since it was "a good *diviner* to tell how deep you must dig, and the quantity and the durability of the supply." *Cultivator and Country Gentleman*, XXXIV (July 8, 1869), 13. Ordinary drivewells could be installed in a half-day's time for about $2 per foot including the pipe. 123 U.S.S.C., *Records and Briefs*, I, 145, 267; 1 *Federal Cases*, 870. Some farmers installed as many as ten wells "in their kitchens, cellars, yards, and fields; wherever they want water, they drive a tube and put on a pump." *Scientific American*, new series, XLVIII (May 26, 1883), 320.
11. 122 *U. S. Reports*, p. 48; *National Live-Stock Journal* (Chicago), III (November 29, 1887), 756. Some estimates ran as high as two million wells. *Rural New-Yorker*, XLVI (November 26, 1887), 788; Des Moines, *Iowa State Register*, November 17, 1887.
12. 123 U.S.S.C., *Records and Briefs*, I, 158, 256, 265; *Prairie Farmer* (Chicago), LIX (June 11, 1887), 373; Green, *American Driven Well*, p. 17.
13. Keokuk (Ia.), *Gate City*, November 16, 1887; *Western Rural* (Chicago), XX (May 20, 1882), 160; *Prairie Farmer*, LIX (June 11, 1887), 373.
14. Cowing & Company, *American Driven Well*, pp. 9–10.
15. *Prairie Farmer*, LIX (June 11,

1887), 373; *National Live-Stock Journal*, III (November 22, 29, 1887), 738, 756. Green assigned one-half his patent to the Andrews Brothers of New York City in order to have them take over much of the litigation expenses. 123 U.S.S.C., *Records and Briefs*, I, 1, 89, 243; *Rural New-Yorker*, XLVI (November 26, 1887), 788.

16. 1 *Federal Cases*, p. 869; 11 *Federal Reporter* (St. Paul: West Publishing Co., 1885), p. 591.

17. Patent law under the amended Act of 1839 stated that no patent could be held invalid except on proof of abandonment of such intention to the public, or that purchase, sale, or prior use had been in effect for more than two years prior to the application. 122 *U. S. Reports*, p. 76; *New Jersey Law Journal* (Plainfield), X (December, 1887), 375.

18. 11 *Federal Reporter*, p. 591.

19. Des Moines, *Iowa State Register*, January 7, February 4, 1879.

20. *Western Rural*, XX (May 20, 1882), 160.

21. *Scientific American*, new series, LVIII (January 21, 1888), 37; *Western Rural*, XXV (November 26, 1887), 769. Suits were brought against farmers in many sections of the country, even as far west as the state of Oregon. *Ibid.*, XXI (October 13, 1883), 361.

22. *American Agriculturist* (New York), XLII (May, 1883), 221.

23. *Nebraska Farmer* (Lincoln), new series, IV (January, 1880), 3.

24. *Western Stock Journal and Farmer* (Cedar Rapids, Ia.), IX (April, May, 1879), 76–78, 101.

25. *Ibid.*, IX (April, 1879), 78. This journal made such offensive comments about the patentees that a libel suit for $25,000 was filed in New York for injury to their names and character. *Ibid.* (March, April, 1879), pp. 55, 77.

26. *Minnesota Farmer and Stockman* (Minneapolis, St. Paul), II (January, 1879), 114; *American Agriculturist*, XLII (May, 1883), 221; *Moore's Rural New-Yorker* (Rochester), XXXVI (January 27, 1877), 60.

27. *Western Rural*, XX (July 22, 1882), 233; XXI (May 26, 1883), 167.

28. 94 *U. S. Reports*, p. 780; 95 *U. S. Reports*, p. 355; *Michigan Farmer* (Detroit), new series, VIII (February 2, October 9, 1877), 8, 2.

29. *Western Manufacturer* (Chicago), VI (April 15, 1879), 980–81; Des Moines, *Iowa State Register*, March 26, 1879, March 9, 1881.

30. Des Moines, *Iowa State Register*, March 26, 1879; Keokuk, *Gate City*, March 15, 1881. The Minneapolis Board of Trade stated in a resolution in 1877 that the Minneapolis Millers alone would pay one and a quarter million dollars royalty, and the country at large about 36 millions, if this patent were sustained. *St. Louis Times*, July 17, 1877, p. 1.

31. 11 *Federal Reporter*, pp. 591–92; 12 *Federal Reporter*, p. 871.

32. 122 *U. S. Reports*, pp. 47–70.

33. 123 U.S.S.C., *Records and Briefs*, I, 34, 55; *Western Rural*, XXI (May 19, 1883), 162.

34. *Western Rural*, XXI (May 26, 1883), 167; *American Agriculturist*, XLII (May, 1883), 221. In Iowa an organization of 85 farmers was established in 1879, in Butler and several other counties; by 1881 it had collected and spent nearly $8,000 on this case. An organization in Minnesota contributed to the expense of the trial, and farmers in Michigan also gave their moral support to the contestants. *Burlington Hawk-Eye* (Ia.), April 27, 1879; *Minnesota Farmer and Stockman*, II (January, 1879), 114; Des Moines, *Iowa State Register*, March 26, 1879; Benjamin F. Gue, *History of Iowa from the Earliest Times*, III, 140–42.

35. 122 *U. S. Reports*, p. 76; *American Agriculturist*, XLII (July, 1883), 346.

36. 16 *Federal Reporter*, pp. 401–402; 123 U.S.S.C., *Records and Briefs*, I, 17–18, 25, 319, 326–27, 390.

37. 11 *Federal Reporter*, p. 596; *Cultivator and Country Gentleman*, XXXIV (September 30, 1869), 253; *Western Rural*, XXI (October 13, 1883), 361.

38. *Working Farmer* (New York), IX (June, 1857), 88.

39. 16 *Federal Reporter*, p. 402; *Western Rural*, XXI (May 19, 1883), 162. This type of well was common in early America; and according to Charles W. Marsh of Harvester fame,

it was also seen in foreign countries where such wells were mauled into the ground in order to secure water for both man and beast. *Farm Implement News* (Chicago), VIII (April, September, 1887), 13–15, 16–17. Judge Oliver P. Shiras was one of the few jurists who favored the farmers in patent suits. In their long struggle with barbed wire monopolists he decided one of the basic cases against them at Dubuque in 1888. *Dubuque Daily Herald*, January 6, 1888; Des Moines, *Iowa State Register*, January 6, 1888. See Ch. XIII, pp. 244–45.

40. "Instances in the Supreme Court . . . in which the result on a patent was different from the result in an earlier decision, are extremely rare, and can be counted on the fingers of one hand." Two of the most noted were the incubator and the driven well cases. Patent Office Society, *Journal*, XIX (August, 1937), 619.

41. 123 U.S.S.C., *Records and Briefs*, I, 60, 70, 79, 89, 97–99. Farmers were urged to "tar and feather" royalty collectors who came into their communities. *Western Rural*, XX (May 20, 1882), 160.

42. 122 *U. S. Reports*, pp. 40, 70, 71, 75; 15 *Federal Reporter*, p. 109; *Cultivator and Country Gentleman*, LII (June 2, 1887), 443. Sustaining of a reissued patent was something "not generally expected of the Supreme Court." *Scientific American*, new series, LVI (June 4, 1887), 352.

43. Des Moines, *Iowa State Register*, May 28, June 1, 1887; *Farm Implement News*, VIII (June, 1887), 30; *National Live-Stock Journal*, III (November 29, 1887), 756. Farmers in Illinois were advised to cease fighting and pay the royalty fees. Although this tax on the water supply would no doubt "be a hardship for the poor men to have to pay," argued one newspaper, it was a necessary burden if they were to enjoy the benefits of our system of patent laws. *Freeport Daily Journal* (Ill.), August 19, 1887.

44. *Farm Implement News*, VIII (October, 1887), 20. In Missouri "whole communities have been agitated and worried by the intolerant exactions of agents representing the owners of the driven well patent." *Age of Steel* (St.

Louis), LXII (November 26, 1887), 5.

45. *Western Rural*, XXV (November 26, 1887), 769; *National Live-Stock Journal*, III (October 25, 1887), 676. Williams county had 300 members; Marion, 200, and Tuscarawas, 34. Dues ranged from $1.50 to $4.00. *Western Rural*, XXV (November 26, 1887), 769.

46. *Western Rural*, XXV (November 26, 1887), 769.

47. *National Live-Stock Journal*, III (November 22, 1887), 738.

48. Nelson W. Green to Rufus Osborn, Boston, October 14, 1887 in the *Michigan Farmer*, new series, XVIII (November 21, 1887), 4; *Western Rural*, XXV (December 10, 1887), 810.

49. *Michigan Farmer*, new series, XVIII (November 21, 1887), 4.

50. It was estimated that there were between 2,000 and 3,000 drivewells in Henry and Whiteside counties, and probably around 500,000 in the whole state. *National Live-Stock Journal*, III (September 20, 1887), 597; *Freeport Daily Journal*, August 19, 1887.

51. *Freeport Daily Journal*, August 19, November 23, 1887; Keokuk, *Gate City*, November 16, 1887.

52. Eleven farmers, according to the *Waterloo Reporter*, subscribed from $100 to $200 apiece; in all, about $2,000 was contributed toward the expense of the Iowa suit in the Supreme Court. *National Live-Stock Journal*, III (November 29, December 6, 1887), 756, 771.

53. Des Moines, *Iowa State Register*, June 1, 1887; *Western Rural*, XXV (July 30, December 10, 1887), 494, 810; *A Memorial and Biographical Record of Iowa* (2 vols.; Chicago: Lewis Publishing Company, 1896), I, 364.

54. Des Moines, *Iowa State Register*, November 17, 1887.

55. It was shown that Green's drivewell was in use in Independence, Milwaukee, and in Preble and Cortland, New York, for some time prior to his application for a patent. 123 U.S.S.C., *Records and Briefs*, I, 17–18, 25, 390, II, 9; *Scientific American*, new series, LVIII (January 21, 1888), 37; *Cultivator and Country Gentleman*, LII (November 24, 1887), 893.

56. Des Moines, *Iowa State Register*, November 17, 1887.
57. 123 *U. S. Reports*, pp. 267, 275.
58. *Prairie Farmer*, LIX (November 19, 26, 1887), 748, 764; LX (February 25, 1888), 124.
59. *Orange Judd Farmer* (Chicago), IV (October 20, 1888), 254.
60. *Freeport Daily Journal*, November 23, 1887; Keokuk, *Gate City*, November 16, 1887.
61. *Farm and Home* (Springfield, Mass.), VII (December 15, 1887), 422. When the final decision was rendered, a number of Iowa citizens who had furnished bonds for the patentees in the Hovey suit were called upon to pay $10,000 in costs. *National Live-Stock Journal*, IV (October 9, 1888), 644.
62. *Prairie Farmer*, LX (February 25, April 28, 1888), 124, 267.
63. *Orange Judd Farmer*, IV (October 20, 1888), 254.
64. *Michigan Farmer*, new series, IX (September 5, 1878), 1-2. Birdsell built his first combined threshing and hulling machine in 1855-1856, although his patent was not granted until February 3, 1858. *Ibid.*
65. *Ibid.*, XVI (August, 1858), 232; IX (December 19, 1878), 1.
66. *Ibid.*, IX (December 19, 1878), 1.
67. *Ibid.*, VII (July 4, 1876), 216; IX (September 5, 1878), 1-2.
68. Senator Hoar reported he had favored renewal, since the patent had been instrumental in lowering the price of clover seed by as much as $1 to $2 per bushel increasing greatly its use as a valuable fertilizing agency. *Senate Reports*, No. 112, 45 Cong., 2 Sess. (1877-1878), p. 1. Citizens and manufacturers from a number of states were against renewing it in 1879 since it had already been patented twenty-one years; despite Birdsell's alleged financial reverses, the House Committee on Patents recommended that it not be renewed again. *House Reports*, No. 181, 45 Cong., 3 Sess. (1879), pp. 1-2; *Moore's Rural New-Yorker*, XXX (July 25, 1874), *passim*.
69. *Michigan Farmer*, new series, VII (July 4, 1876), 216; VIII (December 4, 1877), 1; IX (December 19, 1878), 1.
70. *Ibid.*, IX (April 15, September 9, 1878), 1, 5.
71. *Western Rural*, XV (September 29, 1877), 309; *Prairie Farmer*, XLVIII (December 8, 1877), 388.
72. *Michigan Farmer*, new series, VIII (February 13, 1877), 4; IX (October 17, 1878), 2.
73. *House Reports*, No. 181, 45 Cong., 3 Sess. (1879), pp. 1-2.
74. *Michigan Farmer*, new series, VIII (February 13, 1877), 4.
75. *Ibid.*, VIII (February 13, 1877), 5; IX (October 17, 24, December 19, 1878), 2, 4, 1.
76. *Ibid.*, IX (February 18, 1878), 8; *Prairie Farmer*, XLVIII (December 8, 1877), 388.
77. Michigan State Board of Agriculture, *Report* (Lansing, 1880), XVIII (1879), 209-17.
78. *Ibid.*, pp. 209-10.
79. *Western Agriculturist and Practical Farmer's Guide*, pp. 52-53; *Cultivator* (Albany), VIII (August, 1841), 135; Des Moines, *Iowa State Register*, January 5, 1881.
80. *Michigan Farmer*, new series, VIII (September 25, 1877), 4; IX (August 1, 1878), 1; *Western Rural*, XVI (August 3, 1878), 244.
81. Michigan State Board of Agriculture, *Report*, XVIII (1879), 214; *Farmers' Review* (Chicago), IV (May 27, 1880), 344.
82. *Prairie Farmer*, XLI (December 10, 1870), 386; *Michigan Farmer*, new series, IX (September 12, 1878), 8.
83. *Prairie Farmer*, XLI (December 10, 1870), 386; XLIII (May 18, 1872), 156; Michigan State Board of Agriculture, *Report*, XVIII (1879), 217; *American Agriculturist*, XXXI (July, 1872), 247; XXXIV (July, 1875), 251.
84. *Moore's Rural New-Yorker*, XVII (October 6, 1866), 318; *Prairie Farmer*, XLI (November 5, 1870), 348; XLIV (May 17, 1873), 156.
85. *American Agriculturist*, XXXI (July, 1872), 247; XXXIII (May, 1874), 167; *Prairie Farmer*, XLIII (May 18, 1872), 156; XLIV (April 26, 1873), 129.
86. *American Agriculturist*, XXXII (April, 1873), 137; XXXIII (May, 1874), 167; XXXIV (July, 1875), 251.
87. *Prairie Farmer*, XLI (December 24,

1870), 401; XLIII (September 14, 1872), 292; XLIV (November 22, 1873), 372; *American Agriculturist*, XXX (September, 1871), 324; XXXIII (May, 1874), 167; XXXIV (July, 1875), 251.

88. Wisconsin State Grange, *Bulletin* (Madison), I (June, July, August, 1875), 5–6, 5, 5; *Western Rural*, XIII (May 29, 1875), 172.

89. Michigan State Board of Agriculture, *Report*, XVIII (1879), 217–19.

90. Michigan State Grange, *Proceedings* (Kalamazoo, 1879), VI (1878), 61; VII (1879), 12–13, 40–41; VIII (1880), 15; *Michigan Farmer*, new series, IX (August 8, 1878), 1.

91. Michigan State Grange, *Proceedings*, VI (1878), 61; Michigan State Board of Agriculture, *Report*, XVIII (1879), 219; *Michigan Farmer*, new series, IX (September 12, December 16, 1878), 1, 4.

92. Michigan State Board of Agriculture, *Report*, XVIII (1879), 217–19; *American Agriculturist*, XXXIX (January, 1880), 5; *Michigan Farmer*, new series, IX (September 30, 1878), 4.

Selected Bibliography

The American Farmer's Hand-Book. Boston: R. Worthington, 1880.

American Husbandry. 2 vols. London: J. Bew, 1775.

Anderson, Oscar E. *The Health of a Nation: Harvey W. Wiley and the Fight for Pure Food*. Chicago: University of Chicago Press, 1958.

Ashby, N. B. *The Riddle of the Sphinx*. Des Moines: Industrial Publishing Company, 1890.

Bardolph, Richard. *Agricultural Literature and the Early Illinois Farmer*. Urbana: University of Illinois Press, 1948.

Barnum, Phineas T. *Swindlers of America*. New York: J. S. Ogilvie, 1903.

———. *The Humbugs of the World*. London: John Camden Hotten Company, 1866.

Bayne-Powell, Rosamond. *English Country Life in the Eighteenth Century*. London: J. Murray, 1935.

Beuscher, Jacob H. *Law and the Farmer*. New York: Springer Publishing Company, 1953.

Bidwell, Percy and John I. Falconer. *History of Agriculture in the Northern United States, 1620–1860*. Washington, D.C.: Carnegie Institution, 1925.

Bierer, Bert W. *A Short History of Veterinary Medicine in America*. East Lansing: Michigan State University Press, 1955.

Bogart, Ernest L. and Charles M. Thompson. *Readings in the Economic History of the United States*. New York: Longmans, Green & Company, 1916.

Bogue, Margaret B. *Patterns from the Sod* ("Collections of the Illinois State Historical Library," Land Series, Vol. XXXIV, No. 1 [Springfield: Illinois State Historical Library, 1959].).

Bordley, John B. *Essays and Notes on Husbandry and Rural Affairs*. Philadelphia: Thomas Dobson, 1799.

Bradley, Orlando C. *History of the Edinburgh Veterinary College*. Edinburgh: Oliver & Boyd, 1923.

Bruce, Philip A. *Economic History of Virginia in the Seventeenth Century*. 2 vols. New York: Macmillan & Company, 1896.

Buck, Solon J. *The Granger Movement, 1870–1880*. Cambridge: Harvard University Press, 1913.

Caird, Sir James. *Prairie Farming in America*. London: Longman, Brown, Green, Longmans & Roberts, 1859.

Calder, Isabel M. *The New Haven Colony*. New Haven: Yale University Press, 1934.

Carriel, Mary T. *Life of Jonathan Baldwin Turner.* Jacksonville(?), Illinois: Privately printed, 1911.

Carver, James. *The Farrier's Magazine.* 2 vols. Philadelphia: Littell & Henry, 1818.

Carver, Thomas N. (comp.). *Selected Readings in Rural Economics.* Boston: Ginn & Company, 1916.

Cathey, Cornelius O. *Agricultural Developments in North Carolina, 1783–1860.* Chapel Hill: University of North Carolina Press, 1956.

Clark, Thomas. *The Rampaging Frontier.* Indianapolis: Bobbs-Merrill Company, 1939.

Cole, Cyrenus. *A History of the People of Iowa.* Cedar Rapids: Torch Press, 1921.

Connor, Lewis G. *A Brief History of the Sheep Industry in the United States.* Washington, D. C.: Government Printing Office, 1921.

The Country Gentleman's Companion. 2 vols. London: n.p., 1753.

Cowing & Company, *The American Driven Well.* New York: Broadstreet Press, 1868.

Craven, Avery O. *Soil Exhaustion as a Factor in the Agricultural History of Virginia and Maryland, 1606–1860.* Urbana: University of Illinois Press, 1925.

Dabney, John. *Address to Farmers.* Salem, Mass.: J. Dabney, 1796.

Dallas, Alexander J. (ed.). *Laws of the Commonwealth of Pennsylvania, 1781–1801.* 4 vols. Philadelphia and Lancaster: Hall & Seller, 1793–1801.

Dana, Edmund. *Geographical Sketches of the Western Country.* Cincinnati: Reynolds & Company, 1819.

Debo, Angie (ed.). *The Cowman's Southwest, being the Reminiscences of Oliver Nelson . . . 1878–1893.* Glendale: Arthur H. Clark & Company, 1953.

Demaree, Albert L. *The American Agricultural Press, 1819–1860.* New York: Columbia University Press, 1941.

Drake, Daniel. *Pioneer Life in Kentucky,* ed. Charles D. Drake. Cincinnati: R. Clarke & Company, 1870.

Drowne, William. *Compendium of Agriculture; or, The Farmer's Guide.* Providence: Field & Maxcy, 1824.

Elliott, R. S. *Notes Taken in Sixty Years.* St. Louis: Brentano Brothers, 1883.

Ellsworth, Henry W. *Valley of the Upper Wabash, Indiana.* New York: Pratt, Robinson & Company, 1838.

Falconer, John I. and Percy Bidwell. *History of Agriculture in the Northern United States, 1620–1860.* Washington, D. C.: Carnegie Institution, 1925.

Faulkner, Harold U. and Felix Flügel. (eds.). *Readings in the Economic and Social History of the United States.* New York: Harper & Brothers, 1929.

Fitzpatrick, John C. (ed.). *The Diaries of George Washington, 1748–1799.* 4 vols. New York: Houghton, Mifflin & Company, 1925.

Flint, Charles L. *The American Farmer.* 2 vols. Hartford: R. H. Clark & Company, 1882.

Flint, Timothy. *The History and Geography of the Mississippi Valley.* 2 vols. Cincinnati: E. H. Flint & L. R. Lincoln, 1832.

Flügel, Felix and Harold U. Faulkner (eds.). *Readings in the Economic and Social History of the United States.* New York: Harper & Brothers, 1929.

Frank, John P. *Lincoln as a Lawyer.* Urbana: University of Illinois Press, 1961.

Gates, Paul. *The Farmer's Age: Agriculture, 1815–1860.* New York: Holt, Rinehart and Winston, 1960.

Gray, Lewis C. *History of Agriculture in the Southern United States to 1860.* 2 vols. Washington, D. C.: Carnegie Institution, 1933.

Greeley, Horace. *What I Know of Farming.* New York: The Tribune Association, 1871.

Green, Nelson W. *The American Driven Well.* Seneca Falls, N. Y.: Pew & Holton, 1869.

Greer, James K. (ed.). *A Texas Ranger and Frontiersman.* Dallas: Southwest Press, 1932.

Gue, Benjamin F. *History of Iowa from the Earliest Times to the Beginning of the Twentieth Century.* 4 vols. New York: Century History Company, 1903.

Guthrie, Edward S. *The Book of Butter: A Text on the Nature, Manufacture and Marketing of the Product.* 1st. ed. New York: Macmillan Company, 1920.

Haberman, Jules J. *The Farmer's Veterinary Handbook.* New York: Prentice-Hall, 1953.

Haaff, Heman H. *Haaff's Practical Dehorner, or Every Man His Own Dehorner.* Chicago: Clark & Longley & Company, 1888.

Haworth, Paul L. *George Washington: Farmer.* Indianapolis: Bobbs-Merrill Company, 1915.

Haynes, Fred E. *James Baird Weaver.* Iowa City: Iowa State Historical Society, 1919.

———. *Third Party Movements Since the Civil War.* Iowa City: Iowa State Historical Society, 1916.

Hays, Samuel P. *The Response to Industrialism: 1885–1914.* Chicago: University of Chicago Press, 1957.

Henderson, William T. *A Book of Curious Facts of General Interest Relating to Almost Everything . . . ,* comp. Don Lemon and ed. Henry Williams (pseud.). New York: New Amsterdam Book Company, 1903.

Hening, Walter W. (ed.). *Statutes at Large: being a Collection of all the Laws of Virginia, 1619–1792.* 13 vols. Richmond: n.p., 1809–1823.

The History of Polk County, Iowa. Des Moines: Union Historical Company, 1880.

Holbrook, Stewart H. *The Golden Age of Quackery.* New York: Macmillan, 1959.

Hopkins, John A. *Economic History of the Production of Beef Cattle in Iowa.* Iowa City: State Historical Society of Iowa, 1928.

Hunter, Robert. *Poverty.* New York: Macmillan Company, 1907.

Iowa State College Staff. *A Century of Farming in Iowa, 1846–1946.* Ames: Iowa State University Press, 1946.

Jarchow, Merrill E. *The Earth Brought Forth: A History of Minnesota Agriculture to 1885.* St. Paul: Minnesota Historical Society, 1949.

Johnson, Clifton. *What They Say in New England and Other American Folklore,* ed. Carl Withers. New York: Columbia University Press, 1963.

Johnston, James F. W. *Notes on North America: Agricultural, Economical and Social.* 2 vols. Edinburgh: Blackwood and Sons, 1851.

Jones, Hugh. *The Present State of Virginia,* ed. Richard L. Morton. Chapel Hill: University of North Carolina Press, 1956.

Kellar, Herbert A. (ed.). *Solon Robinson: Pioneer and Agriculturist.* ("Indiana Historical Collections," Vols. XXI–XXII.) Indianapolis: Indiana Historical Bureau, 1936.

Kingdom, William, Jr. *America and the British Colonies.* London: G. & W. B. Whittaker, 1820.

Lampard, Eric E. *Rise of the Dairy Industry in Wisconsin: A Study of Agricultural Change, 1820–1920.* Madison: State Historical Society of Wisconsin, 1963.

Lawrence, John. *A General Treatise on Cattle, the Ox, the Sheep, and the Swine.* London: Symonds(?), 1805.

Lemmer, George F. *Norman J. Colman and Colman's Rural World.* ("University of Missouri Studies," Vol. XXV, No. 3.) Columbia: University of Missouri Press, 1953.

Leyda, Jay (ed.). *The Complete Stories of Herman Melville.* New York: Random House, 1949.

Lisle, Edward. *Observations in Husbandry,* ed. Thomas Lisle. London: J. Hughes, 1757.

M'Robert, Patrick. *A Tour Through Part of the North Provinces of North America . . . in the Years 1774–1775,* ed. Carl Bridenbaugh. Philadelphia: History Society of Pennsylvania, 1935.

Marquart, John. *600 Miscellaneous Valuable Receipts, Worth Their Weight in Gold.* Lebanon, Pa.: C. Henry, 1860.

Marvel, IK (pseud.). *My Farm of Edgewood: A Country Book.* New York: C. Scribner, 1863.

A Memorial and Biographical Record of Iowa. 2 vols. Chicago: Lewis Publishing Company, 1896.

Merrill, Eliphalet and Phinehas (comps.). *Gazetteer of the State of New Hampshire.* Exeter: C. Norris & Company, 1817.

Miner, Horace. *Culture and Agriculture, An Anthropological Study of a Corn Belt County.* Ann Arbor: University of Michigan Press, 1949.

Mushet, David. *The Wrongs of the Animal World.* London: Hatchard & Son, 1839.

Neilson, Peter. *Recollections of a Six Years' Residence in the United States of America.* Glasgow: D. Robertson, 1830.

Nettels, Curtis P. *The Roots of American Civilization.* New York: Appleton-Century-Crofts, Inc., 1938.

New England Farrier. 3rd. ed. Woodstock, Vt.: David Watson, 1824.

Oliver, William. *Eight Months in Illinois, with Information to Emigrants.* Chicago: W. M. Hill, 1924.

Olmsted, Frederick L. *The Cotton Kingdom,* ed. Arthur M. Schlesinger, Sr. New York: Knopf & Company, 1953.

Osgood, Ernest W. *The Day of the Cattleman.* Chicago: University of Chicago Press, 1929.

Pabst, William R. *Butter and Oleomargarine: An Analysis of Competing Commodities.* ("Columbia University Studies in History, Economics, and Public Law," No. 427.) New York: Columbia University Press, 1937.

Parkinson, Richard. *A Tour in America in 1798, 1799, and 1800.* 2 vols.; London: J. Harding, 1805.

Pelzer, Louis. *The Cattlemen's Frontier.* Glendale, California: Arthur H. Clark & Company, 1936.

Phillips, Ulrich B. *American Negro Slavery.* New York: D. Appleton & Company, 1918.

———— (ed.). *Plantation and Frontier Documents: 1649–1863.* (*Documentary History of American Industrial Society,* Vol. I–II.) Cleveland: Arthur H. Clark & Company, 1909.

Pooley, William V. *The Settlement of Illinois, 1830–1850.* ("University of Wisconsin *Bulletin,* History Series," Vol. I.) Madison, 1908.

Portrait and Biographical Album of Henry County, Illinois. Chicago: Biographical Publishing Company, 1885.

Prose and Poetry of the Live Stock Industry. Denver, Kansas City: National Livestock Historical Association, 1904.

Richardson, James D. (ed.). *A Compilation of the Messages and Papers of the Presidents, 1789–1908.* 11 vols. Washington, D. C.: Bureau of National Literature and Art, 1908.

Robinson, Edward V. *Early Economic Conditions and the Development of Agriculture in Minnesota.* Minneapolis: University of Minnesota Press, 1915.

Robinson, Solon (ed.). *Facts for Farmers, Also for the Family Circle.* 2 vols. New York: Johnson and Ward, 1865.

St. John de Crèvecœur, J. Hector. *Letters from an American Farmer and Sketches of Eighteenth-Century America.* New York: New American Library, 1963.

————. *Sketches of Eighteenth-Century America,* ed. Henri L. Bourdin and others. New Haven: Yale University Press, 1925.

Seebohm, Mabel E. *The Evolution of the English Farm.* Rev. ed. London: Allen & Unwin, 1952.

Sims, Newell L. *The Rural Community, Ancient and Modern.* Chicago: Charles Scribner's Sons, 1920.

Smith, Sir Frederick. *The Early History of Veterinary Literature and Its British Development.* 4 vols. London: Baillière & Company, 1919–1933.

Spang, Henry W. *A Practical Treatise on Lightning Protection.* Philadelphia: Claxton, Remsen and Haffelfinger, 1877.

Spurrier, John. *The Practical Farmer.* Wilmington, Delaware: Brynberg & Andrews, 1793.

Stanwood, Edward. *A History of the Presidency.* 2 vols. Boston: Houghton, Mifflin & Company, 1928.

Symons, George J. (ed.). *Lightning Rod Conference Report.* London: E. & F. N. Spon, 1882.

Taussig, Frank W. *Some Aspects of the Tariff Question.* Cambridge: Harvard University Press, 1915.

Taylor, Carl C. *Rural Sociology.* New York: Harper & Brothers, 1933.

Taylor, John. *Arator, Being a Series of Agricultural Essays, Practical and Political.* 4th ed. rev. Petersburg, Virginia: J. M. Carter, 1818.

Thompson, Charles M. and Ernest L. Bogart. *Readings in the Economic History of the United States.* New York: Longmans, Green & Company, 1916.

Thornton, William W. *The Law of Railroad Fences and Private Crossings, etc.* Indianapolis: Bowen-Merrill Company, 1892.

Thwaites, Reuben G. (ed.). *Early Western Travels, 1748–1848.* 32 vols. Cleveland: Arthur H. Clark & Company, 1904–1907.

Towne, Charles W. and Edward N. Wentworth. *Shepherd's Empire.* Norman: University of Oklahoma Press, 1945.

Tyler, Ransom H. *A Treatise on the Law of Boundaries and Fences.* Albany: W. Gould & Son, 1874.

Udell, Gilman G. *Laws Relating to Agriculture.* Washington, D. C.: Government Printing Office, 1958.

Unger, Irwin. *The Greenback Era.* Princeton: Princeton University Press, 1964.

Van Doren, Carl. *Benjamin Franklin.* New York: Viking Press, 1938.

Vaughan, Floyd L. *The United States Patent System.* Norman: University of Oklahoma Press, 1956.

Wallace, Henry. *Uncle Henry's Own Story of His Life.* 3 vols. Des Moines: Wallace Publishing Company, 1917–1919.

Wallace, Robert. *Farm Live Stock of Great Britain,* assisted by J. A. Scott Watson. 5th ed. rev. Edinburgh: Oliver & Boyd, 1923.

Washburn & Moen Manufacturing Company. *Fence Laws.* Worcester, Mass.: Washburn & Moen, 1880.

Webb, Walter P. *The Great Plains.* Boston: Ginn & Company, 1931.

Weeden, William B. *Economic and Social History of New England, 1620–1789.* 2 vols. Boston: Houghton, Mifflin & Company, 1890.

Weldon, James S. *Twenty Years a Fakir.* Omaha: Gate City Book & Novelty Company, 1899.

Wells, John G. and others. *The Grange Illustrated; or, Patron's Hand-Book.* New York: Grange Publishing Company, 1874.

Wentworth, Edward N. *America's Sheep Trails.* Ames: Iowa State College Press, 1948.

—— and Charles W. Towne. *Shepherd's Empire.* Norman: University of Oklahoma Press, 1945.

Western Agriculturist and Practical Farmer's Guide. Cincinnati: Hamilton County, Ohio Agricultural Society, Robinson & Fairbanks, 1830.

Wiest, Edward. *The Butter Industry in the United States.* ("Columbia University Studies in History, Economics, and Public Law," Vol. LXIX, No. 2.) New York: Columbia University Press, 1916.

Willard, Josiah Flynt (Josiah Flynt, pseud.). *Tramping with Tramps: Studies and Sketches of Vagabond Life.* New York: Century Company, 1899.

Williams, Henry T. (pseud.). *Household Hints and Recipes.* New York: Published by the author, 1880.

Willich, Anthony F. M. (ed.). *The Domestic Encyclopedia; or, A Dictionary of Facts and Useful Knowledge.* 5 vols. Philadelphia: Robert Carr, 1803–1804.

Woodward, C. Vann. *Origins of the New South, 1877–1913.* Baton Rouge: Louisiana State University Press, 1951.

Woodward, Carl R. *The Development of Agriculture in New Jersey, 1640–1880.* New Brunswick: Rutgers University Press, 1927.

Young, James H. *The Toadstool Millionaires.* Princeton: Princeton University Press, 1961.

Index

337

Lightning Source UK Ltd.
Milton Keynes UK
UKHW040952021019
350631UK00029B/63/P